An Introduction to Systems Psychodynamics

This book provides an introduction to systems psychodynamic theory and its application to organisational consultancy, research and training, outlining systems dynamics methods and their historical and theoretical developments.

Systems Psychodynamics is an emerging field of social science, the boundaries of which are continually being refined and re-defined. The 'systems' designation refers to open systems concepts that provide the framing perspective for understanding the structural aspects of organisational systems. These include its design, division of labour, levels of authority, and reporting relationships; the nature of work tasks, processes and activities; its mission and primary task and the nature and patterning of the organisation's task and sentient boundaries and the transactions across them. This book presents a critical appraisal of the systems psychodynamics paradigm and its application to present-day social and organisational difficulties, showing how a holistic approach to organisational and social problems can offer a fresh perspective on difficult issues. Bringing together the theory and practice of systems psychodynamics for the first time, this book provides an examination of the systems psychodynamics paradigm in action.

This book gives an accessible and thorough guide to understanding and using systems psychodynamic ideas for analysts, managers, policy makers, consultants and researchers in a wide range of professional and clinical settings.

David Lawlor, Professional Partner, Tavistock Institute of Human Relations, specialising in research and consultancy practice; co-director, Organisational Consultancy: Working with the Dynamics; Visiting Lecturer, Tavistock and Portman NHS Trust; Group Relations consultant; Formerly, Head, Social Work Discipline, Tavistock & Portman NHS Trust; Principal Consultant, Tavistock Consultancy.

Mannie Sher, Principal Social Scientist, Tavistock Institute of Human Relations; Formerly, Director, Group Relations Programme; Formerly, Board Member, International Society for the Psychoanalytic Study of Organisations (ISPSO); Author, The Dynamics of Change: Tavistock Approaches to Improving Social Systems (2013); Co-Editor, Dynamics at Boardroom Level: A Tavistock Primer for Leaders, Coaches and Consultants.

"The authors of this wonderfully comprehensive book invite us to embrace *systems psychodynamics* to support our leadership, followership and consultancy in organisations. It is essential reading for all who care about understanding and solving the often complex and enduring people and technical problems that exist in the workplace. It challenges us to be curious about the unconscious, to allow ourselves to be affected by what is going on - and not to move into action immediately.

Having previously worked with organisational role consultants in a police force, I can testify that the systems psychodynamics approach described in this book was transformational in the way that it opened our eyes to the unconscious processes in our organisation. We saw, for the first time, what was really going on under the surface, rather than what was apparent above it. This book provides a complete guide. It is both an in-depth analysis of the theories underpinning this approach to organisational development, and a rigorous analysis of how consultants and clients can use an understanding of unconscious group processes to: generate ideas for change, test these ideas in practice, and evaluate the results. Anyone interested in optimising the way the social and technical systems in their organisation work and in their inter-organisational relationships should read this".

— **Stephen Otter,**
QPM, ex Chief Constable and
Her Majesty's Inspector of Constabulary

"Welcome to this comprehensive introduction to the world of Systems Psychodynamics as a frame of reference for both understanding and consulting to organizations of all kinds. The chapters co-authored by the editors and the most original thinkers in the field offers the reader a rare view of the field in its entirety and its essence. This book highlights the challenges of joining the subjective world of experience, where thoughts and feelings beneath the surface are often formative, with the objective world of job and organization design. This task, as this most honest book reveals, is by no means an easy one. But the gains from taking it up, are incalculable. Thinkers and doers, academics and consultants: Read it and learn!"

— **Larry Hirschhorn,**
PhD., Principal Emeritus, CFAR, Author,
The Workplace Within and Reworking Authority

"My training at the Tavistock changed the way in which I view organisations and groups. It presented me with the wide spectrum of colours that exist in real organisational life that once seen cannot be ignored and allowed me to see the true pictures painted by the psychodynamics of organisational life and group relations. This book opens up the history and presence of the work of the Tavistock Institute. Not many people know about the history of the Institute and its influence on the terms and ideas that we take for granted, organisational development being one of them, but it might be a revelation to many to note the deep history of Tavistock thinking and doing and its impact on many systems and organisations. In some ways, the history of the Tavistock is the history of organisational thinking and how it relates to what we know of the mind. There are big ideas in this book presented in a way that is both accessible and illuminating. The Tavistock continues to punch well above its weight. The story of this book and its intended volumes explains why".

— **Lord Victor O Adebowale,**
MA, CBE, Visiting Prof. and Chancellor,
University of Lincoln, Chair, NHS Confederation

An Introduction to Systems Psychodynamics

Consultancy Research and Training

David Lawlor and Mannie Sher

With contributions from David Armstrong, Leslie Brissett, Halina Brunning, Susan Long, Juliet Scott, Philip Stokoe, Mark Stein and Heather Stradling

First published 2022
by Routledge
2 Park Square, Milton Park, Abingdon, Oxon OX14 4RN

and by Routledge
605 Third Avenue, New York, NY 10158

Routledge is an imprint of the Taylor & Francis Group, an informa business

© 2022 David Lawlor and Mannie Sher

The right of David Lawlor and Mannie Sher to be identified as authors of this work has been asserted in accordance with sections 77 and 78 of the Copyright, Designs and Patents Act 1988.

All rights reserved. No part of this book may be reprinted or reproduced or utilised in any form or by any electronic, mechanical, or other means, now known or hereafter invented, including photocopying and recording, or in any information storage or retrieval system, without permission in writing from the publishers.

Trademark notice: Product or corporate names may be trademarks or registered trademarks, and are used only for identification and explanation without intent to infringe.

British Library Cataloguing-in-Publication Data
A catalogue record for this book is available from the British Library

Library of Congress Cataloging-in-Publication Data
A catalog record has been requested for this book

ISBN: 978-1-032-02017-4 (hbk)
ISBN: 978-1-032-02015-0 (pbk)
ISBN: 978-1-003-18150-7 (ebk)

DOI: 10.4324/9781003181507

Typeset in Bembo
by KnowledgeWorks Global Ltd.

Homage: Dr Eric Miller (1924–2002) and Albert Kenneth (Ken) Rice (1908–1969)

Eric Miller

The book in this series is dedicated to the memory of Eric Miller through whose hands innumerable groups of people passed, seeking to benefit from his wisdom and experience of complex group, organisational and social processes. These people acquired deep understanding from Eric, who had a gift for translating complex multi-layered ideas and concepts into useful practical tools. Talking to Eric was a sacred experience leading to the scales falling from one's eyes and relief from exasperation.

At an advanced age, one looks back and ponders the confluence of certain events occurring at the right time. I arrived at the Tavistock Institute in 1971 to work in the Adult Department of the Clinic. Then, and for the following four years, Eric Miller was an enigmatic figure who inhabited the third floor – seen but hardly conversed with. For a junior trainee at the Clinic, there was a class of people about whom one heard a lot, but seldom crossed paths with, until I attended my first Leicester conference and then there he was, the Director, rather awe inspiring in his ability to listen, to contain and to offer insightful thoughts which were often delivered with wry humour that made one think about the relationship between the 'I' and the group that the moment before had lain slightly out of reach, beyond one's understanding. At other moments, he appeared on cue, to assist one's group (in the IG) to offer the idea that all parts of the system, including our own, are part of the totality of the learning organisation, and that we might want to experience the fullness of our participation. Our perspectives were changed, our defences lowered, and our group emboldened to take risks in the name of learning.

Instead of following an academic career in social anthropology, Eric became increasingly interested in the problems of people and organisations. He was a fine teacher and mentor, basing his approach on deeply held values of imparting skills to others so that the legacies of the Tavistock Institute and knowledge of organisational change and social improvement would pass to the next generation. Eric's view was that the field involved very hard work; he was critical of attempts to imbibe the learning without the pain and rigour of genuine maturity in managing the boundary between the one's inner world and the realities of the external environment. Over the years, Eric worked as a consultant in a wide variety of organisations – steel mills, an airline, a Church of England diocese, the water sector in Mexico, hospitals, residential homes, and schools.

Eric played a big part in numerous international development projects – the calico mills in India, rural development in Mexico. And of course, he was the director of the group relations programme for many years providing experiential learning opportunities for thousands of leaders, managers, clinicians and technical experts on the dynamics of groups and systems and on the impact they had on the way individuals took up their roles in their organisations. Eric and Ken Rice worked together in developing the group relations training programme. Eric was convinced of the value in enabling individuals to find authority within themselves; to question assumptions; and to extract themselves from irrational situations imposed by a group. Eric also helped to establish other institutions, including group relations organisations, in America, Finland, Denmark, Israel, India, South Africa and elsewhere. Eric was a co-founder of OPUS (an Organisation for Promoting Understanding in Society), a small educational charity which helps individuals recognise their relatedness to society, which today is chaired by his wife, Olya Khaleelee, with whom he often collaborated.

Eric Miller was a prolific writer and clear exponent of consulting practice. His more widely read books include *Systems of Organisation* (with Ken Rice, 1967) and *From Dependency to Autonomy* (1993). Nearly all the chapters in this series contain references to the work of Eric Miller; the people whose interviews appear in the 3rd book attest to the wide influence Eric had with many around the world.

Albert Kenneth (Ken) Rice

Ken Rice went to Nottingham High School, where he won an exhibition scholarship to Gonville & Caius College, Cambridge. He read mathematics at Cambridge University, but halfway through his studies he abandoned mathematics for anthropology. After university, Ken joined the Colonial Service and served in Kenya for several years before returning to Britain to work as assistant general manager at Lewis's, Birmingham; then personnel manager at G.A. Harvey & Co. in London. From 1945 to 1948, he was a deputy director of the Industrial Welfare Society in London (now The Work Foundation). He married Marjorie Ansell in 1935 and had two daughters.

Ken Rice joined the Tavistock Institute of Human Relations in 1948 and worked there until he died in 1969. It was at the Tavistock that Ken developed his method of critically analysing society, in particular addressing problems facing managers in industrial settings. This culminated in his work in India for the Sarabhai firm at Ahmedabad, where, in a few months, he replanned and reorganised the weaving section of the enterprise, increasing its productivity by 300 percent. This experience was recorded in his book, *Productivity and Social Organization: The Ahmedabad Experiment*.

Ken Rice worked with Eric Miller on several projects, including consultancy to an airline, a public school, the clergy, and for the Prison Commission. Out of this work he developed his ideas about group relations. Ken Rice directed the Tavistock Institute's group relations programme and training events, including the Leicester Conference, from 19xx to 1969. He later wrote a book about his experiences running Leicester, called *Learning for Leadership: Interpersonal and Intergroup Relations*.

News of Rice's work in group relations and the original ideas in his book *The Enterprise and its Environment* spread to the United States. He was employed by the Washington School of Psychiatry for a time; and was later asked to reorganise the Yale University Medical School. He directed the first group relations conference in the United States at Holyoke in 1965.

Ken Rice died suddenly on 15 November 1969, aged 61. His memorial service included tributes from his friends and colleagues, including Jock Sutherland, who described Rice's work at the Tavistock: "Ken's first endeavour with us was to create a small group of senior representatives of industry and administrators which met under the leadership of Wilfred Bion. Bion's influence on Ken remained a profound one and it established his future interest in group experience as a method for the personal development and understanding of those in leadership roles. His pioneering work in this field – perhaps one with quite remarkable potential for the educational needs of our society – was rewarded in the most gratifying way possible, its adoption by a wide range of institutions including industry, government departments and the clergy". The A.K. Rice Institute in the United States was set up by Margaret Rioch, Eric Miller and other colleagues in memory of Ken Rice and to continue the work he had started in America.

Contents

List of figures	xiii
Authors	xiv
Contributing authors	xvi
Foreword	xix

Introduction: The development of systems psychodynamics of organisations and consultancy	1
The history of the Tavistock Institute	13
"Dawn"	26

PART I
Systems 29

1 The systems contribution With Halina Brunning and Susan Long	31
2 The systems psychodynamics approach	47

PART II
Psychoanalytic thinking 63

3 The psychoanalytic contribution	65
4 Application of psychoanalytic concepts	80
5 Working with individuals With Halina Brunning and Susan Long	93

PART III
Group dynamics   115

6   Bion's theory of groups   119
    With David Armstrong

7   Working with groups I   136
    With David Armstrong

8   Working with groups II   152
    With Juliet Scott and Heather Stradling

9   The contribution of group relations I   164
    With Leslie Brissett

10 The contribution of group relations II   180
    With David Armstrong

11 Systems psychodynamics and organisational consultancy   202

12 Defences against anxiety   226
    With Mark Stein

PART IV
Socio-technical systems   245

13 Socio-technical systems   247

14 Summary   261

    References   275
    Index   303

List of figures

0.1	Genealogy of systems psychodynamics.	4
1.1	Open systems diagram.	42
2.1	The circular model of organisational development intervention.	59
5.1	Organisation-in-the-mind.	97
5.2	Four models of coaching.	108
5.3	Six domains of executive coaching.	109
5.4	Coaching in the Covid world.	111
5.5	Politics of salvation/politics of revelation and coaching in a post-Covid world.	112
9.1	Group relations: a method of study of the group-as-a-whole.	165

Authors

David Lawlor, Professional Partner at the Tavistock Institute of Human Relations where he specialises in research and consultancy practice. He is a co-director on the *Organisational Consultancy: Working with the Dynamics* programme. David is a Visiting Lecturer at the Tavistock and Portman NHS Trust. He is an experienced international Group Relations Conference consultant. He was Head of the Social Work Discipline at the Tavistock & Portman NHS Trust and a Principal Consultant at Tavistock Consultancy. David has extensive experience managing and working local authority settings, voluntary organisations and psychiatric hospitals. At the Tavistock Clinic, he trained in organisational consultancy and psychoanalytic psychotherapy. He has delivered a wide range of training and staff development programmes in the care sector. As part of his PhD research, he has evaluated consultancy interventions and examined how to improve the outcome for the client. He is particularly interested in the impact of stressful environments on staff functioning. Author of: Test of Time: A Case Study in the Functioning of Social Systems as a Defence Against Anxiety: Rereading 50 Years on, *Clinical Child Psychology and Psychiatry, Vol. 14 No. 4, 2009;* and with Liz Webb: An Interview with Isabel Menzies Lyth with a Conceptual Commentary, *Organisational and Social Dynamics, Vol. 9 No. 1* (2009).

Mannie Sher, Principal Social Scientist at the Tavistock Institute of Human Relations, London. He manages a portfolio of organisational development and change assignments and consults to Boards and executives on their strategic and leadership challenges. His research and consultancy work focusses on the impact of thought on the dialectic relationship between social constructivism, the unconscious and liberal democracy. Mannie is a practicing psychoanalytical psychotherapist. He has published on subjects of consultancy, leadership, organisational development, social dreaming, ethics and corruption. His latest books are *The Dynamics of Change: Tavistock*

Approaches to Improving Social Systems (2013), published by Karnac Books, and *Dynamics at Boardroom Level: A Tavistock Primer for Leaders, Coaches and Consultants* (2020), edited by Leslie Brissett, Mannie Sher and Tazi Smith, published by Routledge. Mannie is the former director of the Tavistock Institute's Group Relations Programme (1997–2017) and a former member of the Board of the International Society for the Psychoanalytic Study of Organisations (ISPSO).

Contributing authors

David Armstrong, Associate Consultant, Tavistock Consulting, a unit of the Tavistock and Portman NHS Foundation Trust. A social psychologist by background; formerly, Junior Project Officer, the Tavistock Institute of Human Relations, working with Eric Trist, Hugh Murray and Eric Miller on action research projects into the impact of automation on relations at work; Senior Research Fellow at Chelsea College, University of London, and later staff member, The Grubb Institute, working on a major action research study in supporting young people in transition to working life (TWL); Group Relations and Organisational Consultant, Tavistock Clinic. Has had a lifelong practical interest in the links between psychoanalysis and social and organisational life on which he has written widely, published and taught. *Organisation in the Mind: Psychoanalysis, Group Relations and Organisational Consultancy*, edited by Robert French; with Michael Rustin, co-edited *Social Systems as a Defense against Anxiety: Explorations in a Paradigm*.

Leslie Brissett, Director of the Group Relations Programme, Principal Consultant and Company Secretary of the Tavistock Institute of Human Relations in London. Leslie has consulted to conferences across the world in consultant, administrator and director roles. He directed the Leicester Conference between 2016 and 2020 inclusive. In 2020, Leslie directed the first online international group relations conference using video conferencing methodology; it was co-sponsored by five institutions. He has actively pursued institutional partnerships with professors at INSEAD, Harvard and Wharton School and negotiated and signed the Tavistock Institute of Human Relations as the first Institutional Partner of the International Society for the Psychoanalytic Study of Organisations. He lives in St Leonards on Sea, East Sussex, UK, and Dumas, Arkansas, USA.

Halina Brunning is a Chartered Clinical Psychologist, freelance Organizational Consultant, Accredited Executive Coach. She has published extensively on clinical and organisational issues, edited several books, including *Executive Coaching: Systems-Psychodynamic Perspective* (2006), translated into Italian in 2009. She conceived of and edited a trilogy of books which analysed the contemporary world through a psychoanalytic lens: *Psychoanalytic Perspectives on a Turbulent World,* published by Karnac in 2010, 2012 and 2014; co-author with Olya Khaleelee *Dance Macabre and other stories – a psychoanalytic perspective on global dynamics,* to be published by Phoenix Publishing House in 2021.

Susan Long is an Organisational Consultant and Executive Coach. Previously, Professor of Creative and Sustainable Organisation at RMIT University, she is now a Professor and Director of Research and Scholarship at the National Institute for Organisation Dynamics Australia (NIODA); Associate of the University of Melbourne Executive Programs and teacher at INSEAD, Singapore, and the University of Divinity, Melbourne. Susan has over 35 years of experience in Group Relations, having been on staff or directed many conferences. Susan has authored ten books and many articles in books and scholarly journals; she is General Editor of the journal *Socioanalysis* and an Associate Editor with *Organisational and Social Dynamics*. She is member of the Advisory Board for Mental Health at Work with Comcare and a past member of the Board of the Judicial College of Victoria (2011–2016). Susan is a distinguished member of ISPSO.

Juliet Scott is an artist and social scientist interweaving her practice between the disciplines through studio research, organisational curation projects and the creation of dynamic learning environments. When Juliet joined the Tavistock Institute of Human Relations in 2006, she began to make a connection between her interest in objects and the Institute's ongoing work with groups in understanding group relations, organisations and social systems. She now works as artist in residence at the Institute which is a part of her leadership of a wider programme of work dedicated to the arts and organisation.

Philip Stokoe, Director Philip Stokoe Associates; Psychoanalyst in private practice working with adults and couples. Organisational Consultant, to a wide range of organisations. Has been a senior manager in a range of health and social care settings since 1978, finally working in the Adult Department of the Tavistock & Portman NHS Foundation Trust between 1994 and 2012, finishing as Clinical Director from 2007. He has a reputation for teaching and writing across a wide range including psychoanalytic institutions and Politics. His book, The Curiosity Drive: Our Need for Inquisitive Thinking, published by Phoenix Publishing House, 2020.

Mark Stein, Professor Emeritus of Leadership and Management at University of Leicester. Formerly, Senior Lecturer, Imperial College London; Research Fellow, London School of Economics and Brunel University; Researcher and Consultant at the Tavistock Institute of Human Relations. Mark has held visiting or associate posts at the Tavistock Clinic, London Business School and INSEAD, Fontainebleau, where he has been an Adjunct

Professor and Visiting Scholar. Mark has been awarded the European Academy of Management's iLab Prize for innovative scholarship; an Emerald Citation of Excellence; the 'Group & Organization Management' best paper prize; the Gavin Macfadyen Memorial Essay Prize; and the Richard Normann Prize, of which he is the only recipient.

Heather Stradling is a senior researcher/consultant at the Tavistock Institute of Human Relations. Her previous career in the applied arts sector informs current practice within diverse research, evaluation and professional development programmes including as Co-Director of *'Deepening Creative Practice with Organisations'*. Heather is also a psychodynamic counsellor (MBACP) and provides supervision and facilitation for a range of clients.

Foreword

This book is a labour of love and intelligence. The authors, Mannie Sher and David Lawlor, provide the readers with a comprehensive overview of 'Systems Psychodynamics' with an eye towards its origins, its development as a theory and practice, and its currents prospects and challenges. The authorship of the book – the result of collaborations between the main authors and the contributing authors, and among the authors themselves – testifies to the group undertaking, spanning decades, cultures and settings, that gives Systems Psychodynamics its continuing vitality and relevance.

Selecting individual contributions for meritorious mention is a bit like saying which of your children you like best. Well, you love them all, (!) though each has distinctive strengths and points of departure, some of which you resonate with personally. I suspect that you, the reader, upon reading this volume of essays, will have a similar response, a testimony to the breadth of the offerings that lie between the covers of this book, whether virtual or real.

To that end, can I mention David Armstrong's reminder that lurking behind Wilfred Bion's conception of the 'Work Group' is the still to be developed conception of what makes for work-group creativity? If, as he notes, the Basic Assumptions of group life are regressive, pulling people away from reality, the Work Group cannot simply end with the group's contact with reality, but rather how it imagines a reality in a way that enables it to develop a creative response to it. But to imagine is to fantasize, and surely, we who work in the psychoanalytic vineyard know something about fantasy and its developmental impacts. This is surely an important arena for further thinking and working.

Can I also mention the chapter on sociotechnical systems, 'STS'. The authors' inclusion of this chapter reminds us that the Systems Psychodynamics tradition proper has for too long been split off from the sociotechnical. This even though in Eric Trist's imagining they were equal partners in the venture of helping organisations define their valued objectives and the methods for achieving them. Perhaps Fred Emery's storied resistance to psychoanalysis played a role here. In addition, in its heyday, STS took up the thread of social history associated with worker engagement and emancipation – interests and their associated passions that were more closely aligned with the trade-union movement than with psychology. But in today's setting when information technologies dissolve organisational boundaries and blur the line between fantasy and reality – think of the multiplayer game called 'Second life', – we deeply need a Systems Psychodynamics that takes technology and its impacts as among its foremost preoccupations. One additional impact of technology is that organizations today are losing their skins; they are in networks often tethered to other, dissimilar organisations. Think of companies in a particular city that depend on a school system's ability to educate its children, not simply for literacy but for creativity. Was there ever a more fertile field for projection, with each 'node' in a network imagining that the other node – unfamiliar to it and for this reason strange – is the reason for the overall system's stagnation?

And can I also mention the chapter on Organizational Role Analysis co-authored by Susan Long and Halina Brunning. Systems Psychodynamics was born in the 'decade of the group', to use Eric Trist's felicitous term. But while we focus on role, group, and system we cannot forget that people take up roles. Just as their roles influences their behaviour, their personal psychodynamics influences how they take up their roles. Susan Long provides a lovely vignette that helps illuminate this issue. During a role consultation, a defense attorney draws a person juggling balls in the air, but the person lacks facial features. As befits the psychodynamically tuned role consultant, Long wonders if drawing a face without features is meaningful and she asks her client, why the absence? The interplay is exquisite. The client first denies that this absence is important – a signal of a possibly defensive response. But upon further dialogue, the client links it to the way she must keep her often intense emotions in check because everyone in court is scrutinising faces, presumably for signs of truth-telling or lying. The trigger for avoiding faces is in the court room, and in this sense, the drawing reflects the client's situation. But Long's client had internalised it, so that facelessness was affecting her friendships. Long does not elaborate, but there is surely a very personal story here as well. Not all attorneys would respond to this court-induced stimulus in the same way. As we say in our field, Long's client may have had a 'valence' for facelessness. Could it have influenced her choice of work as much as it made her vulnerable to the emotional triggers associated with appearing in court? I wonder if at times, in our insistence on the group perspective, we don't avail ourselves of the knowledge we have, often gained through the hard work of our own individual psychoanalysis, about individual psychological functioning. This is, after all, the heart and soul of psychoanalysis, our mother discipline.

I hope I have persuaded you to dip into this volume of essays and read freely to find those themes, issues, case studies and clinical nuggets that telegraph to you, "I want to be part of the next chapter in his storied venture of extending Systems Psychodynamics into the coming decades". That feeling will be the beginning of your own contribution to the field.

By Larry Hirschhorn

Introduction

The development of systems psychodynamics of organisations and consultancy

This series of books coincides with the centenary of the founding of the Tavistock 'Family' in 1920, which initially was the Tavistock Institute of Medical Psychology (better known as the Tavistock Clinic and now known as the Tavistock and Portman NHS Trust), the parent body of the post-World War II Tavistock Institute. The books are creative testimony to the continuing intellectual contribution of the Tavistock Institute to improving human relations.

An Introduction to Systems Psychodynamics: Consultancy Research & Training, which we have termed 'Dawn', introduces the reader to systems psychodynamics theory and its application for organisations and consultancy. The book explores the current state of knowledge about the practice and application of the systems psychodynamics paradigm, illustrated by several case studies and an account of its historical and theoretical development. The book's authors, together with guest authors David Armstrong, Leslie Brissett, Halina Brunning Marianna Fotaki, Susan Long, Juliet Scott, Mark Stein, Philip Stokoe and Heather Stradling describe the work of the main theorists who have developed the theory and practice and how these ideas have been advanced. The authors show how systems psychodynamics methods and models are attempts to understand the nature of organisational life and at the same time, demonstrate practical application insofar as the models have a built-in problem-solving approach. The authors demonstrate that the work of professionals associated with systems psychodynamics methods have a multi-disciplinary, multi-theoretical and holistic approach to organisational and social problems. Each chapter ends with an exercise to challenge the readers thinking in the application of the ideas.

The second book, *Systems Psychodynamics: Innovative Approaches to Change, Whole Systems & Complexity*, we have termed 'Emergence'; it continues with our in-depth exploration of the application of the following sets of theories, also illustrated with many case studies and an exercise at the end of each chapter. The book's authors and guest authors Eliat Aram, David Armstrong, Coreene Archer, Anne Benson, Mee-Yan Cheung Judge, Camilla Child, Jonathan Gosling, Dione Hills, Olya Khaleelee, Susan Long, Anton Obholzer, Carolyn Ordowich and Bert Painter cover sociotechnical systems and action research, leadership and whole systems, working with

DOI: 10.4324/9781003181507-1

large complex collaborative partnerships, the application of complexity theory, working with leadership, social dreaming, the impact of digitalisation and virtual working, two chapters on evaluation, the professional development of systems psychodynamics consultants and concludes with a chapter on current theoretical developments and conclusions.

The third book, *Systems Psychodynamics: Theorist and Practitioner Voices from the Field*, which we have termed 'Voices from the Field', contains the recorded experiences of eminent Tavistock colleagues who have contributed to the development of the work of systems psychodynamics practice and its evolving methodologies. These narrative interviews engage in what systems psychodynamics consultants think is the purpose of their consultancy and research interventions; what theoretical constructs make up their use of the theories; and ask if there is a difference in how these theories are deployed in practice by different consultants. Models of work have evolved over a 70-year period. The main theoretical constructs are drawn from the fields of psychoanalysis, sociotechnical theory, open systems theory, group relations practice, and latterly, complexity theory. Historically, there has been a divergence in the application of these theories, with some practitioners placing more emphasis on certain aspects of the theory than others. Much of this theory has been developed from detailed individual case studies. In "Voices from the Field", we hear the stories of how consultants have worked with these ideas over time and how their practice has evolved.

In the first book, Gould et al. (2001, Pg. 2–15) make the case that systems psychodynamics is an emerging field of social science, the boundaries of which are continually being refined and re-defined. The central tenet of the systems psychodynamics perspective is contained in the conjunction of the two terms 'systems' and 'psychodynamics'. The *systems* designation refers to the open systems concepts that provide the dominant framing perspective for understanding the structural aspects of an organisational system. These include its design, division of labour, levels of authority and reporting relationships; the nature of work tasks, processes and activities; its mission and primary task; the nature and patterning of the organisation's task and sentient boundaries and the transactions across them.

The *psychodynamics* designation refers to psychoanalytic perspectives on individual experiences and mental processes (e.g. transference, resistances, object relations, phantasy, etc.), as well as on the experiences of unconscious group and social processes which are simultaneously both a source and a consequence of unresolved or unrecognised organisational difficulties (Menzies, 1960; Jaques, 1955). Gould et al. (2001, Pg. 2–15) declare that in the formal sense, the field of systems psychodynamics had its birth with the publication of Miller and Rice's seminal volume *Systems of Organisation* (1967).

Petriglieri and Petriglieri (2020) state that:

> Systems psychodynamic scholarship focuses on the interaction between collective structures, norms, and practices in social systems and the

cognitions, motivations, and emotions of members of those systems. It is most useful to investigate the unconscious forces that underpin the persistence of dysfunctional organizational features and the appeal of irrational leaders. It is also well equipped to challenge arrangements that stifle individual and organizational development.

A proposition in the first and second books will be that because of its multi-disciplinary and multi-theoretical approach; it is problematic for managers, policymakers, consultant practitioners and researchers to find a meta-position in relation to systems psychodynamics methods. A critical appraisal of the systems psychodynamics paradigm and its application to present-day social and organisational difficulties is a necessary challenge. Therefore, the books will be an examination of the paradigm in action. How useful is the existing practice and its theoretical goals to enable managers, policymakers, consultant practitioners and researchers help their clients with organisational problems will be an expected outcome of this book. This question is relevant for the following reasons:

1 The systems psychodynamics paradigm has been widely disseminated in the applied social sciences.
2 The systems psychodynamics paradigm, because of its multi-disciplinary and multi-theoretical base, poses methodological problems for managers, policymakers, consultant practitioners and researchers. This could be summed up as: the systems psychodynamics model is often taken as a given. By this, we mean that the systems psychodynamics paradigm could be experienced and regarded as a concrete representation of organisational and social reality rather than an emergent body of theory that helps make sense of current experiences.

According to Miller (1997, Pg. 188), the conceptual framework evolved at the Tavistock Institute in the 1950s and 1960s. Miller outlines the following as the main theoretical developments. He states that it draws on the two strands of **systems theory** and of **psychoanalysis** with its illuminations of unconscious processes in individuals and groups. See Figure 0.1 that sketches the 'genealogy' of the systems psychodynamics framework (Miller 1997, Pg. 188).

Systems psychodynamics as a distinct paradigm

This book endeavours to raise systems psychodynamics to the level of a paradigm – a new set of ideas and ways of looking at organisational development consultancy.

Producing three volumes may make the paradigm seem like an aggregation of elements rather than an integrated whole. We have located the essence of the paradigm in the combination and integration of two primary bodies of knowledge – psychoanalysis and systems theory – and drawing

4 Introduction

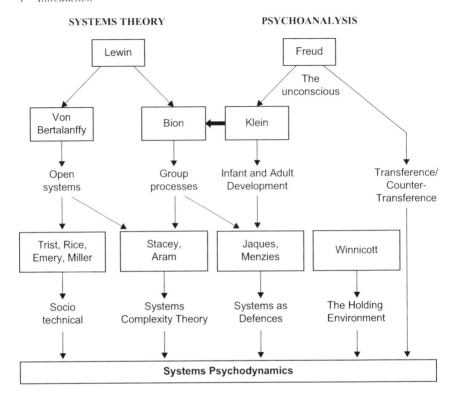

Figure 0.1 Genealogy of systems psychodynamics.

Source: Eric Miller, The Tavistock Institute of Human Relations.

on related theories like complexity theory, organisational theory, leadership theory, group relations theory, political theory, etc. We posit a harmonising coincidence of conceptualisations about the individual, role, group, system, organisation and environment in our systems psychodynamics paradigm as it applies to consultancy practice. This would mean that an organisational development intervention could comprise some or all of the following elements: executive coaching; team building; the technical operations of the organisation, sociotechnical systems of task, matrix, boundary and authority. In the second book, we write about supply chain, both up and down, the market eco-system, the turbulent environment, geo-political conflict, Covid-19, economic depression; evaluation, large group interventions, leadership and followership, social dreaming, art and community harnessing the power of creative practice for personal and social change.

In the third book, we present the work of prominent practitioners and clients who are implementing the systems psychodynamics paradigm and developing it in their practice.

Throughout the series, the authors strenuously hold the view that the systems psychodynamics paradigm means taking a view of and working as far as possible with the total system and not just one part of it; nor does one theory or approach explain the complex nature of organisational systems, organisations of organisations; or systems of systems. The systems psychodynamics paradigm eschews the idea of the individual consultant working alone heroically to effect change. The paradigm in effect changes the function of the organisational development consultant from a leader of change processes to a provider of containment, understanding and facilitation of others to take up their leadership roles responsibly in their change processes.

The multi-disciplinary and multi-theoretical nature of *systems psychodynamics* makes for a complex and sophisticated set of theories and interventions available for a consultant to draw upon. The model is a complex interweaving of different theories that are brought to bear when a consultant is working with a client system. Using the different concepts that make up the model can lead to discussions on the application of psychoanalytic theory and the appropriateness of open systems thinking for organisational theorising. But this would be dissembling the parts that make up the totality of the model. *Systems psychodynamics* could be thought of as akin to a menu that attempts to achieve balance and equilibrium in its constituent parts. By examining only one part of the menu and losing sight of the whole, ends up with an incomplete picture of the whole system, or in this case, the *systems psychodynamics* model.

We conclude from this that the *systems psychodynamics* model should be constituted as a paradigm. Duberley and Johnson (2000) offer this interpretation of Kuhn's formulation of a paradigm:

> It is a set of beliefs, values, assumptions and techniques centred around successive exemplars of successful practical application. A paradigm serves as a regulative framework of metaphysical assumptions 'shared by members of a given community' (Kuhn, 1970) which specifies the character of the world and its constituent objects and processes and which acts as a 'disciplinary matrix' by drawing the boundaries for what a community's work is to look like. As such, paradigms are 'universally recognised scientific achievements that for a time provide model problems and solutions to a community of practitioners' (Kuhn, 1970). Each 'practitioner community' is characterised by a consensus, into which neophytes are socialised through their disciplinary training. This consensus is grounded in a tradition that bases their work around a shared way of thinking and working within an established network of ideas, theories and methods. Each paradigm therefore has its own distinctive language which offers a unique means of classifying and construing the objects encountered during scientists' engagements with the world.

Bearing in mind the above definition, from the authors' review of the literature as detailed above, the work of the *systems psychodynamics* community of professional practitioners has attempted over the last one hundred years to develop a new paradigm for understanding organisational life and the nature of work. The paradigm has incorporated into the model several theories and categorisations of phenomena from other disciplines to construct both a model of the world of organisations, individuals and groups and a theory of practice.

It is the theory of practice that presents problems for research, practice and theory development. It can be seen from the literature that the development of theory and practice has led to several different strands that can be identified as *systems psychodynamics*. These different strands of the *systems psychodynamics* paradigm place different emphases on the differing theoretical concepts underpinning their practice. Miller (1993) makes this same point, 'there has been no single *systems psychodynamics* role model: for example, Jaques (1951), Sofer (1961) and Rice (1963) all describe their positions differently. Commonalties, however, are more important'. Miller argues that the differing projects that the *systems psychodynamics* were engaged in led to the generation of different theories as the demands of the 'laboratory of real life' required solutions from the action research/consultation processes.

The differing strands of both practice and theory mean that it is possible to position oneself within the systems psychodynamics paradigm and not adhere to all the theoretical propositions. Jaques (1995 a,b, Pg. 343–349) is an interesting example of this. Jaques is cited many times in the literature for his innovative work in Glacier Metals, yet some 40 years later, he 'recants' his earlier position with regards to psychoanalytic perspectives on organisations. Does this mean that he no longer subscribes to the systems psychodynamics paradigm? Or are his later contributions an addition to the paradigm or the attempt to create a new one? Another example of this is Stacey (2001), who attempts to develop systems theory from a complexity perspective. Gould et al. (2001) rightly points out that Stacey is serving a 'timely reminder that we need to consider new approaches that may challenge or complement our traditional thinking. He (Stacey) writes from the unique position of 'complexity theory' as applied to organisations. The difficulty here is trying to ascertain how the paradigm is extended. Gould does not sound sure whether complexity theory lies inside the boundary of the systems psychodynamics paradigm or beyond it and outside within its own paradigm. But it should also be noted that Stacey was not the first writer associating himself with both systems psychodynamics thinking and complexity theory. Morgan (1993) explores the relevance of Prigogine's ideas of the whole being contained in part, fluctuation at a distance from equilibrium and dissipative structure. According to Stacey (1993), "Prigogine is the chemist who has shown how non-linear feedback systems develop unpredictable new forms of behaviour when they are pushed far from equilibrium. There is a fundamental relationship between states of bounded instability or chaos, on the one hand, and innovation or creativity, on the other: systems can only be creative through experiencing instability".

As the systems psychodynamics model is applied science, it is difficult to set boundaries around its theoretical starting and finishing points. The application of theory in the field inevitably leads to the generation of a new theory or the reinterpretation of old theory.

Palmer (2002), through a critique of three case studies, attempts to identify the paradigm limits of systems psychodynamics practice. He proposes that the following are the core concepts of systems psychodynamics practice:

1 The individual and the mechanisms of defence (Klein, 1959)
2 Role (Reed and Armstrong, 1988a, b)
3 Group processes (Bion, 1961, 1967a, b, c)
4 Use of social systems as defences against anxiety (Jaques, 1955; Menzies, 1960, 1989a, b)
5 Boundary (Rice, 1965)
6 Systemic (Miller, 1990)
7 Open system (Miller and Rice, 1967; von Bertalanffy, 1950a, b)
8 Sociotechnical system (Trist and Bamforth, 1951)
9 Organisation in the mind (Lawrence, 1999; Stokes, 1994; Hutton, 1997; Armstrong, 2005a, b, c)
10 Authority and power (Rice, 1965; Reed and Armstrong, 1988a, b; Jaques, 1989)

Linked to the core set of theories and practice is:

1 Working with groups
2 A temporary holding environment and container for client anxieties
3 Working with or in the transference
4 Working with the countertransference
5 Working through
6 Defining and clarifying boundaries
7 Designing new forms of organisation
8 Designing experiential learning events

Working with groups

Working with groups is often a preferred method of diagnosis and intervention. This practice draws upon Bion and the *Leicester Conferences – A Working Conference for the study of organisational life*, involving a distinctive form of process consultancy in which the consultant works interpretatively with the 'material' presented by the client group.

A temporary holding environment and container for client anxieties

Providing a temporary safe environment (Bion's notion of 'container') for the client (individuals, teams, management groups or boards) to address and work through anxieties.

Working with or in the transference

The transference being all the thoughts, feelings and phantasies that are invoked in the client–consultant relationship. The consultant uses these experiences to understand organisational life that is normally outside the client's awareness.

Working with the countertransference

Interpreting and using the consultant's own feelings, phantasies, impulses and behaviour as indicators of having become not only in but part of the client system.

Working through

In psychodynamic psychotherapy, working through is seen as the process of repeating, elaborating, and amplifying interpretations. It is believed that such working through is critical towards the success of therapy. In the consulting relationship we can apply the same methodology but apply it to helping the client deal with the emotional, intellectual and technical issues that they are facing. Working through also allows resistance to change or difficult emotions to surface in the consultant/client relationship. Instead of interpretations as in the clinical setting, organisational consultants are likely to offer a working hypothesis as to what might be occurring in the system.

Defining and clarifying boundaries

Organisational boundaries are the demarcation between the organisation and its environment. There are many structural types of organizational boundaries: vertical, horizontal, external, and geographic. In analysing the organisation we ask where are the boundaries drawn. Why is the boundary drawn there and not there? What is permitted to cross and what is controlled? An organisational consultant seeks to find the underlying rationale that lies behind why boundaries are drawn where they are and managed as they are.

Designing new forms of organisation

The six most common approaches to organisational design include simple, functional, divisional, matrix, team and network designs. A company will choose their organisational structure based on their needs. The organisational design will reflect a structure that aligns to the business at any given moment in time. A consultant's key task is exploring the nature of the design and its suitability to the primary task and purpose of the organisation.

Designing experiential learning events

Experiential learning comprises of learning activities, both inside and outside the organisation that are designed to actively engage organisational members to learn by doing, and then reflecting on the process and experience and actively creating their own understanding. By engaging organisational members in hands-on experiences and reflection, they are better able to connect to the dynamic processes in their system to order to effect desirable change.

The following activities or ways of thinking and relating make up the systems psychodynamics paradigm:

1 Working with projective identification.
2 Introjective identification and re-projection via an interpretation or intervention.
3 Working through helping the client recognise resistance to change and the associated fears to change processes.
4 Defining and clarifying boundaries. Articulating and enacting a coherent array of boundary roles and task systems is functional for organisational work.
5 Designing new forms of organisation, based on the open systems model (Miller and Rice, 1967).
6 Designing experiential learning events; training in group relations.

The *environment* in the systems psychodynamics model is extremely important. Trist and Murray (1997) specifically make the connection between sociotechnical systems and the socio-ecological model. They refer to the turbulent field that most organisations now find themselves in and make the point that over-bounded systems can no longer survive in the modern world of globalisation.

> No organisation, however large, can go it alone in a turbulent environment. Dissimilar organisations become directly correlated. They need to become directively correlated. They need to be linked in networks. A new focus of the Institute's (systems psychodynamics) work has been, therefore, the development of collaborative modes of intervention for the reduction of turbulence and the building of inter-group networks that can address 'meta-problems' at the 'domain' level …The socio-ecological approach is linked to the socio-technical because of the critical importance of self-regulating organisations for turbulence reduction.

It is further linked to the socio-psychological approach because of the need to reduce stress and regression. Primitive levels of behaviour can only too easily appear in the face of higher levels of uncertainty.

(Trist and Murray, 1997, Pg 16)

The metaphor of systems, individuals, groups and organisations operating more like network pathways with overlapping boundaries could be applicable. Boundary location would be less determinate, boundaries more porous with osmotic permeable membranes. The consequence for the individual is that much work would be carried out in a multiplicity of roles and tasks and with the membership of multiple overlapping systems.

But the use of any metaphor or symbol for organisational life can easily lead to a reification process. Instead of regarding a group or boundary as a heuristic concept, one to be worked with and developed through thought and dialogue, it can easily become fixed and institutionalised and be rendered meaningless and dead.

Holding in mind of all three domains that make up the systems psychodynamics model, the *socio-psychological, the sociotechnical and the socio-ecological* is necessary but not easy. Sometimes it may feel too much to encompass in both one's 'methodological kit bag' let alone in one's core practice. It is important not to be driven into one domain and occupy it professionally and 'turns a blind eye' to what one is not facing theoretically or practically in how one might engage with the client system as a whole and including the environment in which it operates.

Hoggett (1996), in his review of the *Unconscious at Work* (1994), draws attention to the perception that the *group relations* tradition has remained frustratingly marginal to the concerns of those British practitioners to whom they should have an enormous relevance – change agents in organisational and social systems, managers and policy makers in the human services. He notes that those working within the systems psychodynamics tradition of group relations seem to have remained hermetically sealed from the social developments around them. He claims that there has been a failure on the part of the systems psychodynamics to engage with the *political* dimensions of welfare systems, particularly with the rise of marketisation of welfare systems. According to Hoggett, this lack of a political perspective has led to a crude interpretation of the concept of the *primary task*. He argues that the concept of a **primary task** is inevitably value laden and that practitioners such as consultants need to locate the interpretation of the *primary task* within a social context.

Hoggett may well have identified an important social process which present-day practitioners of the systems psychodynamics model now find themselves in, namely, that the permanent 'white water' or turbulent field forces them into a narrow definition of the task. But it may well be that echoes of the earlier difficulties that the Tavistock Institute faced with its work on the *sociotechnical* still reverberate. Trist and Murray, in their Historical Overview (1993, Pg. 1–34), write of the difficulties encountered:

> The socio-technical perspective was entirely novel. ..... Efforts to bring about changes in this new direction have encountered resistances of profound cultural and psychological depth. These can be more readily understood when their basis in unconscious processes is recognised, for they disturb socially constructed psychological defences in management and worker alike and threaten established identities. The loss of the familiar, even if beset with 'bad' attributes, often entail mourning. The possibly 'good' may threaten because it is untried. Change strategies must allow for the fact that working through such difficulties takes time. Moreover, intensive socio-technical change threatens existing power systems and requires redistribution of power.

It may well be that difficulties lie in the nature of the work; consultancy assignments procured by competitive tendering lead to a watering down of attempts to deal with the powerful forces that resist change. Consultants in their thinking can unconsciously set limited goals for the consultancy. Discrete work with sub-systems may be possible but large-scale system change may now seem a utopian ideal of the founding fathers of the Tavistock Institute tradition. Hoggett argues that the definition of *primary task* as the task that must be carried out for the institution to survive is limiting the definition to certain interest groups. Who defines the 'task' is the point he is making. Within the group relations model, it would be those 'authorised' in role to make such decisions, but this evades the issue of how they are authorised and whom this authorisation represents. But since 1996, there is evidence from the Tavistock Institute of Human Relations that large-scale change interventions can be successfully applied.

Loewenthal (1996, Pg. 1248), in her review of the Unconscious at Work (1994), draws attention to the fact that there are no discussions of evaluations of consultancies of the kind described in the book. She notes the relative isolation of the work described from other apparently relevant areas of activity such as occupational psychology, clinical psychology and social psychology. According to Loewenthal, there is a need for the validation of the system psychodynamic approaches. She states that more assessments are needed of the effectiveness of systems psychodynamics-based approaches to consultancy and intervention.

> There is usually at least one desirable ultimate outcome, which should be specifiable and measurable. As Leiper (1994) says, professionals are being asked explicitly to evaluate the work they do. It should be possible to show the extent to which, for instance, members of institutions using consulting from systems psychodynamics consultants felt that since the

consultancy, they were clearer about their task, or had agreed a more realistic task, or were clearer about authority structures, or had achieved other of the several outcomes described in The Unconscious at Work. This could further increase the acceptability of the ideas and practices in this very important work.

To fill the gap outlined by Loewenthal, we have included two chapters in the second book, *Systems Psychodynamics: Innovative Approaches to Change, Whole Systems & Complexity,* on the evaluation of consultancy.

The history of the Tavistock Institute

The early history of the Tavistock Institute overlaps with that of the Tavistock Clinic as many of the staff from the Clinic worked on new, large-scale army psychiatry and social reconstruction projects during the World War II, and it was because of this work that the Institute was created. During the Second World War in England, several innovative psychiatrists and social scientists were brought together to solve practical social problems by combining social science and psychiatry. They were committed to seeing what further application their learning could have beyond the conditions of war. As Trist and Murray relate, "Undertaking practical tasks that sought to resolve operational crises generated insights that led towards new theory ... a new action-oriented philosophy of relating psychiatry and the social sciences to society had become a reality in practice" (Trist and Murray, 1990a, b, Pg. 3–4).

During the war, staff from the Tavistock Clinic played key roles in British Army psychiatry. According to Sofer (1972), there were three main strands in the Tavistock war-time work. One was the area of group selection of officers. Here the emphasis moved from attempts to identify personality attributes of prospective leaders to the simulation of problematic situations requiring leadership and to the observation of personal behaviour in those situations. Secondly, the group developed new forms of therapy which revolved around working in groups and organisations and systematically drew the attention of patients to the link between personal behaviour and unsatisfactory social environments; this led to the development of therapeutic communities. The approach to therapy is summed up as:

> ... an attempt to use a hospital .... as a community with the immediate aim of full participation of all its members in its daily life and the eventual aim of the resocialisation of the neurotic individual ....The daily life of the [hospital] community must be related to real tasks, truly relevant to the needs and aspirations of the small society of the hospital, and the larger society in which it is set.... full opportunity must be available for identifying and analysing the inter-personal barriers which stand in the way of participating in a full community life.
>
> (Main, 1946)

DOI: 10.4324/9781003181507-2

Thirdly, in civil resettlement work, they constructed and manipulated specially designed transitional communities as bridges between war-time experiences and civilian life.

Working with colleagues in the Royal Army Medical Corps and the British Army, they were responsible for innovations such as the War Office Selection Board (WOSB) and Civil Resettlement Units (CRUs). The CRUs were designed to deal with the problems surrounding the repatriation of former prisoners of war. The central notion was to develop a programme within regional residential units which would enable these to act as transitional communities through which men might hope to gain help. The units were to be run so far as possible on a basis of participation and self-government rather than impersonal military authority, see Curle (1947). The Tavistock group also worked on psychological warfare. The group that formed around the WOSBs and CRUs were fascinated by this work with groups and organisations and sought to continue research in this field after the war. Various influential figures had visited the WOSBs during the war, so there was scope for consultancy work, but the Clinic staff also planned to become a part of the National Health Service when it was established, and they had been warned that such consultancy and research would not be possible under the auspices of the NHS. Because of this, the Tavistock Institute of Human Relations (TIHR) was created in 1947 to carry out organisational research when the Clinic was incorporated into the NHS. The Rockefeller Foundation awarded a significant grant that facilitated the creation of the TIHR. WOSBs left an important legacy in the forms taken by selection for management traineeships after the war. Ronald Hargreaves joined the Unilever industrial concern and, on his recommendation, collaborated with the Unilever personnel department in improving selection procedures based on the learning from WOSBs.

Dicks (1970), in his review of the work of the Tavistock Clinic and the Tavistock Institute over a fifty year period describes the early work of the Institute as follows: "in the first four years seventy projects were undertaken, ranging in size from a single discussion and report to work extending over three years. There were two main projects, the first, led by Elliott Jaques, was an intensive study of the psychological and social forces affecting the group life, morale and productivity of a single industrial community; the second, led by A.T.M. Wilson, was single study of communication in industry, which was undertaken with the collaboration of a number of firms together representing a wide range of industries". Wilson describes how studies on the organisation of work groups in coal mining aimed to generate new principles of work organisation. A parallel research programme in India, led by A.K. Rice, compared work between developed and underdeveloped countries. This work demonstrated that it is possible to re-design a sociotechnical system in the manufacturing industry to satisfy the technologist as well as the human needs of the workers and to adapt to constraints.

In the early years of the TIHR, income was derived from research grants, contract work, and fees for courses. During the 1950s and 1960s, the TIHR carried out several signature projects in collaboration with major manufacturing companies, including Unilever, the Ahmedabad Manufacturing and Calico Printing Co., Shell, Bayer and Glacier Metals. They also conducted work for the National Coal Board. The focuses included management, women in the workplace, and the adoption (or rejection) of new technologies. Projects on the interaction between people and technology later became known as the sociotechnical approach. According to Cooke and Burnes (2013), the management field 'Organization Development' (OD), is said to have been invented in the mid-1950s in the USA. Some contribution post-1958 by the UK Tavistock Institute of Human Relations (TIHR), and to a minor extent, in its World War II 'group relations' work is acknowledged. Otherwise, OD depicts its US 'founding father' Kurt Lewin (1890–1947) as its historic mainspring. A new primary source (Tavistock Clinic, 1945), the TIHR's originating funding proposal to the Rockefeller Foundation, proposes all the components of OD, without mentioning Lewin et al. Thus, Cooke and Burnes, in their archival research, argue that what was to become OD was invented in the Britain of 1945, not the USA of the 1950s.

Research units

In the TIHR's early years, there were four main units: Programme Groups A and B within a Committee on Human Resources; Organisation and Social Change; the Operations Research Unit and a Committee on Family and Community Psychiatry.

The Human Resources Centre (HRC) and the Centre for Applied Social Research (CASR) were established in the 1950s, and in 1963 the Institute of Operational Research (IOR) was established in conjunction with the British Operational Research Society. The Centre for Organisational and Operational Research (COOR) was created from a merger of the HRC and the IOR in 1979.

The Self-Help Alliance project begun in the 1980s led to further work in evaluation and the creation of a dedicated unit, the Evaluation Development Review Unit (EDRU) in 1990.

Key figures

The Institute was founded by a group of key figures from the Tavistock Clinic and British Army psychiatry, including Elliott Jaques, Henry Dicks, Leonard Browne, Ronald Hargreaves, John Rawlings, Mary Luff, Harold Bridger and Wilfred Bion, with Tommy Wilson as chair. Other well-known people that joined the group shortly after were Isabel Menzies, J.D. Sutherland, John Bowlby, Eric Trist and Fred Emery. Although he died before the TIHR was formally established, Kurt Lewin was an important influence on the work of the Tavistock: he was a notable influence on Trist and contributed an article to the first issue of the Tavistock Institute's journal *Human Relations*.

Abraham (2013) points out that 'The Tavistock Group' was a term coined by Eric Trist, which included the 'first generation' of staff at the Tavistock Institute of Human Relations during the late 1940s–1950s. It was responsible for initiating different types of enquiry into organisations: identifying organisational culture, work and organisational design, and organisational strategy in different environments which are all reflected in management theory today. Members of the Tavistock Group also developed different kinds of collaboration with managers and organisations: from full action research engagement at all levels in the organisation to advising managers on how to support and engage with their employees. The different management theories of the Tavistock Group built on one another's insights so that the whole group was more than the sum of its parts and each stream of work tended to reflect those of the others.

The term *systems psychodynamics* evolved to describe the work that had its origins after the Second World War with the establishment of the Tavistock Institute of Human Relations in London and included the influential work of Kurt Lewin at the Massachusetts Institute of Technology (MIT) and the National Training Laboratories in the United States (Nossal, 2007, Pg. 43). This work helped develop a coherent and integrated approach to consulting to organisations. Systems psychodynamics ideas continued to be improved through the work of Ambrose (1989); Armstrong, (2005a,b,c); Bain (2000); Chapman (1999); Allcorn and Diamond (2003); French (2000); Gabriel and Carr (2002); Gilmore and Krantz (1985); Hirschhorn (1993, 1997); Huffington et al. (2004); Lawrence (1997); Long et al. (1997) and Sullivan (2002).

Ideas, hypotheses and theories emerging from the early work of the Tavistock

The first research projects designed to explore, test and develop the theories and ideas emerging from war-time experiences were funded by grants from the newly formed post-war Industrial Productivity Committee in the UK and the Rockefeller Foundation in the USA. It was only later that the Tavistock Institute began to offer consultancy services (as distinct from externally funded research) to organisations (Trist and Murray, 1990 a, Pg. 1–34). The ambition was that these consultancy projects would deliver insights leading to increased productivity and performance. This hope was realised and many of the concepts entered the mainstream of management theory and consultancy practice internationally. The early projects of the Tavistock Institute provided the major pillars of the theory that continue to be elaborated to this day and differentiate what is unique in the systems psychodynamics approach. For a detailed historical overview on the foundation and development of the Tavistock Institute to 1989 by Eric Trist and Hugh Murray (1990 a,b), here you will find a detailed description of the early years and the work undertaken. The early work of the Tavistock Institute of Human Relations brought together staff from different disciplines to find ways to apply psychoanalytic and general systems theories to group and organisational life. Action research from the outset was a key element in the way the TIHR worked. Through early collaboration with commerce and industry, the Institute developed new participative approaches to organisational change and development. Some of the pioneering approaches to theory and practice included sociotechnical systems design aimed at helping clients grapple with emerging changes in their organisation's context, its technology, job, work and organisational design, all of which had the objective of joint optimisation of their technical and psycho-social resources. This was initially developed through collaboration in English coalmines (Trist and Bamforth, 1951), followed by work in Indian textile mills (Rice, 1953), among many other fields in Europe, North America and Australia. Fraher (2004a and b) quotes Jean E. Neumann, core faculty of the Tavistock Institute's Advanced Organisational Consultation (AOC) Programme, who reflected on the process by which the term *systems psychodynamics* came into use:

> Both Eric and I wanted to discourage consultants from thinking that the role taken by a consultant at a group relations event was the only, or even preferred, role to take in working with organisations. I wanted to emphasize the idea that what an organizational consultant needed to do was apply psychodynamics to the diagnosis of, and intervention into, issues relevant to any organizational change and development project. A range of roles, theories and approaches could be used for the application of psychodynamic theory to organizations and other systems (e.g. between groups and organizations and within communities). Psychodynamics, instead of psychoanalysis, was important because AOC faculty considered other depth psychologies relevant as well.
> (Neumann, 1999)

Fraher states that the first mention of the term *system psychodynamics* in print form was in 1993 in the Tavistock Institute's *1992/93 Review*. The Institute's annual Review provided a candid overview of the work of the Tavistock Institute, including the activities, developments, interests and concerns of Institute staff over the year. Having observed that the Group Relations Programme emerged in the 1960s based on "the Institute's innovative work in bringing together open systems and psychodynamic perspectives to the study of group and organisational processes", Miller noted nonetheless that "the Tavistock Institute's own activities in this field have not been expanding" (*1992/93 Review,* 1993, p. 42). He concluded that it was necessary to "redevelop this heartland area of the Institute" (*1992/93 Review,* 1993, p. 42) and recommended a new strategy, termed *system psychodynamics,* with which to accomplish this. System psychodynamics was as much an organisational strategy as it was an integration of theoretical approaches. Miller noted that "the two main thrusts of the emergent strategy are to enlarge the nucleus of staff competent to work with the 'system psychodynamics' perspective and to take roles in the educational activities of the Programme and, during 1993–1994, to extend the range of these activities to include events specifically designed for industrial, commercial and other sectors and not confined to the experiential method" (*1992/93 Review*, 1993, p. 42). In response to this observation, three external Programme Advisers were appointed in early 1992, Wesley Carr, Tim Dartington and Olya Khaleelee and, along with former Tavistock staff member Isabel Menzies Lyth and then current staff member Jean Neumann, they undertook those tasks. So, the term *system psychodynamics*, which later transformed into *systems psychodynamics*, came into existence.

Fraher makes the case that the systems psychodynamics conceptual framework has at its roots psychoanalysis, the development of group relations theory and systems theory incorporating sociotechnical theories.

Major projects

Below we outline some of the major projects in which the theories, which constitute the model, were developed:

1 The Glacier Project and Social Defence Theory and Nurses Training Programme
2 Coal mining and Socio-Technical Systems
3 Open Systems Theory and Task, Role and Sentient Groups
4 Group Relations Theory: The Group Relations Training Programme

The glacier project and social defence theory and nurses training programme

Elliott Jaques headed the first Institute project with the Glacier Metal Company, which lasted for 17 years (Jaques, 1964). It became known as the Glacier Project and is renowned among its other discoveries for Jaques' hypothesis about the use of some social structures as a defence against anxiety. This theory was elaborated by Isabel Menzies and her work with the nurses training programme in a British teaching hospital (Menzies, 1960), and as Gould et al. (2001, Pg. 2–15) points out, has been demonstrated many times over by other consultants working with organisations. For most systems psychodynamically oriented practitioners, social defence theory provides one of the vertices through which the client organisational system can be considered. The work by Jaques on culture change and organisation development, originally developed in heavy industry (Jaques, 1951), but with broad applications, was grounded in understanding of how unconscious processes work in organisational life and how social defences against anxiety inhibited progress (Jaques, 1951a, b.; Menzies Lyth, 1993).

Coal mining and sociotechnical systems

Coal mining was the second research project of the Tavistock Institute, led by Eric Trist, and it was in this project that the term *socio-technical system* was first identified (Trist and Murray, 1990a, Pg. 1–34). Through the coal-mining project, Trist and Bamforth (1951) detailed the complex interactions between the technological aspects of a task system and the social impact of these upon the workers. Where technology had previously been split off into the jurisdiction of the engineers, Trist and Bamforth recognised the relevance and importance of studying the technical system in all of its dimensions alongside the social system of work groups and discovering the impact and interdependence of one upon the other (Trist and Bamforth, 1951). Rice continued to develop Trist's sociotechnical systems perspective in his experimental research in the Calico Mills in Ahmedabad in India, which began in 1954. As Trist and Murray relate, 'This led to developments that continued for 25 years showing that the sociotechnical concept was applicable in the culture of a very different kind of society' (Trist and Murray, 1990a, Pg. 1–34).

It was these two main research experiments that led to the establishment of the field of sociotechnical studies led initially by Trist, Emery and others in the early 1960s (Fraher, 2004a; Trist and Murray, 1990a). Emery and Trist went on to research the organisation in relation to its environment, highlighting the role of the turbulent environment (Emery and Trist, 1963) and implications for shaping that environment through collaborative activities.

Open systems theory and task, role and sentient groups

In their classic text, *Systems of Organisation*, Miller and Rice (1967, Pg. 3) draw together the ideas and theories derived from the Tavistock research and consulting projects (in particular their own, but inclusive of the theories already presented) of the previous 20 years. The theories presented in their book form the second pillar of the systems psychodynamics approach: open systems theory and thinking. Miller and Rice (1967) liken the systems of an organisation to those of a living organism and its interactions with the environment: simply stated, these are import –> conversion –> export systems upon which the organism (or the organisation) depends for its survival.

The development of group relations theory: the group relations training programme

Fraher (2004a, Pg. 50) recounts that the post-World War II period could be classified as the birth of the field of group relations because many people excitedly experimented with the knowledge gained from their war-time experiences. Central to this exploration were Bion and his fellow members of the Tavistock Clinic and Tavistock Institute in England and Lewin and the National Training Laboratory (NTL) in the United States. The NTL's contributions were pivotal with the development of its human laboratory, an experiential method of studying groups in 1947.

In London, Bion continued to make significant contributions to social psychiatry through his conduct of psychotherapy groups at the Tavistock Clinic and developed his theory of group behaviour. Fraher quotes Trist (1985), who wrote the following observation of Bion's methods for taking groups: "Several features characterized Bion's group 'style'. He was detached yet warm, utterly imperturbable and inexhaustibly patient. He gave rise to feelings of immense security — his Rock of Gibraltar quality. But the Rock of Gibraltar is also powerful and he exuded power (he was also a very large man)" (Pg. 30).

In Kleinian terms, Bion seemed to be inviting, whether consciously or not, the group's projective identification with him. That is, he made himself available for the group to disown their uncomfortable feelings and project them onto him as a means of understanding the group's unconscious behaviour (Gabriel, 1999, Pg. 119). As Trist (1985) put it, "He made it safe for the group to dramatize its unconscious situation" (Pg. 31). In his articles, Bion outlined his theories of group behaviour that were based largely on observations he made while working with small groups over the years. He hypothesised that groups have two modes of operation. One mode he called the productive *sophisticated group,* more commonly called a *work group.* The work group focused intently on the group's task and maintained close contact with reality. The other mode of group operation Bion called *basic assumption.* Its primary task was to ease the group's anxieties and avoid the pain or emotions that further work might bring. Bion identified three types of basic assumption modes: basic assumption of *dependence* (baD), basic assumption of *pairing* (baP) and basic assumption of *fight-flight* (baF) (Bion, 1961).

Bion's theories continued to be interpreted and evolved by other theoreticians who applied his theories to working with groups. Rice, Miller, Bridger, Trist, Menzies and other social scientists affiliated with the Tavistock Institute carried Bion's theories about covert group dynamics, such as unconscious defence mechanisms, into their continued exploration of how best to understand organisations.

Group Relations theory evolved alongside Miller and Rice's elaboration of open systems theory and is inclusive of it. The three main influences upon its early development were: the work of Bion, Von Bertalanffy's 'open systems' perspectives and Lewin's theories and models of experiential learning in groups that were pioneered at Bethel, Main, with the establishment of the National Training Laboratories (Bridger, 1990a, b; Fraher, 2004; Miller, 1990).

While the use of the word 'theory' is commonplace (Gould, et al., 2001, Pg. 2–14), others write about the applied learning from the Group Relations

Training Programme (GRTP) (Stapley, in Gould et al., 2001, Pg. 2–14). Theory and applied learning go together. The GRTP is an experiential educational programme designed to study group behaviour and organisational systems through experiential learning. The foremost event of this programme is the Leicester Conference. See https://www.tavinstitute.org/wp-content/uploads/2017/02/about-Group-Relations.pdf.

The systems psychodynamics perspective

Psychoanalytical theory is one of the key components that constitute the underpinning philosophy of the systems psychodynamics approach (Abraham, 2013; Cilliers and Koortzen, 2005; Czander, 1993; De Board, 1978). However, Freud, the father of psychoanalysis, wrote very little about work. Czander (1993, Pg. 7) said that from "a psychoanalytical perspective, attachment to work is considered the result of the gratification of conscious and unconscious fantasies whose analyses present insights into how organizations change". A further contribution to the systems psychodynamics perspective is Klein's Object Relations theory (Czander, 1993; Miller, 1993; Rice, 1965). This theory places less emphasis on instinct and regards individuals as object-seeking, thus permitting an inclusion of "environmental or cultural factors in a systematic theory" (Czander, 1993, Pg. 43–73). Object relations theory highlights how people use one another to stabilise their inner lives and helps to create an understanding of how psychodynamic processes within people shape the relationships between them (Hirschhorn, 1988, Pg. 162–181). This perspective supports the premise that groups and organisations are social systems and that the collective – groups or organisations – are social entities with identities that are separate from the elements which constitute their make-up. Organisations are cooperative enterprises that function in harmony (Czander, 1993, Pg. 1–8). This view moves the organisation from being primarily a rational system to a view that organizations are "filled with intangibles that are complex sets of social relations" (Czander, 1993, Pg. 1–8). This perspective is, according to Koortzen and Cilliers (2002), a rejection of the economic view of work within a group or organisation. Kets de Vries (1992) also contends that there is growing support for the view that logical/rational models of organisational functioning are limited because non-rational forces influence leadership and group behaviour.

Gharajedaghi (1985) views organisations as open systems – another important element within the systems psychodynamics perspective. Open systems is described by Miller (1993, Pg. 3–23) as systems that "exist and can only exist by the exchange of materials with their environment". Miller (1993) elaborates on the contribution of Von Bertalanffy's (1950) concept of *equifinality* – the achievement of an outcome that can be reached through a variety of different means and routes. The theories of open systems enable the evaluation of relationships between the social and technical elements of organisations, as well as the relationships between the part and the whole, and the whole and the external environment (Miller, 1993, Pg. 3–23; Rice, 1965, Pg. 10). Wells (1980, Pg. 165–198) reports that the group-as-a-whole perspective emerges from the open systems framework, and that this perspective "assumes that individuals are human vessels that reflect and express the group's gestalt". Group-as-a-whole refers to the collective that forms when systems operate as one, forming a psychodynamic relation, relatedness and interconnectedness – implying that no event happens in isolation (Cilliers and Koortzen, 2005, Pg. 52).

The systems psychodynamics perspective is a process that takes account of the psychological nature and covert behaviour within systems (Cilliers, 2005, Pg. 52–53). Czander (1993, Pg. 43–73) suggests that this perspective heightens awareness to better understand the covert meaning of organisational behaviour, and thereby understand the deeper and unconscious challenges faced by leadership. The systems psychodynamic consultant engages in an analysis of among others, but not limited to, interrelationships between such constructs as anxiety, social defences, projection, transference and counter-transference, valence, resistance to change, boundaries, role, authority, leadership, relationship and relatedness, and group-as-a-whole (Bion, 1961, Pg. 29–190; 1962, Pg. 1–99; Hirschhorn, 1993, Pg. 182–197; Long, 2006). The consultant is aware of, hypothesises about and interprets dynamic and covert aspects of the system and its sub-systems with a specific focus on relatedness, representation and authority (Cilliers, 2005, Pg. 52). To interpret appropriately, the consultant recognises attitudes, phantasies, conflicts and anxieties prevalent that trigger social defences and pattern relationships – determining how these affect task performance (Czander, 1993, Pg. 43–73; Hirschhorn, 1993, Pg. 182–197). Projection of unwanted feelings, a valency in the system to adopt a defence and containment on behalf of the group, are all products of the covert nature of group dynamics (Cilliers, 2005, Pg. 52–53). Furthermore, understanding how unconscious anxieties are reflected in structures and organisational design is also reviewed by the systems psychodynamics consultant (Czander, 1993, Pg. 43–73; Hirschhorn, 1993, Pg. 182–197; Krantz, 1990, Pg. 49–64). This stance studies the system as a reality *and* as a 'system-in-the-mind'/'group-as-a-whole' (Wells, 1980, Pg. 165–198). Cilliers and Koortzen (2000, Pg. 2–9) sum up the systems psychodynamics approach as studying organisational behaviour from the perspective of "the organisation as a system having a life of its own which is both conscious and unconscious, with subsystems relating to and mirroring one another" (Colman and Bexton, 1975; Czander, 1993; Hirschhorn, 1993; Miller, 1990; Obholzer and Roberts, 1994).

The 'outside-in' perspective and 'inside-out' perspective

Petriglieri and Petriglieri (2020) suggest the tension in systems psychodynamics theory and practice is the result of between an 'outside-in' perspective, focused on institutions' influence on individuals, and an 'inside-out' perspective, focused on leaders' influence on institutions. They suggest that the marginalisation of systems psychodynamic scholarship, positing that its marginality is both a social defence for organisation studies as a whole and a generative feature of the systems psychodynamics approach. The first tension they identify concerns the focus of inquiry. Systems psychodynamic scholars examine the boundaries of people's inner and social worlds, "working simultaneously from 'the inside out' and 'the outside in' with neither perspective being privileged" (Gould et al., 2001, Pg. 4). But there is a tendency to either focus on how systems of organisation affect individuals ('outside-in') or on how individuals affect systems of organisation ('inside-out'). From the literature, it would seem, the focus is either studying organisations psychoanalytically or to psychoanalyse organisations, as they quote Gabriel (2016) puts it. The 'inside-out' perspective focuses on how powerful individuals have on systems. Kets de Vries (1994), echoing Zaleznik (1989), calls the 'leadership mystique' that dominates organisations. 'Inside-out' scholars treat leaders as people who shape structures, processes and cultures in ways that reflect and amplify their inner world, their history and aspirations, neuroses and preferences, or who, on occasion, can make the organisation less about them and more focused on its work.

The most researched and built upon among 'outside-in' systems psychodynamic constructs is social defences. Social defences are "collective arrangements, such as an organizational structure, a work method, or a prevalent discourse, created or used by an organization's members as a protection against disturbing affect derived from external threats, internal conflicts, or the nature of their work" (Petriglieri and Petriglieri, 2010, Pg. 47). Many 'outside-in' studies informed, and emerged from, scholars' consulting to organisations. Consulting and researching from this perspective is to help organisations' members understand themselves and their systems while finding better ways to organise. But Gabriel (2016), adds that consultants and scholars must not limit their interventions to 'psychoanalysing organisations' that is, generating insights into people's motives and attitudes in the workplace. They must also help change the structures and norms that sustain those motives and attitudes (Neumann and Hirschhorn, 1999). It may be that doing only one of the two can lead to failure. When they surface anxiety without facilitating change to the structures that provoke it, consultants make people hopeless. When they only recommend new structures, those structures might not work because they do not contain anxiety. It is our belief that the study of this unconscious behaviour and dynamics leads to a deep understanding of organisational behaviour.

Tavistock group and methods

Sofer (1972) describes the work of what he calls the Tavistock group. It is a helpful description of what later constituted the systems psychodynamic approach. Although when he was writing in 1972, the term systems psychodynamics was not used, his depiction still stands. He states, Tavistock group consultants often join one or more groups within an organisation and use their understanding in the service on an agreed task, usually involving a current interdepartmental crisis or an organisational change in process of introduction. This type of activity has been variously described as action research, social consultancy, or socio-therapy. It involves the study of an organisation or parts of organisations through methods derived or adapted from sociological/social psychological research and psychiatry. This type of intervention differs from direct management interventions. The Tavistock group consultant works in close association with line management but is not a member of it. The relationship with the organisation is temporary. The consultant pays attention to the forms and processes of social interaction and to perceptions and feelings in addition to the content of the interaction and explicates these forms and processes of interaction in collaboration with the client organisation. The consultant may define their responsibility and role as clarification and one of interpretation of behaviour, not as advice on executive action. The consultant concerns themselves with the quality of decision making and the steps taken in reaching decisions rather than with the correctness or otherwise of any particular decisions taken. The consultant questions the prevailing institutions and structures rather than regarding themselves as obliged to work within the framework they provide. This work does overlap with management consultancy. But the Tavistock group consultant is different, however, in the emphasis on social processes (including unconscious motivations and feelings), in the attempt to understand dynamic processes and the task of clarifying, interpreting and studying behaviour rather than taking the initiative in recommending specific changes.

Tavistock group consultants draw on a range of theories, from Lewin, Freud and Bion. Lewin's interest in participative democracy is a strong underlying influence. Freud's influence is in the assumption that is made that persons are significantly affected by personal motivations of which they are unaware, the unconscious. These working concepts are supported by the understanding that shared anxieties and unconscious collusions underlie social defences in social institutions. Tavistock group consultancy involves interpretative comments, observations on face-to-face group behaviour, whether in committees, project groups, or group relations conferences and they tend to be influenced by Bion's theories of group dynamics. Another strand in the Tavistock group approach is the attention paid to the structural properties of the organisation. This strand is mostly evident in sociotechnical interventions. Rice (1958, Pg. 4) states that the basis is:

> While industrial production systems are of necessity, designed in accordance with technological demand, there has been a tendency to project the technological into the associated work organisation. The assumption is then made that there is only one work organisation that will satisfy the conditions of task performance. This has meant treating groups and

individuals as though they were machines .... Where, as frequently happened the resulting work organisation has failed to satisfy the social and psychological needs of its members; their attitudes to task performance have inhibited the full realisation of technological potential and lowered productivity.

Rice describes how he intervened in helping management make changes in their production system. This involved changes towards a group centred method of working; internally, it led to more or less autonomous work groups of workers taking responsibility for groups of machines, the groups of workers being themselves largely mutually selected. At management, the changes included clearer segregation of functions and levels of management and between governing and operating systems; increased delegation; the creation of new roles; movement of personnel between roles; the formalisation of new types of executive meetings; and the institution of management conferences. Although Rice is not explicit, he regarded a measure of help in this restructuring as part of his task as a consultant. He took account of conscious and unconscious attitudes and processes, including ambivalence towards him, and at some points discussed these with the client where he thought this would help them face painful changes. A contemporary account of the Tavistock group methodology is given by Sher (2013) who demonstrates a down to earth and reality-based yet deeply reflective focus on approaching problems within organisations and social systems.

"Dawn"

Systems psychodynamics, both theory and practice, is an evolving field within the social sciences and consultancy practice. In this volume, we introduce the reader to some of the key theories and practices that make up the model. A significant aspect of the systems psychodynamics model is the combining of systems concepts and psychoanalytic concepts. Psychoanalytical theory is a key set of theories and practices of the systems psychodynamics approach (Czander, 1993; De Board, 1978). Czander (1993, Pg. 7) said that from "a psychoanalytical perspective, attachment to work is considered the result of the gratification of conscious and unconscious fantasies" and he suggests that it is "these fantasies and their analysis that present insight into how the organisation can change". Object Relations Theory (Czander, 1993; Miller, 1993; Rice, 1965) sees a person as object-seeking, therefore allowing for "environmental or cultural factors in a systematic theory" (Czander, 1993, Pg. 43). According to Hirschhorn (1988), object relations theory shows how psychodynamic processes within people shape the relationships between them. Within the systems psychodynamics model, groups or organisations are social systems that constitute a social entity with an identity that is separate from the elements which make it up.

An organisation is an open system (Gharajedaghi, 1985) and is defined by Miller (1993, Pg. 10) as systems that "exist and can only exist by the exchange of materials with their environment". Miller (1993) added the contribution of Von Bertalanffy (1950) of equifinality, which is an end result that can be gained through diverse methods. The theories of open systems enable consultants to gauge the associations between the social and technical elements of the organisations as well as the relationships between the part and the whole, and the whole and the external environment (Miller, 1993; Rice, 1965). Wells (1980, Pg. 114) recalls that the group-as-a-whole perspective emerged from the open system framework and that this perspective 'assumes that individuals are human vessels that reflect and express the group's gestalt'. Group-as-a-whole refers to the collective that forms when systems operate as one, forming a psychodynamic relation, relatedness and interconnectedness.

Czander (1993) suggested that the primary task of the systems psychodynamics model is to heighten awareness so as to better understand the

DOI: 10.4324/9781003181507-3

hidden significance of organisational behaviour, and thus comprehend the profounder and unconscious processes that consultants encounter. Krantz (2006) argues that while the unconscious is a source of destructiveness, it is also the source of creativity, and by allowing the unconscious to emerge, acknowledging it and linking it to conscious aims, can create a generative organisational environment.

In this first volume of *An Introduction to Systems Psychodynamics*, the reader is introduced to some of the key theories and applications of systems psychodynamics research and consultancy. We examine the systems contribution, the practice of systems psychodynamics consultancy, and the application of psychoanalytic theories to organisations. The practice of organisational role analysis and coaching in working with individuals is introduced. This is a key consultancy practice within the systems psychodynamics approach.

A predominant set of ideas originate from the work of Bion and his theories of group dynamics. We set out the important ideas that Bion (1961) has contributed to the systems psychodynamics model. The design and practice of Group Relations Conferences (GRC), which owes a debt to Bion, and later Rice's developments of Bion's theories to GRCs, is explored in this volume. Closely connected to the seminal work of Bion is the work of Isabel Menzies (1970) and Elliott Jaques (1955). Their ground-breaking work on social defences as a defence against anxiety is shown to be highly relevant to both our contemporary organisations and social structures. The sociotechnical systems theories were discovered through the research and consultancy in the mining industry in the English coal fields by Trist and Bamforth (1951) in the late 1940s. These sets of ideas have had an enormous influence on organisational design all over the world.

Part I
Systems

Systems thinking is a huge, highly differentiated area (Cabrera, 2014; Cabrera and Cabrera, 2015; François, 2004; Midgley, 2003; Schwarz, 1996). With the growing complexity in the natural, social, economic and political realms, systems thinking has application for a multiplicity of purposes. An awareness of systems thinking has developed in the last 30 years or more. We note that there is a mixture of systems thinking applications in different areas. Systems thinking is interdisciplinary; it covers academic, theoretical and practical domains.

The view of organisations as open social systems that must interact with their environments in order to survive is known as the systems theory approach. Open systems theory (OST) states that organisations are influenced by their environment. The environment consists of other organisations that exercise many forces of a commercial, political and social kind. The environment also offers resources that sustain the organisation and lead to change and survival. OST was developed after World War II in reaction to earlier theories of organisations, such as the human relations perspective of Elton Mayo and the administrative theories of Henri Fayol, which treated the organisation largely as a self-contained entity. Almost all modern theories of organisation utilise the open systems perspective. The open-systems theory also accepts that all large organisations contain multiple subsystems, each of which receives inputs from other subsystems and turns them into outputs for use by other subsystems. The subsystems are not necessarily represented by departments in an organisation, but might instead resemble patterns of activity.

Organisations that exist in dynamic environments must be open systems in order to maintain homeostasis. An open organisation monitors its environment and collects information about environmental changes that are seen as input. Input can also be thought of as a form of feedback. The most important information is negative input, according to systems theorists, because this information alerts the organisation to problems that need to be corrected. Negative input tells the organisation that it is doing something wrong and that it must make adjustments to correct the problem; positive input tells the

DOI: 10.4324/9781003181507-4

organisation that it is doing something right and that it should continue or increase that activity.

Within the systems psychodynamics model, socio-technical systems thinking is very pertinent. Socio-technical systems thinking brings together: human relations, psychodynamics, action research and the theory of open systems. The human relations movement saw the importance of relationships within the workplace and the lived experience of employees within it. Psychodynamics which originates in psychoanalytic theory was applied to understanding group and organisational behaviour. Action research involved the application of quantitative and qualitative methodology within the scope of the human relations school, while the theory of open systems derives from the work of von Bertalanffy and other early systems thinkers.

In Chapter 1, we describe the relationship between systems thinking, complexity theory and systems psychodynamics. Complexity theory originates in biology and borrows significantly from mathematics, physics and chemistry. We introduce the reader to systems thinking, general systems theory, the open systems approach to organisations, systems dynamics and learning organisations, developments in socio-technical theory and design (STSD).

In Chapter 2, we explore the systems contribution of the systems psychodynamics approach. We examine what are the consultations about; systems psychodynamics consulting; working methods and application of theory.

1 The systems contribution

With Halina Brunning and Susan Long

In this chapter, we describe the relationship between systems thinking, complexity theory and systems psychodynamics, theories which originate in biology and borrow significantly from mathematics, physics and chemistry (Coveney and Highfield, 1995; Gell-Mann, 1994; Gleick, 1987; Goodwin, 1995; Kauffman, 1995; Prigogine and Stengers, 1984; Waldrop, 1992). We describe how ideas from these new sciences were taken into theorising about organisation and management during the 1990s (Allen, 1998; Stacey, 1991, 1992, 1993; Stacey et al., 2000).

While Tavistock Institute researchers had gone deep into the local, industrial social systems that shaped the 20th-century workplace, similar work on our virtual, remote, distributed, volatile work realities have taken place, but they have not been widely written about. Contemporary human industrial work is no longer only located in Europe and North America. Industry has moved to the Far East where labour costs on average are 10% of Western labour costs. But Tavistock methods like worker participation, autonomous work groups, socio-technical systems in China and India, for instance, are being introduced. We include examples of current systems psychodynamics consultancy and the development of local consultants and other organisational change agents in China.

> **Extending Tavistock systems psychodynamics philosophy and practice into new environments**
>
> The Tavistock Institute has researched and consulted mainly in the West and parts of the East like India. An invitation to work in China provided an opportunity to examine the transferability of systems psychodynamics ways of working that are strongly Anglo-Saxon in orientation, language and concept. How well would Tavistock approaches translate in an environment with a 2,500-year history of Confucian and Taoist philosophies? Confucianism emphasises personal and governmental morality, the correctness of social relationships, justice and sincerity that is the basis of Chinese tradition and belief, with strong family loyalty, ancestor veneration and respect of elders. Taoist philosophy emphasises living in harmony with the Tao, literally the

'Way' – personal improvement through effortless action, naturalness, simplicity, spontaneity, compassion, frugality and humility, harmonising human behaviour in accordance with the alternating cycles of nature. Taoism differs from Confucianism by offering spiritual explanations and does not emphasise rigid rituals and social order.

The cultural and spiritual atmosphere in China is one of having and being aware of one's place in the order of things, acceptance of rewards and sanctions of life that are instilled from birth through the family, education, religion and state policy. Within these constraints, the personality is formed and the nature of human social relations and individual life's ambitions are bound together. The result is social conformity that is meant for the greater good, on the one hand, and a tension for the search for personal contentment through developing individual insights and free expression of feelings on the other.

How then do Tavistock systems psychodynamics philosophy and practice resonate with Chinese traditional behaviour and culture? The invitation to work in China was said to link with the President of China's dissatisfaction with educational systems that emphasise control and 'correct answers' and do not encourage enquiry, questioning and independent thought. Generally, independence of thought does not fit well with tradition, but as China grows in strength and influence in the world, it recognises the need for independent thinkers to challenge but not undermine social and political norms. In other words, to use Tavistock language, how will the Chinese in groups and teams maintain their individual sense of themselves, think independently and fearlessly with personal authority and remain faithful to the task of the groups of which they are members? Tavistock systems psychodynamics methods examine the inherent tensions between individual desire and responsible group membership.

These tensions are examined usually in small bounded groups that are familiar to most people in China (comparable to the family) and in large social political groups which, in China, are the preserve of few people. New tensions are appearing because of increased individuality in a money-oriented consumerist society that loosens ties to tradition and increases anomie and social dislocation.

Teams from the Tavistock Institute have worked on teaching and training programmes in China. The programmes are conducted in English with simultaneous translation. This presents immediate obstacles, for no matter how accurate the translation is, communications must pass through another language before they can be understood and then responded to. Another challenge is language construction and tone of voice, which are the basis of establishing power, dominance and control between speaker and spoken to. In China, these controlling elements in speech are pronounced; subtlety and irony have less prominence, which in China can lead to insult and humiliation. Making your audience lose face does little to improve its learning.

Our experience of working in China is about confronting an impatience for learning, often expressed as wanting to get things right and to be perfect immediately – wanting to bridge the gap between not knowing and knowing without struggling with the slower assimilation of ideas. Tavistock team members often feel pulled into giving more, before what has already been given, is digested. Our programme of studying group dynamics combines traditional teaching methods like lectures with experiential group work like social dreaming, small study groups and inter-group events that enable 'living' and 'seeing' the hidden dynamic forces at play. This learning process cannot be hurried; it is sometimes painful and always only partial. It produces substantial frustration for the programme participants.

The situation in China is one of choosing between 'catch up' or development. The timescales for each are different and there is a desperate sense that time is short. The uniqueness of China and the Chinese people themselves makes it difficult to find one's bearings in China coming from the free world where the trend is to re-engage with ancient values, like so many people do with yoga or acupuncture or use Chinese herbs for healing. The Chinese people seem intent on pursuing money and appear to be losing touch with ancient values. The pace of change in China is ferocious, gratification must be immediate and there is pressure for the new to displace the old. It is almost as though the Chinese and the West are going in opposite directions, and as we cross each other, it often feels like a clash of cultures. In our experience, the concept of boundaries is hard for Chinese people to grasp both conceptually and experientially and that provides us with a constant challenge of what it means to work with a fundamentally different concept to that which we are used to and are informed by. Ancient traditions help us learn to be patient and this is a constant every-day lesson.

The Tavistock Institute was invited to bring its well-established ideas to China; one result is that the Tavistock Institute is emerging from its China experience enriched by the magnificence, beauty and continuity of Chinese culture from which paradoxically many Chinese seem to be turning away.

Much of the Tavistock's work accompanied the first generation of computers and automation and the Tavistock Institute has wrestled with the social consequences of mass redundancy. Human relations having accelerated exponentially, driven by social media, is a subject of research interest and we describe how systems psychodynamics contributes to our understanding of contemporary organisations and the digitalised world. We describe the stark choices facing society and organisations in how we bring our technology – socio-technical analysis, action research, group relations conference learning and systems psychodynamic ways of understanding – to bear on contemporary but culturally different western and eastern organisations.

We link the work of the early pioneers of systems psychodynamics associated with the Tavistock Institute and the institutional memory it carries. Their deep engagement with public sector organisations to its developmental work with globalised economies and the virtual digital worlds that threaten to make work irrelevant will be covered here. We highlight approaches to consulting that provide the private sector, the globalised economy and the virtual world with an understanding of unconscious processes and systems psychodynamics so that people can see the impact of the rapidly changing world, increased velocity of algorithms and machine learning. With the traditions of the Tavistock Institute's methodologies, organisations, sectors and societies will be better informed of the futures they are creating.

Systems and systems thinking

Systems and Systems thinking is a large and highly varied field (Cabrera and Cabrera, 2015; François, 2004; Midgley, 2003; Schwarz, 1996). The idea of systems thinking has application for a number of purposes, given the increasing complexity of the natural, social, economic and political dimensions. Interest in learning how to 'systems think' has grown over the last couple of decades among those outside the 'discipline'. In reality, there is less a single discipline of systems thinking than there is an amalgamation of systems thinking applications in different realms. Systems thinking is interdisciplinary in nature and very much both scholarly/theoretical and applied in its application. Systems thinking is the ability or skill to perform problem solving in complex systems. System theory or systems science is the interdisciplinary study of systems in which system thinking can be learned. A system is an entity with interrelated and interdependent parts; it is defined by its boundaries and it is more than the sum of its parts (or subsystems). Changing one part of the system affects other parts and the whole system, with predictable patterns of behaviour. Systems theory is the interdisciplinary study of systems. A system is a cohesive conglomeration of interrelated and interdependent parts which can be natural or human made. Every system is bounded by space and time, influenced by its environment, defined by its structure and purpose, and expressed through its functioning. A system may be more than the sum of its parts if it expresses synergy or emergent behaviour. It may be possible to predict changes in patterns of behaviour. For systems that learn and adapt, the growth and the degree of adaptation depend upon how well the system is engaged with its environment. Some systems support other systems, maintaining the other system to prevent failure. The goals of systems theory are to model a system's dynamics, constraints, conditions and to elucidate principles (such as purpose, measure, methods, tools) that can be discerned and applied to other systems at every level of nesting and in a wide range of fields for achieving optimised equifinality. Equifinality is the principle that in open systems a given end state can be reached by many potential means, also meaning that a goal can be reached in many ways. Systems theory is manifest in the work of practitioners in many disciplines, for example, the works of biologist Ludwig von Bertalanffy, linguist Béla H. Bánáthy, sociologist Talcott Parsons and Fritjof Capra's study of organisational theory, and in the study of management by Peter Senge, in interdisciplinary areas such as Human Resource Development in the works of Richard A. Swanson, and in the works of educators Debora Hammond and Alfonso Montuori.

As a transdisciplinary, interdisciplinary and multi-perspectival endeavour, systems theory brings together principles and concepts from ontology, the philosophy of science, physics, computer science, biology and engineering, as well as geography, sociology, political science, psychotherapy (especially family systems therapy) and economics. Systems theory promotes dialogue between autonomous areas of study as well as within systems science itself. In this respect, with the possibility of misinterpretations, von Bertalanffy believed a general theory of systems "should be an important regulative device in science", to guard against superficial analogies that "are useless in science and harmful in their practical consequences". Others remain closer to the direct systems concepts developed by the original theorists. For example, Ilya Prigogine of the Centre for Complex Quantum Systems at the University of Texas, Austin, has studied emergent properties, suggesting that they offer analogues for living systems. The theories of autopoiesis of Francisco Varela and Humberto Maturana represent further developments in this field. Important names in contemporary systems science include Russell Ackoff, Gregory Bateson, Anthony Stafford Beer, Peter Checkland, Brian Wilson, Robert L. Flood, Allenna Leonard, Fritjof Capra and Michael C. Jackson.

The formal origins of systems theory date back to the middle 20th century and draw from two interconnected threads. There were the physicists and biologists, such as David Bohm (1951, revised 2012) and Ludwig von Bertalanffy (1950), and there were the group dynamicists and organisational developers, such as Stafford Beer (1959), Russel Ackoff (1972, 1974, 1978, 1981), Fred Emery (1965, 1969, 1996), Eric Trist (1997), Reg Revans (2011), and, to some extent, Kurt Lewin (1944; Lewin and and Cartwright, 1951). The basic issue all sought to understand was the relationship between an event and its context: past, present and future. Although they each took a different route, they built on each other's concepts and established the basis of the rich range of systems approaches that are available today.

Organising the field: waves of systems thinking

There is a large set of methods, theories, applications, approaches and tools under the systems framework. Gerald Midgley (2000, 2003) has contributed an organising framework that demarcates the literature into three distinct 'waves'. While these waves represent distinct 'eras' in systems thinking, each successive wave builds off its predecessor as the methods and approaches from later waves do not supersede each other. Leleur (2014) explains that the approaches within each wave are today "used concurrently when seeking to make sense of complex problems; thus the waves ... have successively contributed to expanding and enriching systems thinking" (Pg. 22).

Midgley (2000) explains that the first wave of systems thinking, "hard systems", incorporated "insights from both the quantitative and human relations branches of applied science, amongst other traditions" (Pg. 191). This wave was characterised primarily by expert, quantitative modelling. It began the 1950s and was the dominant approach through the 1970s. These early systems theorists (including Bertalanffy) were conceived of systems in very physical terms, employing biological and computational metaphors (Burton, 2003). The second wave, soft systems, aimed to address such disparities perceived in the early systems thinking field. As one scholar explained, "the limits of the physical metaphor (and for Midgley, the non-systemic traces of reductionism and mechanism) were reached, paving the way for a focus on social metaphors deemed more applicable to human systems" (Burton, 2003). Scholars and practitioners emphasised qualitative modelling in the context of participatory practices. The third wave, critical systems thinking, emerged during the 1990s. It rectified the methodological split between the first and second waves by advocating methodological pluralism and avoided the positivist, functionalist, 'expert' orientation of some systems thinking approaches in favour of increasing participation of stakeholders and affected parties (Jackson, 2000). This wave acknowledged power relationships in systems approaches and emphasised the value of methodological pluralism. The fourth wave conceives of systems thinking as a conceptual framework and model for thinking about and learning about systems of all kinds, scientific, organisational, personal and public. Fourth-wave systems thinking highlights the crucial relationship between systems (the basic unit of how the natural world works) and thinking (the process of constructing mental models of real-world phenomena and evolving them based on feedback) to better approximate reality. Finally, the fourth wave embraces the plurality of systems thinking methods while espousing an all-important underlying structure to unify all those methods (Cabrera, 2014); it enables universality and pluralism to coexist.

What is systems theory?

Chen and Stroup (1993) sum up systems theory as follows: At the core of systems theory are the notions that:

1 A 'system' is an ensemble of interacting parts, the sum of which exhibits behaviour not localised in its constituent parts, i.e. "the whole is more than the sum of the parts".
2 A system can be physical, biological, social or symbolic, or it can be comprised of one or more of these.
3 Change is seen as a transformation of the system in time, which, nevertheless, conserves its identity. Growth, steady state and decay are major types of change.
4 Goal-directed behaviour characterises the changes observed in the state of the system. A system is seen to be actively organised in terms of the goal and, hence, can be understood to exhibit 'reverse causality'.
5 'Feedback' is the mechanism that mediates between the goal and system behaviour.
6 Time is a central variable in system theory. It provides a referent for the very idea of dynamics.
7 The 'boundary' serves to delineate the system from the environment and any subsystems from the whole system.

System-environment interactions can be defined as the input and output of matter, information and energy. The system can be open, closed or semi-permeable to the environment. Bertalanffy's discussion serves to reconcile the competing traditions of general system theory, cybernetics and system dynamics.

Open systems approach to organisations

Open systems

The contribution of the biologist von Bertalanffy (1950a, 1950b) was open system theory. In several papers and books between 1945 and 1968, the German biologist Von Bertalanffy put forward the idea that organisms, as well as human organisations and societies, are open systems. The model of the organism, which can exist and survive only through continuous interaction with the environment, as the source of its intake and the recipient of its outputs, offered a much more satisfactory paradigm for organisation of the enterprise than the closed system model implicit in most previous theories of organisation. The model was quickly adopted and developed in organisational analysis and change. It underlined the significance of boundaries and their management. Thus, leadership was defined as a boundary function mediating between inside and outside (e.g. Miller, 1959, 1976; Miller and Rice 1967; Rice 1958, 1963, 1965).

Perhaps the most complete as well as the most complex approach to understanding human organisations is one based on OST. OST is the framing perspective used in the Tavistock model for understanding the structural aspects of an organisational system. These include its design, division of labour, levels of authority and reporting relationships; the nature of work tasks, processes and activities; its mission and primary task; and, in particular, the nature and patterning of the organisation's task and sentient boundaries and across them.

It also showed the importance of subsystems, each with its unique character and primary task, and each related to the enterprise as a whole. In open system theory, human organisations are regarded as open systems because they consist of a number of component subsystems that are interrelated and interdependent on each other. They are open because they are connected by feedback links to their environment, or supra systems of which they are a part.

Each subsystem within a system and each system within its environment has a boundary separating it from other subsystems and other systems. Within each system or subsystem, people occupy roles, they conduct sets of activities, and they engage in interrelationships with others both within their part of the system and in other parts of the system and in other parts or other systems. Each subsystem within a system and each system within an environment is open in the sense that it imports materials, labour, money and information from other systems or subsystems and in turn exports outputs, money and information to other systems or subsystems.

Open systems explanations of managing and organising, therefore, focuses attention on:

a Behaviour of people within a subsystem or system.
b Nature of boundary around a subsystem or system.
c Nature of the relationship across the boundaries between subsystems and systems.
d Requirements of managing the boundary.

The open system concept provides a tool for understanding the relationship between:

a The technical and the social aspects of an organisation.
b The parts and the whole organisation (for example, the individual and the group, the individual and the organisation).
c The whole organisation and the environment.

From this we can see that OST views the organisation as a system, just as it would a person, a tree, or any other living thing. The social organisation could be a pair of people, a large family, a temporary group, one department in an organisation, or an entire organisation. In this model, organisations are designed (consciously or otherwise) so that they can take in resources (input), do something with them (throughput or conversion), and generate some valued result (output).

From this basic model come the following ideas:
The first idea is that there is a:

1 **Primary task, a primary sense of purpose.** The work that must be done if the organisation is to survive (Rice, 1958). This primary task also helps create a sense of purpose that may be more or less articulate, and there may be some important differences of opinion about it, but there certainly will be an effort to have a shared overall goal. The primary task shapes the organisations sense of meaning, which in turn can help members of the organisation develop a sense of being valuable. Further exposition of the concept of the primary task is addressed later in the chapter.

The second idea is that organisations need to be:

2 **Self-regulating.** This means that the people in the system want to feel they have a sense of control over their lives and jobs. Clear feedback is needed, so people will know what happened as a result of their actions; these feedback loops allow adjustments to be made. Ideally, the feedback loop will be as short as possible. Information also needs to get into the system so that people 'on the front line' can solve problems and deal with difficulties quickly.

The third idea is that:

3 **Internal and external boundaries** need to be managed. There are always issues of 'in' and 'out', and who are members of which teams and how they relate around the task. A reasonable degree of autonomy is needed, neither too much nor too little. Within and between the boundaries, there will be various mechanisms for getting the work done – for managing the workflow.

Primary task

The next theoretical development in the socio-technical/open system model was that of Rice (1958). The concept was the primary task; this concept grew out of his action research in India. In his work with the Jubilee Mill in Ahmedabad Rice (Rice, 1958) describes his action research thus:

> In the experiments, attempts were made to take into account both the independent and interdependent properties of the social, technological and economic dimensions of existing socio-technical systems, and to establish new systems in which all dimensions were more adequately interrelated than they had previously been.

This primary task, in system terms, is the task that each system or subsystem is created to perform. Rice saw it as the rallying point for effective co-operation from people in the system.

> The performance of the primary task is supported by the powerful social and psychological forces which ensure that a considerable capacity for co-operation is evoked among the members of the organisation created to perform it. As a direct corollary, the effective performance of a primary task can provide an important source of satisfaction for those engaged upon it.
>
> (Rice, 1958)

Rice gave three other assumptions about task organisation, which although written nearly 40 years ago, are relevant to discussions on work satisfaction.

i A task should be so organised that it is a 'whole task'.
ii Those engaged in the task should be able to control their own activities.
iii Tasks should be so organised that people can form satisfactory relationships.

Since 1958 the concept of primary task has had further refinements and developments. Rice redefined primary task as the task that an institution at any given time 'must perform to survive' (Miller and Rice 1967; Rice, 1963). Miller and Rice (1967) add:

> The primary task is essentially a heuristic concept, which allows us to explore the ordering of multiple activities (and of constituent systems of activity where these exist). It makes it possible to construct and compare different organisational models of an enterprise based on different definitions of its primary task; and to compare the organisation of different enterprises with the same or different primary tasks. The definition of the primary task determines the dominant import-export system.

Lawrence (Lawrence and Robinson, 1975) have further refined the concept by making explicit according to Miller (1993), the 'hitherto partly implicit distinction between':

1 The normative task as the task that people in an organisation ought to pursue (usually according to the definition of a superordinate authority).
2 The existential primary task as that which they believe they are carrying out.
3 The phenomenoligical primary task which it is hypothesised that they are engaged in and of which they may not be consciously aware.

The importance of boundaries in the open systems model

In Systems of Organisation: Task and Sentient Systems and Their Boundary Control (Miller and Rice, 1967), the Tavistock model for organisations as open systems is clearly delineated. The following is a summary of the points made for understanding organisational processes and systems:

1 Boundaries are where change is felt and made or allowed to happen and where conflict is felt and managed.
2 Organisations in relatively stable environments can be more highly bounded or 'structured'. They can have more specialised parts, a lot more autonomy between the parts, localised measures of successful performance, limited channels of communication and many policies and procedures.
3 Organisations functioning in relatively more dynamic environments should have characteristics in the other direction: less division of labour, more interaction between the parts, more concern for how well the whole unit is doing, more communication, fewer policies.
4 A principle in OST is that it is best for an organisation to be correctly bounded, whatever that means for them at a particular time.
5 Over-bounded systems fail to adapt as well or as quickly as they should; under-bounded ones suffer from confusion and conflict.
6 Boundaries are established over time through the managerial process. They should be built around such considerations as:

Task, territory, time, transactions and teamwork

The following are concepts that are part of open systems thinking for organisational analysis:

Task: What's getting done? How complex is it? Who is dependent on whom? Where are the similarities in skills? What constitutes a whole piece of work? Where are the natural supervisory connections?
Territory: What are the physical considerations within the workspace? How does geography affect the people and the workflow?
Time: What are the likely rhythms? In what cycles do outputs function? Who else is working in the same time frames?
Transactions: How can frequent boundary crossings be avoided so the work can be done more easily? How can we keep the needed skills and resources within the team? How can we keep the providers as close as possible to the users of a service?
Teamwork: What's a good size for the group? What are the natural identity and membership connections? Where do people get their personal supports from? How much stress is there?

(Miller 1959)

According to Katz and Kahn (1966), the open-system approach identifies and maps the repeated cycles of input, transformation, output and renewed input and represents the adaptation of work in biology and in the physical sciences by Von Bertalanffy and others (See Figure 1.1). Bastedo (2006) makes the point that OST refers simply to the concept that organisations are strongly influenced by their environment. The environment consists of other organisations that exert various forces of an economic, political or social nature. The environment also provides key resources that sustain the organisation and lead to change and survival. OST was developed after World War II in reaction to earlier theories of organisations, such as the human relations perspective of Elton Mayo (1933) and the administrative theories of Henri Fayol (1949), which treated the organisation largely as a self-contained entity. Virtually all modern theories of organisation utilise the open systems perspective. As a result, open systems theories come in many flavours. For example, contingency theorists argue that organisations are organised in ways that best fit the environment in which they are embedded. Institutional theorists see organisations as a means by which the societal values and beliefs are embedded in organisational structure and expressed in organisational change. Resource dependency theorists see the organisation as adapting to the environment as dictated by its resource providers. Although there is a great variety in the perspectives provided by open systems theories, they share the perspective that an organisation's survival is dependent upon its relationship with the environment.

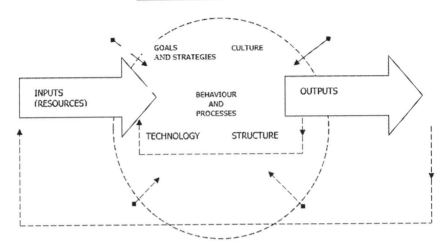

Figure 1.1 Open systems diagram.

Source: Adapted by David Lawlor.

Properties of a system

A system is an assembly of parts wherein:

1 The parts or components are connected in an organised way.
2 The parts or components are affected by being in the system and are changed by leaving it.
3 The assembly does something.
4 The assembly has been identified by someone as being of special interest (Peters and Beishon, 1972).

Around the early 1970s, Checkland (1999) at the University of Lancaster developed the following list of essential properties of a system:

1 An ongoing purpose (which may be determined in advance – purposeful – or assigned through observation – purposive)
2 A means of assessing performance
3 A decision-taking process
4 Components that are also systems (i.e. the notion of subsystems)
5 Components that interact
6 An environment with which the system may or may not interact
7 A boundary between the system and the environment that may be closed or open
8 Resources
9 Continuity

These definitions are relatively old, and the systems field has broadened considerably since they were formulated. Nevertheless, they still provide a good base from which to understand the fundamental nature of systems and systems-based inquiry. Thirty years on, their main disadvantage is that they promote the idea that a system is always an observable concrete 'thing' (e.g. a manufacturing supply chain) rather than the possibility that a system may be an assembly of concepts, ideas and beliefs.

Systems concepts include:

1 System inputs
2 System hierarchies
3 The idea of a system environment
4 System functions and processes
5 System outputs
6 Goal-directed behaviour
7 A definable boundary
8 Information and information flows

Systems theory and the integrated perspectives school

Both Scientific Management and Human Behaviour approaches have been criticised for their failure to integrate organisational structure, technology and people with the larger environment in which organisations exist. The Scientific Management theorists concentrated on organisational structure and work design with little attention to people and organisational environments. The Human Behaviour theorists were concerned with people but also tended to ignore influences beyond organisational boundaries. In reaction to these criticisms, a number of organisational researchers have developed **Integrated Perspectives** viewpoints. These theorists attempt to explain how people, technologies and environments integrate to influence all that happens in organisations. The Scientific Management and Human Behaviour viewpoints, according to their critics, had failed to integrate organisational structure, technology and people with the larger environments in which organisations exist. The Integrated Perspectives approaches attempted to explain how people, technology and environments interact to influence goal-directed behaviour.

Integrated perspective theories: process and environmental approaches

Process and environmental approaches to organisational theory attempt to describe how complex processes such as decision-making influence the internal operation of organisations and are influenced by external environments. Researchers using these perspectives seek to explain how human and technical systems interact with the broader environments in which organisations operate and, in so doing, seek to test basic assumptions from both Scientific Management and Human Behaviour viewpoints. To describe the process and environmental approaches, we explore the decision-making approach of Herbert Simon; sociotechnical integration as described by Eric Trist and Kenneth Bamforth; contingency theory as introduced by Joan Woodward, Paul Lawrence and Jay Lorsch; and systems theory as explained by Daniel Katz and Robert Kahn. Finally, the new organisation science and learning organisations using the work of Margaret Wheatley, Peter Senge and Gareth Morgan. The theories attempt to explain how people, technologies and environments integrate to influence goal-directed behaviour.

Holding on to the social *and* the technical

Even though Trist and Bamforth (1951) introduced the term socio-technical in a production system context, there has been a shift away from the technical towards the social aspects of socio-technical in recent decades. Today, socio-technical system theory typically deals with topics such as motivation, process improvement and job satisfaction, self-managing teams, job design and enrichment, job rotation and empowerment through communicative participation, and so on. Along this line, we argue that present STS models have lost their original, and important perspective. Furthermore, it is crucial to bring the origin into focus again, not by itself, but as a vital part of the two-sided value creation process that will strengthen companies' competitive edge.

STS and eco-systems

In short, because of the capacity to connect, work systems are now complex eco-systems that extend beyond an organisation and its employees. Organisations rely increasingly on technologically enabled integration and optimisation of a network of multi-faceted connections that are integral to each involved organisation's ability to perform effectively and carry out its strategy. The design of any organisation extends well beyond the organisation's boundaries to include its lateral connections with many elements within the eco-system. Organisation designers must expand focus from bounded organisations to the design of eco-systems. The design of the technical system that links together the members of the eco-system will have to occur interactively with the design of the eco-system's social system.

From an OST perspective, a definition of a human or social ecosystem (Trist et al., 1997) is provided by Merrelyn Emery (1993):

> An ecosystem in social science is a community of systems, usually organizations and individuals, who occupy a particular section of the extended social environment, a task environment. In human affairs, the first task of the community of human systems that constitutes the ecosystem is to

work towards adaptation to their econiche so that it and they can function productively within it. That means that the relationship between the community of systems and its task environment, and the relationships between the members of the community itself, must be adaptive. When and only when all these relationships become adaptive, can the human ecosystem said to be in an adaptive, evolving relationship with its social environmental econiche.

Summary

Reality consists of sets of interacting problems, systems of problems we call 'messes'. As previously noted, problems are abstractions extracted from reality by analysis. Therefore, education for practice should develop and apply methodology for dealing holistically with systems of problems. Because messes are complex, this requires an ability to cope with complexity. It is much easier to deal with complexity through design in practice—for example, in designing a skyscraper—than in dealing with it academically in a classroom or research facility. The theory of complexity is not required for dealing with complexity in practice; design can handle it too.

(Ackoff and Greenberg, 2008)

Systems psychodynamics theories of organisation and management originate in biology, mathematics, physics and chemistry. Tavistock Institute's engagement with contemporary organisational life combines industrial social systems that shaped the 20th-century workplace with virtual, remote, distributed, volatile work realities of the 21st century. Contemporary human industrial work is no longer only located in Europe and North America but has moved to the Far East where Tavistock methods of worker participation, autonomous work groups and socio-technical systems are being introduced. First-generation computers and automation influenced the Tavistock Institute to wrestle with the social consequences of mass redundancy. 'Human relations' has accelerated exponentially, driven by social media; systems psychodynamics contributes to our understanding of contemporary organisations and the digitalised world. Society and organisations benefit by using Tavistock technology – socio-technical analysis, action research, group relations conference learning and systems psychodynamics. Tavistock thinking illuminates contemporary but culturally different, western and eastern organisations. Tavistock Institute's deep engagement with public sector organisations and in developmental work with globalised economies and the virtual digital worlds leads to an understanding of the impact of unconscious processes, increased velocity of algorithms and machine learning. The traditions of the Tavistock Institute's methodologies enable organisations, sectors and societies to be better informed of the futures they are creating.

Exercise

Your organisation has been asked to design a new IT system for a large complex eco-system like Health and Social Care. Budget is £40m–£50m and timescale is two years. Identify the need, the optimum scope of the system, the benefits, the users and the limitations. Using an Open Systems model, how would you set about researching IT needs, making your recommendations, implementing the installation and providing training and after-sales service? Describe your assumptions and behaviours in terms of the theory of open systems theory. What open systems theory and concepts do you think you would find useful?

2 The systems psychodynamics approach

There is a wide spectrum of consultation practice encompassed by the systems psychodynamics paradigm. Bain (1982, Pg. 35–46), as quoted in Gould (2001, Pg. 8), provides a useful taxonomy. He notes that the organisational consultant engages in an analysis of the inter-relationships of the following:

1. Boundaries
2. Roles and role configurations
3. Structures and organisational design
4. Work culture and group processes

Gould (2001, Pg. 8) delineates how a consultant would work from within the systems psychodynamics paradigm:

> A consultant working on these aspects of the organisation would be alert to, and selectively interpret the covert and dynamic aspects of the client organisation and the work groups that comprise it, often with a focus on relatedness and how authority is psychologically distributed, exercised, and enacted, in contrast to how it is formally invested. This work would include a consideration of attitudes, beliefs, phantasies, core anxieties, social defences, patterns of relationships and collaboration, and how these in turn may influence task performance. Further, in a manner similar to group relations training conferences, the consultation work would focus on how a variety of unwanted feelings and experiences are split off and projected onto particular individuals and groups that carry them - that is, their process roles as distinct from their formally sanctioned role - on behalf of the organisation.

Czander (1993, Pg. 204) considers the entry into the client system as an important process. He reflects that crossing of the organisational boundary by the consultant into the client's system is a point for analysis of boundary-related issues in the consultant–consultee relationship. He points out that systems psychodynamics consulting maintains that an external boundary forms around all organisations and sub-systems within the organisation.

DOI: 10.4324/9781003181507-6

According to Czander (1993, Pg. 204), assessment of the boundary issues will give the consultant information on the following aspects of organisational functioning:

a Areas of authority in the organisation
b How it is delegated
c Sub-system dependency and autonomy
d Clarity of task definition
e How the organisation manages multiple tasks
f How the organisation manages its boundaries
g Clues concerning the nature of the request for a consultation
h Issues that precipitated the request for consultation
i Organisational resistance towards intervention and change

What is the consultation about?

In systems psychodynamics consultancy methodology, the idea of crossing the boundary is central (Czander, 1993) since it is at that point that consultants are immediately subject to projective identification by the system, and who are themselves also introjectively identified with aspects of the system. The capacity of the consultant or teams of consultants to work with this process is a key skill. In systems psychodynamics consultancy, boundary management in the consultant–consultee relationship has a significant place. Czander (1993, Pg. 186) suggests that there are three major activities in which the consultant engages during the beginning of any consultation. The first focuses on the nature of the contract between consultant and organisation; the second is the consultant's capacity to view and understand their entry into the organisation as a microcosm of the organisation's capacity to manage its boundaries; and the third is the consultant's capacity to conduct an analysis of the dynamics and unconscious forces at play in the consultant–client relationship.

Systems psychodynamics consulting – working methods and application of theory

From the literature, the following core concepts make up the systems psychodynamics paradigm:

1 Boundary maintenance and regulation (Emery and Trist, 1960; Miller and Rice, 1967)
2 Task analysis (Emery and Trist, 1960; Rice, 1963)
3 Authority and leadership (French and Vince 1999; Obholzer and Roberts, 1994; Rice, 1965)
4 Role definition (Reed and Armstrong, 1988a,b)

5 Inter-organisational relations (Aldrich, 1971; Chin, 1961; Emery and Trist, 1965)
6 Sub-system dependency and autonomy (Argyris, 1964; Emery and Trist, 1960; Schein, 1988)
7 Psychoanalysis (Armstrong, 1997; Bion, 1961; Jaques, 1955; Klein, 1959; Lawrence et al., 1996; Turquet, 1975)

Working methods

Palmer (2002) sees the following elements as constituting systems psychodynamics practice; working with groups is often a preferred method of diagnosis and intervention. This practice draws upon Bion (1961) and the Leicester Conference – A Working Conference for the Study of Organisational Life (Miller, 1990). This involves a distinctive form of process consultancy in which the consultant works interpretatively with the 'material' presented by the client group. Systems psychodynamics has the notion of a temporary holding environment and container for client anxieties whether the 'client' is individuals, teams or management groups. Working with or in the transference is crucial, the transference being all the thoughts, feelings and phantasies that are invoked in the client/consultant relationship. The consultant uses these phenomena to understand organisational life that is outside the client's awareness. Linked to this is working with the countertransference; that is, interpreting and using one's own feelings, phantasies, impulses and behaviours as indicators of having become not only in, but of, the client system.

The working through of these dynamics helps the client recognise resistance to change and the associated fears to change processes. There is a need to define and clarify boundaries. It is assumed that articulating and enacting a coherent array of roles and task systems is functional for organisational work. Helping design new forms of organisation, based on open systems models (Miller and Rice, 1967) can be part of the consultancy task. Often designing experiential learning events based on group relations methods are used in the consultancy intervention.

The necessary skills, methods, aims and working practices of a systems psychodynamics paradigm of organisational consultancy involve developing the capacity for reflection on the emotional experience of task-related work. These skills, methods, aims and practices can be better understood and mastered by examining how individuals and teams debate and communicate within the organisation and how they help or hinder work on the primary task of the team and organisation. A systems psychodynamically oriented consultant will have a realistic rather than a rigidly defensive relationship to the emotional aspects of work. This awareness will help staff gain greater insight into the limits of what is possible to work on.

Czander and Eisold (2003, Pg. 475) draw attention to what distinguishes psychoanalytically oriented or systems psychodynamics consulting from other types of consulting. They maintain that it is the consultant's capacity to use the three major aspects of psychoanalytic practice:

a   The deciphering or translating of unconscious thoughts and feelings.
b   The understanding of resistances and defence mechanisms.
c   The assessment of transference and countertransference reactions.

> Psychoanalytic consultants, like general consultants, face an array of ambiguities during the interview process. Should they gain entry, they have the advantage of being able to pay careful attention to the complex, shifting and sometimes contradictory dynamics associated with this process. They face from the start the disadvantage of promising an exploratory and uncertain process that many clients will not understand or want. But, by contrast, they offer a sophisticated and flexible instrument that can succeed where others have failed.

The knowledge of dynamic forces in systems by the systems psychodynamics consultant can enrich the entry, contracting and intervention phase of the work. Czander and Eisold (2003, Pg. 485) suggest the creation of two distinct phases of the consultation process. This would give rise to two separate contracts, a diagnostic contract and an intervention contract. But crucially, more time and effort should be given to the diagnostic phase than to the intervention because a correct assessment is necessary for a successful consultation. The adage 'how you start determines where you end up' is important to keep in mind. Czander and Eisold (2003, Pg. 486) summarise the importance of diagnosis to achieve a better understanding of the true nature of the underlying problem; understand the conscious and unconscious transference reactions the client is having to the consultant. An accurate understanding of this can help avoid working at cross-purposes that may sabotage the possibility of a successful consultation. The diagnosis aids in a better understanding of the underlying 'collective wishes' associated with the presenting problem and the forces that will have to be mobilised in the organisation to bring about significant change:

> The key to a successful consultation is being able to respond to the 'real underlying problem' of the organization, the 'problem' that the consultant has been able to lay bare, and at the same time gratify the desire and the need for the client to develop its true, inherent potential. This does not mean that the organization cannot be challenged to confront some of its most cherished assumptions, but that the consultant and the organization must come together in a spirit which responds to some underlying collective passions and desires.

There is no simple answer to the pressure that a consultant meets when entering an organisation. The strength of the systems psychodynamics consultant is the capacity to pay attention to the transference and countertransference reactions that are an inevitable part of the contact and the relationship. If the consultant can take up a position in the client's mind where these encounters are observable and available for reflection, they could have access to very rich data on the organisation's real and hidden difficulties. The strength is offering a process of reflection and exploration that not only is not a 'quick fix solution' but which also engages the organisation in thinking about itself. Czander and Eisold (2003, Pg. 481) examine some of the transference and countertransference issues typically associated with consultation failure. They point out that a frequent problem is that consultants will be 'captured' emotionally by one segment of an organisation or by an individual with whom they have established a special relationship. This then blinds the consultants to vital aspects of the larger system so that interventions can be destructive. Czander and Eisold suggest that during the diagnostic phase, a psychoanalytically oriented consultant needs to have an understanding of the psychodynamics associated with the presenting problem – or as they put it, why has the presenting problem been chosen to represent the organisation's dilemma?

There are three reasons for stressing the diagnosis:

1 To arrive at a better understanding of the true nature of the underlying problem.
2 Understand the conscious and unconscious transference reactions the client is having to the consultant.
3 To arrive at a better understanding of the underlying 'collective wishes' associated with the presenting problem, the forces that will have to be mobilised in the organisation to bring about a significant change.

Systems psychodynamics consultants focus on working with the client to:

a Enable them to feel and think through the presenting problem.
b To form their own diagnoses and generate their own solutions.

In the systems psychodynamics paradigm, the task of consultancy is to consider the relations between processes operating across the boundary of different levels of a system. The distinctive emphasis in the systems psychodynamics model is to bring processes outside of ordinary consciousness into clear focus and understand their meaning. In systems psychodynamics organisational consultancy, the consultant is continually asking, "what is it that is generating emotional experiences that are being registered by the consultant and by the client?" (Armstrong, 2005a). The consultant aims to enable the client to gain awareness of what is happening below the surface within the organisation and to help the client rehearse and examine the significance of this awareness and meaning for policy, planning, decision-making and action. The consultant carries out the consultancy process by the practice of attending to, reflecting on, and making links from the emotional experiences presented through the consultant's engagement with and in the organisation and in the roles the consultant has taken or is given. Diagnosing the source of the problem is not easy because there can be layer upon layer of resistance to changes in structure. Menzies Lyth (1991) enunciates this dynamic process within institutions that a consultant will meet in which the presenting symptoms in an assignment may appear discrepant with the emotional charge that accompanies them and which has led the organisation to seek consultancy in the first place.

> The defensive system collusively set up against these feelings consists, first, in fragmentation of the core problem so that it no longer exists in an integrated and recognisable form consciously and openly among those concerned. Secondly, the fragments are projected on to bits of the ambience of the job situation, which are then consciously and honestly, but mistakenly, experienced as the problem about which something needs to be done, usually by someone else. Responsibility has also been fragmented and projected often into unknown others, 'Them', the authorities.
>
> (Menzies Lyth, 1991, Pg. 361–378)

To promote the client's development, the consultant believes in enlarging understanding, bringing to awareness those aspects of the client's experience that are often hidden, un-reflected upon, unformulated or simply ignored as not relevant. The consultant helps the client reflect on the fit between the motives and intentions driving the action and decision-making in the system. Following on from this, the consultant works to help the client deal with internal resistances, defences and blind spots. Enlarging the client's grasp on the human realities of work and the system is a hallmark of the systems psychodynamics model. The consultant is always a participant in working with the experience that the client brings. The consultant works to help the client be open to new insights and motivations. The model suggests that a primary preoccupation of the systems psychodynamics consultant is in helping the client to extend the repertoire of what can be thought about in charting new courses of action for the system. This might be particularly true in relation to organisational structures.

The skills, methods, aims and working practices linked to their application in the systems psychodynamics model of organisational consultancy include asking questions and probing for clarity and understanding of the client's issues. They pay attention to both the 'hidden' and 'open' messages that the client is giving. The consultant attempts to understand the client's perspectives and needs. To gain good information, the consultant builds trust and credibility with the client. They will test out with the client their understanding of the work group and its primary preoccupations. Once having a clear grasp of the difficulties, the consultant will negotiate and agree a contract with the client on the task of the consultation. Part of this negotiation will be an exploration and clarification of expectations of the consultant and client in the consulting relationship. It is important that in the negotiations, agreement is reached on the need for time to be set aside to process, examine and review the work of the consultant and the client. The contract should reflect that the consultation is a collaborative relationship between the client and the consultant. Contracts should agree rules around confidentiality. Most important but often neglected is agreement on the evaluation of the consultancy (see Chapters 17 and 18).

Systems psychodynamics consultants spend time gathering information and, most importantly, via the relationship with the client, communicating that they are interested in:

1. Day-to-day problems of the client.
2. Objectives of the client and methods to achieve them.
3. Philosophy of the client.

In this process, the consultant shows that they are actively supportive of the client's work and helping the client diagnose a problem. This may entail a constructively critical stance of the client's work, but it also demonstrates an interest in the client's work. All these activities help the consultant in collaboration with the client to make an analysis of the dynamic in the client's system and help the client understand it. Hopefully, the build-up of trust and credibility helps the consultant communicate effectively with the client on the nature of the difficulties. This helps the client think about change. The consultant demonstrates their capacity to help the client by staying on task in the consultancy session. This will inevitably mean the recognition of conflict and confrontation in the consultancy session. The exposition of conflict and tensions within the system allows for the client to develop objectives for the organisation and the consultancy interventions. At the back of the consultant's mind, and often at the forefront, is how to help the client manage their development and evaluate achievements and activities. The encouragement by the consultant for the client to be pro-active in the consultancy session encourages autonomy and avoids an unhealthy dependency. Therefore, the consultant needs to work at being creative and innovative in working with the client. When an impasse occurs, the consultant can then act as a catalyst and overcome inertia to help the client work on serious problems. This may mean the consultant has to help the client see that they need to plan how to gain more resources. Throughout this process, the consultant is helping clients recognise and define their needs. The client may not recognise the resources, i.e. personal skills, finance, organisational, etc., that are available. This may be due to denial or splitting within the system, where due to unconscious dynamics, the 'obvious' cannot be seen. The move should be to support the client in selecting or creating solutions to problems. But the consultant also must assist the client adapt and carry out solutions to identified problems and evaluate solutions.

Case study

At an exploratory meeting with a CEO and Head of HR, the consultant team discuss an initiative to help the company examine its leadership capabilities and address their challenges over the next five years.

The pair from the company explained their concerns over whether the existing executive committee was properly geared up to drive the company towards its hoped-for five-year target. They were hoping that HR, with the help of the consultants, may develop the company's top leadership to enable growth to the next business level and achieve and maintain a high market share. The CEO said the company had a high-risk strategy to grow to $20b and 28–30 thousand employees in four to five years. That would mean doubling the size of the company that still behaves like a start-up. To be sure, they said, over the past 15 years, the company has matured and achieved huge profitability. It was a success story, but they feared would be unlikely to continue. In the realm of its technology, the company was the leader, a lead which could be maintained for another seven years at most. About 20% of the budget was invested in R&D, but they had to take account of Moore's Law, which states that:

> ... in the history of computing hardware, the number of transistors on integrated circuits doubles approximately every two years. The law is named after Intel co-founder Gordon E. Moore, who described the trend in his 1965 paper. His prediction has proven to be accurate, in part because the law is now used in the semiconductor industry to guide long-term planning and to set targets for research and development. The capabilities of many digital electronic devices are strongly linked to Moore's law: processing speed, memory capacity, sensors and even the number and size of pixels in digital cameras. All of these are improving at roughly exponential rates as well. This exponential improvement has dramatically enhanced the impact of digital electronics in nearly every segment of the world economy. Moore's law describes a driving force of technological and social change in the late 20th and early 21st centuries. It predicts that chip performance would double every 18 months, being a combination of the effect of more and faster transistors. Although this trend has continued for more than half a century, Moore's law should be considered an observation or conjecture and not a physical or natural law. Sources in 2005 expected it to continue until at least 2015 or 2020. However, the 2010 update to the International Technology Roadmap for Semiconductors predicted that growth will slow at the end of 2013, when transistor counts and densities are predicted to double only every three years.

The CEO and HR Director continue that their challenge as a successful company now is to keep up with Moore's Law, doubling the capacities of their products every two years, and aiming to become a $25b–$30b company. Currently, the company feels like a family business, but as it grows, paradoxically, the leaders fear losing control. Many current leaders were present at the start-up and they still manage/lead in the 'old way' while the company grows big rapidly and the structure gets more cumbersome. Growth also increases mistrust among members of the executive committee.

The CEO described the company's commitment to innovation, customer relations and social responsibility. The culture, he said, was to review the manufacturing process relentlessly in order to find and fix the flaws in their products. R&D, sales, engineering and operations are organised in a flexible matrix style. The company is part of an extended and complicated supply chain (about 2,500 suppliers) and the company's success depends in large part on the efficient functioning of all the suppliers in the supply chain. The company places huge importance on 'looking after' their suppliers.

The company, the Director of HR said, has an ethos of 'extraordinariness' and it has to have extraordinary leaders, but the second tier of leaders, the heads of divisions and departments seem lost. "We need to develop a particular leadership style in the second tier, and we do not know what we are looking for. Our company cannot grow to the next level without extraordinary leaders. We have recruited people from outside and the majority have failed. They were good people, but they leave because they cannot tolerate the culture or the culture extrudes them. The executive committee, on the other hand, lacks self-confidence and is resistant to change. Our problem is that we are behaving like a start-up with the founders feeling they must control everything. We are a 30-year-old company and are at risk of becoming a dinosaur. Growth strategy needs to be linked to the integration of the company leadership at all levels".

In preparing the company leaders for future leadership roles, a leadership development programme was suggested based on an in-depth and extended exploration of the group dynamics at team, executive, board, company, sector and global levels. We explained that the programme they were asking for should consist of addressing underlying dynamic leadership issues that focus on groups, not individuals, as the arena for change. This would involve deepening understanding of the expectations of all parts of the company, with a focus on business, i.e. environmental and eco-system pressures, organisational strategies, and the practical challenges of producing the highest levels of technology. The programme should also focus on the gaps between strategic and policy decisions and operational implementation and other inconsistencies in the company, like taking up a more mature role in the supply chain relationships. The consultants suggested to the CEO and Director of HR that people, teams and groups and the company-as-a-whole would be more effective as industry leaders if people as members of groups/teams, i.e. the company's sub-systems, increased their ability to use systems psychodynamics thinking and better understand the hidden, sometimes unconscious, determinants of individual, group, organisational, sector and global behaviour.

Our diagnostic process involved interviewing all the members of the executive committee followed by working with the committee for six months before meeting the second-tier leadership. It was necessary diagnostically to win the trust of the executive committee to work dynamically. Doing so helped us understand the disruptive competitive dynamics between the first and second tiers of leadership. The design of our programme would have to include addressing these competitive dynamics. The aim of any leadership development programme would be to improve understanding and skills of integrating the two leadership levels, reduce the extent of the competitive dynamic, develop the ability to listen and accept the views and opinions of others; to act on behalf of and represent others authoritatively, remain true to themselves, and engage more authentically with other people's hopes, fears, frustrations and disappointments, etc.

The leadership development programme took nine months of diagnostic work to ready the top levels of leadership for the potential disruption to the different systems as they negotiated a difficult change process while continuing with normal day-to-day usual business. The programme was intended to help the 75 top leaders discover more about what goes on in the company's boards, different units, sections and teams, their rivalries and resistances. It would mean taking account of the many unsaid things in their relationships; learn why their groups get into 'group-think' mentality; avoided listening to minority voices; considering that being an effective leader also requires being an effective follower perhaps in the space of two consecutive meetings; paying attention to the spiritual elements at work, for example, by holding onto the company vision of contributing towards a better world without losing sight of profitability and cost-reduction challenges.

The diagnostic phase would involve interviews, sometimes two or three interviews with each member of the executive, that covered all aspects of leading a highly technical and complex global business. Based on these interviews and meetings with the executive, we eventually came up with the following definition of the Primary Task of the leadership development initiative, which was agreed by the executive:

> *To identify personal, group and cultural barriers to achieving greater leadership capability in the company's leaders and working on these barriers in order to reduce their impact on individual and group leadership performance.*

Splitting phenomena

During the attempt to implement change, the client system will probably be subject to splitting. This splitting may be due to the changes disturbing the social defence system. The splitting may take place in the organisation; i.e. the organisation or its leadership can be split into highly idealised good parts and highly vilified bad parts. These processes, if attended to by the consultant, will aid the client in understanding that the unconscious refers to the hidden aspects of organisational life. This will give the consultant the opportunity to assist the client to understand that by projection, the organisation gets rid of something unwanted into specific other parts of the systems. Understanding that an organisation is a complex place where good and bad, right and wrong are inextricably linked, helps in extending the client's leadership capability. This is in opposition to a tendency to perceive parts of the organisation as either 'good' or 'bad'. In this process, the client may begin to understand that their authority is often attacked for no good reason. Through 'spoiling' behaviour, aspects of the organisation may become impaired, weakened, damaged and diminished. Menzies Lyth (1991, Pg. 361–378) describes this process very well:

> I think what may be happening is something like this. There is within the job situation a focus of deep anxiety and distress. Associated with this there is despair about being able to improve matters. One meets this same process frequently in psychoanalysis when a patient feels himself to be up against an intractable problem and believes he cannot manage the feelings associated with it. Such defensive reactions to institutional problems often mean the institution cannot really learn. The solutions tried before had failed, but they will work this time, it is believed, as though there is a kind of magic about them. Effective resolution can only come when the institution, with or without the help of a consultant, can address itself to the heart of the matter and not only to its ambience, and introduce relevant changes there.

Change and anxiety

Change processes for the organisation can entail significant anxieties for staff, and it is the job of the consultant to help the client tune into these. This will mean more awareness of the defences against anxiety which are embedded and part of the system. The client will then become aware that the system resists efforts to change it. Work by the consultant can then focus on understanding that the change processes expose staff more directly to anxiety. This anxiety may show itself when the sub-systems in the organisation, such as teams or groups of managers, use other sub-systems as repositories for anxiety, criticism, blame, denigration, or other unwanted feelings. If the work is progressing well, this may mean the client understanding that in a well-functioning organisation there will be a capacity among staff and managers to think about the emotional impact and significance of the work undertaken with respect to the primary task. It will be a timely reminder to the client and the organisation that the primary task is the core work the organisation must do to survive. Time can be spent on understanding how the system performs its primary task. This may lead to the discovery that work groups can and do sometimes avoid carrying out the primary task. This growing awareness that anxiety can arise in any part of the system and can have origins in the personal history of individuals, the demands of the task and the demands of the client group or wider social system.

But how should the consultant help with this growing awareness of defences, off-task behaviour and underlying anxieties? The client will need to understand that containment describes a basic dimension of human experience, that is, how the relationship between emotion and its 'containment' is experienced or avoided, managed or denied, kept in or passed on so that its effects are either mitigated or amplified. This work will deepen the client's understanding and awareness of what is happening below the surface within their organisation.

Consciousness and unconscious processes

Systems psychodynamics consultants work with unconscious processes by paying attention to processes taking place outside of ordinary consciousness; by considering the relations between conscious and unconscious process; by raising awareness of unconscious anti-task tendencies that could be understood and mastered; by helping clients look at the 'value' of experience and implied motives or intentions.

Consultants develop formulations; by this, we mean a translation of what is happening. Consultants offer formulations to the client as a basis for further exploration; a formulation is a provisional answer to the question: 'why is this happening?' The offering of a formulation entails risks, facing hostility and working through resistances. Interpretations involve making speculative links to other elements of the client organisation's situation, narrative and history.

Miller (1997, Pg. 191) describes the methodology of the consultant thus:

> The feelings evoked in the organisational consultant about the role one is being put in and the way one is being used provide data about underlying processes in the client system. The other influence is the recognition that as, with the analyst, it is an important function to provide for the client system a 'holding environment' (Winnicott, 1965) by serving as a safe container who can accept and survive the anxieties and sometimes hostile projections coming from the client system.

From our earlier elaboration of the projective identification/introjective identification processes, we can see how interpretation along systems psychodynamics lines illuminates Miller's statement above on consultants' methodology. The framework that holds this in place is the proposition that it is necessary to have a theory of a 'container/contained' (Riesenberg-Malcolm, 2001) relationship between consultant and client, as well as attending to the practical application of structures and organised work groups.

Systems psychodynamics consultants listen and tune into everything their senses are picking up from a meeting with a client. The consultant pays attention to the shifting feelings they become aware of in themselves. In particular, the unexpected or surprising, the practice of letting oneself be open to the associations that come into one's mind as one listens to or observes the client, is a distinctive feature of the systems psychodynamics method – images, memories, recollections of earlier material, questions, etc.

The six basic stages in the organisational development consultancy cycle

Kolb and Frohman's (1970) formulation of seven basic stages in the organisational development and consultancy cycle is a well-known and popular set of ideas within the organisational consultancy community:

Jean Neumann (1997) gives a comprehensive account of the negotiating entry and contracting process. She explains the use of Kolb and Frohman

(1970) and gives examples of its application from her consultancy practice. She states (Pg. 26) that negotiating and contracting take place in the real world, and she offers the following guidelines for negotiating and contracting while acknowledging the complexity of completing the initial stages of work.

> **Guide Line One:** Negotiate entry and contracting by keeping in mind the whole of the organisational development cycle as well as possible multiple cycles that might follow on.
> **Guide Line Two:** Ensure that the conditions necessary for the consultant to undertake professional consultancy are agreed at the point of entry and contracting.
> **Guide Line Three:** Craft and entry and contracting process that honours the unique characteristics of the organisational client while completing the overall task of this initial stage of work.
> **Guide Line Four:** Avoid engaging in diagnosis and intervention during entry and contracting.
> **Guide Line Five:** Avoid beginning work as a consultant without a contract and fee agreed.

Jean Neumann adds that successful entry and contracting requires the consultant to cross the geographic and social boundaries relevant to the immediate purpose of the potential consultant agreement. There is a need to develop a mutual understanding with an authorised person.

The spiral starts with a narrow base (engaging with a small number of people during entry and diagnosis) and widens as the top is approached (as the number of people engaging increases) with an arrow to indicate that an organisational development and change initiative consists of on-going cycles of diagnosis, planning, intervening, reviewing and so on that extend further and further into the organisation until a point is reached when client and consultant agree that the requisite change capacity has been achieved to enable the client to proceed independently. The Team Development and Individual Development activities spin-off out of the sequence of stages but are integrated with them too (Figure 2.1).

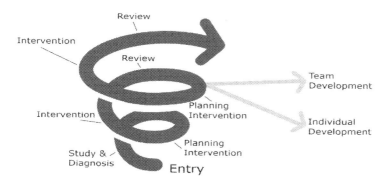

Figure 2.1 The circular model of organisational development intervention.

Summary

Systems psychodynamics consultation practice analyses the inter-relationships of boundaries, roles, structures and organisational design, work culture and group processes. Systems psychodynamics consultation selectively interprets the overt, covert and dynamic relationships of the client organisation and the work groups that comprise it. Systems psychodynamics consultancy focuses on how authority is psychologically distributed, exercised and enacted. Systems psychodynamics consultancy considers attitudes, beliefs, phantasies, core anxieties, social defences, patterns of relationships and collaboration and how these influence task performance. Systems psychodynamics consultation focuses on how unwanted feelings and experiences are split off and projected onto other individuals and groups that then carry the unwanted feelings on behalf of the organisation. Crossing an organisational boundary by the consultant into the client's system is a point for analysis of boundary-related issues in the consultant–consultee relationship. Assessment of boundary issues gives the systems psychodynamics consultant information on areas of authority in the organisation; how authority is delegated; sub-system dependency and autonomy; clues about the nature of the request for a consultation; organisational resistance to intervention and change. The act of boundary crossing into an organisational system is subject to projective identification by the system, just as the consultant introjectively becomes identified with aspects of the system. The beginning of the consultation focuses on the nature of the contract between consultant and organisation and the consultant's capacity to view and understand their entry into the organisational system. The key educative task used in systems psychodynamics consulting is 'insight' into the psychodynamics or covert processes as well as the structural properties of the system in the organisation. Working with and in the transference is crucial, involving thoughts, feelings and phantasies in the client/consultant relationship. Systems psychodynamics consultancy aims to understand organisational life that is outside the client's awareness.

Exercise

You represent your employing organisation at a regional partnership of six organisations engaged in a community development project to design apprenticeships for unemployed youth.

Thinking about how you would use systems psychodynamics approaches, how would you understand and address the following:

a Identifying the roles of each partner.
b Identifying the shared goals of the partnership in relation to the parent organisations.
c The different contributions of each partner.

d Managing the potential conflicts in the partnership.
e Achieving good levels of collaborating.
f Developing a common culture without losing sight of each partner organisation's unique contribution.
g Evaluating the change process for all parts of the system, including the young people.

Part II
Psychoanalytic thinking

Part II covers the influence psychoanalysis has had on the development of the social sciences at the Tavistock Institute since its inception. Key to this development is the theories of Melanie Klein and the Object Relations School of Psychoanalysis in Great Britain. The essence of this influence was the formulation that humans are primarily motivated by the need for contact with others, the need to form relationships. This formulation represents a significant development of Freud's formulations that humans are motivated by sexual and aggressive drives.

Chapter 3 underlines the importance of object relations in the individual's capacity for self-reflection and exploration in the relationship with 'the other'. This idea of self-examination applies equally to groups in their relationships with other groups and to systems in their relationships with other systems ad infinitum. Therefore, whatever unit is the focus of study – the individual, the mother-infant pair, the parent-child triad, the family, the community, the state or indeed, the world – the spotlight is cast externally, on the interactive elements in the relationships between the partners, and internally, on the self, and the way the self (or family or group) perceives the relationship between it and others. This involves holding at least three constructions in mind simultaneously – the self, the other and the relationship between the two.

Chapter 4 explicates key psychoanalytic concepts that are in everyday use by consultants to assist them in understanding and helping their clients and helping their clients understand the forces acting on them. These forces, at first, may be difficult to grasp if one's thinking and attitudes have been influenced by other forms of professional or technical training or life experiences.

Bion's theory of thinking, concepts of linking, container-contained, alpha function and basic assumptions link to Klein's ideas on projection and introjection. These are especially relevant and can be applied as well as to individuals and their relationships, as to complex organisational systems and their inter-organisational relationships. We have added the views of Philip Stokoe to our work on psychoanalysis and appreciate his novel and creative ways of applying the understanding of psychoanalytic theory in working with groups and organisations. Stokoe suggests that the key to what Bion calls 'alpha function' is the continuous activity of the K-drive (which he calls

DOI: 10.4324/9781003181507-7

'curiosity'). Stokoe shows how that K (Knowledge) is an innate drive like L (Love) and H (Hate) and that the K drive is responsible for the development of consciousness as it acts like a computer programme that requires constant explanation to what is happening to us; we are continually asking ourselves, 'what's going on here?' The answers appear in the form of 'unconscious phantasy'; they are images of ourselves in relation to others or parts of others. If we are able to 'learn from experience' (Bion, 1962), those explanations are continually modified, and they accumulate to create the conscious mind.

Finally, in Chapter 5, Halina Brunning rounds off Part II with a piece on executive coaching, also known as organisational role analysis. She provides a helpful ecology of systems psychodynamics coaching, which pays attention to the individual's role in the organisation and increases the coachee's capacity to use multiple perspectives in making sense of and meeting work challenges and contributing to organisational purpose.

The three chapters in Part II serve as a basis of understanding the systems psychodynamics approach to work with systems, organisations and environments in an integrated way, developing new ideas and methods and building on the strong foundations of rigorous psychoanalytic thinking.

3 The psychoanalytic contribution

With Marianne Fotaki

History

According to Arnaud (2012), the psychoanalytic approach sets out to study the unconscious in all its forms and can, therefore, be legitimately applied to organisations, understood as systems that are constructed, lived and managed by individuals, each of whom has specific capacities and a specific unconscious. Arnaud shows that a prolific current of research focusing on the psychodynamics of work, leadership and organisations has taken form over approximately the last 70 years. He states that the richness of this current remains in evidence today and is shown in the interest in applying psychoanalysis to research work on management. First, psychoanalysis can aid researchers to develop a more profound comprehension of organisational functioning by considering the effects of the unconscious. Second, it can guide them in different fields of intervention by transposing aspects of the analytical treatment and integrating transference. Last, it can allow them to re-question managerial ends from a slightly 'askew' point of view informed by psychoanalytic ethics and recognition of the 'subject'. His article aims at examining these issues and offering psychoanalytic theory as a paradigm for the study of management. Fotaki et al. (2012) summarise the contribution of psychoanalysis to contemporary organisations. The aim is to draw attention to psychoanalysis as a critical theory with wide explanatory power and a potential for thinking about organisational practice in new ways. Psychoanalysis does so firstly by reviewing the impact it has on illuminating group dynamics, leadership dysfunctions and socially sanctioned institutional defences. This chapter outlines future developments in the psychoanalytic studies of organisations about: (i) greater conceptual inclusivity and crossing the boundaries between the humanities and science; (ii) the study of affect and emotion in organisations; (iii) an integration of psychoanalytical insights with social theory via psycho-social approaches and 'systems psychoanalysis' and (iv) linking psychoanalysis to discourses of power and the politics of life.

Developments in the 1950s and 1960s by the Tavistock Institute of *open systems* and *socio-technical* theory as a way of viewing organisations were influenced by the psychoanalytic strand in Figure 0.1 (see Introduction, Pg. 4).

Here a key figure was Melanie Klein on her theories of infant development and its continuing influence on adult relationships (e.g. Klein, 1946, 1952, 1959), and object relations theory. According to Hinshelwood (1989), the object relations school includes Fairbairn (1952), Winnicott (1990) and Balint (1968) and others among the Independent Psychoanalysts (Kohon, 1986). Object relations is a variation of psychoanalytic theory that diverges from Sigmund Freud's formulation that humans are motivated by sexual and aggressive drives, suggesting instead that humans are primarily motivated by the need for contact with others, the need to form relationships.

Basic concepts in object relations

Whereas Freud talked about stages of development – oral, anal, genital – Melanie Klein talked about positions, the paranoid-schizoid position and the depressive position. These describe two oscillating mental states experienced throughout life. In the context of object relations theory, the term 'objects' refers not to inanimate entities but to significant others with whom an individual relates, usually one's mother, father or primary caregiver. Regarding internal objects, we internalise, take in, or introject, external experiences, others and aspects of others. Mental representations of the relationships between self and others are laid down in the mind from infancy onwards. These internal templates affect the way we perceive and react to other people in the present. This is the basis of transference. In some cases, the term 'object' may also be used to refer to a part of a person, such as a mother's breast, or to the mental representations of significant others. Object relations theorists stress the importance of early family interactions, primarily the mother–infant relationship, in personality development. It is believed that infants form mental representations of themselves in relation to others and that these internal images significantly influence interpersonal relationships later in life. The term 'object relations' refers to the dynamic *internalized* relationships between the self and significant others (objects). An object relation involves mental representations of:

1. The object as perceived by the self.
2. The self in relation to the object.
3. The relationship between self and object.

For example, an infant might think:

1. "My mother is good because she feeds me when I am hungry" (representation of the object).
2. "The fact that she takes care of me must mean that I am good" (representation of the self in relation to the object).
3. "I love my mother" (representation of the relationship).

Internal objects are formed during infancy through repeated experiences with one's caregiver. The images do not necessarily reflect reality but are subjectively constructed by an infant's limited cognitive abilities. In healthy development, these mental representations evolve over time; in unhealthy development, they remain at an immature level. The internal images have enduring qualities and serve as templates for future relationships. However, these internal representations are not merely faithful copies of external experience but are modified, distorted, altered by one's own wishes and impulses e.g. a parental figure may be represented as more benign or more hostile than they really are. We imbue or project something of ourselves onto them. Thus, an internal object can be a mixture of the real external mother and aspects of oneself. This term 'internal object' is often used when describing internal versions of people, like 'figures' in the mind which interact in various ways with other objects and the self. Thus, we take our experience of important figures into our minds, where they are felt to have a forceful reality of their own. They may be experienced as benign, in which case they are felt to support or comfort us, or they may be felt to be hostile, disappointed or accusing: they are then felt to persecute us. These objects also relate to each other. They may be felt to join together or to be attacking each other, as for example, if my mother *in my mind* is felt to be jealous of my love for my father *in my mind*. Or they may be felt to be in harmony. These internal objects are affected by our relationship with our external objects, but they are not identical with external objects. A view of someone can alter radically depending on the state of mind without any reference to any actual change.

Central to object relations theory is the notion of splitting, which can be described as the mental separation of objects into 'good' and 'bad' parts and the subsequent repression of the 'bad', or anxiety-provoking, aspects. Infants first experience splitting in their relationship with their primary caregiver: the caregiver is 'good' when the needs of the infant are satisfied and 'bad' when they are not.

Initially, these two aspects of the object (the caregiver) are separated in the mind of the infant, and a similar process occurs as the infant comes to perceive good and bad parts of the self. If the mother is able to satisfactorily meet the needs of the infant or, in the language of object relations, if the mother is 'good enough', then the child begins to merge both aspects of the mother, and by extension, the self, into an integrated whole. If the caregiver does not satisfactorily meet the infant's needs, the infant may repress the 'bad' aspects of the mother and of the self, which can cause difficulty in future relationships.

Development and history of object relations

Object relations theory is composed of the diverse and sometimes conflicting ideas of various theorists, mainly Melanie Klein, Ronald Fairbairn and Donald Winnicott. Each of these psychoanalysts placed great emphasis on the mother–infant bond. This is seen as a key factor in the development of a child's psychic structure during the first three years of life.

Klein is often credited with founding the object relations approach. From her work with young children and infants, she concluded that they focused more on developing relationships, especially with their caregivers than on controlling sexual urges, as Freud had proposed. Klein also focused her attention on the first few months of a child's life, whereas Freud emphasised the importance of the first few years of life. Fairbairn agreed with Klein when he posited that humans are object-seeking beings, not pleasure-seeking beings. He viewed development as a gradual process during which individuals evolve from a state of complete, infantile dependence on the caregiver towards a state of interdependency, in which they still depend on others but are also capable of being relied upon. Winnicott stressed the importance of raising children in an environment where they are encouraged to develop a sense of independence but know that their caregiver will protect them from danger. He suggested that if the caregiver does not attend to the needs and potential of the child, the child may develop a false self. The true self emerges when all aspects of the child are acknowledged and accepted. For a more detailed application of the ego psychology or contemporary Freudian school and its application to organisations, Czander (1993) gives a very comprehensive exposition.

Klein's proposition was that the infant is instinctively programmed to seek pleasure and comfort and to avoid pain. The infant polarises its world accordingly. The maternal breast is, at one moment, a good object to be cherished, and at another, a bad object to be destroyed. Early anxieties related to this splitting are complicated by discovering that the 'good' and the 'bad' breast are manifestations of the same breast/person. The defences developed against these intolerable anxieties at this stage remain a permanent part of our psychic life alongside the emergent feelings of guilt, reparation and love. They find expression, for example, in processes of splitting and projection. To deal with the conflicts and complexities of our internal world, we populate our external world with representations of good and evil, friends and foes, and the various other manifestations of 'not-me' or 'not-us' that enable us to hold on to a more consistent self-image.

The psychoanalytic perspective refers to individual experiences and mental processes (e.g. transference, resistances, object relations, phantasy), as well as on the experience of unconscious group and social processes, which are simultaneously both a source and consequence of unresolved or unrecognised difficulties. According to Gould (2001, Pg. 4–5):

> From its earliest days psychoanalysis has been interested in the nature of group and organisational processes. For example, in Group Psychology and the Analysis of the Ego (1920), Freud linked certain dynamic aspects of the church and the army to his earlier hypotheses regarding the origins of social process and social structure, namely, in his analysis of the primal

horde (1913). However, despite this early interest in group psychology, neither he nor colleagues carried this line of theorising much further. Bion's work and the Kleinian concepts that it is based on, are still the touchstone.

Psychoanalytic ideas are useful in understanding both individual experience and group and organisational dynamics. From psychoanalysis, the systems psychodynamics approach draws upon a variety of working principles, for instance.

The unconscious

Halton (1994, Pg. 11–18) describes the contribution that psychoanalysis has made to the systems psychodynamics approach, "looking at an institution through the spectrum of psychoanalytic concepts is a potentially creative activity which may help in understanding and dealing with certain issues. The psychoanalytic involves understanding ideas developed in individual therapy, as well as looking at institutions in terms of unconscious emotional processes". He describes the application of psychoanalytic concepts (mainly Kleinian) to organisations:

1   The unconscious
2   The paranoid-schizoid position
3   Envy
4   Projective identification and countertransference
5   The depressive position

The unconscious is a part of our minds that we are not aware of and which interferes and affects our behaviour. We know the existence of the unconscious through studying ordinary behaviour in our everyday existence e.g. we have dreams, we make 'slips' of the tongue or we forget. Psychoanalysis puts forward the principle that there are hidden aspects of human mental life that, while remaining hidden, nevertheless influences conscious processes. Ideas, which have a valid meaning at the conscious level, may at the same time carry an unconscious hidden meaning. Similarly, in organisations there are processes that are outside of awareness – unconscious – that operate under the surface. These processes are made up of a mixture of phantasy and real experiences. The real experiences shape and influence the hidden phantasies that are influencing both individual behaviour and group behaviour.

The contribution of Melanie Klein – the paranoid schizoid position and the depressive position

Klein outlined two different 'positions': the paranoid-schizoid position and the depressive position. The notion of 'positions' is important. They can be thought of as two different states of mind, each of which is composed of an arrangement of anxieties and other feelings, defences and ways of relating to objects. It is in the Kleinian paranoid-schizoid position that the process of projection and introjection are primary processes used by the infant to defend against persecutory anxieties of annihilation. It is important to bear in mind that these processes are unconscious and they operate in phantasy. Through the paranoid-schizoid position, Klein developed a conceptualisation of an unconscious inner world, present in everyone, peopled by different figures personifying differentiated parts of the self or aspects of the external world. Splitting and projection are the predominant defences for avoiding pain; Klein referred to this as the *paranoid-schizoid position* ('paranoid' referring to badness being experienced as coming from outside oneself, and 'schizoid' referring to splitting). Contained within these hypotheses is the idea that these infantile processes are a part of normal development: 'The processes of splitting off parts of the self and projecting them into objects are thus of vital importance for normal development as well as for abnormal object relations' (Klein, 1946). It is the infant's first means of organising their experiences. To manage anxiety, the world is divided into 'good', which they try to own and to be, and 'bad', which they expel and place outside themselves, in the object. 'Good', for the infant matches 'me', and is made up of good object/good me; 'bad' matches 'not me 'and comprises of bad/object/bad me'. To sum up, what happens in the paranoid-schizoid position, a quotation from Segal (1964, Pg. 67) gives the central points:

> As the processes of splitting, projection and introjection help to sort out his perceptions and emotions and divide the good from the bad, the infant feels himself to be confronted with an ideal object, which he loves and tries to acquire, keep and identify with, and a bad object, into which he has projected his aggressive impulses, and which is felt to be a threat to himself and his ideal object.

The mechanism of projective identification seeks to make the object like oneself, whereas the mechanism of introjective identification is an attempt to be like the external object by taking it into oneself.

The stage of integrating the good and bad perceptions is called the *depressive position*. According to Halton (1994, Pg. 17):

> because giving up the comforting simplicity of self-idealisation, and facing the complexity of internal and external reality, inevitably stirs up painful feelings of guilt, concern and sadness. These feelings give rise to a desire to make reparation for injuries caused through previous hatred and aggression. This desire stimulates work and creativity and is often one of the factors which leads to becoming a 'helping' professional.

In the depressive position, objects are no longer only good or only bad, as they are in the paranoid-schizoid position, but are seen as containing a more accurate blend of qualities and functions. The person, therefore, has more ambivalent feelings towards objects; someone with whom they can feel angry, even hate, is the same someone who is loved. Therefore, feelings of concern and remorse about the loved one begin to arise because the person comes to realise that the object that is hated and wants to attack is also the object that is loved. Accepting responsibility for all these conflicting and contradictory feelings and the need to make reparation are major struggles throughout life. Having achieved the depressive position, the individual is able to see both themselves and others more or less as they really are. The depressive position is never fully achieved or worked through. The anxieties pertaining to guilt, as well as situations of loss which reawaken depressive experiences, are always with us.

To sum up, according to Jaques (1951), "projective identification unconsciously puts internal objects, good or bad, or good or bad impulses, into persons (or things) in the external world. Introjective identification takes persons and things in the outside world into the self so that what one does comes not from oneself but from the internalised other influencing one's behaviour". In all organisations the process of introjection, introjective identification, projection and projective identification are operating under the surface and are largely unconscious.

Emotional pain

A key psychoanalytic idea is emotional pain. The systems psychodynamics approach argues that we all tend to protect ourselves from psychic pain and emotional disturbance. For example, social work, nursing, policing and medicine and teaching will inevitably bring people into contact with distressing life events – such as mental illness, violence, child abuse, death, loss and bereavement. Individuals can often feel overwhelmed by such painful feelings, so can an organisation as a social system feel overwhelmed. To protect itself and the individuals within it, barriers or defences may be erected to stop the pain getting through or at least filtering it. These organisational defence systems can act as a protective factor for staff. But they can also mean that off-task behaviour can take place. The *primary task* can be subject to anti-task activities. Here, management's purpose is the support of staff so that their values and principles inform them in the execution of the primary task. If enough attention can be paid to maintaining staff in on-task activity, the organisation would feel itself purposeful and effective. Too much defensive activity can lead to a sense of uselessness and a fall in morale.

Splitting

The tendency to split continues through into adult life. In organisations, we see it in relation to how different parts of the system can be perceived and experienced. "That's a good place to work; that's a bad place to work". How does this splitting get maintained when there may be no discernible cause or real difference in the way a group performs? Splitting in organisations can take a collective form: groups of individuals or even most organisational members may collectively split the organisation or its leadership into highly idealised good parts and highly vilified bad parts. Invariably, good parts are invested with love and *introjected*, while bad parts become legitimate targets of hate via *projection* and are scapegoated. *Projection* often accompanies *splitting* and involves locating feelings in others rather than in oneself.

Systems psychodynamics consultancy and organisational work transpose the individual model of development to institutional and group processes. Therefore, splitting associated with the paranoid-schizoid phase can occur between groups within the institution. Halton (1994, Pg. 15) points out how:

> ... structural divisions into sections, departments, professions, disciplines are necessary for organisations to function effectively. However, these divisions become fertile ground for the splitting and projection of negative images. These gaps between departments or professions are available to be filled with many different emotions - denigration, competition, hatred, prejudice, paranoia. Each group feels it represents something good and that other groups represent something inferior. The less contact there is with other sections, the greater the scope for projection of this kind. Contact and meetings may be avoided in order unconsciously to preserve self-idealisation based on these projections. This results in the institution becoming stuck in a paranoid-schizoid projective system. Emotional disorder interferes with the functioning of an organisation, particularly in relation to tasks which require co-operation or collective change.

Projective identification

Halton (1994, Pg. 11–18) states that an individual's personal unconscious plays only a subsidiary role in organisational functioning. The link between personal behaviour and organisational dynamics is the psychoanalytic concept of *projective identification and introjective identification*. Here systems psychodynamics practitioners find the concept of projection very useful. Projection is a psychological mechanism that allows us to get rid of the feelings that we find unacceptable into another individual or group. We psychologically export the things we cannot tolerate into another part of the system. The roles, which are on the boundary of systems, can be very prone to projection and attack. "I'm so pleased that my group is not like that group"; or "I wish my group were more like that group". Projective identification is a difficult concept to understand. What purpose projection serves is a question we have to ask ourselves. The first reason is to get rid of intolerable feelings and secondly to have control over the recipient of the projections. It is important to bear in mind that we all use this mechanism sometimes. We can all recall sounding like our parents. Also, when projective identification is used greatly, it appears to be the best possible solution for what feels like overwhelming anxiety, threatening psychological collapse. But the act of projecting important aspects of the person, or group or organisation, leads to a diminution in their capacity to think and know themselves, and they are consequently weakened. Groups or organisations that experience denigration via projection from other groups and then identify with this denigration are often seen as the failing part of the organisation. Likewise, the projecting group also diminish themselves by not owning an aspect of their own functioning.

Most managers have to endure projection from the staff that they are accountable for. The systems psychodynamics approach proposes that unconscious projection into others can have a very powerful effect on the recipient. Often they begin to act out and behave from the projection and in this way confirm the reality for the projector and develop a culture and set of beliefs within the organisation that such events have not only a psychic reality but also a practical manifestation. A vicious cycle begins that confirms the projection and maintains the balance of splitting. Some splitting is inevitable and sometimes necessary for individuals to cope and for groups to stay together (Foster, 2001, Pg. 81–90). But systems psychodynamics consultants would say that it is important to make sure the splitting is not excessive, as the putting of feelings into others also has the effect of depleting the group that has got rid of them. In some way, they can be emotionally impoverished – they never have to grapple with the feelings that they find hard to bear – they just export them.

Another important purpose of projective identification is to communicate states of mind. This is important for consultants to realise that whether it is primarily to communicate or it is primarily to get rid of bad feelings, projective identification always happens between people. The consultant by paying attention to projective identification either to themselves or between sub-systems can pick up on the pressures and solutions that the organisational system is using. It is important that consultants can distinguish what comes from the client system and what comes from them and their personal history. This is best achieved either through some experience of therapy and consultation with colleagues. Consultants need to pay attention to how their responses and defences can be mobilised.

Introjective identification

The concept of introjective identification is barely mentioned in the psychoanalytic organisational consulting literature other than in relation to projective identification. Freud (1922) used the concept of identification to explain the relationship between leaders and followers. Followers identify with their leaders and 'take in' their characteristics through a process of identification and the leader takes the place of their ego-ideal – 'that is the person I would ideally like to be'. Projection and projective identification are more fully taken up in the literature. An exception is Elliott Jaques (1951), who links the two processes and demonstrates how they operate in social relationships. Introjection and introjective identification are complementary to the mechanism of projection and projective identification. Through introjection, individuals take attributes of other people into themselves, and the 'other people' become part of their inner world of imagination, hopes and desires. In introjective identification, the person's internal make-up is made up of a whole society of different 'characters', called internal objects.

Bion (1967) developed Klein's theory, stressing the *function* of this introjected object, which is essential to make feelings thinkable, understandable and therefore tolerable. He describes how it is necessary, for healthy emotional development, to have the experience of a parental object (it is often the mother) who can receive a cluster of sensations, feelings and discomforts that the child cannot give a name to and is, therefore, unable to think about. The function of this parental object, defined by Bion (1967) as 'alpha function' or 'reverie', involves keeping in mind, giving a meaning, making thinkable those feelings for the child. To fulfil this function, it is necessary that the parental object should be able to tolerate the psychic pain the child cannot tolerate themselves. After repeated experiences of this containment, such a function can be internalised by the child as they grow and develop and gradually become able to deal with these processes within their own maturing mind. Of particular importance for psychoanalytically orientated consultancy is the *quality* of introjective processes and, specifically, the introjection of a function.

Czander (1993) suggests that for organisational theorists, the most significant aspect of Kleinian theory is her conceptualisation of how one perceives. Klein (1959) suggests that the external world is seen in terms of internal concerns and that one's experiences in the external world will reinforce some anxieties and diminish others. This suggests that organisations, as external realities, will have significant impacts on the internal worlds of employees, something that psychoanalytically oriented consultants are aware of and need to pay consistent attention to those dynamics. This suggests that consultants should pay attention to management's capacity to promote the containment of primitive feelings and emotions that are inevitable in systems that are undergoing stress and change.

Envy

Klein places envy in a dominant position in her theory. The group of analysts associated with Klein found themselves working with an apparently innate propensity for conflict and confusion in their patient group in which the *good object is attacked for its goodness* (Rosenfeld, 1947, 1952; Segal, 1950). Obholzer (1994, Pg. 43–45) describes the operation of envy within the workplace. He argues that envy is one of the key destructive phenomena in institutional processes, particularly in relation to figures in authority. Typically, the envious attack on the leader is led by the member of staff with the highest naturally occurring quantum of rivalry and envy. This person is unconsciously *set up*, by means of projective identification, to express not only their own destructive envy but also that of other group members. Stein (1993, 1997, 2000a, 2000b, 2003, 2005, 2007) has shown how the concept of envy has been somewhat neglected in the systems psychodynamics consultancy literature and describes its application to the commercial sector.

Fotaki, in the piece below, helpfully introduces the ethics of care and its connections to feminist psychoanalysis. In the consulting relationship, the ethical stance of the consultant is crucial and bringing care and compassion to the practice is vital. Fotaki introduces us to contemporary thinkers on how care can be understood.

Why care matters for organisations and society? Feminist psychoanalytic approach

Marianne Fotaki

Care is both a human ability and a human need: it is about considering the needs and interests of others (Fotaki et al., 2020). We all require care for growing and flourishing as being cared for provides a sense of security to individuals and fosters positive attachments among them. Though care is fundamental to social life, care activities that form the foundations of the economy are often undervalued and made invisible (Fraser, 2016). Care practices are enforced and sustained through subjectivation where social norms shape and structure subjects' attachments and their ways of relating and feeling (Fotaki et al., 2020). The feminist approaches to psychoanalysis enable us to unearth psychic mechanisms, including affect and fantasy, that individuals rely on and deploy, along with discursive strategies, when they both enact and disrupt the existing symbolic norms on which power structures rest.

This short contribution draws on various insights by feminist psychoanalytic writers to focus on the affective nature of psychic mechanisms and the physical body to highlight their key role in supporting various social discourses concerned with ethics of care. Psychoanalytic feminist thinking does this by offering a conception of embodied identity as relational: focusing on cohabitation, sharing and respect for the other. This originates in the key assumption that we do not exist as autonomous and separate individuals.

Care has been often addressed in the context of ethics and gender. Feminist ethical theory reflects a wide range of perspectives, combining various angles of feminist theory with broader socio-political, philosophical and cultural analyses, including Marxism (Federici, 2012), post-colonialism (Mohanty, 2003), psychoanalysis and post-structuralism (Fotaki and Harding, 2017). The proposed ethical framework offers a notion of ethics based on interconnectedness and relationality as an intersubjective phenomenon sustained by social norms, discourses and political arrangements. It, therefore, eschews any form of exclusion by virtue of being both contextually (socially, politically and translocally) embedded and materially embodied (Fotaki and Harding, 2017).

The feminist psychoanalytic understanding of relationality elucidates how it is concerned primarily with inter-subjectivity (Benjamin, 2004) while encompassing both intrapsychic and interpsychic reality. It has origins in Freud's theory of social life as depending on individuals' ability to sublimate their sexual instincts and use them to bond within successively larger communal groupings. Yet, in contrast to the traditional single-person focus in psychoanalysis (for example, in Freud's drive theory), feminist relational approaches take their inspiration from a two-person concept modelled on the mother/child dyad. As early as the 1920s, Melanie Klein introduced this concept to psychoanalysis as a centrepiece of her theory on human development. Jacques Lacan re-read his theory through a linguistic prism, explaining why we cannot exist socially except in relation to an important other. People who care about us early in life and with whom we form libidinal ties are the literal others, while the social institutions and symbolic values onto which we transfer our affect are the big Other standing for a given symbolic order, according to Lacan (2006). It is in relation to literal (loved ones) and symbolic others (community, nation, etc.) that we strive to remake the world that surrounds us when we engage in political activities (Fotaki, 2010).

Judith Butler's work proposes a concept of the social based on a re-interpretation of Lacanian notions of the unconscious psychic life (termed the imaginary and the real) and the symbolic as a system of social norms, rules and discourses to introduce political considerations into psychoanalysis. She integrates insights from Lacan's and Foucault's work to identify intrapsychic aspects of power that eluded Foucault, while focusing on social dimensions that tend to be absent from psychoanalytic theories (Butler, 1993, 1997). Butler's engagement with post-structuralism and psychoanalysis allows her to develop the notion of relationality through subjectivation – a space that is co-created between the self and the other (through a subjection to the other and the symbolic order). Yet since this is how we become subjects, we cannot evade but must rather acknowledge this condition of mutual dependency, fully recognising its ethical and political implications. This existential vulnerability and precarity, which Butler developed from reading Melanie Klein's work, suggests that the subject's implication in the other and her dependency on the other for intelligibility carry the potential for altruism as well as harm (Fotaki, 2019). Butler's idea of relationality, therefore, entails an ethical obligation towards the irreducible other and differs from identification-based empathy. She takes inspiration from Emmanuel Lévinas about the face of the other belonging to the sphere of ethics in positing that our infinite capacity for being injured obliges us to protect the other.

Yet if the face of the other, in its defencelessness and precarity, is at once a call to kill and a call for peace (Benjamin, 2004), then the possibility for violence creates its own responsibility. Without this possibility, no ethical stance would be involved. But how do we arrive at "the felt experience of the other as a separate yet connected being with whom we are acting reciprocally?" (Benjamin, 2004, Pg. 6). In her own conception of relationality, which she terms 'thirdness', Benjamin, a psychoanalyst feminist, offers a clinical category (as a mental space) that has social significance as a space in which subject and other are intertwined without one prevailing over the other.

Bracha Ettinger's (2006) theory of the matrixial borderspace and trans-subjectivity, might help re-envisioning coexistence with the unknown and unknowable other, since this, as she argues, is our primary condition that we carry within ourselves. Proposing an ethics of 'difference', based on connectedness, co-existence and compassion towards the other, she develops psychoanalytic insights further by grounding them in our corporeality: the matrixial borderspace as both a symbolic and material entity, imply an absence of separateness of the subject from the other. Her ideas are unknown in management and organisations (Kenny and Fotaki, 2015) or organisational consultancy practice.

The relational reconsideration of subjectivity vis-à-vis the other outlined above, which brings together insights from diverse feminist psychoanalytic thinking, has powerful implications for both ethics and the ethics of care. It indicates that caring and relating share conceptual and ontological resonance because everything we do involves care. And it is only through relating to others that we gain a sense of value and significance since, literally and metaphorically, we do not exist without the other. As we cannot exist but in relation to others, we have to make these relational links that tie us to others explicit and strive for their inclusion in public policies (Fotaki, 2017). Care is always political as it concerns the issues of distribution among various recipients of different types of care and considerations of care work involved in producing and providing it (Tronto, 1995), which must be built into the logic of caring institutions. This implies reconsidering ethics of care not as a matter of personal choice but a social issue which accounts for the needs, contributions and prospects of women along with many different actors.

Further, rethinking the notion of compassion, cohabitation and care may help us envision new, inclusive forms of opposing exclusion and 'othering' in organisations and society through research, teaching and specific interventions and policies. Fotaki and Harding (2013) show in relation to gender, for instance, that the very instability of organisational structures, norms and dominant discourse, opens up the possibility to change these norms in the symbolic social order. This indicates how contemporary approaches which undervalue care can and must be transformed towards inclusivity and valuing all lives as equivalent to make our societies liveable.

Summary

> As a practice and sensibility, psychoanalysis remains attuned to superficiality; it constitutes a search for depth on the surface of things.
>
> (Lippitt, 2005)

Psychoanalysis aids in developing comprehension of organisational functioning by considering the effects of the unconscious. Psychoanalysis illuminates group dynamics, leadership dysfunctions and socially sanctioned institutional defences. Kleinian object relations theory diverges from Freud's formulation that humans are motivated by sexual and aggressive drives, suggesting instead that humans are primarily motivated by the need for contact with others, the need to form relationships. Basic concepts in object relations include the paranoid-schizoid position and the depressive position – two oscillating mental states experienced throughout life. The term 'objects' refers, not to inanimate entities but to significant others with whom an individual relates, usually one's mother, father, or primary caregiver. 'Internal objects' are figures that have been internalised, taken in, via introjection. Mental representations of the relationships between self and others are laid down in the mind from infancy onwards. The term 'object' refers to a part of a person, such as a mother's breast, or to the mental representations of significant others, early family interactions, primarily the mother-infant relationship, in personality development. Central to object relations theory is the notion of splitting, which can be described as the mental separation of objects into 'good' and 'bad' parts and the subsequent repression of the 'bad', or anxiety-provoking, aspects. The caregiver is 'good' when the needs of the infant are satisfied and 'bad' when they are not. If the caregiver does not satisfactorily meet the infant's needs, the infant may repress the 'bad' aspects of the mother and of the self, which can cause difficulty in future relationships.

Object Relations theorists include Melanie Klein, Ronald Fairbairn and Donald Winnicott, who emphasised the mother-infant bond as a key factor in the development of a child's psychic structure during the first three years of life. Fairbairn posited that humans are object-seeking beings, not pleasure-seeking beings. Development was viewed as evolving from a state of complete, infantile dependence on the caregiver towards a state of interdependency. Winnicott stressed the importance of raising children in an environment where they can develop a sense of independence but know that their caregiver will protect them from danger.

Early anxieties relating to splitting are complicated by discovering that the 'good' and the 'bad' breast are manifestations of the same breast/person. Defences developed against these intolerable anxieties at this stage remain a permanent part of psychic life alongside the emergent feelings of guilt, reparation and love. The psychoanalytic perspective refers to individual experiences and mental processes (e.g. transference, resistances, object relations, phantasy), as well as to the experience of unconscious group and social processes.

> Whereas all human sciences advance towards the unconscious only with their back to it, waiting for it to unveil itself as fast as consciousness is analysed, as it were backwards, psychoanalysis, on the other hand, points directly towards it, with a deliberate purpose — not towards that which must be rendered gradually more explicit by the progressive illumination of the implicit, but towards what is there and yet is hidden.
>
> Foucault (1970, Pg. 374)

Emotional pain is a key psychoanalytic idea – we protect ourselves from psychic pain and emotional disturbance.

Exercise

1 Psychoanalysis has been scientifically controversial since Freud's discovery. What scientific principle, what kind of hypothesis, supports continuing research in psychoanalysis?
2 Denial, suppression and splitting are enabled by what psychological mechanism?
3 How do 'good' and 'bad' objects get reconciled?
4 How does object relations theory differ from Freud's development theory?
5 What does 'object-seeking' mean to you?
6 When a 'good' internal object is attacked because it is 'good', what emotional process is in play?

4 Application of psychoanalytic concepts

With Phillip Stokoe

Although psychology and pedagogy have maintained the belief that a child is a happy being without any conflicts and have assumed that the sufferings of adults are the results of the burdens and hardships of reality, it must be asserted that just the opposite is true. What we learn about the child and the adult through psychoanalysis shows that all the sufferings of later life are for the most part repetitions of earlier ones, and that every child in the first years of life goes through an immeasurable degree of suffering.

(Klein, 1961)

The purest form of listening is to listen without memory or desire. Every session attended by the analyst must have no history and no future. What is 'known' about the patient is of no further consequence: it is either false or irrelevant. If it is 'known' by patient and analyst, it is obsolete. The only point of importance in any session is the unknown. Nothing must be allowed to distract from intuiting that. In any session, evolution takes place. Out of the darkness and formlessness something evolves.

(Bion, 1967)

Working in the transference and countertransference

Through the process of projective identification and introjective identification (see Chapter 3, Pg. 10, 11), recipients of a projection react to it in such a way that their own feelings are affected: they unconsciously identify with the projected feelings, as in hostage situations like the Stockholm Syndrome, a condition in which hostages develop a psychological alliance with their captors during captivity (Jameson, 2010). The state of mind in which other people's feelings are experienced as one's own is called *countertransference*. Projective identification frequently leads to the recipients to act on the projection. In practice, the consultant may take the presenting problem as the main issue for research and change when further work should be done on diagnosis, e.g. a hospice sought consultancy to help staff cope with the impact of a high number of deaths among patients. It later transpired that the underlying difficulty was the challenge of succession due to the retirement of long-standing senior leaders. The issues of succession were displaced into another level of the system, i.e. the patients. Death among the patients was real enough, but it served as a defence against facing and acknowledging the imminent change in the leadership. Therefore, paying attention to projections and emotions that are aroused in the consultant is an important diagnostic capability on crossing a boundary.

The systems psychodynamics of organisational consultancy emphasises transference and countertransference. Many client statements relate to skills, methods, aims and working practices and their application. In the process of understanding the consultancy task, the consultant learns about the organisations' patterns of conscious and unconscious functioning through attention to their own experiences of being with the client as they work with the consultant. In the consultancy relationship, the consultant's countertransference is an important source of information about the unconscious life of the organisation. The consultant's capacity to think about and interpret transference and countertransference is an important skill and is part of helping consultees develop their own capacity for thinking about work-related emotional experiences. In the transference, consultants have access to the organisation via the notion of 'the organisation-in-the-mind' of the client (see Chapter 5, Pg. 6). As the consultant and client work with each other, the image of 'the organisation-in-the-mind' evolves as they engage with the organisation day by day. Psychoanalytically oriented consultancy aims to identify the projective processes at work and trace the projections to their source, but this is not enough. What was previously unbearable and therefore projected needs to be made bearable. It is painful for the individual or group or institution to have to take back less acceptable aspects of the self which had previously been experienced as belonging to others. For example, legitimate criticisms may arise from within an organisation, for example, criticism of a colleague may not simply be intrusions by malicious outsiders.

As we saw earlier in Chapter 3 introjective identification can take two forms, introjective and projective. When a consultation is going well, there is a rapid oscillation between introjection and projection. As the client speaks, it could be an individual (for role consultation) or a team, staff group or some other organisational configuration that is being consulted to; the consultant will become introjectively identified with these organisational members, e.g. in working with staff of a child care institution, the consultant may feel upset on behalf of the staff who are subject to abuse to the extent that they may not look forward to meeting with some of the children, fearing that they may not be able to hear what the children have to say, as the consultant is so identified with the staff and their experiences of abuse. The consultant having taken in (introjected) the projections and understood them from the inside, will re-project this aspect of feeling, thought or sensation to the client and interpret it. But what the consultant is most aware of is the projective phase, i.e. the aspect of the client functioning that is dysfunctional in some way. These dysfunctional aspects of the client system are what, in an analysis, would be the damaged objects of an individual patient. In an organisational consultancy, these damaged objects may well be aspects of the personalities of the staff members, but for an organisational consultant the important data is what meaning does this shed on the functioning of the organisational system. The consultant by careful consideration of the transference and countertransference, from the primitive introjective and projective processes, can then make an interpretation. This understanding by the consultant and the giving of an effective interpretation can help the client to make further connections that can be understood. This relationship can help deepen the client's understanding of their dynamic processes. Therefore, it is important for the consultant to reflect on and digest the projective and introjective processes they are subject to on crossing the boundary and on the continuing relationship with the client system.

Containment

Containment (Riesenberg-Malcolm, 2001) is a term whose meaning can be either taken for granted or misconstrued. Sometimes it is seen, even in relation to supervision, as synonymous with control, taking charge or putting the lid on a difficulty from outside, as the fire brigade might 'contain' a fire or the police a riot. It can also be debased to mean little more than collusive support. It is a concept that is highly relevant to consultants as it has implications for the management of organisations and the management of consultants. The theory of containment is closely linked to the concepts of projective identification, introjective identification and transference and countertransference. It derives from Klein's original description of projective identification in which one person, in some sense, contains a part of another. From this, Bion (1959) developed a theory of development based on the emotional contact of infant with mother. By extension, we can see a theory of consultancy contact akin to psychoanalytic contact.

Bion's theory of thinking

From these ideas, Bion (1959) developed a theory of thinking. Bion's (1959) concepts of linking, container-contained, alpha function and basic assumptions are underpinned by the concepts of projection and introjection. Bion postulated that relationships were characterised by six elemental emotional links. They are defined as positive signs of love (L), knowing (K) and hate (H), as in the conditions of A loves B, B knows C and C hates D, and in their negative forms of minus L, minus K and minus H (Bion, 1962, 1970). With regards to the latter negative forms, Bion described these as forces which attack linking. He related the links to projective processes. For example, in a role consultation, a client complains about the aggressiveness of the executive of the organisation, which reminds her of her internal warring parents from childhood. Later, she joins a working group that is led by a female and male pair who work collaboratively and fairly and make the members of the working group feel they are making a positive contribution. In the working group, the male and female leaders provided more containing processes, which enabled her to contribute effectively. In the hierarchical structure, attacks on linking predominate and in the professional context, alpha elements are paramount. She feels more encouraged and collaborative, which enables her to feel more purposeful and useful. This illustrates how the internal world and external world interact to either promote alpha functioning or more chaotic beta elements.

Containment in consultancy

As consultants, we often see one department pitted against another rather than exploring each other's functions and how they can help each other in the overall task of the enterprise. These destructive attacks originate in the paranoid-schizoid phase in which the individual or the group or enterprise has part-object relationships, i.e. the 'bad' department or the 'good' department, as opposed to the whole enterprise containing both departments.

When consultants attempt to link organisational relationships together, the emotions that are aroused are hated. The emotion is felt to be too powerful to be contained. In the mind of the members of the organisation, the experiences of putting together emotions is felt to be intolerable as it stirs up complicated feelings in all of them. Consequently, the members disown these feelings and project them into other parts of the system. The idea that emotion itself is hated has resonance in consultancy projects; for example, pointing out that the so-called 'good' and 'bad' departments are part of the same enterprise will lead to some attack on the consultant as the act of linking is felt to be too emotionally powerful. Keeping the departments separated by being characterised as 'good' and 'bad', feels safer. Bion gives a perspective on emotional links when he says, "When two characters or personalities meet, an emotional storm is created" (Bion, quoted in Hinshelwood, 2003, Pg.181). There is resistance to being 'stormed' by others, and people take protective action from it. One of the tasks of the consultant, through interpretation, is turning chaotic feelings and thoughts into something more manageable.

A psychoanalytic contribution to systems psychodynamics

By Philip Stokoe

The provision of containment is the provision of a process. The key to it is what Bion called alpha function. I have suggested that this is the continuous activity of the K-drive (which I prefer to call 'curiosity') (Stokoe, 2020). Bion made it clear that K is an innate drive like L and H but I'm not aware that many writers have described the consequence of this idea other than Fisher

(2006). My suggestion is that the K-drive is responsible for the development of consciousness because it acts like a computer programme that requires us constantly to explain to ourselves what is happening to us, we continually ask ourselves, 'what's going on here?' (Kay and King, 2020). The answers appear in the form discovered by psychoanalysts and called 'unconscious phantasy'; they are images of ourselves in relation to others or parts of others. If we are able to 'learn from experience' (Bion, 1962), those explanations are continually modified, and they accumulate to create the conscious mind. Following this thinking, we can imagine the mind to be in a state of balance when there is an equal tension between the activities of the three drives. K, in its continuous background function that I believe to be the same thing as alpha function, is the reason that the baby finds himself turned towards reality in the face of the failure of the hallucination of the breast to enable him to tolerate the frustration of hunger (Freud, 1911); nothing in the context of the pleasure principle would account for such a change in direction. The continuous background presence of K is the reason why we are able to release ourselves from the paranoid-schizoid position (of course, in doing this, we are re-enacting that original move towards the reality principle, which is the trigger for the development of the depressive position). A way to imagine the paranoid-schizoid position in terms of drives is that L and H dominate the psyche, splitting experience into either extreme good or extreme bad and K, which represents a threat to this state of mind, is reduced merely to that background activity called alpha function. Perhaps I should explain why K represents a threat to the P/S position: it is because the only tolerated perspective is certainty; K, by definition (what is going on here?), represents uncertainty. It is the release of K from this suppressed position that instantly shatters the artificial split and restores the individual's view of the world to one of complexity and 'shades of grey'. Curiosity or the urge for knowledge generates a capacity to tolerate uncertainty.

In the process of containment as described by Bion, the baby feels contained by mother but only because mother, herself, feels contained by an internalised image of herself as loved by a loving couple and this sense is reinforced by the response of the baby, whose reaction, which is to become quieter, confirms the belief that mother can provide containment. In other words, it is not a simple mechanical process like putting a frightened animal in a cage, it is a dynamic engagement at several different levels, but it is the activity of K, not L or H, that makes it work. Where we encounter a team or an organisation in a state of anxiety, we will usually find ourselves engaged with a paranoid-schizoid state of mind. The first thing we must do is to reduce that level of anxiety and, whatever activity we decide upon will achieve this purpose in direct proportion to the extent to which the system feels contained. Unlike the animal in a cage, the contained is able to engage with the container; there can be a reciprocity, an intercourse can take place. The cage is merely a concept that fits within a paranoid and split universe; it is unyielding, which means it is certain. It will come as no surprise that human beings in a paranoid environment prefer the certainties, even those of a cage, to the uncertainties of engagement with reality.

In 1994, I created a method of working with teams and organisations while working at the Tavistock & Portman NHS Trust. It was the result of many years working as an organisational consultant in which I found myself with a team in which there was no shared concept of a human being, let alone a team. These clients found it almost impossible to use the standard consultation approach I'd been trained to do. My 'invention' was a brief intervention lasting ten weeks consisting of two sessions during a once-weekly space of about 3½ hrs. The first session, lasting 90 minutes, was a lecture and discussion, then there was a ½ hour break followed by an open experiential group meeting for 90 minutes; the teacher had transformed into a consultant during that break and there was no agenda, it was not reflective practice or staff support, the task was merely to observe whatever came up in that context. The training was a psychoanalytic and systems-based delivery of a model of the development of the mind and of thinking which was then applied to the context of groups and teams and finally to the concept of organisations based on my Healthy Organisation model (Stokoe, 2011, 2020). This came to be called the Short Course Intervention and it ran at the Tavistock until 2012, when I left and has continued to be run from my private practice. During the years at the Tavistock & Portman NHS Trust, it was extremely successful (more than 60 interventions were completed) and required the creation of a team to meet the demand. I think that the provision of a taught model provided a form of containment, but I want to describe an event that happened early on in its history which captures the need for containment. Following that, I shall offer a few thoughts about the relevance of such models of work for the future.

The occasion I have in mind was when we started the first of what turned out to be a long series of work with organisations working with the homeless. My colleague had taken on this client and telephoned me on the way back from her first meeting with the staff team. Now it should be said that this colleague was a principal social worker with many years' experience as a manager and as a consultant (also with a consultancy training at the Tavistock). She was extremely upset and said she was shaking as she was speaking to me. She had run several versions of the course and was used to there always being a certain hostility from one or two people, usually on the lines of psychoanalysis being a discredited system or that it was white and middle class and had no relevance to their work. She conveyed that this was a continuous assault in a way that threw her into confusion and loss of any confidence. Eventually, she said this, "I was so shocked because, in the introductory part, after they'd filled in the questionnaire, they had all shared that what they had in common was a Christian faith and the view that this work was a vocation. The viciousness of the attacks on what I was saying came as such a shock following this".

The first thing to say about my thinking at this point is to explain the questionnaire. I had set the intervention up with the view that we needed the means to get useful feedback, something that would tell us whether we were achieving what we aimed to achieve. The principle upon which the whole thing was built was that the emotional and psychological impact on workers from their work can damage practice and the individual if it is not processed. Processing is what we would demonstrate, and we would aim to show the client team that the emotional material, when understood (i.e. spoken about, attributed to its true source – the work, not the worker – and properly described), becomes important information that can turn a struggle into an interesting and satisfying engagement. If it isn't processed in this way, we would predict that individuals would interpret this material in ways that would distort their view of the work, either the clients, their colleagues, their managers, other professionals or even the social context in which they worked. Therefore, a simple attitude survey of team members' views of these groups taken before the start and at the end, when analysed by a blind rater, should show change and the change ought to seem to be in the direction of reality.

So, they had been asked about how they viewed these 'others' in the context of their work and then the next thing was a shockingly 'unchristian' assault on the tutor/consultant. I found myself feeling both protective of my colleague and wanting to confront these people. In our later debriefing with our team, it seemed that we could see that the emotional impact on my deputy, when interpreted as information about the client team, made some sense. Free association to the work with the homeless revealed an awareness of how very different this client group was (n.b. this was in the days before the drastic removal of basic support for immigrants, which has flooded the streets with a different category of homeless). We knew that this work was continuously destroyed as the workers felt they had 'rehabilitated' a client enough to offer them accommodation in a flat, only to find their client had gone back to alcohol and completely trashed the flat. We found ourselves wondering what the effect must be of believing this work to be a vocation. This revealed another hypothesis that the rejection of the offer to their clients could be thought of as an attack against homes or, perhaps more accurately, against a couple. If your 'other' is God, it's difficult to complain about your lot. We thought it would be more appropriate and potentially containing to model a provision of a service by an ordinary couple rather than this other version. Consequently, I joined my colleague in running the rest of the intervention and we made it a protocol always to send two consultants whenever we worked with homeless teams.

In fact, the outcome was extremely good and the explanation of the reason we'd arranged to work as a couple facilitated a very moving discussion about how impossible it felt to every individual to admit how hurt they were by the constant rejection of their help. The following is taken from one of those individual's before and after questionnaire in the category, 'how you feel about your clients'. In the before, she had written, "I consider myself privileged to be given the opportunity to serve these victims of society". In the 'after' questionnaire, she'd written, "These are extremely difficult and challenging clients. Weirdly, now that I've been able to see this, I'm finding the work more interesting and that has also allowed me to get to know my clients better".

In my view, the thinking and consequent action of sending in two of us was a good example of the process of containment in which a mother metabolises the projections from her baby and is able to work out what he needs and provide it. We created a sense of thoughtful containment where we could have made the mistake of omnipotently facing down the 'attacks'. The result was a very sensitive and frequently very moving intervention. The client group seems to have felt the same because we only received requests for work via word of mouth and, by 2010, we'd worked with most of the homeless organisations in London.

We might consider that a containing environment makes it possible to reduce anxiety by allowing a space for genuine thinking. In the post-truth

> political climate, such spaces will be essential to restore a capacity to face reality. In a world of climate change and pandemics, our contribution must be to offer places in which reality can be addressed; these are places that begin with the assumption that nothing is certain and that the most successful approach is the one that begins with a question, "What's going on here?"

Consultancy relationships

A proposition would be that one could readily transpose the notion of container-contained relationship to the consultancy relationship. Because the consultant can take up a position akin to the mother-infant dyad and receive complex and often confusing communications from the client, and by taking them in makes sense of them and give them back to the client in a less toxic form. The client is then able to reflect on this feedback or interpretation and, with the creation of thinking space, can contemplate and reflect on the situation. This then may involve taking appropriate action within the organisational system. If this normal interplay of projection–introjection and re-projection does not take place, then the client will continue to feel overwhelmed by the system difficulties that led to the need for consultancy. If the consultant feels overwhelmed by the communications from the client system – there will be a lack of capacity in the consultant/container to process the raw material and the container/consultant will be rendered ineffective. This highlights the need for consultants to receive regular supervision on their work so that they have the space to digest the projections they are taking in (see Volume 2, Chapter 12 on professional development).

Thought

Systems psychodynamics stresses the capacity to develop reflective thinking in individuals, groups and organisational systems. This was influenced by Bion's (1967) later psychoanalytic writings on thinking and the development of the mind. For systems psychodynamics consultants, the capacity to think about work involves reflecting on the relationship between:

a   The nature of the task difficulties in undertaking the work.
b   The symbolic significance of communication associated with the work process.
c   The individual and the aims of the wider organisation.
d   The small workgroup and the aims of the wider organisation.

Management in a well-functioning organisation ensures the provision of constant opportunities for staff to think about the task of the organisation.

88 *Psychoanalytic thinking*

A consultant promotes the capacity for learning from experiences on the part of the client.

Emotional experience

Armstrong et al. (1994) suggest in their paper *'What does management really mean?'* that in the psychoanalytic approach, there is a fundamental recognition of the centrality and significance of emotional experience in all human endeavour, both at a conscious and unconscious level. The open systems model lets us see the inter-relatedness of emotional experience. With this view, emotional experience is not bounded by one's own individual skin, is not the property of the individual alone. Rather, it is bounded by the system or systems in which individuals interact in collaboration or in conflict with each other and with their context.

Unconscious phantasies and the organisation-in-the-mind

Mental images or pictures-in-the-mind are prevalent and hugely influential in groups, organisations, culture and society. Here is an example of intergroup myths and assumptions:

> In a meeting of the purchasing department to discuss relationships with their suppliers, the group expressed strong negative views about the supplier's national characteristics. This was an attempt to explain to themselves the over-bearing temperament and lack of compromise of the supplier. This was the result of the department being oblivious to the strident national characteristics of the members within its own group. This dynamic of denial and projection of unacknowledged feelings and behaviour of the department amplified the supplier's strident behaviour. The reason for this projective process is that on both sides there is a denial of their mutual dependency. Both sides behave as if they don't need each other which in reality is totally untrue. The inability to accept their painful need for each other leads them to behaving aggressively towards each other through mutual projection and introjection. The purchasing group denies its own aggression; the suppliers have a capacity to combine with and act out the group's projected aggression.
>
> In this instance, the meeting suggested that the supplier may be using its unique product capability to hold the company to ransom and raise prices unfairly. The meeting does not recognise its own threats to the supplier. The group may be aware of its behaviour, but the meeting does not speak about it; instead, negative or difficult behaviour is attributed solely to the outside supplier. The group's aggression may be outside of awareness, i.e. unconscious, but it operates under the surface, a mixture of group phantasy and real experience with the supplier that influences relationships with the supplier.

Introjection and identification

The process of introjection and identification with a stable and reliable system through good leadership and management is crucial to the employees and the organisation-as-a-whole. This enhances the organisation's capacity for reality-testing and the binding and integration of experience. Unhealthy or perverse cultures (Long, 2008; Stein, 2000a, 2000b, 2003, 2005) may cause enormous anxiety and can lead to organisational and social disintegration, whereas consistent and reliable leadership which is in touch with reality with the external world promotes confidence and well-being.

Organisationally, these internalisations show themselves in good products, high-quality services, and healthy values, leading to effective inter-personal and group and inter-group relationships, which are linked to the execution of the primary task. Organisationally, group and inter-group relationships are seldom neutral. A group or team or department that is dependent on another group, team or department for its inputs will inevitably have strong feelings, positive and negative, about the group that it is dependent on. All experiences that are perceived or remembered, whether consciously or unconsciously, are internal in that they are 'in-the-mind' with a memory and feeling attached to them.

Containing leadership

Organisationally, a containing leadership involves participative decision-making, planning and collaboration, i.e. designing an organisation through the participation of all the players and stakeholders that leads to high productivity *and* the well-being of people. In other words, working relationships optimally express expectations and hopes of the participants so that their working relationships are characterised by collaboration rather than conflict. Concentrating solely on technology fails to meet the emotional needs of both designers and users; it undermines responsible autonomy and leads to failures of internal structures that are more likely to overwhelm an organisation.

This complex interaction of internalised figures and experiences continues throughout life between the world of these internalised figures, which are termed as 'pictures-in-the-mind' or feeling and attitudes, and real experiences of people and situations in the external world of reality, through repeated cycles of projection and introjection. Important internalisations are those derived from parents, school and friends. Experiences that become a powerful part of the group or organisational 'mind' or culture are enacted as myths or legends and may be experienced by the system concretely through rituals and symbols, such as logos and letterheads, buildings, websites, mission statements, statements of vision, straplines, 'this is the way we do things here', soundbites, the type and quality of the leadership, rules and norms.

The Relational Terrain

Izod (2017) contributes what she terms the Relational Terrain as a development that enhances our understanding and application of psychoanalytic and systems thinking. It comprises a set of distinct and interrelated conceptual and practice-based approaches to participating in organisational life, understanding group processes and consulting to change. These approaches have at their core the capacity to sustain a mind-ful connection with work (Izod and Whittle, 2009, 2014), through developing and negotiating meaning with others. Izod investigates four theoretical fields as comprising this Relational Terrain:

1. A socio-ecological field, considering the changing nature of systems and their relatedness to ever more turbulent environments and emphasising the capacity to build and sustain the connection between systems and their environments.
2. Theories of human development derived from object and social relations and specialists in infant development.
3. Group processes principally through the work of Bion (1961), and later developments of his work in Group Relations and consulting.
4. The nature of the role.

Izod conceptualises the Relational Terrain as an intervention within the theoretical framework known as systems psychodynamics but she proposes a shift of emphasis within this framework which is twofold:

1. A shift away both from Klein's theories on innate drives, which are object-seeking in the face of persecutory anxieties, giving rise to the defensive mechanisms of projection/projective-identification and splitting and from Bion's conceptualisation of the group as defending itself from the primitive anxieties evoked by working as a group and working to the task.
2. A shift towards an approach which acknowledges that innate drives are socially oriented, that they are dependent on real experiences with real people, and that are connection-seeking and relationship-oriented.

Izod (2017) contends that this proposal allows for an approach to group understanding that views group behaviour in developmental terms, where the unconscious is concerned with patterns of lived interactions as they become enacted in the behaviour of the group.

Relational

Izod (2017) gives the following definition and sources for the term relational. She points out that it has prolific usage and is being applied frequently to describe practices in the 'human process' range of interventions which put people and relationships first. She is specifically using the term as it derives from the concept of the 'Relational Turn' where it has been used since the 1980s across a range of professional discourses. In sociology, the emphasis is on the Relational Turn as the study of the social relationship itself; psychoanalysis, as an 'expanded theory of interaction', is a turn to theories "whose basic assumption is that development and unconscious phenomena are marked primarily by relationship and not drives".

Fields in which these ideas have been introduced (or re-emphasised) include psychoanalytically informed organisational consulting and role consultation, coaching, counselling and psychotherapy, group psychotherapy and group analysis, pedagogy; leadership, applications of the Relational Turn in social and political theory, psychoanalysis, welfare practice, interventions in groups and organisation, and in teaching, learning and social research. Collectively, the Relational Turn emphasises process and the co-creation of knowledge through the interconnectedness of people and systems, shared meaning-making, multiplicities of truths and pluralities of voices in the absence of any singular reality. In bringing relational psychoanalytic theories to the task of consulting to groups and organisations, Izod (2017) is concerned with enabling groups to find and sustain conditions under which they can work to best effect. This entails developing a capacity to stay connected to the task, to one's colleagues and clients, and to one's own emotional and mental state. She views Benjamin's (1998, 2004), thoughts on recognition 'being able to sustain connectedness to the other's mind while accepting his separateness and difference' (2004, Pg. 8) as key developmental and operational issues in group and organisational life. These issues are central to Izod's relational practice. Izod has found that a consultancy stance which joins with the client system and offers a careful attention and attunement to the dynamics at play can provide such a developmental experience of connection.

Summary

Understanding of unconscious processes in groups and organisations is further enriched by the theory of **basic assumptions** (Bion 1948–51, 1961) (see Volume 1, Chapter 6). Awareness of these unconscious processes helps in understanding the resistances that change can generate and therefore in being prepared for them. Moreover, because uncertainty or ambiguity about work tasks tend to make groups more vulnerable to basic assumptions disturbances, definition of the **primary task** is critical in organisations design (Miller and Rice, 1967; Rice, 1953 a,b, 1958, 1963).

Miller (1997) says that taken together, this set of concepts form the '**socio-technical system psychodynamics**' framework. Miller then describes how these sets of concepts are used in consultancy practice. The conceptualisation of the consultancy role as shown in the diagram (see Volume 1, Introduction), reflects the influences of the psychoanalytic strand in the early development of the Tavistock Institute. According to Miller (1997), some practitioners saw organisational consultancy as a macro-version of psychoanalysis and the term '*sociotherapy*' was sometimes used (Sofer, 1961). All practitioners, because of the connotations of illness and treatment did not take this up. But the nature of the psychoanalytic relationship heavily influences the way consultants practiced. Miller (1997) describes this as an ongoing collaboration in which the consultant and client work together in gaining a deeper understanding of the system and generating possible courses of action. The decision to act (or not) rests with the client; both jointly review the outcomes and, if appropriate, move to the next phase. It is an action research approach. Again, according to Miller, there are two more specific influences. First, the *transference* is central to the analytic method. That is to say, the analyst in the analytic method becomes a screen onto which the patient projects underlying and perhaps unconscious feelings towards key figures in the patient's earlier life. In the analyst, this evokes *countertransference*: the analyst either has the experience of becoming the fantasised character in the patient's internal drama (a process of projective identification), or the projections resonate with some parallel dynamic in the analyst's own inner world. Correspondingly, the feelings evoked in the organisational consultant about the role one is put into and the way one is being used provide data about underlying processes in the client system. The other influence is the recognition that, as with the analyst, it is an important function to provide a 'holding environment' (Winnicott, 1965) by serving as a safe container who can accept and survive the anxieties and sometimes hostile projections coming from the client system.

Exercise

1 Describe a situation when in your role, you were 'projected into'. What happened? How did you understand what was happening?
2 What did it feel like to be 'unseated' from your role?
3 What efforts were necessary to help you get back into your role?
4 How are Bion's concept of 'containment' and Winnicott's of 'holding environment' similar?

5 Working with individuals

With Halina Brunning and Susan Long

The contemporary phenomenon of executive coaching was re-defined as *organisational role consultation* by the Grubb Institute because 'coaching' implies differential powers between coach and coachee and expert practice, whereas the term *organizational role consultation* (ORC) more accurately describes the 3-way integrated focus on the person, the role and the organisation. When working with individuals, the ORC consultant will always have in mind that the client is part of a larger system, e.g. a team, an organisation, community and society. The consultant will explore with the client what is occurring at the interface between the individual-in-role and their professional or technical environment. Role consultation is the work of helping clients better understand their individual and organisational roles. It is a process by which the consultant and client scrutinise and attune the client's behaviour in an understanding of the role, including its conscious and unconscious determinants, to enhance the client's effectiveness in relation to the needs and desires of the organisation and its environment.

Coaching for leadership

The systems psychodynamics coaching model provides for developmentally and psycho-educationally focused reflection and learning opportunities to the individual leader, to study, become aware of and gain insight into how task and organisational performance are influenced by both conscious and unconscious behaviour (Brunning 2006; de Vries, 2007; Huffington et al., 2004; Newton et al., 2006). Consciousness refers to objectivity and rational behaviour, and unconsciousness to 'the organisation-in-the-mind', which contains the system's unconscious defences and irrational behaviours (Armstrong, 2005b).

The systems psychodynamics leadership–coaching model investigates how the following behavioural constructs manifest in the leader's work life (Cilliers and Koortzen, 2005; Czander, 1993; Gould et al., 2001; Hirschhorn, 1988; Klein, 2005):

Anxiety – defined as the fear of the future; anxiety acts as the driving force ('dynamo') or a paralysing force in the relationships between an organisation's leaders and employees.

- **Task** – the basic constituent of work. The leader's pursuit of the primary task indicates a level of containment of anxiety. Any diversions into off-task or anti-task behaviour would indicate confusion and free-floating anxiety.
- **Role** – is the indicator of the boundary surrounding work and position and between the leader, employee and organisation. The role of leadership encompasses managing the boundaries between what is inside and what is outside the organisation.
- **Authority** – the formal and official right to perform a given task, authorised from above (the organisation, manager, leader), or laterally (colleagues), below (subordinates) and from within (self-authorisation).
- **Boundaries** – task, time, territory, are regarded as boundaries which need maintaining and adjusting according to changing contexts. Boundaries promote containment and provide security and predictability.
- **Identity** – the ways clients feel and think about themselves; the ways they are thought of by others and the influences of these identities on behaviour and organisational culture.

At the beginning, one might start with a role analysis which aids diagnosis for the coaching relationship and issues that the client is facing (Newton et al., 2006). The focus is not solely on the person as in psychotherapy (McKenna and Davis, 2009) or on the organisation, but rather on the person-in-role within the organisation and their interactions (Huffington et al., 2004). One gains information on how the organisation impacts the person and the taking up of the role. The client may be asked to describe their job description and content, measured according to performance management criteria. This usually is called the *normative, or formal or official, primary task* (Lawrence, 1977). The client's interpretation of and meaning that they give to the task of their role and activities is called the *existential primary task*; and the task that can be inferred from people's behaviour and of which they may not be consciously aware is called the *phenomenalogical primary task*. (Brunning, 2006; Obholzer and Roberts, 1994). The discrepancies that may emerge between these interpretations of the role help the coach and the client focus on what needs to be done to be more effective in role. (Newton et al., 2006). A useful question is: 'what is happening with you in your role now?' To ensure the smooth flow of the discourse in the here-and-now relationship between coach and client, sessions start with where the client feels themselves to be emotionally and cognitively at that moment in time. Therefore, the coach at the start of the sessions may say something like: "where would you like to begin?" Unlike a formal business meeting, in the systems psychodynamics model there is no formal set agenda (de Vries, 2007). This approach aims to work with the emerging conscious and unconscious dynamics as they become apparent in the relationship.

Coaching for leadership involves an intense discourse (Campbell and Gronbaek, 2006; Mackay, 2019). The role of the coach involves taking a reflective stance from a meta-position on the boundary, alert to the client's behaviour, making sense of the client's experience and thoughts and using appropriate concepts where necessary (Campbell and Huffington, 2008). This is done by formulating working hypotheses, defined as an integrative statement of 'searching into' (Schafer, 2003) the leader's experiences and by constantly re-visiting this content in the light of further and new emerging evidence (Campbell, 2007). Clients are encouraged to be curious, to associate freely, to explore a variety of related feelings, patterns, defences and images and metaphors and to move between different levels of thinking (Jaques, 1990; Kegan, 1994), thereby enabling clients to access their own unexplored conscious and unconscious experiences of their role. This might include attitudes, beliefs, wishes, conflicts, hopes, rivalry, aggression and patterns of relationships and collaboration. They can investigate how their feelings and emotions may be invested in others, e.g. the CEO or subordinates or sub-systems, e.g. other departments. Understanding these dynamics can enable the client to be and feel more integrated and less depleted (Blackman, 2004; Neumann et al., 1997; Shapiro and Carr, 1991; Stapley, 1996, 2006).

Revelation versus Salvation

Gordon Lawrence (1994, 2000) suggested that the psychodynamically oriented approach to coaching has an emphasis on "revelation" rather than "salvation". In adopting a psychodynamic stance the role of the executive coach becomes one of trying to assist the executive in making sense of their work experiences, rather than solely facilitating goal achievement, skill development or teaching management tools and techniques. Gordon Lawrence (1994) presents the idea of salvation originally from the "rescue phantasy" that can operate in therapeutic situations when the therapist loses sight of the task and becomes involved in trying to save the patient from whatever psychic ill they may be experiencing. The politics of revelation is preoccupied with the conditions and resources for the exercise of transformation that come from inside the person or system. This is brought about through the people revealing what may be the truth of their situation to themselves and taking authority to act on their interpretation. Gordon Lawrence (1994, 2000) outlines ideas on the possible changes in consultancy practice from the politics of salvation to those of revelation. This is coming about through the changes in the methodologies employed, and the resultant conceptualizations of the natural sciences. The politics of salvation can be clearly seen in the missionary effort of the churches. The idea was to convert the heathen—that is, save them for Christ.

The Politics of Revelation

Gordon Lawrence (see http://www.psychoanalysis-and-therapy.com/human_nature/free-associations/lawren.html) argued that totalitarian-states-of-mind are nurtured by the politics of salvation which, by their nature, pre-empt divergent thinking. By contrast, the politics of revelation are more a state of being than doing. By revelation Lawrence meant the work of being available for experiences whether psychotic-like or not, generating working hypotheses on these experiences and making interpretations on the significance of the experiences. It is through the politics of revelation that individuals come to recognise that they are having experiences, which derive from the paranoid-schizoid and depressive positions. Such people are those in institutions who have minds and thoughts and are capable of thinking and having dreams. Lawrence went on to point out that individuals who are committed to the politics of revelation are always striving towards, what Bion (1970) termed, 'O', which signifies the original 'thing in itself' of an experience. 'O' represents absolute truth, which can never be known by any human being, but it is the journey to attain a version of it, which makes us pre-eminently human. 'O' is more possible to attain if we can find a sense of and respect for the unconscious, for otherness, for mystery and death (Weatherill, 1994) which are present in our lives no matter how hard we try to make them absent. The systems psychodynamics approach encourages exploration and discovery as part of the coaching process, rather than following a fixed coaching formula and agenda. The coach must therefore refrain from responding to the client's projections that the coach can somehow 'save' the client from their work problems, or that the coach has the powers to convert them into a high performing executive. Instead, the coach engages the client in a collaborative process that educates and informs; the revelations arising from their work become the basis for action and learning.

Introduction to Systems psychodynamic theories

Executive coaching is concerned with enhancing the effectiveness of the executive's professional practice. The work of the executive coach is often about helping the executive improve their ability to provide leadership to what are often complex, social systems. Hence, the executive coach must take into consideration the multitude of personal, organisational and environmental factors that influence behaviour and performance. To those seeking to coach others in an organisational context, systems psychodynamic theories and approaches can usefully inform and add depth to the practice of executive coaching. Psychodynamic theories recognise the centrality and significance of emotional experience, while the systemic approach contributes recognition of the essential inter-relatedness of emotional experience (Hutton, Bazalgette and Armstrong, 1994). The combined theories provide a framework for understanding how emotions impact on the functioning of work or the socio-technical system. Mersky (1999, p.1), uses psychoanalytic thinking in her organisational development consulting work, describing her consultancy stance. "I use many models – one of which is the analytic role ideal. I think of this ideal as observing clear and appropriately bounded role and set of role relationships; managing and learning from countertransferential feelings toward the client system; and working – in Bion's (1967, p. 17) terms – without "memory and desire". The consultant attempts to function as a non-threatening 'container' for the clients projections and – through them and other sources of data, both organizationally objective and emotionally internal – develop an understanding of the underlying issues and dynamics in the system".

Organisational role analysis

In organisational role analysis (ORA) the role is considered as the link between the individual and the organisation. There is a clear distinction that can be made between role and personality of the individual. A proposition is that when people are in conflict, often it is because roles and personality become merged and therefore confused. The role we are in will determine the way we behave. In the ORA model it is argued that people change their behaviour depending upon the role they are in and how they understand their roles. It is possible that people become stuck in their definition of roles. The ORA is an approach that promotes growing collaboration and problem-solving. An important aspect of the ORA model is the notion of system. A system is a set of relations that over time has developed rules. The roles taken by individuals connect parts of the system. Systems thinking examines the containing frame and how the container influences what is contained. In organisations, the role is the frame or container and the behaviour is what is contained. To place the role under scrutiny is to place the system that contains it under the same scrutiny.

For Hirschhorn (1997), the transitional object is the 'organisation-in-the-mind', which can be surfaced with the client through the ORA process. The emotional relationship between consultant and client gives clues as to the nature of the organisation-in-the-mind of the client. If, in the meeting, the consultant feels anxious or fearful or any other feelings, this may be a clue to the nature of the client's 'organisation-in-the-mind' (Figure 5.1).

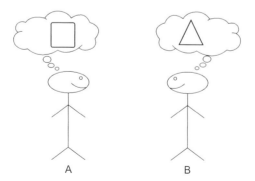

Figure 5.1 Organisation-in-the-mind.

Source: Bruce Reed, The Grubb Institute.

Organisation in the mind

Organisation in the mind is the picture which all organisational members and others will have in mind when interacting across boundaries (Armstrong, 2005b). In the diagram above, individuals A and B, talking to each other, have a different picture of the organisation in their minds. Different aspects of organisation's primary task may be held by different professions or groups within the same organisational system who may then get into conflict with each other, e.g. in the prison service, the prison officers responsible for security and safety and the health care staff responsible for health and wellbeing of the prisoners, often are in tension, misunderstanding and miscommunication.

Because the material surfaced in the ORA process is powerful and potentially volatile, it is necessary that the boundary structures made up of task, time and setting boundaries, which contains the work, are resilient and strong. According to Bazalgette and Quine (2014, Pg. 194) of the Grubb Institute, the value of working with the idea of 'organisation-in-the-mind' frees the client from thinking about the way things ought to be, so they can engage creatively with the way organisational life actually is in order that future plans and intentions can be more realistically planned and achieved. The practical outcome of working with the ORA method is that it is a way of helping clients to reflect on their experiences, to analyse and learn from them, to bring about change. Factors involved in taking up the consultant's role in the ORA process include exploring the 'organisation-in-the-mind' thus enabling the client to discover their 'organisation-in-the-mind' and how their idea of it informs and influences their behaviour in their role(s). The concept of the 'organisation-in-the-mind' ideally should free the client from the pressure of feeling that it is all up to them – differentiating role from personality and abandoning the heroic/charismatic model of leadership.

The consultant explains the process and describes the idea of 'organisation-in-the-mind'. The client is invited to start at any point with a presenting issue, or with a critical incident, or by describing or drawing a picture of the organisation as they see it with themselves in it. The consultant listens and reflects and in due course presents ideas about what is going on. This is a cyclical process throughout the ORA. The client can test these ideas for themselves and seek more evidence in the intervening weeks to confirm or disconfirm these ideas.

Dependability is provided both physically and psychologically. This provides the dependable 'holding environment' for the 'organisation-in-the-mind' to be exposed as fully and as richly as possible. The consultant tries to keep to the same room arrangements, to start and end on time and to avoid altering dates. For the client to learn to 'see' the organisation in their own mind, it is important that the consultant works in a way, which reflects back to the client the impressions and implications of what the client is conveying. The consultant can also be a 'memory' for the client in later sessions, when new happenings and events in the client's workplace may blot out material which needs to be recalled.

This enables the client to relax and to allow those inner, symbolic representations of the organisation to surface. The 'holding' is done in such a way that the client trusts the coach and the coaching organisation, so that they are able to let go of their wish to manage the situation or suppress their image of the 'organisation-in-the-mind' and allow their feelings, anxieties, thoughts and ideas about their organisation and its workings to emerge and to be examined. When this clarification of their many feelings occurs, the client can begin to test the external realities of their situation and work at how they can be addressed, taking note of the real state of the organisation or department, the processes by which the organisation or department sustains itself in its context and considering all those involved. The client can contemplate how to take up their role more effectively as a manager or leader.

Case study

The client speaks about the value of role consultation for him, his executive team and for his organisation

As a senior executive of a public sector organisation, I am often asked how my regular role consultation helps me in my role. This question comes from line managers, peers, line reports and friends in the pub, all expressing a high level of curiosity. My stock response has been to say it is 'difficult to explain'.

I have worked with my role consultant for over six years, and having thought about the question, I realise that the principal benefit of the support I receive is to provide me with thinking time and the discipline of treating that thinking time as a priority because of the leadership challenges I face in my role. These insights would be impossible to acquire without the benefit of skilful, professional judgement and experience that is available through the role consultation.

I sometimes wonder how often people find time in busy schedules to think about the strategic issues they face individually and organisationally. I suspect only a minority would answer affirmatively. At times, dealing with complex organisational choices daily makes me break into a sweat. The role consultation has given me the equanimity and confidence to confront these complex strategic challenges; it has enhanced my leadership skills and abilities and allowed me to consider the unique dynamics of my organisation in a way that would otherwise have been impossible.

Imagine the following scenario which routinely affects executives in all sectors. You are sitting in an executive meeting discussing a difficult issue that has been presented to the meeting on countless previous occasions without arriving at a resolution. Each member of the executive has a different interest in the issue, and often those interests are in competition with each other. Stalemate is reached and rather than a decision being made, the issue is postponed for discussion to a later meeting, delegated to another group or simply dropped off the agenda, leaving those involved in the preparation of the proposal bruised and disempowered, their efforts rendered pointless. If that is a familiar scenario, I would, firstly, encourage the executive team to seek consultation as a team, but if that is not possible, I would recommend individuals to seek role consultation (or executive coaching). The support would be invaluable in allowing you as a member of your executive team to understand the personal, group, organisational and political/environmental dynamics that are forcefully paralysing the meeting. You would also acquire the confidence to assist the executive to find a way through any negative dynamics towards a resolution. My role consultation regularly focuses on the dynamics of power and control, envy, jealously and rivalry. The ability to understand these dynamics as they play out between members of the executive has given me the skills to ask open-ended questions that often help unlock even the most difficult issues. As with all public sector organisations facing swingeing austerity measures in recent years, my executive has had to make reductions in the workforce. Where do we cut? Who should we make redundant? Where should we invest our reducing assets? These challenges result in acute emotional reactions in the executive; members fight to protect their silos often resulting in stalemate. I have taken the model offered by my role consultant into executive meetings – i.e. the confidence to ask: "what dynamics are playing out here that we are getting caught up in that prevents us making progress towards decision-making?" as opposed to the fruitless ritualised questions of "what are we going to do?" that gets us nowhere. Asking open-ended questions allows the executive to unblock itself to think and to acquire an understanding of the broader organisational dynamics that hamper decision-making at board level. My role consultation has been helpful and supportive for improving my role effectiveness and the effectiveness of the executive team, which in turn has impacted favourably organisational performance. We are successful in moving forward managing difficult issues rather than continuing to bang our heads against a wall.

In times of austerity and significant reductions in public spending, there are voices arguing that role consultation is an unaffordable luxury. My response is to say that if ever there is a time that organisations need to invest in their leadership with the skills to grapple with complex issues, it is in times of austerity, as it is then, rather than when times are good, that leaders need to demonstrate extraordinary leadership capabilities.

The experience of the ORA consultant is that, in a session with a client, the dynamic between the client and the consultant and the way the client relates to the consultant, the kinds of incidents that are described by the client – all provide evidence, which enables the 'organisation-in-the-mind' to become apparent to both. That enables the client and consultant together to devise ways of testing what is going on in the organisation and why the client experiences their role in the system in the way they do.

Organisational role analysis

Susan Long

Organisational role analysis (ORA), as I use it, is an exploration of a role using the Transforming Experience Framework and a psychodynamic approach. It was first developed by staff at the Grubb Institute in London and involves a collaborative exploration between a coach/organisational consultant and a client or client group using associative and systemic thinking.

The aim is to uncover the dynamic nature of the role. The underlying belief is that by understanding this the solution to any problem will begin to reveal itself.

I will discuss some of the theory, frameworks and methods used in ORA and then will walk through how I use ORA with a client or client group.

The theoretical underpinnings of the method are important, because there is no exact recipe to follow. There are principles and guidelines and if you understand these, the role exploration follows.

The associative unconscious

Just imagine – all the words, signs, symbols, images and ideas known to a human community and potentially able to be in that community. Imagine them in a vast network of interconnection – a network studied by semiotics – where all are connected through threads of associations, a tapestry of meaning. Just as in a dictionary, where all words are described in terms of other words, all associated and connected; just as in mathematics where numbers are interconnected and gain their meaning in relation to one another; just as in nature where organisms in ecological niches interconnect to form ecosystems; so, imagine this network of words, ideas, signs, images and symbols.

This is the associative unconscious (Long and Harney, 2013). Its entirety is not available to any one member of that human community; an individual thinker or imaginer has access only to part. This is due to their individual experience, education, capacity – the whole of their background. Much of the network may not be available to most because of personal memory, repressions, intolerances, social taboos. Whole sections of a community may not have access to large sections of the network because of group or societal beliefs. The idea of gay marriage, for example is there, but was not thinkable to most 50 years ago. So too, many ideas in science are there in nascent form, but the technology may not yet be available for such ideas to be realised. The network is there – past, present and future – implicit or, as the scientist David Bohm says, *implicate* in that network (Bohm, 1980). Hence, in a particular community – a scientific, artistic or even an everyday colloquial community – the same idea may emerge in quite different places because of the readiness of that community to receive it; and the capacity of thinkers to think and intuit those ideas.

But although the network seems to exist in its own right – a system of thoughts, ideas, symbols and signs, it is not independent of living experiencing people. It exists between and within them. The logic of the associative unconscious is grounded in experience, in the connected nature of existence.

The only way to access broad swathes of the associative unconscious is for members of the community to pool their ideas, images, signs, symbols and experiences. Think of the idea of a house. You may have an image, a word association with bricks or wood, or a home and family. You may remember experiences of being in houses – their smells, the feel, the surroundings; your emotions. But a fuller meaning of house and all its connections, that themselves have connections, is achieved by sharing images, signs and symbols about houses with others, because each experience, each set of associations and connections is different. Access to the associative unconscious is via stories, art, discussions, scientific or otherwise. I use socioanalytic methods including reflective practice and social dreaming for such access (Long, 2013; Long and Manley, 2018).

There have been many social dreaming matrices held online during the Covid-19 pandemic. Many dreams quite directly lead to the fears and anxieties participants have been experiencing. Dreams of being out of control, of distorted and ill bodies, of dead relatives and associations of a vengeful nature and a gleeful virus. Other dreams of water and waves are associated to in terms of a second wave of the virus. There have been some dreams of hope, babies and new beginnings. Deeply in these dreams there have been ideas about the loss of effective parents – perhaps a notion in the associative unconscious that we are at a time of great change where a new generation has to find ways of being in the world that are more about co-creation, adaptation and symbiosis than control.

Abductive logic

ORA, as I use it applies what Charles Peirce describes as abductive logic (Peirce, 1931, Pg. 58). In a general sense, abductive reasoning begins with a set of observations and derives what might be the most probable explanation for their occurrence. It uses everyday hunches and guesses based on past experiences: "The hole in the front lawn must have been made by the dog; he's done it before".

But in the philosophy of science, the meaning is not so much about justification for conclusions reached, as about hypothesis formation. Abductive logic for Peirce is the first step in scientific knowledge – the only step that is creative and is the basis for hypothesis creation. It begins with what he terms 'a surprising fact'. Some observation surprises us and we seek an explanation. We form what Gordon Lawrence later refers to as a 'working hypothesis'. In surprising circumstances ideas may 'come out of the blue' or 'from left field'; from obtuse associations and connections and may be used as a likely explanation when there are no others. Peirce's formula:

> A surprising fact C is observed
> If H is true, then C would be a matter of course, not surprising
> So, H hypothetically can be true

This can subsequently be tested using deductive and inductive reasoning and scientific method. But to reach the surprising fact is not simple, because habitual perceptions fill in gaps, and we see or hear what we expect to see or hear most of the time. Observing surprising facts requires an open mind and as Bion following, Keats, the poet, puts it – to use negative capability – to be without memory, desire or an irritable search after meaning; a state of mind completely in the present. Then once the surprising fact is noted, a meaning becomes available through associations and connections.

Ginzberg (1983) calls this conjectural knowledge. He explains the method with reference to an Italian art historian of the late nineteenth century – Morelli – who developed a new way of authenticating paintings. Prior to Morelli's work, paintings were authenticated by an artist's typical choice of subject or setting. Morelli looked to the small details – the way an artist painted a hand, a fingernail or an ear; the small stokes of the brush or pen; elements of the painting that emerged as Morelli himself said – 'by force of habit, almost unconsciously' from the artist and could not be deliberately replicated. Freud read Morelli's work as a young man; his book being in Freud's library and Ginzberg and Davin (1980, Pg. 11) say:

> But what significance did Morelli's essays have on Freud, as a young man, still far from psychoanalysis? Freud himself tells us: proposal of an interpretative method based on taking marginal and irrelevant details as revealing clues. Here details generally considered trivial and unimportant, 'beneath notice', furnish the key to the highest achievements of human genius.

Interestingly, or perhaps pertinently, Morelli was originally a physician, as was Freud, and Ginzberg points out how medicine primarily uses conjectural methods and abductive logic. It involves the use of surface clues to find underlying causes. Ginzberg compares the methods of Morelli and Freud and also of detectives, exampling the work of the imaginary Sherlock Holmes, who, despite author Conan Doyle's claiming Holmes as deducing his solutions, actually uses abduction. Doyle was also a physician. This abductive logic or conjectural method seems to be a primary way in which psychoanalysis works. Small omissions or unusual connections are noted in a patient's associations – verification comes later with insight and mutative change. So too with ORA and system change.

Case example

During an action research project in a prison, the research team had made a rule that no one member of the team would go into an area with prisoners by themselves. If escorted by prison staff they would always go in twos in order to debrief together later. On one occasion I broke the rule as my colleagues were not available during a visit. It was a high-security unit for sex offenders. Although passing without overt incident, it proved to be quite traumatic for me as the social worker whose role I was exploring, upon our leaving the unit, spelled out for me in some detail the crimes committed by the inmates with whom I had been talking. Suddenly the details of the ways in which they had looked at me or had spoken to me became shocking. In all of this, the most surprising fact for me was that she convinced me to go into the unit with her when I had been clear about the rule, which I had made for safety of the team. Was it just my own hubris or my struggling after meaning?

Later upon debriefing, I realised the extent to which I had been subjected to a projective identification from the social worker. That is, she wanted me, perhaps unconsciously, perhaps not, to directly experience what she felt in role. She had earlier said that her role was hard to describe and I should come with her to observe as she did her rounds. I had agreed despite our rule of not going alone. My experience reflected what she experienced in her work – only she had had time to build the defences that I was woefully lacking. I got the full brunt. I had been seduced into going into the unit, groomed, as it were, into being the person who might know her pain in role.

Working socioanalytically

Just as with psychoanalysis, socioanalysis works conjecturally in the first instance. It involves:

- Noticing the surprising
- Finding patterns
- Allowing new ways of seeing
- Hunches

These methods generate meaning through understanding the clues – finding patterns in seeming chaos or unconnected occurrences. They work with the unconscious in dreams, drawings, photos films, music, associations, metaphors and patterns (right brain) to come to 'the surprising fact' Their aim is to generate 'working hypotheses' – the first step in scientific enquiry.

They give access to the associative unconscious: the infinite of thought, through abductive logic. They are methods that generate associations and find interconnections using chaotic seemingly unconnected 'bits and pieces' of human phenomena as clues.

As interpretivist methods exploring subjectivity (see Shapiro and Carr, 1991), they become validated through the insights they provide and the actions they support and engender. In the case of ORA, they enable clients to find the systemic purpose of their roles and to make changes.

Case example

A client – a defence lawyer – drew her role as juggling many coloured balls. Such an image is not uncommon in roles with many complex demands. She was able to discuss this complexity quite openly and had drawn the role quite consciously in this way. However, she had not drawn any features on her face. Was this surprising? At first, she dismissed the absence of features saying it was not important; the drawing was simply schematic not representational. But upon my insistence she explored the meaning of being faceless in a court setting and how such facelessness came into her roles outside the court, sometimes losing her friends, and how being expressionless in court was seen as professional. She said that the way her clients looked and their expressions in the dock had a great effect on judges and juries, and she always advised them on their expressions. And, upon further reflection she said that although she kept her emotions in check, they nonetheless were often quite intense. This led to a discussion about the importance of her feelings in a case and her reactions to a particular 'bullying' male prosecutor.

The transforming experience model (transforming experience into authentic action in role)

This is a model, not a theory. It makes no hypothetical predictions but gives guidance for an exploration of the dynamics within organisational systems. I owe my understanding of this to the former Grubb Institute and its staff, then becoming the Grubb Guild, now closed. I use the model as background to ORA. The model describes five domains of experience: the experience of being a person, the experience of being in a system, the experience of being in a role, the experience of being in a context, and the experience of source. These are not necessarily exhaustive domains but are central to organisational analysis. Here I will just touch on the model as it is explained more fully in a book I edited – *Transforming Experience in Organisations: A Framework for Organisational Research and Consultancy* (Long, 2016).

Role is central in the model because it is in a role that a person can take actions on behalf of the organisation and instigate change. Roles mark the place where people in an organisation stand in relation to one another. This is different from relationships between persons. The relation between roles is always mediated by the tasks associated with the roles. One may have quite different experiences as a person and in role. Often workplace and ethical dilemmas are experienced because the role calls for one thing when the personal experience or values call for another.

Each of the domains puts pressure on the person in their role, and the person in role makes decisions that can influence each of the domains. Role analysis can explore the experiences in each of the domains, find surprising observations and patterns and develop working hypotheses about the dynamics surrounding the role, the system and its context; and working hypotheses about how the person takes up the role and is influenced by source. Source is the deepest values by which a person in role operates. It may be religious, is certainly spiritual and provides a guiding source of decisions and actions. Source may have to be discovered because it is mostly unconscious even though having conscious presence in a set of purposes and values or in a deity.

Conducting a role analysis

Setting up and discussing your approach is important for the client. It establishes the context for the work. In light of the TEF model, you must remember that you and your client, or clients, are not simply exploring a work role but are yourselves taking up roles in a system with a context and source. Exploring the here and now of the ongoing role analysis along with the work role explored is part of the process.

I discuss:

- Confidentiality
- The setting
- Collaborative work
- Roles in the work – my own and the client
- Elaboration, associations and amplification
- When interpretation and by whom – meaning making
- Developing working hypotheses
- TEF model
- Time and place for our sessions

- Number of sessions
- Costs
- Any other considerations.

In starting we consider together:

- What role/roles are to be worked with?
- Describing the role, the system and context
- Role drawing
- Working with a challenge in the role
- Hypothesis about the role – how is it serving the system?
- Are there any connections between the work role explored and the ORA system as it is unfolding?

I work through a consideration of the experience of person, role, system, context and source; not necessarily in that order, and often we move from one back to the other. Through role biography (Long, 2006, 2013) and an exploration of finding, making and taking a role (Kapoor, 2016; Quine and Hutton, 1992) we develop working hypotheses about the person in the role – how is the role being taken up? What are the demands of the role? What is the fit between person and role?

Working with the experience of the system might involve: understanding purpose, tasks, authority and accountability in the system; looking at the culture of the organisation and its sub-groups; that is, thinking about artefacts, values, behaviours and assumptions (Bion, 1961; Schein, 2016). Then developing hypotheses about the system in light of the organisational purposes.

Working with the experience of the context considers social, physical, economic, political, environmental and technological contexts and developing hypotheses about the effect of these contexts on the system, role and person.

Working with source may take my client and I into personal, systemic and contextual purposes, values and meanings and how these affect the way role is taken up and used.

At different points of the role analysis we review the various hypotheses and how our own role relations are developing.

Using ORA in an organisation

Each of the following I have done:

- A client or client system may wish to explore a series of roles and how these interact;
- Several roles in a system may be analysed to get a deeper sense of the system;
- Different roles may be involved in role dialogue;
- Teams may explore differing perceptions and conceptualisations of the many roles in the team, and yet these may go undiscussed because the discussions become personalised and blames given to persons, rather than complexities in roles; and
- Organisational processes such as induction or performance assessments can use short forms of role analysis. In the former to understand anticipations from a role, in the latter to separate out the changes needed to roles from the success or not of the person occupying the role (see Long et al., 2010a).

Case example

In a hospital department, an action research team that I led explored the experiences of different team members from the experience of their roles. We found that many of the difficulties experienced in the departmental teams resulted from their not finding ways to communicate the needs of each role to others. For example, patient appointment times seemed never to be co-ordinated between cardiologists and radiologists such that patients could not be seen by both groups on the same day, and many would have to travel from country areas into the city on several occasions. The attempts to co-ordinate successfully always became doomed. We engaged them in an open space process that allowed them, as a self-organising system to bring forward this and other issues, where their experiences in roles could be openly discussed together and solutions were found. They had to then rethink their team leadership processes where, in workshops, they each drew pictures to depict their understanding of the other roles in the team, especially the leadership roles. This led them to a deeper understand of what the leadership roles demanded and how they might make changes (see Long et al., 2010b).

Executive coaching

Halina Brunning

The challenge

The chief objective of this section is to reflect upon the current practice of a systems psychodynamics approach to executive coaching and to predict the likely after-effects that the 2020 pandemic might exert upon the theory and application of executive coaching.

The second objective is about forming hypotheses about the likely new developments over the next five to ten years, envisioning their application and utility, whilst linking executive coaching to the systems psychodynamics paradigm and the overall theme of this book.

These two objectives will be addressed in the following four steps.

Step one

Towards an ecology of systems psychodynamics coaching

The history of psychodynamic and systems psychodynamics coaching is given a useful contextual background by examining the typology of coaching proposed by Roberts and Jarrett (2006, Pg. 3) (See Figure 5.2) who studied the key differences between the main approaches to coaching currently practiced in the UK.

> The grid shown in diagram 1 is based on their interviews of leading practitioners of different kinds of coaching regarding the main aims and focus of their work. The primary aim of the coaching intervention is shown on the vertical axis, with insight at one end of the spectrum and outputs (e.g. higher sales) at the other. The horizontal axis indicates whether the primary focus of the coaching is on the individual or on the organization or organizational role.

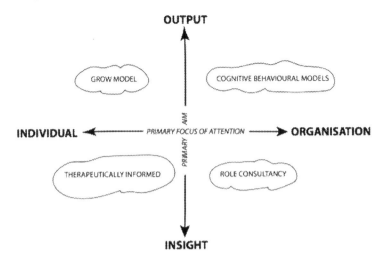

Figure 5.2 Four models of coaching.

Source: Copyrights V.Z. Roberts and M. Jarrett (2006, Pg. 3–40) and modified by Kristof Bien (2020).

The information gathered in quadrants "shows that these are not rigid categories but clusters of types of coaching interventions. A striking finding was that whereas most of the leading approaches to coaching fell fairly clearly into one or other quadrant, psychodynamic coaching found a place in both lower quadrants: the more purely 'therapeutically informed' approach on the left and the systems psychodynamics (role consultancy) approach on the right. The top two quadrants are based on goal attainment, whereas the bottom two quadrants are based on meaning-making" (Roberts and Brunning, 2007, Pg. 253–254).

This point will be re-visited at the end.

Step 2

The 'steady state'

It is possible to identify the goals of psychodynamic coaching by looking again at the typology of models of coaching. "Therapeutically-informed coaching will have as its core goal the development of personal insight by the coachee: to bring into conscious awareness what has previously been outside their awareness. The primary goal of role consultancy is to increase the coachee's capacity to use multiple perspectives in making sense of and meeting work challenges and contributing to organizational purpose" (Ibid., Pg. 263).

Role consultancy includes developing a deeper understanding of their role: which system(s) or sub-system(s) they are in, which boundary or boundaries they are on, the sources of their authority and how they are using it, how well the organisational design of their role and system match the requirements of the primary task and so on. In addition, the coachee becomes more aware of systemic defensive processes of which they are a part, which makes for a greater level of choice about how they will act. "They may of course also develop personal insights along the way, but these are not the primary goal of the coaching" (Ibid., Pg. 264).

One illustration of this approach is the six-domain model of coaching (Figure 5.3). In this version of the P/R/O model the three basic elements of Person, Role and Organisation are opened up also to include more information about the client's personality, life story, set of skills, talents and competencies brought into the role. All six domains are contemporaneously present during the coaching sessions, and any or all of them constitute a legitimate and appropriate focus of work. The six domains are in continuous dynamic motion, as if they were a set of six interlinked cogwheels, each able to affect the movement of the neighbouring cogs. Thus, a disruption in the domain of 'current organisational role' is likely to affect the domain of 'life story' and vice versa. Each domain can influence others in ways that are either harmonious or disharmonious, all are thus interconnected (Brunning, 2001).

This coaching approach to the development of the individual and as well as the role within the organisation has been relevant and appropriate from the start of the Millennium until recently. It survived despite the first dramatic disruptor in the form of the 2007/8 financial crisis. It can, however, be said that this model no longer fully holds as it is not meeting the challenges of the current major disruptor that the coronavirus pandemic created, mainly due to its narrow focus on the coachee individual development.

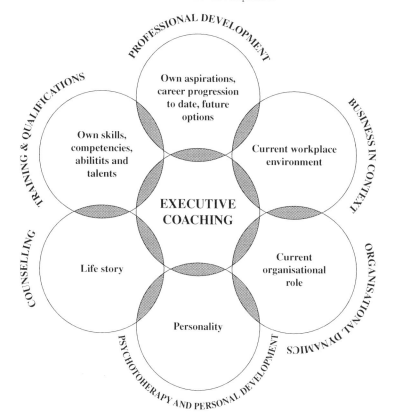

Figure 5.3 Six domains of executive coaching.

110 *Psychoanalytic thinking*

Step 3

Covid 19, the second major disruptor

Early in 2020 the coronavirus shook the world and changed all assumptions, presumptions and rules upon which the globalised world is based (Brunning and Khaleelee, 2021; Denworth, 2020). In less than six months the established structures, solid, famous and wealthy firms and organisations faltered. Unemployment and uncertain futures threaten many industries and millions of workers in the developed world. (Leighton, 2020; News of companies that have gone bust in the UK, 2020). No statistics are available to ascertain the damage in the developing world by June 2020. Human omnipotence has been severely attacked, exposing the precariousness of human condition (de Vries, 2020), and the fourth humiliation of humankind was affecting our capacity to recover, proposes Nagel (2020), linking it to the first three humiliation blows to human narcissism at the hands of science, originally identified by Freud, with the current crisis being the fourth humiliation as it shows us that we are not the masters of nature and earth – neither technologically, nor morally, writes Nagel. Links between the causality and the pandemic are also difficult to admit to warns Western (2020). Have we as the human race painted ourselves into a corner?

Covid-19, capable of causing a multi-organ failure in affected individuals, slowly reveals its power to also cause a multi-system failure in other human constructions: be it the way we live and interact, how we trade and govern ourselves as nations, or states, and interconnect our global dependency worldwide. The interlinks of nature-human-technology acting as an ecosystem must now be seriously considered (Western, 2020). According to Western, the time for eco-leadership has arrived (2019). Articles are being written on the post-Covid leadership style (Hobbs, 2020), and questions are being asked about what can coaching offer and how can it change to be of use (Association for Coaching, 2020; Parsadh, 2020).

These dramatic environmental changes necessitate a different approach to coaching due to the need to consider implications of the roles taken up by the leadership, the workers and especially the organisations – an urgent task for the industry.

Considering the fragility and vulnerability that has been recently exposed and experienced by humanity, by some of the most powerful countries as well as business and commerce globally (McQuaid, 2020a; Pattison, 2020), changes are inevitable in the way work will be delivered and how coaching will be applied, if at all.

Power and vulnerability form a strong dynamic bond (Brunning, 2014; Brunning and Khaleelee, 2021), an invisible frame within which all interactions are located, and as such this frame must be addressed in any recovery effort. Organisations will be restructuring, relationships between workers and their bosses will alter (Leighton, 2020; McQuaid, 2020b), the focus on the ecology within which organisations exist will need to be urgently considered (Western, 2020).

In the immediate Covid-19 recovery period an augmented and updated six domains model might be suitable as the executive coaching framework based on systems psychodynamics (see Figure 5.3). Attention is being drawn here to the pairing between the coach and the client, which might occur or cut across any section of the organisation, including the business in context, leadership, human resources, and workplace environment. Consideration must also be given to the issues of global ecology and the cross-section/interdependency between the environment and the business.

Furthermore, Figure 5.4 represents the interim coaching model proposed as a remedy for the immediate aftermath of the Covid-19 impact. The essence of this application resides in the external ring showing how power fused with vulnerability wraps around the organisational system affecting all intervening domains. Denying this potent pairing of power with vulnerability will not allow a proper recovery to take place in any of the organisational domains.

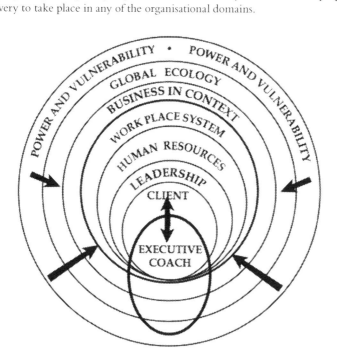

Figure 5.4 Coaching in the Covid world.
Source: copyrights HB (2020).

Step four

The post-Covid world of systems psychodynamics coaching: tentative predictions

In the opinion of this author coaching might not automatically survive as an industry unless it can position itself adequately to reflect the new reality. Systems psychodynamics coaching, if posited differently, might have a unique ability to assist the leaders of industries.

This I see as a process of a coach accompanying the leaders with the task of addressing their own and the organisational power and vulnerability dynamics. This aim could be achieved by considering Gordon W. Lawrence's two concepts: the politics of salvation and the politics of revelation (See Figure 5.5). Lawrence differentiated "the politics of salvation as holding power imposed from the outside on individual or systems, the politics of revelation as being preoccupied with the conditions and resources for the exercise of transformation that comes from inside the person or system and are brought about through (...) revealing what may be the truth of their situation to themselves and taking authority to act on their interpretation" (Lawrence, 2000, Pg. 173). Lawrence further claimed (2006, Pg. 97–112) that the politics of salvation can only lead to change as they are born of conscious thinking and deal with what is already known, whereas the politics of revelation can achieve a transformation as they are based on unconscious thinking and self-authorisation in search of the unknown.

With this thought in mind I propose a new diagram in memory of Gordon W. Lawrence's creative thinking that might point us towards the future of transformation in a post-Covid world.

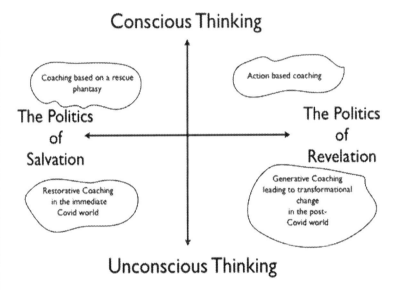

Figure 5.5 Politics of salvation/politics of revelation and coaching in a post-Covid world.

Source: Copyrights HB (2020).

A final thought

It is possible to envisage that systems psychodynamics coaches may have the capacity to communicate with industry leaders on subjects psychological, philosophical, organisational and global. This might work if the coaching conversation is located within the lower right quadrant of this diagram linking the unconscious thinking with the politics of revelation thus leading to generative transformational change. These deep conversations might influence the leadership to re-examine afresh old assumptions, including rescue phantasies, so that old thoughts and acts, including dreams, and with it also meaning can become transformed and therefore transformational in re-learning how to live and work in the new post-Covid world order.

Summary

Executive coaching at the Tavistock Institute is referred to as *organizational role consultation* because 'coaching' implies differential powers between coach and coachee and expert practice. *Organizational role consultation* more accurately describes the 3-way integrated focus on the person, the role and the organisation. The client is always part of a larger system – a team, an organisation, community and society. Role consultation occurs at the interface between the individual-in-role and their professional or technical environment. Role consultation helps clients better understand their individual and organisational roles by the understanding of conscious and unconscious determinants. Role consultation aims to enhance the client's effectiveness in relation to the needs and desires of the organisation and its environment. Role consultation relies on group relations theory, open systems theory, psychoanalysis and leadership studies. The goal of role consultation is an understanding of the realm of the role and the context, the organisational system within which the role is embedded and expected to function. Role consultation is a joint exploration where the power relationship is one of equals and the consultant and client jointly investigate 'what is going on' as a means of devising a way forward. Better understanding leads to better judgement, and thence to more effective behaviour. Systems psychodynamics consultants tend to focus on developing leadership capability. Role consultation sessions help develop capability to think under demanding conditions, to be resourceful and collaborative and to take up leadership or management roles successfully. Role consultants provide developmentally and psycho-educationally focused reflection and learning opportunities to the individual leader, to study, become aware of and gain insight into how task and organisational performance are influenced by both conscious and unconscious behaviour. Consciousness refers to objectivity and rational behaviour, and unconsciousness to the image of 'the organisation-in-the-mind', which contains the system's unconscious defences and irrational behaviours. Organisational role consultation provides a professional context for leaders and managers to examine and articulate their current working experiences; analyse them in their organisational setting so as to sharpen up the meaning of those experiences in terms of purpose, systems and boundaries; grasp opportunities to find, make and take up their organisational roles more effectively; and transform their contribution towards achieving the corporate aims of their organisations. A clear distinction is made between role and personality. When people are in conflict, often it is because roles and personality become merged and therefore confused. Working with the idea of 'organisation-in-the-mind' frees the client from thinking about the way things ought to be, so they can engage creatively with the way organisational life actually is in order that future plans and intentions can be more realistically planned and achieved. Role consultation is a way of helping clients to reflect on their experiences, to analyse and learn from them, in order to bring about change. Each new role consultation session is a fresh start and should not be regarded as phases to be worked through.

Exercise

1 Every role consultation session starts with (i) prior agreement on the phase for working-through; (ii) at client's own unique choice of starting point. Which approach do you follow? Why?
2 What does 'organisation-in-the-mind' really mean? For you? For your organisation?
3 What is the difference between psychotherapy and role consultation?
4 What is the difference between role consultation and organisational consultation?
5 How can the role consultant work effectively with a client without meeting other people in the organisation?

Part III
Group dynamics

Part III includes chapters that examine Bion's understanding of groups and the influence of the unconscious on the life of groups. Chapter 6 describes the life of Bion, his role in World War I and how that period of history influenced his ideas on the importance of mobilising the inherent forces in groups – the dynamics – to achieve the aims of groups, whether the task is therapeutic – treating group members for their psychological problems – or whether the group is engaged in a consciously devised task, like a committee or a work team. This chapter describes Bion's short-lived experiment at the Northfield Military Hospital, which was the forerunner of the therapeutic community. That experiment reshaped many traditional hierarchical organisations and contributed to creating new organisational structures in which responsibility for decision-making, working arrangements and accountability was devolved from the formal hierarchy to the people who were directly involved in the work. This shift was encapsulated in Bion's statement that the patients in the hospital should be related to as "soldiers who happened to be patients, rather than as patients who happened to be soldiers". This was a revolutionary idea that did not sit easily with the military authorities or even Winston Churchill. Yet, this idea transformed management and leadership theory in later decades and challenged accepted notions of social stratification, in which people "were to know their place" in the hierarchy.

In this chapter, David Armstrong writes about Bion's basic assumptions, and Bion's brilliant extrapolation of Freud's theory of the unconscious as applied to groups. Armstrong challenges the general tendency of dynamically oriented consultants to emphasise the basic assumptions at the expense of examining the conscious goal-oriented work group. All layers of consciousness and intentionality must be examined simultaneously with the objective of integrating them.

Chapter 7 moves towards 'application' of systems psychodynamics to teams with contributions from David Armstrong, Juliet Scott and Heather Stradling. This chapter also introduces us to sociotechnical systems, which examines the interactions between people in groups and the technologies they encounter; and investigates the interactions between the psychological, social and environmental factors as well as structural and technical elements of organisations. The chapter describes the contribution of Eric Trist on how groups shape the work patterns of organisations and their attitudes and behaviours of group members to their jobs. Also, in this chapter, the reader will come across the idea of self-managing teams that has proved so popular in Western ideas on work design, to working with large groups, comprising cross sections of organisational stakeholders, working together on organisational issues of strategic importance and change. Armstrong offers a piece of the evolution of the Work Group from his consultation with a faith organisation, searching for the 'multiplicity of meanings' found in stories and objects that sometimes lead to states of spiritual deprivation. The Work Group in this distinctive forum, with the technology of its own, opened the possibility of a shared engagement – an 'autonomy of exploration' and the shift from cooperation to collaboration.

Chapter 8 moves to organisational development consultation within the systems psychodynamics paradigm, citing Isabel Menzies Lyth seminal work with the nursing profession, introducing ideas of the functioning of social systems as a defence against anxiety. Obholzer challenges one-sided consultancy as having little value in "commenting on the existence of unconscious group processes and speculating about the origin and meaning without addressing issues of what's to be done to address them, by whom, in what role, with what authority and in what time scale".

Chapter 8 introduces us to Eric Miller on the methodology of the consultant and the role of transference and countertransference, a derivative from the psychoanalysts' role, i.e. the way the consultant is used and experienced and also the feelings evoked in them, offering evidence of underlying and unstated issues and feelings in the client system – that which is repressed by the client may be expressed by the consultant.

Also, in Chapter 8, we meet Juliet Scott and Heather Stradling, who write about the use of art in organisational consultancy and change through integrating the power of storytelling, power and politics, the unconscious and performance. They describe embodied practice and interventions, including visual and multi-media arts, dance, theatre and performance art; anticipating further possibilities such as the use of sound to bring a new sensitivity and choreography that draws attention to questions of inclusion and exclusion. Scott and Stradling describe how art can deepen understanding of psychodynamic concepts and approaches and artistic practice can be used to support the development of organisations.

Chapter 9 moves to the distinguishing Tavistock Institute phenomenon of group relations – the professional development forums concerned with experiential learning about group and organisational behaviour. Group relations was invented at the Tavistock Institute and is the product of the convergence of psychoanalysis and sociotechnical systems and design theories. Leslie Brissett and David Armstrong contribute from their experiences of group relations conferences. This chapter describes the heart of group relations theory that organisations and groups generate anxiety among its members, anxieties that trigger a variety of defence mechanisms some of which are rooted in the individual and others in the organisation. While defensive mechanisms relieve immediate anxiety, they also promote and immerse individuals and groups in a fantasy world where emotions dominate, often leading to poor decision-making and miscalculations. Group relations conferences help reveal how these processes and dynamics evolve and how they can be worked with. The chapter describes the key conceptual ideas and methods that establish group relations theory and practise as a distinct paradigm as well as how new group relations conference events were and are developed that reflect the changing environments and nature of organisations in the second half of the 20th century and the beginning of the 21st century.

David Armstrong, in a piece on group relations and the ethical imagination puzzles over boundaries of group relations, what it covers and what it does not; arguing about the fundamental issue of applicability – what follows from the learning about group relations in the social and organisational worlds we inhabit. Armstrong talks about an imaginative deficit or creative withdrawal referring to the origins of group relations as a practical necessity born of war, in the selection of officers, responding to soldiers withdrawn from the front or prisoners of war returning to civilian life. Attending to these groups of people, the Tavistock Group of psychiatrists and social scientists were confronted with developing new ways of working, evolving methods that had few precedents. The Tavistock Group started their endeavours by engaging with people to explore their problems more deeply and understand their conflicts and dilemmas. Armstrong defines his practise as working simultaneously with two sides of group functioning – the generative and the resistant – striving never to fall into the binary trap of linear cause-and-effect explanations.

Chapter 10 brings us to a core systems psychodynamics concept of *social systems as a defence against anxiety* and allied concepts of *container and contained*. The work of Isabel Menzies Lyth, Elliott Jaques and Wilfred Bion are significant here on building on Freud's ideas of aggregating bonds as elements binding individuals into institutionalised human associations serving as defences against psychotic anxiety. This chapter describes how anxieties originating in people's responses to their work tasks, stimulating primitive anxieties, leads to a collective defence which in turn becomes part of the culture and structure of the organisation.

The chapter also addresses other key concepts like projection and introjection and projective identification and introjective identification. Understanding these concepts and having a working knowledge of them is central to the thinking of the systems psychodynamics consultant, which is achieved by a combination of personal psychotherapy and regular supervision. The chapter describes other important concepts like unconscious phantasy, splitting, transference and countertransference in the consultant–client relationship. The chapter also focuses on achieving results for the client and not being content with explaining the presence of unconscious dynamics: what is the point of working with social defence systems if it is structured into the very being of the organisation? Among the ways forward are suggested reflection and learning opportunities to allow for the development of an awareness of the whole organisation and its interconnected parts. With awareness, defences become conscious rather than remaining unconscious and maladaptive aspects of the social defences can change.

6 Bion's theory of groups

With David Armstrong

History

The influence of Wilfred Bion

Having qualified in medicine in 1930, Bion spent seven years in psychotherapeutic training at the Tavistock Clinic. He wanted to train in psychoanalysis, and in 1938, he began a training analysis with John Rickman, but World War II brought this to an end.

The entire group at Tavistock had, in fact, been taken into the army and were working on new methods of treatment for psychiatric casualties (those suffering post-traumatic stress, or 'shell shock' as it was then known). Out of this, his pioneering work in group dynamics was associated with the 'Tavistock group'. Bion's papers describing his work of the 1940s were compiled much later and appeared together in 1961 in his influential book, *Experiences in Groups and other papers* (1961). It was less a guide for the therapy of individuals within or by the group than an exploration of the processes set off by the complex experience of being in a group. The book quickly became a touchstone work for applications of group theory in a wide variety of fields.

The Northfield Experiments

Manpower shortages during the war severely hampered British military success. It was during this desperate time to get rehabilitated soldiers back to the battlefield that much of Bion and his colleague's experimentation with groups took place at a treatment facility called the Northfield Hospital. Trist (1985, Pg. 14) recalled the following:

> Northfield was a large military psychiatric hospital, which functioned as a clearing house. According to a man's condition, he would be discharged from the army, return to his unit or found alternative military employment. The need for manpower was at its height. Any method was welcome which would encourage a body of disaffected men displaying a bewildering variety of symptoms in different degrees of acuteness, to

re-engage with the role of being a soldier in an army at war. Methods so far tried had yielded poor results.

In response to this need, Bion devised a therapeutic community, outlined in a document called the 'Wharncliffe Memorandum' in 1939. The premise of the therapeutic community was to use the entire hospital environment as a therapeutically engaged social system to treat patients by shifting the focus from individual treatment to that of group process, leadership concepts and social obligation.

Paramount was the notion that the group analyses its own dynamics rather than waiting for outside direction from authority figures. This philosophy becomes a central tenant in the field of group relations and, therefore, in systems psychodynamics.

Events that transpired at the Northfield Hospital had a widespread impact on the field of psychiatry both during and after the war. Many of the so-called invisible college returned to their former employer, the Tavistock Clinic. Much of the clinic's post-war work was based on the experimentation that this interdisciplinary group from the invisible college conducted at the Northfield Hospital during the war years (White, 2014). The Northfield Experiments took place at Hollymoor Hospital, Northfield, Birmingham, during World War II. The first experiment was conducted by Bion and Rickman. The second evolved gradually; many people contributed to its success, including Foulkes, Main and Bridger. The experiments were an important landmark in the evolution of theory and practice in group psychotherapy and in the therapeutic community movement. They were not carried out solely as responses to the need for mass treatment of neurotic disorders among army personnel; antecedent factors, the theoretical orientation of the practitioners and the nature of army life were equally important. The two experiments differed in pace and in recognition of the needs of higher-order systems, particularly the military hierarchy. They shared many underlying concepts, including responsibility to society, the therapeutic use of groups (including the hospital community) and an emphasis on process (Coombe, 2020). Experimentation with experiential group methods and the development of a therapeutic community laid the foundation for the emergence after the war of a new field called group relations.

Bion in *Experiences in Groups and Other Papers* (1961, Pg. 16) describe how in 1942, while Northfield was serving as a military hospital, he and John Rickman set up the first Northfield experiment. Bion and Rickman oversaw the training and rehabilitation wing of Northfield and ran the unit along the principles of group dynamics. Their aim was to improve morale by creating a 'good group spirit' (esprit de corps). Though he sounded like a traditional army officer Bion's means were very unconventional. He was in charge of around 100 men. He told them that they had to do an hour's exercise every day and that each had to join a group: "handicrafts, Army courses, carpentry, map-reading, sand-tabling etc.. … or form a fresh group if he wanted to do so". While this may have looked like traditional occupational therapy, the real therapy was the struggle to manage the interpersonal strain of organising things together rather than simply weaving baskets. Those unable to join a group would have to go to the restroom, where a nursing orderly would supervise a quiet regime of "reading, writing or games such as draughts ... any men who felt unfit for any activity whatever could lie down". The focus of every day was a meeting of all the men, referred to as a parade.

> A parade would be held every day at 12.10 p.m. for making announcements and conducting other business of the training wing. Unknown to the patients, it was intended that this meeting, strictly limited to 30 minutes, should provide an occasion for the men to step outside their framework and look upon its working with the detachment of spectators. In short it was intended to be the first step towards the elaboration of therapeutic seminars. For the first few days little happened; but it was evident that amongst patients a great deal of discussion and thinking was taking place.
>
> (Bion, 1961, Pg. 16)

The experiment had to close after six weeks, as the military authorities did not approve of it and ordered the transfer of Bion and Rickman (who were members of the Royal Army Medical Corps. These ideas on the psychoanalysis of groups were then taken up and developed by others such as S.H. Foulkes (1948, 1957), Rickman (1957), Bridger (1985, 1990a, b), Main (1946) and Patrick de Maré (1972). S.H. Foulkes, who was more successful at gaining the support of the military authorities, started the second Northfield experiment, which was based on the ideas of Bion and Rickman and used group psychotherapy, the following year. The experiments were important in the development of therapeutic communities. Among his interesting findings was that in a group, the standards of social intercourse lack intellectual content and critical judgement. This observation agrees with Gustave Le Bon's findings about groups which he mentioned in his book *The Crowd* (1896).

Another interesting observation was that whatever a group member says or does in a group illuminates that member's view of the group and is an illumination of that member's personality. If the contributions of the group and its members can be made anonymously, then the foundations for a system of denial and evasion are established. And perhaps one of the most important findings in his experiments was that whenever a group is formed, it always seeks a leader to follow. The group then searches for someone who has questionable attributes with his or her mental health. Initially, the group will search for someone who is paranoid schizophrenic or someone who is malignant hysteric. If the group is unable to find someone with those attributes, the group looks for someone with delinquent trends and a psychopathic personality. Otherwise, the group would just settle on the verbally facile high-grade defective.

The basics

Bion's (1961) theory of group behaviour has become the foundation of the Tavistock model of group behaviour. Bion (1961) viewed the group as a separate yet collective entity. For the most part, groups emerge from the acceptance or agreement that a common goal (positive or negative) exists. This manifest aspect of a group is Bion's work (W) group (Bion, 1961). Bion (1961, Pg. 63) held that "people come together as a group for the purposes of preserving the group". Rice (1965, Pg. 17) defined the primary task of a group or sub-group as "the task it must perform if it is to survive". Even though groups form, as stated, at an overt level to achieve a common goal, there are also latent or covert aspects within the group that are real (Bion, 1961; Rice, 1965; Banet and Hayden, 1977; Czander, 1993; Miller, 1993). They contended that though there is a conscious effort on the part of the group members to pursue the common objective, there are often unconscious hidden agendas that interfere with the completion of work tasks.

Furthermore, they suggested that individuals are often unaware of the controls in play, which help to separate their stated intentions from their hidden agendas. The hidden agendas of the individuals within the group collectively make up the latent (covert) aspects of group behaviour, which are referred to by Bion (1961) as the basic assumptions (b/a) group (Bion, 1961; Rice, 1965; Banet and Hayden, 1977; Czander, 1993; Miller, 1993). This covert aspect of the group, though frequently disguised, is a latent motivating force for group members (Banet and Hayden, 1977). This relates also to Bion's (1961, Pg. 65) description of group mentality:

> Group mentality is the unanimous expression of the will of the group, contributed to by the individual in ways of which he is unaware, influencing him disagreeably whenever he thinks of behaves at variance with the basic assumptions.

The group's culture is a function of the conflict between the individual's desires and the group's mentality (Bion, 1961). Thus, the group's culture emerges and regulates group members' behaviour and provides evidence of the basic assumptions operative within the group.

Bion's work on group processes (*Experiences in Groups*, 1961) was based largely on developments in object relations theory pioneered by Melanie Klein (1928, 1935, 1940, 1945, 1946, 1948, 1952, 1955, 1957, 1959). The essential element of Bion's theory of group life was to differentiate between behaviours and activities geared toward rational task performance (the work [W] group), and those geared to emotional needs and anxieties (the basic assumption [b/a] group). In addition to noting the importance of Klein's general theory of development centring on the paranoid/schizoid and depressive positions, Bion also explicitly set out to articulate the relevance of other central Kleinian concepts for an understanding of the human group, including projective identification, splitting, psychotic anxiety, symbol formation, schizoid mechanisms and part-objects. It was this influential work that provided the major psychoanalytic underpinnings of what has become known as the Tavistock, and hence systems psychodynamics, approach to the theory and practice of both group relations training and organisational theory and consultation. Work groups may avoid carrying out the primary task. The functioning of a group is best understood by reference to Bion's basic assumptions. An organisational group that is in a basic assumption mode is likely to display 'anti-task' behaviour.

The systems psychodynamics approach thus recognises two groups at play, viz. the W group and the b/a group. Both groups are real, operating and present simultaneously (Bion, 1961; Rice, 1965; Miller, 1993). Banet and Hayden (1977) depicted the W-group as being outwardly focused on the task; while the b/a group is inwardly focused on itself, and this creates an inevitable tension which is balanced by various behavioural and psychological structures like individual defence systems, ground rules and group norms.

Therefore, to truly understand behaviour (whether of the individual or the group) one should first understand the inner state. An underlying premise of the systems psychodynamics consultancy stance is that unconscious forces affect individual behaviour and individuals and groups behave in ways that are not always rational and obvious (Rice, 1965). Furthermore, individuals influence and are influenced by all group members, affected by not only the rational but, more often, the emotional and non-rational elements present in the group (Czander, 1993). It is often the state of anxiety that causes the development of a variety of defence mechanisms (Czander, 1993; Hirschhorn, 1993).

Case study

Improving morale and generating organisational change through a 'good group spirit' (esprit de corps)

A major leadership challenge is managing the inter-personal and inter-group strain of organising things together. Often, in a group charged with a task, the standards of social intercourse may lack intellectual and emotional content and critical judgement. Group-as-a-whole consultants generally take the view that the behaviour of a sub-system is a fractal, i.e. it mirrors the behaviour of the larger formal system. During a three-year consultancy intervention based on the creation of six action learning sets (ALSs) it emerged that Bion's basic assumptions (b/a) of dependency and fight/flight were the same paralysing basic assumption processes that were present in the formal systems of the company where they could not be grasped (or worked with) so easily.

During the first few meetings on one ALS, comprising 11 geographically-dispersed senior engineers and physicists of a global high-tech company, the participants asked how structural and technical issues they were tasked with rectifying would be translated into active change processes across the company? These participants of the ALS recognised in themselves a cynical rejection of the deeper meanings of collective responsibility, a defence against change (despite claiming that they wanted to 'change') and were skeptical of any 'psychological' explanations of their behaviour. But they understood that the future success of the company depended on the six ALSs – totaling 65 top leaders in the company – taking up their leadership roles differently from the way they had done in the past, especially in their relationships to their bosses on the Board. They were anxious that taking up their authority to make and implement company-wide decisions would result in push-back, cynical reactions from their bosses and possible threats to their career progression. The Board and the ALS could be said to have been locked in an oedipal struggle for dominance. The ALS expressed a need to learn more about the dynamics of leadership in group and inter-group functioning, including their own tendency to project their hostility into the Board whom they experienced as critical of their business judgements and leadership capability.

The overt source of the ALS's, anxiety was the Board's decision to move about 100 senior technical personnel to a subsidiary manufacturing site abroad: for some, it was a decision already taken; for others, it seemed they would be given the choice of whether or not they would be transferred. No one really knew the full situation. The absence of a clear decision (whether to move the 100 senior personnel) and the subsequent feeling of a lack of candidness between the two tiers of management was affecting the motivation of the personnel involved. They felt that in a matrix organisation such as theirs, early alignment between product line, programme development and staff deployment was needed; no one wanted a last-minute default decision.

Concerns about operational performance were expressed. The deployment, it was said, may have been due to a sense of 'stuckness' at Board level. No one in the ALS seemed able to divine the Board's intentions. In the discussion, ALS members said that the transfer plan was not just about relocating workers; it would involve relocating manufacturing functions too. They were doubtful this deployment could happen because alignment between the two sites had not been formally agreed. The ALS discussed how the overseas subsidiary had developed a unique method for achieving an essential light source, but could not deliver on the size of the product order, thus causing delays to manufacture and to customers. Headquarters wanted to help the overseas subsidiary, but their help had set up strong negative reactions in the subsidiary, which felt blamed for various acquisition problems, including an underestimation of the time needed to solve the light source problem. There were fears that the centre of gravity of manufacturing would be moved from the subsidiary to Headquarters.

The ALS's decided to research the distribution of responsibility and identify respective roles of the subsidiary and Headquarters'. Headquarters people were hesitant and did not fully trust the subsidiary to deliver the product on time because they lacked engineering power and capability. Conceptually, and from an engineering point of view, the two organisations were different – the subsidiary was good on physics; Headquarters was good on project management, engineering and integration of large-scale systems.

Headquarters representatives in the ALS said they feared there would be job losses and there was concern over the Board's inability to come up with a viable plan. This led to self-protective behaviour among Headquarters people in the ALS. A proposed transfer plan had not been aligned between the two sites, and therefore, it held little chance of being realistically implemented. There was no agreement with the plan with the relevant stakeholders (R&D, program management, supply chain, manufacturing, customer service). The plan had become dogmatic and the facts could no longer be seen objectively. The ALS Headquarters participants were taking up strong positions and constructive dialogue was absent. The ALS participants said they did not want to be responsible for repeating previous failures. The Design & Engineers had produced a plan, but the boundaries of operation had not been agreed or accepted at the necessary levels. The Headquarters people could not see that the subsidiary was a parallel organisation that was not connected structurally to production lines at Headquarters in Europe. Programme management had no control of the subsidiary's technologies. There was no joint alignment and trust between them had been lost.

From an engineering point of view, parts of a manufacturing system should never be located over two sites, especially if they have a complex interface, so the challenges for the ALS were how to align the split sites – the subsidiary and Headquarters. Generally, subsystems should only be designed, integrated and tested at other sites when there is a sufficient level of modularity (meaning the degree to which a system's components may be separated and recombined with flexibility and variety in use) in the overall architecture, and the subsystems are self-contained and modules have a low dependency on other sub-systems to realise their performance and function. For example, the ALS referred to the current transfer plan not including a self-contained testable module. Parts of the system function were completed in one city and other parts in another city. "Either we go for it fully or not at all – we cannot go halfway". Preferences were stated for organising along the subsidiary's model of leaving the system integration at Headquarters in Europe and have integral module development organised at other company sites. The ambition of some members of the ALS was to transfer everything to the overseas subsidiary, but there were two incompatible forces operating against that idea – a systems engineering force and the force of the needs and wishes of the people. Each time at the point of transfer, there would be further delay. There was no credible transfer plan; it could not be discussed because none of the 1200 engineers believed in it.

The ALS (one of six ALSs) discussed the state of paralysis on the transfer question in the organisation. No one seemed willing or able to decide and the paralysis trickled down into the organisation, leaving team leaders and others to sort out technical and relationship problems as they arose, which they could not do because there was no agreed framework. Interpersonal rivalries added to the difficulties because some people objected to be line managed by certain other people and senior management refused to face the problem and make decisions.

The ALS agreed: (i) to research the problems posed by the re-organisation of manufacturing. They decided to ask people in their lines of accountability and departments for their views on the Headquarters-subsidiary relationship, the problems associated with the acquisition and their thinking about possible solutions; and (ii) that the Board too was a 'prisoner' of a 'stuck' dynamic and the ALS agreed to approach the Board for discussions on the Headquarters-subsidiary relationship. (iii) They agreed to report back at the next ALS.

The following meeting of the ALS heard a status report of the work transfer from the European Headquarters to the overseas subsidiary. All those who had been involved in the research noted that the lessons about the dynamics on inter-group functioning learned from the previous ALS meetings had been helpful in their research. Those reporting back said it had become clear to them that it was impossible to expect to obtain 100% clear-cut directions, nor were they requested to provide 100% clear-cut answers when dealing with cutting edge technology or the subsequent organisational impacts. A calm descended on the ALS as they and their stakeholders realised it would take time and close collaborative effort in the matrix along both vertical hierarchical and horizontal collegial lines for the transfer to succeed. The question *"What do we expect from ourselves?"* would drive the ALS towards clarity; they said it was pointless waiting till they got it served up!

Representatives of Headquarters and the subsidiary, who previously had been at loggerheads with each other, reflected on their learning in the ALS and how it had helped them apply principles of surveying, listening, reviewing, collaborating, analysing and taking action in their discussions on company strategic direction with the Board and in their consultations with their staff members on the distribution of work between the subsidiary and Headquarters. As a result, discussions proceeded to be held widely on both sites on the status of work distribution, remaining unclarities and been cleared up, and a way forward was found to resolve the timing needs of both sites. Proposals were discussed and accepted and later confirmed more widely throughout both organisations. Members of the ALS agreed to follow up decisions by creating a monitoring group that would last for as long as the work distribution processes, defining criteria and meeting pre-conditions were active.

Members of the ALS exchanged ideas, wrote up notes and comments on the merger of the subsidiary and Headquarters and the subsequent management of the combined organisation and the cost and value creation that would accrue from an integrated organisation. A presentation based on their research and dissemination would be made at the next Whole Community Conference, involving up to 120 people.

The ALS asked the Board to nominate a 'champion' to sponsor the activities of the ASL.

Members of the ALS spoke about how, through resistance and conflicts with their consultants, the participants had come through after they had lost their focus so that it could now represent the whole community on issues of the acquisition, integration and cooperation and manufacture. The participants thought back to how they had formed themselves into a working group in the Open Forum through which the leadership development programme had kicked off. The ASL agreed that it had shifted gradually towards discussing topics that they had found difficult to share. They agreed that their report to the Board did not have to be about 'hard' issues, i.e. – improving engineering processes, but instead, it could be about 'soft' issues, i.e. – how people work with others organisationally and inter-organisationally. The group struggled and broke through from the tangible, practical and technical to how they worked together internally in the company and externally with the subsidiary. The consultants encouraged the ALS to create an inter-active learning session with its audience at the upcoming Whole Community Conference to focus on why so many meetings had been characterised by avoiding discussions on sensitive topics, such as how we work together – our successes and our problematics. In discussions with the Board, both the executives and the ALS agreed to disagree where issues and opinions could not be reconciled.

Theory

The dynamic in the ALS moved from basic assumption dependency ("we can't decide until the Board decides") to basic assumption fight-flight ("you guys – the subsidiary referring to headquarters and headquarters referring to the subsidiary – just don't get it. How can we trust you?"). At first, the dominance of these two basic assumptions prevented work from being achieved, but, through interpretation by the consultants, as the ALS became more reflective it was able to develop a stronger Work Group mentality. At first, the ALS retreated from the boundaries of the company, retreating into themselves, becoming a closed sub-system. Regular forceful meetings, reminders of their responsibilities overall to the company helped the ALS realise that as a sub-system it was meant to relate on a number of levels simultaneously – to each other as representatives of diverse parts of company; to the other ALSs in the programme; to the Board (their bosses) and to the community as a whole. Membership of the ALS with its commitment to relating between the ALSs across their boundaries helped it see that it was a microcosm of the whole system of which it was a part; that the way they related to each other mirrored the way the formal system related to its parts. The approach of the project was to regard the ALSs as 'temporary learning institutions' and ensuring that their learning was transferable and transferred to the formal system through regular meetings with members of the Board. Greater ownership of the unconscious dynamic processes in the formal system was available mainly in the 'temporary system' and they could be worked with more easily there. The basic assumptions became clear in the ALSs where they could be seen to be the same basic assumption processes in the formal system, but which the formal system could not get hold of.

Basic assumption mentality in groups

Bion (1961) claimed that in basic assumption mentality, the group's behaviour is directed at attempting to meet the unconscious needs of its members by reducing anxiety and internal conflicts. There are three basic assumptions giving rise to specific complex feelings, thoughts and behaviour: basic assumption dependency, basic assumption fight-flight and basic assumption pairing.

a **Basic assumption dependency (b/aD)**
   In b/aD, the group behaves as if its task is to only provide for the satisfaction and needs and wishes of its members. The leader is expected to look after, protect and sustain the members of the group, to make them feel good and not to face them with the demands of the group's real purpose. Dependency on the leader inhibits growth and development.

b **Basic assumption fight/flight (b/aF/F)**
   The assumption here is that the group experiences danger or 'enemy', which should either be attacked or fled from. However, the group is not prepared to do either. Members look to the leader to devise some appropriate action; their task is merely to follow. For instance, instead of considering how best to organise its work, a team may spend most of the time in meetings worrying about rumours of organisational change. This provides a spurious sense of togetherness while also serving to avoid facing the difficulties of the work itself. Alternatively, such a group may spend its time protesting angrily without planning any specific action to deal with the perceived threat to its service.

c **Basic assumption pairing (b/aP)**
   Basic assumption pairing is based on the collective and unconscious belief that, whatever the actual problems and needs of the group, a future event will solve them. The group behaves as if pairing between two members within the group, or perhaps between the leader of the group and some external person, will bring about salvation. The group is focused entirely on the future but as defence against the difficulties of the present. For example, for a work team, this may take the form of an idea that improved premises would provide an answer to the group's problems, or that all will be well after the next away-day. The group does not want to work on present problems but only in sustaining a vague hope as a way out of its present difficulties.

   Marion McCollom Hampton (1999), in Organisation in Depth, has pointed out how Bion's theory has been developed through the identification of other types of basic assumption groups. Turquet in 1974 made an additional assumption, which has been added to Bion's original findings; Oneness (also referred to as We-ness), which draws its inspiration from Freud's discussion of the 'oceanic' feeling. Lawrence et al. (1996) hypothesised a fifth basic assumption, the basic assumption 'Me-ness'.

d **One-ness (b/aO)**
   One-ness is also referred to as 'we-ness'. Turquet describes this basic assumption as occurring when "members seek to join a powerful union with an omnipotent force, surrendering self for passive participation, thus experiencing existence, well-being and wholeness" (Turquet, 1974, Pg. 357). Lawrence, Bain and Gould (1996a) added that group members experience existence only through membership of the group. Thus, by being passive and sublimating the self to the union of the group, the individual experiences existence and wholeness. This type of behaviour

is typical when a group is striving towards cohesion and synergy (Banet and Hayden, 1977; Koortzen and Cilliers, 2002).

e **Me-ness (b/aM)**
According to Lawrence this is almost the opposite of the basic assumption 'one-ness', a denial of the existence of the group because all groups are seen as impure, contaminating and oppressive (Lawrence, et al., 1996). This basic assumption is about a retreat into individualism. This retreat, according to Koortzen and Cilliers (2002), is an attempt to avoid the outer world (reality) and find solace in the inner world. The tacit assumption of the members is that the group is to be a non-group. In other words, only the individual is important and the group is of no importance (Koortzen and Cilliers, 2002). Lawrence, et al. (1996) suggested that within this assumption, there is the denial and exclusion of the outer environment and a focus on the individual's own inner reality. These additional developments are still being debated and clinical and consulting evidence practice will hopefully confirm or disconfirm their viability as working concepts.

Conditions for success

The work group mentality and basic assumption group mentality

Bion identified two core processes in the life of a group, namely the basic assumptions mentality and the work group mentality. Both processes are operating simultaneously in the group. The work group mentality is engaged with reality and orientated to achieving the primary task. But as we have seen from the descriptions above, the basic assumption mentality is habitually unconscious and avoiding working on the task. A group in basic assumption mode can be described as off task. The basic assumption mentality is a defensive process to avoid facing painful and conflicted feelings and thoughts in the group. Bion describes 'Work-group mentality' (Bion, 1961, Pg. 173) as the disposition and dynamics that characterise the life of a group, to the extent that its members are able to manage their shared tensions, anxieties and relationships, in order to function effectively; the outcome is a 'capacity for realistic hard work' (Pg. 157). Whereas 'Basic-assumption mentality' (Pg. 173), by contrast, describes the state of a group that is taken over by strong emotions – anxiety, fear, hate, love, hope, anger, guilt, depression (Pg. 166) – and has, as a result, lost touch with its purpose, and become caught up in an 'unconscious group collusion' (Eisold, 2005, Pg. 359); the outcome is 'stagnation' (Bion, 1961, Pg. 128).

French and Simpson (2010) summarised Bion's thoughts on work group and basic assumptions as follows:

> central to what follows is the idea, that these two mentalities always co-exist: "there is no Work Group without a Basic Assumption Group

running concurrently" (Gosling, 1994: 5; his capitals). As a result, neither is stable, let alone permanent, and there is always the potential for movement in a group's emotional life. Bion argued that this movement can occur at two levels. In basic-assumption mentality, "shifts and changes from one [assumption] to another" (Bion, 1961: 160) are sometimes rapid, with "two or three changes in an hour", but at other times spread out, with "the same basic assumption ... dominant for months on end" (p. 154). At this level, therefore, individual basic assumptions 'alternate' (p. 96) or 'displace each other' (p. 188) – but the underlying basic-assumption state remains unchanged. At a more fundamental level, however, there can also be a shift in the dominance of one mentality over the other, that is, a shift from basic-assumption mentality to work-group mentality, or the reverse.

Armstrong (2005c) contends that working with Bion's framework requires constant attention to this paradoxical tension, always recognising that these mentalities "are co-dependent, each operating as a silent, unconscious complement to the other" (Pg. 145). Bion argued that work-group mentality can never exist in a pure form: it is always "pervaded by basic-assumption phenomena" (Bion, 1961, Pg. 154); but also that work-group functioning is not, as one might expect, always 'obstructed' or 'diverted' by basic-assumption mentality. There are also occasions when it can be 'assisted' (Pg. 146) or 'furthered' by the basic assumptions (Pg. 188). Miller, for example, suggests that "fight-flight may be appropriate for a sales team and dependency for a hospital; any other basic assumption would interfere with the task and generate a dysfunctional group culture" (Miller, 1998, Pg. 1504; see also Gosling, 1994; Stokes, 1994, Pg. 25–26).

As for the basic assumptions, Bion believed that only one can dominate at any one time:

> The emotional state associated with each basic assumption excludes the emotional states proper to the other two basic assumptions' (Bion, *1961*, Pg. 120). He described the excluded or 'inoperative' basic assumptions as 'the victims of a conspiracy' between work-group mentality and the 'operating basic assumption' (p. 102). Alternatively, a group may become caught up in what Bion called the 'dual' of the basic assumption, where, for example, a dependent group behaves as if it is now the leader who is dependent on them: 'I do not nourish or sustain the group so they nourish and sustain me.

Lawrence, et al. (1996) describe a W group as one:

> in which all participants are engaged with the primary task because they have taken full cognisance of its purpose. They cooperate because it is their will. They search for knowledge through using their experiences.

They probe realities in a scientific way by hypothesis testing and are aware of the processes that will further learning and development. Essentially, the W group mobilises sophisticated mental activity on the part of its members, which they demonstrate through their maturity. They manage the psychic boundary between their inner and outer worlds. They strive to manage themselves in their roles as members of the W group. Furthermore, the participants can hold in mind an idea of wholeness and interconnectedness with other systems, and they use their skills to understand the inner world of the group, as a system, in relation to the external reality of the environment. In a W group the participants can comprehend the psychic, political, and spiritual relatedness in which they are participating and are co-creating. The W group is an open system. The major inputs are people with minds who can transform experiences into insight and understanding.

Basic assumptions

David Armstrong

"The Dreaming Consultant"
In Memory of W. Gordon Lawrence
Israel 2014

The kind of question that interests me is "what has our preoccupation with Basic Assumptions led us to neglect"? One answer, I think, is "the deeper dynamics that underpin Bion's 'Work Group'".

If one goes back to Bion's early war time work, before *Experiences in Groups*, (Leaderless Groups, the Northfield Experiment, Recruitment Nomination), his focus is much less on the 'regressive' end of the spectrum, much more on his belief in and commitment to drawing out the group's capacity for recovering a sense of internal agency (Armstrong, 2014). This, he sees, as compromised not only by the group's own internal dynamics but also by an organisational and societal or community collusion: "some sort of equilibrium of insincerity", he says. "achieved by patients, doctors and community alike" (Bion, 1948, Pg. 181). It is this latter that constitutes the regressive pull that Bion is later to explore in *Experiences in Groups*.

The paradox is, though, that the originality of Bion's dissection of the nature of this regressive pull, his account of the basic assumptions and their dynamics and its extraordinary hold on successive generations of practitioners, has tended to draw attention away from the countervailing developmental push behind W, the work group, and hence the deeper sources of the group's capacity for internal agency.

I don't think that Bion himself was altogether free from this tendency; maybe a consequence of his post-war analysis with Melanie Klein and/or the growing significance of his experience with more psychotic patients.

Recall that for Bion, Ba's and W (basic assumptions and work group) are terms deployed to capture and define two aspects or modes of mental activity identifiable in but not necessarily confined to all group life and always in interplay, just as conscious and unconscious processes are always in interplay. Moreover, even in *Experiences in Groups*, despite its more regressive focus, it is noticeable how Bion continually stresses, as he writes, "I think one of the striking things about a group is, that despite the influence of the Ba's it is the W group that triumphs in the long run". Hence his disagreement with Freud that "groups have never thirsted after truth, only illusion" (Bion, 1961, Pg. 135).

Elsewhere he notices how in his experience "the psychological structure of the work group is very powerful and it is noteworthy that it survives with a vitality that would suggest that the fears that the work group will be swamped by the emotional states proper to the basic assumptions are quite out of proportion". Yet, when he first describes the work group he makes it sound curiously bloodless as if it were a purely intentional object created for a specific purpose and structured in accordance with rational means/ends relations:

> When a group meets it meets for a specific task and in most human activities today cooperation has to be achieved by sophisticated means. Rules of procedure are adopted; there is usually an established administrative machinery operated by officials who are recognizable as such by the rest of the group and so on.
>
> (Bion, 1961, Pg. 98–99)

Maybe the 'and so on' hints at a short circuit in Bion's thinking here because nothing less 'vital' can surely be imagined than this oddly bureaucratic description. Later, Bion goes some way to repair this impression, distinguishing three elements in the mental phenomena of W that, he says, are linked together just as the emotions in the basic assumption group are linked together. These are:

- The idea of development rather than full equipment of instinct.
- The idea of the value of a rational or scientific approach to development.
- Acceptance of the validity of learning by experience (Bion, 1961, Pg. 98–99).

Bion suggests that what underlies the bringing together of these elements and evokes the work group is "the development of thought designed for translation into action, since action inevitably involves contact with reality and reality compels regard for truth and therefore scientific method". I think, however, that this description tends rather to show its age, begging what will later become important and contested issues, about the location and nature of 'reality' or the limitations and scope of a 'rational or scientific approach'.

It is as if W is still being characterised too much in terms of ego functioning, without reference to maybe deeper, if not instinctive, at least basic human drives, operating unconsciously.

I want to suggest, albeit hesitantly, two such drives, both of which and particularly (maybe only) the first were to become increasingly prominent in Bion's later, more psychoanalytic writing:

1. A latent awareness of, curiosity about and search for truth (an offshoot of Melanie Klein's 'epistemophilic instinct') in relation to both internal and external reality. In *Experiences in Groups*, Bion sees this unconsciously driven commitment as itself an element that fuels and accounts for both

the hostility of the group to interpretation and the eventual way in which interpretation can manage to make a difference.
2   What Jonathan Lear refers to as a 'basic fact about us': that we are 'finite erotic creatures', finite in the sense of being vulnerable, subject to limitation and loss; erotic in the Platonic sense of a "reaching out to the world (and to others) in yearning, longing, admiration and desire for that which (however mistakenly) we take to be valuable, beautiful and good" (Lear, 2008, Pg. 119–120). (One might think of this as an enlarged concept of 'attachment'.)

I am not suggesting that such an extension or reworking of Bion's characterisation of W shifts the way in which we may conceive of the basic assumptions as such. I am suggesting that it may profoundly affect the ways in which we understand the processes that energise the emergence of basic assumptions as they surface in group, organisational and social life.

One might think of the relation between Ba's and W on the lines of Freud's distinction between life and death instincts, or in my terms, 'developmental push' and 'regressive pull'. To understand the tension between them, one needs to scrutinise, acknowledge and do justice to the unconscious claims of each; as to just what it is that triggers this tension, externally and/or internally.

And herein lies the rub in respect of the practice of Group Relations. For, as many practitioners see it, the whole purpose of Group Relations conferences and events is to elicit regressive processes, make them available for scrutiny. Correspondingly, the more developmental side gets a look in, one might suggest, only in members' readiness to stay the course. As one practitioner recently put it:

> the Leicester model strips away ordinary social defences that keep experience of the primitive stratum of group life out of awareness. Then, being able to observe and interpret these forces is where the learning resides and where the W group manifests… What makes our method so effective and so unique is (i) the razor-sharp focus on authority; (ii) the regression induced by the framework—learning about unconscious processes and irrationality through direct experience of them.
>
> (Krantz, 2014)

(Note here the elision between 'unconscious', 'primitive' and 'irrationality', which, in my view, drains the 'work group' of its vitality as it drains the 'unconscious' of its creativity.)

One might think of Social Dreaming as turning things upside down, that is, as bracketing out, or rather shifting the focus away from the regressive undertow of Group Relations, in order to release a more developmental, creative and playful aspect of unconscious life. As Gordon Lawrence was to put it in one of his later papers:

> Followers of the Tavistock tradition have always believed in the existence of the unconscious in social systems; nevertheless it comes across as negative and joyless …. Practitioners can become blind to the positive aspects of the unconscious, (as) the source of thinking and creativity.
>
> (Lawrence, 2003, Pg. 621)

The other side of Krantz's 'uniqueness', perhaps?

Sustaining the results

To maintain a work group mentality is the main aim of a consultative intervention. To achieve this, a consultant should be mindful of the powerful sway of the basic assumption mentality in the group. The keeping in mind of the primary task and how a group will fall into off task activity if overwhelmed by basis assumption processes is an important task of the consultant. The consultant can observe and comment on the group's basic assumption behaviour and how off task it may be. This may then help the group maintain its work group mentality. But groups will always be susceptible to basic assumption behaviour as it is the unconscious life of the group.

Sensitising organisational members to group processes is another way to sustain learning. Sometimes, running a short Group Relations Conference internal to the organisation can help open people eyes and minds to the complexity of group life. These Group Relations Conferences can be designed around a task that is relevant to the organisations change issues, thus aiding the change process and simultaneously helping people understand how groups operate at two levels, the work group mentality and the basic assumption level. Or staff may wish to attend an external Group Relations Conference such as the Leicester Conference.

Burning questions

To interpret or not to interpret the group dynamic? Basic assumption activities, how should one proceed?

Groups working on the primary task often get into problems which hamper with and even stop them getting to grips with their stated aim. Groups are certainly engaging in two tasks at once: one, the maintenance of the stated task of the group, which is accurately regarded and necessitates its members, their conscious collaboration and the use of their intellect and patience; the other, the fulfilment of emotional needs that are hidden and largely unrecognised. If the work of the group is genuinely hindered by basic assumption activity, then scrutiny of this situation may facilitate the group getting back to its task. But it may be more useful to build on the group's aspiration to have a consultant who can help them stay on task. This intervention by the consultant makes use of the sophisticated basic assumption dependency. In deciding to focus on the 'here and now' problems in the group there are various issues to consider. Does it take the group away from work group mentality by encouraging regression? Does it change the way the consultant is perceived and experienced in the group? If the consultant can keep in mind the core task of encouraging on-task activity, then the group can via introjection take in and identify with a consultant who can stay in role. Here the consultant needs to manage the boundaries. It is worth keeping in mind that unless it is a study group or therapy group then its primary purpose is not the examination of its communication system. This is only of interest if it is hindering the pursuit of the primary task. Helping the group regain ownership of its primary task is probably the most important function of the consultant.

Summary

When using group interventions in organisation change programmes, hypotheses should be made in a supportive manner. The hope is that they will encourage reflection and with some small degree of anxiety promote change and learning. But participants should not be so anxious that they become unskilled in their roles. The wish is to combine thinking and feeling to better understand the groups that they are members of.

Exercise

1. What basic assumption processes tend to interfere with your work group?
2. Which basic assumption do you think predominates?
3. What do you think would help the group stay on task?
4. What valencies do you see being mobilised within individual members of your group?

7 Working with groups I

With David Armstrong

> A self-managed team has the capacity and authority to make key decisions about the way it does its work — how it sets its goals, how it holds itself accountable, even defining why the team exists. Such a team has a sense of engagement; a greater sense of responsibility and its members have a higher stake in their mission; their buy-in becomes that much greater.
>
> (Jeff Russell: https://russellconsultinginc.com/about-russell-consulting/staff/)

The application of systems psychodynamics theory to teams and working groups

Why groups are important aspects of organisational life?

Significant psychological needs are met by membership of a group, for instance, a sense of identity, affection and closeness, achievement, recognition of skills, being rewarded for one's contributions to the group. Group membership provides a sense of belonging; being included is a crucial aspect of individual's membership of a group and the satisfactions that derive therefrom. Membership of groups also provides opportunities to influence and exercise power and take up authority. An organisation is made up of groups of people; these groups are the working sub-units of organisations which mostly form the focus of systems psychodynamics-oriented consultants. Most activities of the organisation require coordination through the operation of group and inter-group working. Therefore, consultants need an understanding of the nature of groups if they hope to influence the behaviour of their organisational clients. The literature and research on groups is wide and diverse. Here we are going to focus on the systems psychodynamics set of theories and practices. The power of the group was shown clearly in the Hawthorn experiments at the Western Electric Company (Roethlisberger and Dickson, 1939). It was shown that the working group developed patterns of informal social relations and codes and practices (norms) of what constituted proper group behaviour.

DOI: 10.4324/9781003181507-13

The systems approach to organisations and management also recognizes the importance of groups in influencing behaviour at work. The concept of the organisation as a sociotechnical system and the organisation as part of its environment is concerned with the interaction between the psychological, social and environmental factors, as well as structural and technical requirements. Trist identified how technological change in the coal mining industry had brought about changes in the social structures of the miners' groups (Trist et al., 1963). Groups, therefore, help shape the work patterns of organisations, and the attitudes and behaviours of group members to their jobs. From the coal mining studies, important developments emerge in relation to work design and job enrichment as a form of work organisation based on self-managed work groups and team working. This involves a sociotechnical approach with technological processes, production methods and the way in which work is carried out and integrated with the social system of the organisation, including informal group structure. Individual members of self-managing groups appear to have higher levels of job satisfaction, although the effectiveness of self-managed groups appears to be less efficient because decision-making takes more time, but overall, research shows that in the longer-term quality improves and remains at a higher level than leader-led groups (Cohen and Ledford, 1994).

Why are self-managed teams so popular?

Sagoe (1994) argues that self-managed teams are workers who have been organized into teams based on relatively complete task functions. They make decisions on a wide range of issues, often including such traditional management prerogatives as:

1. Who will work on which machines or work operations?
2. How to address interpersonal difficulties within the group?
3. How to resolve quality problems?
4. Also, these teams usually consist of 5–15 employees, who:
   a Produce an entire product instead of sub-units
   b Learn all tasks and rotate from job to job
   c Take over vacation scheduling, order materials, etc.

Such groups are self-regulating and work without direct supervision.

From these definitions, it can be determined that self-managed teams are relatively small groups of employees given substantial responsibility for planning, organizing, scheduling and production of work products or services. Self-managed teams, however, are more than just another way of directing groups. The concept, according to Mathusamy et al. (2005), involves nothing less than, the complete restructuring of the jobs that people do. Mathusamy et al.'s (2005) conceptual model of innovation dynamics in self-managing work teams suggests that the presence of self-leadership at the team level enhances innovative behaviour, and consequently, team performance. The literature supports the view that employees that are empowered and autonomous have a greater degree of control over their work. This degree of control means that employees feel comfortable in their role to be innovative in their own work environment (Thamhain, 1990; Tang, 1999; Zwetsloot, 2001; Amar, 2004; Mostafa, 2005; Muthusamy et al., 2005; Nystrom et al., 2002; cited by Smith et al., 2008).

The objectives of using self-managed teams are to improve the efficiency and effectiveness of specific tasks. This approach achieves these objectives by having self-managed team members look beyond their individual task concerns to the needs of specific groups and the entire organization. The group assumes greater autonomy and responsibility for the effective performance of its work. Key features of the self-managed work group include the following:

1 Specific goals (the "What") are set for the group but members decide the best means (the "How") by which these goals are to be achieved.
2 Group members have greater freedom and choice and wider discretion over the planning, execution and control of their own work.
3 Collectively members of the group have the necessary variety of expertise and skills to successfully undertake the tasks of the group.
4 The level of external supervision is reduced, and the role of the supervisor becomes more one of giving advice and support to the group.
5 Feedback and evaluation are related to the performance of the group-as-a-whole in addition to individuals.

The introduction of self-managed work groups may result in a marked reduction in stress (Hall and Savery, 1987). Our understanding of the importance of group membership and group dynamics to the organisation and the individual members highlights the need for the systems psychodynamics consultant to have a sophisticated understanding about group processes and how to intervene effectively in systems of groups.

Here we need to acknowledge that there is a convergence of psychodynamic theories, social systems theories and group relations theories to produce an overarching systems psychodynamics theory and its application to organisational consultancy. The aims of the early scientific pioneers in this field to combine conceptual frameworks that are usually segregated still holds true today. This 'integration of the social sciences' to make a contribution to new systems psychodynamics theory and practice is not easy, and often the temptation is to stick to one set of practices and theories in order to manage the complexity of contemporary organisations and the complex environments they inhabit. We still believe that it is a worthwhile ambition to attempt to cover the integration of psychoanalysis, field theory, social anthropology, social psychology, engineering and mathematics. This inevitably is a task that is never completed. It is through the work of academics, consultant practitioners, managers and members of organisations and their capacity to reflect on their experiences that help develop and refresh this process.

The convergence of two bodies of practical theory and theoretical approaches, i.e. 'sociotechnical systems' and 'group relations' – led to the formation of an overarching integrated theory of systems psychodynamics (Rice, 1963; Miller and Rice, 1967; Trist and Murray, 1990, 1993). The sociotechnical systems approach to job and organisational design considers interconnections between psychological, technical and economic factors alongside the inter-relationships between workflows, tasks and roles.

The group relations approach applies the object relations school of psychoanalysis, field psychology and social systems theory to the understanding of small groups, inter-group relations, large group and institutional dynamics. Sociotechnical and group relations theories, when applied to management development and organisational change, can be better understood through leaders and managers attending group relations conferences in the Tavistock tradition on the study of authority, leadership and organisation. The link between the two theories offers practical solutions to organisational problems via the use of systems psychodynamics informed consultancy. Ideas about 'anxiety and defences against anxiety', 'role', 'authority', 'boundary' and 'task' take on special meanings and are pivotal to both sociotechnical systems and group relations theories because attention is paid simultaneously to the structure of tasks and motivational dynamics of individuals and groups. Concepts and elements that make up the systems psychodynamics paradigm may give the impression that they have a discrete and finite boundary but this would be to miss the point of the nature of the paradigm. The systems psychodynamics paradigm from its early history has been an interdisciplinary field. Researchers and practitioners have attempted to integrate the developments of group relations theory, psychoanalysis and systems (open) theory and the integration of these primary concepts within the systems psychodynamics paradigm for effective organisational consultancy. For the sake of exposition of the theories, they are presented as discrete entities, but the application of the systems psychodynamics model brings the theories together as a way of thinking-in-practice.

Within systems theory, organisations are viewed as open systems and the organisation is understood as a social system. The sociotechnical model of organisations is the primary model for understanding organisational design. Systems theory is concerned with boundaries and their regulation. To engage with the organisation, the consultant needs to understand its structure. Connected to the organisational design will be an appreciation of its primary task – what it must do in order to survive. Consideration of the organisational design and its boundary systems of control and regulation will involve an assessment of how it manages its inputs and outputs to its environment. Within the systems theory framework, boundary maintenance and regulation and task analysis are aspects of the organisations functioning that will be relevant to a systems psychodynamics consultant. A consultant will monitor the organisation's functions and direction regarding its primary task. How the organisation relates to those inside and outside the group or organisation will provide important diagnostic material on organisational functioning. The examination of how the organisation pursues its aims and primary task will involve thinking about how roles are defined and taken up. Role definition may well need some inquiry on inter-organisational relations and how sub-systems within the organisation relate to each other and their degree of dependency and autonomy. Systems theory, as we have stated, involves thinking about an organisation's conversion process, the converting of inputs to outputs, linked to a primary task – the task that must be performed to survive.

Working with large groups

A large group intervention is a participative meeting, conference or event where a large number of participants (10–2,000) comprising a diverse cross-section of an organisation's stakeholders come together to work on real organisational issues of strategic importance to help bring about fast change. According to Rice (1965), since World War II, many institutional conferences have adopted a pattern whereby speakers address the whole conference, and then discussion of the lectures takes place in small groups, which subsequently reassemble in plenary session to report back to the total membership. In 1947, at a conference run jointly by the Tavistock Institute and the Industrial Welfare Society, this technique was modified in that there were few speakers, and they only set themes, leaving members to decide the content of the conference. Many variations are now common; in some, the small groups are given a specific question or different ones for different groups; in others, usually the larger conferences, sections have their own speakers. 'Buzz' sessions (in which members form small units of from two to six persons without moving out of the conference room), role-playing, socio-drama, brains trust, panel discussions, and debates are among techniques that have been used with success. All are attempts to establish organisational mechanisms that will allow an individual member to make their views heard without exposing them to the difficulty of addressing a large group.

Work with the whole system

In contrast to most early work in organisational development (OD) that had focused on small groups (French and Bell, 1995), Emery and Trist developed a theory of sociotechnical systems that emphasized the importance of work with a whole system to accomplish change. They developed what later came to be recognized as the first truly large group intervention to enable a large number of organizational members (from two merged British aircraft engine makers; see Bunker and Alban, 2014, Pg. 409) to work together "to consider what kind of new company they wanted to become". Emery and Trist (1960a) eventually labelled this process of searching for a desired future as the Search Conference, and it went on to be developed as a formal large group intervention (Emery and Purser, 1996).

The importance of considering the whole organization began to be articulated more fully in the 1970s when Beckhard and Harris (1987) started to write systematically about intervening in whole systems, an insight that was later developed by Weisbord (1987). He and Janoff used this in the development of a large group intervention called Future Search (Weisbord and Janoff, 1995).

Large group interventions enable hundreds, even thousands, of people to gather for the purpose of planning strategic change and exploring its implications. Having all stakeholders together in the same room creates a broader information base, improves cross-functional working, facilitates simultaneous planning and implementation, and maximises 'whole system' (or organisational) learning.

A large group intervention is more than a mass attendance meeting or conference. It is part of a wider strategic process that includes pre-event work (designing the intervention, often by a design team that is a microcosm of the large group), and post-event activities such as implementing the plans, monitoring progress and modifying the plans if necessary. In some cases, a series of events may be called for. Regardless of the method employed, interventions are always customised to meet the circumstances.

There are at least 20 different large group intervention methods (Bunker and Alban, 1997).

Martin Leith (2004), in his Guide to Large Group Intervention Methods, points out that meetings are an essential part of organisational life, particularly those convened to plan the organisation's future. He argues that most business meetings, perhaps as many as 70%, are considered by participants to be unproductive.

Search conferences

Search Conferences were developed in the 1960s by Eric Trist and Fred Emery of the Tavistock Institute of Human Relations based on open systems principles. The Search Conference methodology has evolved over the years since Emery and Trist reported on the Barford Conference the original Search Conference, in 1960 (Trist and Emery, 1960a). Search Conferences pre-date Future Search by more than 20 years. Although the two methods share certain key features, there are several significant differences.

A Search Conference is frequently used as a 'front-end' planning process prior to a complete redesign of the system aimed at making it democratic and participative. The Participative Design Workshop process, which is closely related to the Search Conferences method, may directly follow the conference or be an integral part of it (Emery and Emery, 1993; Weisbord and Janoff, 1995; Emery and Purser, 1996).

Future search

Ronald Lippitt and Eva Schindler-Rainman's developed large-scale community futures conferences held in North America during the 1970s. Lippitt and Schindler-Rainman developed the method to get the whole system in the room and focus on the future, not on problems and conflicts. Trist and Emery saw the importance of thinking globally before acting locally and of having people manage their own planning (Weisbord et al., 1992). There is a commitment to democratic ideals and their embodiment of the 'action research' tradition of Kurt Lewin (1948). Future Search looks at a progression of events from the past to the present and into the future, whereas Search Conferences are concerned with finding the best fit between the system and its environment. In a Search Conference, more of the work is done in the large group. Future Search has members of the wider system (external stakeholders such as customers, suppliers, parent company) take part in the entire event. Full participation in a Search Conference is restricted to members of the system in focus. Although stakeholders from outside the system may be invited to participate in the first part of the conference, it is more usual for information from these people to be obtained through a pre-conference environmental scan. The Search Conference method places more emphasis on the rationalisation of conflict than Future Search.

People, whole systems and planning

Future Search is a learning laboratory for getting everybody involved in improving their own system.

Future Searches enable people to experience and accept polarities and to bridge barriers of culture, class, age, gender, ethnicity, power, status and hierarchy by working as peers on tasks of mutual concern. The Future Search process interrupts the human tendency to repeat old patterns – fighting, running away, complaining, blaming or waiting for others to fix things. And it gives everyone a chance to express their highest ideals. Instead of trying to change the world or each other, Future Search aims to change the conditions under which people interact.

Case illustration

Introjection, introjective identification and search conferences

The concepts of introjection and introjective identification, the companion concepts to projection and projective identification, have long interested this writer because they help to understand the relationship between consultant and client and, through those concepts, gain a deeper perspective of the client's issues than traditional methods allow. Put simply, the client in the telling of their story, places (projects) pressure on the consultant to accept (introject) their version of the story so that the consultant agrees with the client's version of the organisational dilemmas being faced. The problem is that other people in the organisation, whom the consultant meets, in the telling of their stories, also place pressure on the consultant to believe that their version of the story is the true and proper one. The strength of the projections and introjections and the different levels of authority that accompany them can throw consultants off course or find they are getting caught up in taking sides for and against different people in the organisation. What may be happening here is that different aspects of the problem are split up into fragments and individuals and sub-systems identify with the fragments and hold them to be a true idea of what is happening. This can lead to the consultant team identifying with the different projected fragments. To avoid this splitting, the consultants may initiate a Search Conference that deliberately allows for diverse points of view, opinions, perspectives and judgements to be expressed, leading to the creation of a small number of clusters of core organisational issues on which work in small groups can begin at once. A Search conference respects the multiple views of as many segments of the organisation as possible, leading to the construction of a workable framework of exploration and constructive strategic debate and planning of up to six or seven core issues that the organisation must face if its future business development is to succeed. Bringing the whole system together in this way enables a more coherent view of the split projections.

One such Search conference occurred in an assignment with a global manufacturer of High-Tec lithography technology which turned out to be difficult yet extremely rewarding because the review and rebuilding process over a period of 18 months with the organisation's top 120 people led to resolving a billion-euro technological problem. About 70 top leaders/managers participated in the 2-day Search conference and came up with 100 practical suggestions as core issues they thought the organisation needed to address. Through a process of debate, argument, negotiation and compromise, the 100 ideas were whittled down to 6 over-arching organisational strategic dilemmas: the value (supply) chain, unlocking value (of the company), new product development, diversification, expanding leadership, partnership collaboration, and instituting a multiplier effect. Some disappointment was felt because the pet topics of some people were not considered to be major dilemmas. Everyone signed up to serve in one group and focus on one 'dilemma' of their interest and contracted to meet once a month, sometimes, more, with consultants. Part of the contractual arrangement was to report back regularly to the Executive committee of the company on their progress, but also to negotiate from their leadership roles with the executive committee the urgency of the need for collective change. Among the core issues was one connected with the development of new technologies for creating Artificial Intelligence and a digitalised rapid means of international communications. For this to occur, relationships between many suppliers and innovators had to be re-defined, and bottlenecks smoothed out across departmental, professional, organisational and national boundaries, by no means a simple goal to achieve, given the influences of strong personalities and embedded cultures in different parts of the global company and its eco-system.

During the assignment, I got ill. On a visit to a physician, I was asked: "Why do you think you got ill?" I was somewhat blind-sided by this question as it seemed the doctor was deliberately linking my mind to my body. My thoughts turned to the concept of introjection – what aspects of the client's culture, way of being, had I taken into myself to make me ill? I explained to my doctor how I thought I was over-identified with the client's global ambitions and dilemmas and simultaneously had introjected the client's injurious competitiveness, hostility, mistrust and humiliating behaviour. My physician said it was plausible – my loving over-identification with the client blinded me from my introjection of their noxious atmospheres as our work uncovered the destructive aspects of the client's functioning and their interactions with people that it could not/would not see for itself.

I reflected on the impact of my consultancy with the client and the client's impact on me. My colleague frequently challenged me on my tendency to get caught up in a heroic role providing salvation to dysfunctional inter-personal relationships, unconsciously offering myself as (i) an alternative better leader or (ii) a sacrificial lamb. She added that by internalising the client's projection of a wish for a perfect product achieved through flawless leadership, I had enacted the ultimate sacrifice of myself so that the company, freed from any guilt feelings over the negative effects of its product on people and society, could push forward with new unheard-of technologies in their quest to free humankind from the 'chains of reality'. This could be understood as the messianic dynamic in the organisation with which I had identified and which was also mirrored in the consultant team dynamic, each one identifying with different parts of the system.

Naturally, throughout the assignment, the consulting team asked ourselves whether our work was useful or not. Some of our clients thought we were useful in opening conversations to the level they never had before; others felt our approach did not match their needs. Did we bring any influence to bear in resolving the client's technical challenges for producing a new light source? Did we manage to throw 'new light' on the company's quest for world leadership and domination in its sector? What was the extent of our sacrifice to achieve this? Our consultancy ended abruptly when it had another nine months to run, and we wondered if our challenging the messianic dynamic had led to their defensive reaction leading to the ending of the contract early. It was too painful to give up their idea as saviours. It seemed to us that the leadership dynamics at the top, the level of competitiveness and unhappiness with certain key suppliers and our insistence on facing those dilemmas and their consequences led the executive to 'sacrifice' us. The executive committee, as much as they wanted their supplier to 'hurry' with solutions to the problem, could not tolerate the haste with which we charged them to examine their own defensiveness and disengagement dynamics. And so, having left, we wondered whether our work had helped the committee to free itself from their own internal obstructiveness and resistance, or was their extrusion of us the catalyst for the committee to realise its need for change. Consultants working with large systems that are subject to splitting processes highlight the need for regular supervision to help understand and work with the inevitable introjective and projective processes that get enacted in the consultant team.

Five years later, the following report appeared in https://innovationorigins.com/unveiling-of-new-iphone-with-ultra-fast-chip-from-an-asml-machine/ (13 October 2020; accessed 22 December 2020):

> At long last, the time has come: Tonight at 7 pm Apple is expected to announce that the iPhone with a chip from the latest chip machine from ASML will go on sale in November. This chip is a true technological masterpiece from an obscure little village in The Netherlands. They have achieved something no other tech company in the world can match.
>
> The machine, uses extreme ultraviolet light, (EUV for short), for the manufacture of the chip. EUV is a kind of light that cannot naturally exist on earth. The reason is that it is so fragile, that it is absorbed by the air immediately after it is created. It can be found in space though.
>
> The EUV light burns a pattern of the circuits onto the chip which is made up of one hundred extremely thin layers with separate patterns (all of which are burned in with EUV) to run separate digital processes and commands. In total, the chip has 8 billion circuits (transistors), which are activated electrically to transmit millions of zeros and ones. This means that one can record and edit films on one's phone because it can handle huge files and the processing power is extremely high.

The evolution of a work group

By David Armstrong

I was invited by an American colleague to work with her in planning a Small Group Consultation for Senior Clergy (Bishops, Presbytery Leaders and Conference Ministers) in the United States. The Consultation was planned as a selected follow-up to be a leadership programme on "Developing Leadership Roles, Now and into the Future".

The context

The Consultation was intended to reach into less conscious, more latent elements in members' organisational experience, with the stated purpose of "providing opportunities for members to further explore how the inner world of their organization is affecting and affected by their leadership".

The overall shape of the programme circled around two main sequences of events. One centred on the idea of 'organisation-in-the-mind', involving members using drawings or constructions to imaginatively capture 'the emotional world of my own organization and my own part in it': the other a version of role analysis, working with critical incident material offered by members from their current working experience. There were also opportunities for sharing organizational and personal preoccupations and challenges, for end of day and overnight reflections and for private reflection and reading.

Throughout the first two days, we were struck by the sense of freedom with which members seemed able to work, by their imaginativeness, readiness to share associations and absence of defensiveness.

For example, towards the end of the sessions on 'Organisation in the Mind', following the work around their individual representations, we invited members to see if, working now from the set of pictures they had individually drawn, they could use these to come up with a collective representation of what might be being configured about the state of the Church in America as a whole. Within about half an hour and to the accompaniment of a good deal of back chat and jokiness, they presented an attempt at a three-dimensional structure with a rectangular frame made out of strips of paper, which constantly threatened to collapse and had to be held up, like a puppet on a string. Inside this paper frame were several colourful but amorphous objects, representing the individual images from their earlier drawings. It seemed, one might say, to interpret itself as if quite without façade, inviting not so much association as recognition, something like, on occasion, the imaginative play of Winnicott's child patients, simultaneously setting a shared unconscious ball rolling.

At the end of the second day, the programme included an open discussion around some readings which had been sent out to members just before the Consultation and which we had invited them to review in private earlier that afternoon. This was lively, spirited and enquiring. At some time during this discussion, as the conversation turned to the theme of anxiety and defence, I found myself wondering aloud what people might identify as the core anxiety that the Church might exist to contain and what social defences might be mobilised against this. At the time, this was left in the air, not so much a question to answer as to open something out. (Recall Bion's quote from the French surrealist poet Andre Breton, 'la reponse est le malheur de la question'.)

Turning point

On the afternoon of the third day, for one and a half hours before and after dinner, we had scheduled a session called simply Open Exploration. Manifestly, at the time, we introduced this as an opportunity for members to work on something relevant to their learning but not so far included in the programme, as they saw it, which they would plan and lead by themselves. It would be up to them to decide on a theme and a method, during which time we would not take part but just sit on our own outside. We set the group two guidelines: that the event should be in line with the stated purpose of the Consultation as a whole and should be collaborative and not dependent on us. We would participate in the event, once designed, but as members and not staff.

The group worked on the design for nearly the whole one and a half hours before dinner. We had previously arranged that they would let us know as and when they were agreed and would brief us beforehand, and, privately, we had reserved the right to reject or not take part in any proposal made if we felt it did not meet the two criteria, we had set.

At the time the group had agreed a design, though we were not briefed in detail about it, taking this on trust, we gathered that it had brought together two strands in the group's discussion: first, an interest in the question posed earlier about the core anxiety the Church might exist to contain and/or defend against; and second, the spontaneous idea of drawing on and making use of a particular method they were familiar with from the practice of religious study.

Lectio Divina

The method they chose and adapted and which neither of us was familiar with is known as *Lectio Divina*. This is a traditional and long-standing Benedictine practice, where a story or passage of scripture is chosen as the stimulus to a process of meditative reflection or rumination, something akin perhaps to a theological version of free association or response.

So, what happened?

When we came back to work after dinner, the room had been rearranged. The chairs were clustered in a semi-circle in front of a long narrow table covered with a red cloth (in fact, a scarf belonging to the Presbytery leader). On this was a dish with pieces of bread, a small flask of oil and a few crossed sticks. These were placed either side of a wooden book stand, on which was an open book. (In retrospect, this arrangement had something of the look of a revisionist communion table.)

To the left of the table was a flipchart on which was written an overview of the process, which the Presbyter, presiding, talked us through.

There were to be four main steps, during which we would all take part:

- Listening and associating to a chosen biblical text, to be read on three separate occasions by one or other member, each reading to be followed by a posed question or task.
- Interviewing each other in pairs (and one trio) on one's own responses to the questions asked.
- Reporting back, with each member of a pair presenting the other's response.
- A whole group conversation between the seven of us.

The chosen text, unannounced, was the following Old Testament story (Elijah and the Widow of Zarapeth, 1 Kings 17: 7–16):

> Sometime later the brook dried up because there had been no rain in the land. Then the word of the Lord came to him: "go at once to Zarapeth in the region of Sidon and stay there. I have directed a widow there to supply you with food". When he came to the town gate a widow was there gathering sticks. He called to her and asked, "Would you bring me a little water in a jar so I may have a drink?" As she was going to get it, he called, "and bring me please a piece of bread".
>
> "As surely as the Lord your God lives", she replied, "I don't have any bread, only a handful of flour and a little olive oil in a jug. I am gathering a few sticks to take home and make a meal for myself and my son, that we may eat it and die".
>
> Elijah said to her, "Don't be afraid. Go home and do as you have said. But first make a small loaf of bread for me from what you have and bring it to me, and then make something else for yourself and your son. For this is what the Lord, the God of Israel says: 'The jar of flour will not be used up and the jug of oil will not run dry until the day the Lord sends rain on the land'".
>
> She went away and did as Elijah had told her. So, there was food every day for Elijah and for the woman and her family. For the jar of flour was not

used up and the jug of oil did not run dry, in keeping with the word of the Lord spoken by Elijah.

During the first reading, we were told to listen for words and images and to note them down I wrote down 'I don't have any food', 'two sticks', 'myself and my son', 'die', 'won't'.

After the second reading, we were asked two questions to think on silently: 'where do you see yourself in the story' and 'where do you see your organisation';

I thought of the death of my father when my brother and I (two sticks?) were 14 and my mother was left to bring us up on her own.
    I thought of my own organisation, the Tavistock and its tradition and their being at risk of dying (drying up)

The text was read a third time, and we divided into pairs and a trio. Each was to interview the other with four questions in mind:

- What are the nature and source of anxiety in this story?
- Where do you see these in the life of your organisation?
- Where do you see these in yourself as a leader?
- How in the story is anxiety dealt with?

I cannot now recall exactly the details of what my pair and myself exchanged. For my pair, his focus seemed to turn around themes of 'strangeness': *a strange land, a strange context, the drought of imagination, the stranger in a new community, the Bishop as 'stranger'*. For myself, I seemed preoccupied with feelings around the memory of my mother's struggle and faithfulness, following my father's death and her tenacity in keeping his image, the feel of his presence alive for his children. Organisationally, I had this uneasy sense, coming towards the end of my professional life, that the organisation and tradition I had spent my working life within might not last and how this had led to a shift of direction towards a focus on trying to recapture something perhaps lost, bring it alive again to pass it on. Was this operating as a defence against anxiety or a way of containing it that was active, not passive?

In the ensuing whole group conversation, one was brought aware of the multiplicity of meanings found and made from this story, much of which seemed to turn around themes of spiritual deprivation, the role of 'stranger', revelation versus salvation, the 'blindness of faith' (this both from a religious perspective but also from Bion's more psychoanalytic vertex), the death of the father, how to lead in a strange land. From my own experience, it was extraordinarily invigorating and suggestive, for example, in leaving open and ambiguous a question about the institutional embodiment of 'faith': defence or container, which emerged as perhaps the central struggle of the 'Church' within a dying or dried-up religious landscape. (Again, although I am putting this within a religious context, I did not see it as unique to this institutional frame.)

More specifically here, though, what I want to draw attention to is the way in which this event, opened up by ourselves as staff but 'found and made' (like Winnicott's transitional objects), by **the group of members**, working alone, elicited an imaginative response that linked the emphasis and methodology of a secular tradition, represented by the programme as a whole, with a religious or spiritual discipline, in the process reaching, to my mind, a level of depth which as staff we had neither explicitly anticipated nor elicited.

It may be interesting in this connection to note how earlier in the programme the members had signally failed to take up an invitation afforded to organise an early morning slot we had set aside for Morning Prayer. This was to be dependent on one or other member being prepared to lead it. In the event, however, no one was so prepared. My colleague and I just waited in silence, sitting in the designated room. There were various reasons members had cited for this apparent 'anomaly'. But one might wonder whether, unconsciously, it represented a maybe defensive splitting between the two frames of reference underlying the programme, religious and secular. From this perspective, the members' imaginative response now could be a movement towards a kind of re-integration, a bringing together of what was initially to be kept apart.

A working hypothesis

Provisionally, I suggest that one might take this event and the opportunity it opened up within the programme, as a 'turning point' in the evolution of 'W' (Bion's work group), marking a transition to a new and distinctive 'practice', in which the members took ownership for themselves of the territory the programme as a whole sought to open up, drawing now on a distinctive 'technology' of their own, but in a way which seemed to create a kind of third space, opening the possibility of a shared engagement, beyond the boundaries of each discipline of enquiry, theological or psychoanalytic. One could perhaps characterise this dynamically as a movement away from the 'dependency of learning' to the 'autonomy of exploration'; simultaneously, given the suspension of the role boundary between members and staff, a shift from cooperation to collaboration, which was to affect both the quality of staff member relations and the ways in which the group was to sustain itself over time, across a series of six follow-through meetings by phone over the ensuing three to four years.

One year after what I have been describing, I had begun working on a paper, to be given at the ISPSO Annual Meeting in Granada, on "Psychoanalytic Study and the Ethical Imagination: the making, finding and losing of a tradition". In the course of working on this, I was to come across a distinction drawn by Eric Trist between two related but contrasting modes of socio-analytic engagement: one more consultancy-driven, foregrounding client-centred problems or concerns within specific bounded contexts, the other more open-ended, with what Trist characterised as an 'existential quality', recalled from the wartime projects of "experiencing those with whom he works as travellers on a common journey rather than as clients who have requested his particular help". Where the problem or dilemma is experienced as "his also, belonging to both as members of the wider society which it permeates". I think it is something approximate to this shift, albeit, within a rather different working context, that evolved within this programme, transforming simultaneously both the group culture and the nature of our engagement.

> There is so much more that one might choose to make (that the reader might choose to make) from this experience. But what is in my mind here and now is Elisha Davar's comment on Winnicott:
>
>> Intrinsic to Winnicott's ideas is the capacity for authentic, imaginative play. To use Winnicott's ideas well you need to have a capacity to be able to play with your own thoughts. A play space is necessary for the creation of a symbolic universe. Yet by no means everyone knows how to play with their imagination. The letting go of a previously held mind set can prove to be quite a formidable task. To use his theory well, you need to trust it to guide you to a place - and here I mean a mental conception of space - where you will come to know of something, though it is not quite what you had originally imagined.
>
> It appears though that the 'group', like the 'child', does not always need to **know** Winnicott to *use his theory well.*

Summary

Significant psychological needs are met by group membership – a sense of identity, affection and closeness, achievement, recognition of skills, rewards for contributing to the group. Group membership provides a sense of belonging, inclusion and satisfaction; opportunities to influence, exercise power and take up authority. The primary working sub-units of organisations are groups of people. Most activities of organisations require coordination through the operation of group and inter-group working. The concept of the organisation as an open social system, as a sociotechnical system, and the organisation as part of an eco-system is concerned with the interaction between the psychological, the social and the environmental, as well as the structural and the technical. Groups shape the work patterns of organisations and the attitudes and behaviours of group members to their jobs. Systems psychodynamics involves applying sociotechnical approaches to technological processes, production methods, the way work is carried out and integrated with the social system of the organisation. Work design and job enrichment is based on self-managing work groups and team working which provides higher levels of job satisfaction, improved quality that remains at higher levels than leader-led groups. Self-management involves the complete restructuring of the jobs that people do in small groups of employees with substantial responsibility for planning, organizing, scheduling and production of work products or services. Self-managing teams, with greater control over their work enhances innovative behaviour and team performance. Self-managing teams look beyond their individual task concerns to the needs of the groups and the entire organization; there is a marked reduction in stress. Systems psychodynamics consultants have a sophisticated understanding of group processes and how to intervene effectively in systems of groups. There is a convergence of social systems theories and group relations theories to produce an overarching systems psychodynamics theory and its application to organisational consultancy. The group relations approach applies psychoanalysis, field psychology and social systems theory to the understanding of small groups, inter-group relations, large group and institutional and environmental dynamics. The sociotechnical model of organisations is concerned with organisational design, boundaries and their regulation. Large group interventions are participative, comprising a diverse cross-section of an organisation's stakeholders, come together to work on real organisational issues of strategic importance to help bring about rapid change.

Exercise

1 Explain why leader-led groups achieve higher levels of performance in the short term and self-managing groups in the long term.
2 What values underpin leader-led groups and self-managing (or semi-autonomous) groups?
3 What anxieties do you think are associated with these two types of groups?
4 What do you think is the relation and contradictions between leader-led groups and organisations as open systems?
5 What is your experience of a shift in emphasis from the 'organisation' to the organisation-in-its-environment as the unit of study?
6 What is your experience of Large Group Interventions? What do they achieve, if anything?

8 Working with groups II

With Juliet Scott and Heather Stradling

The application of group relations

Organisational and social applications of group relations training

From its earliest days psychoanalysis has been interested in group and organisational processes. Fenichel (1945) noted that human beings create social institutions to satisfy their needs as well as accomplish tasks. Institutions then become external realities, independent of individuals, which affect them in significant ways. The beginnings of a psychodynamic theory of group and organisational processes had to wait for a fully worked-out object-relational perspective that could provide the necessary interactive constructs i.e. Klein (1959) and Bion (1961). Bion's theory of groups differentiated between behaviours and activities geared towards rational performance (the work [W] group) and those geared to emotional needs and anxieties (the basic assumption [ba] groups: fight-flight [baF], dependency [baD] and pairing [baP]. Other central Kleinian concepts that were applied to group processes were: projective identification, psychotic anxiety, symbol formation, schizoid mechanisms and part objects. Other theories that were integrated were organisational and systems theory. The Tavistock approach to group training and organisational consultancy co-evolved and crystallised. The central tenet of the Tavistock Model is the term systems psychodynamics. 'Systems' refer to open systems concepts for understanding the structural aspects of an organisational system i.e. design, division of labour, levels of authority, reporting relationships, the nature of work tasks, process and activities, its mission, and primary task, the organisation's task and sentient system. 'Psychodynamics' refers to the psychoanalytic perspective on individual, group and social processes from the work of Klein and Bion.

The primary task of Group Relations conferences is to provide members with opportunities to study the nature of leadership and authority and the interpersonal, group and intergroup problems encountered in their contexts. This study is entirely experiential – there are usually no lectures. To implement the task, participants are involved in a number of group events (i.e. plenaries, small group, the large group, the intergroup, the institutional event, review and application groups, etc.) which provide opportunities to examine their experiences and behaviour in them and in the conference as a whole. The basic staff role is to provide consultation by taking up a stance of neutrality and offering interpretations of covert and unconscious processes, with an emphasis on transference and countertransference manifestations. However, the Group Relations conference model has been used as the basis for a wide range of organisational interventions. The basic approach is to utilise one event or combination of several events derived from Group Relations conferences, with a membership composed of individuals who comprise a natural work group, or groups, or the totality of an organisation. This contrasts to the typical Group Relations conference in which participants are, for the most part, strangers from different organisations.

From Bion and group relations thinking

Systems psychodynamics brings together the contribution of social psychology (Lewin, 1936 a,b; 1947 a,b,c,d) and psychoanalysis (Bion, 1961). The aim of group relations is to 'encourage an analytical and critical approach to the way people perform their roles in the groups to which they belong' (Trist and Sofer, 1959). From Bion, we have the concepts of the 'work group' and the 'basic assumptions group', which allows us to understand the tension between the conscious and unconscious life of a group.

Work group

We will focus on Bion's ideas and later developments of the work group which until recently had been rather neglected. The work group is that aspect of group functioning that has to do with the real conscious task of the group, e.g. plan a programme, review activities, study, etc. The work group can define its task. The structure of the group furthers the attainment of its task. With a work group mentality, members of the group cooperate as separate and discrete individuals. Membership is experienced as voluntary and the individual's own interests are closely identified with those of the group. Brazaitis (2017) summarises Bion's model; *all groups engage concurrently in two aspects or mentalities: work group activity and basic assumption activity.* The prevalence of one mentality over the other depends on the state of the group, its current pressures and the context. That is, a group might well engage in mostly work group activity until it loses resources, e.g. staff, budget; is tasked with a high profile, high stakes deliverable and is given a tight timeline to deliver results. These stressors could make the group members exceedingly anxious such that their group behaviour regresses into predominantly basic assumption mentality activity while the work group activity recedes to the background. According to Bion (1961), basic assumption activity is triggered by anxiety and is more likely to manifest when a group is under significant stress.

Work group activity includes the rational, task-oriented and goal-directed aspects of group life. When group members are engaged in working together to create a product, devise a growth strategy, generate ideas for new markets, or implement action steps in a project management plan, they are exhibiting work group activity. In work group mentality, a group is working together to achieve goals, produce results and demonstrate effective performance.

> The work group constantly tests its conclusions in a scientific spirit. It seeks for knowledge, learns from experience, and constantly questions how it may best achieve its goal. It is clearly conscious of the passage of time and of the processes of learning and development.
>
> (Rioch, 1975)

According to Brazaitis (2017), Bion's understanding that groups and teams can be working hard at their task (or think they are) while paradoxically also engaging in behaviour that is obstructive and anti-task is one of the most important ideas in the field of group dynamics. That is, Bion was one of the first to put forth the idea that groups and teams can engage in overt processes (working on goals, producing deliverables, fulfilling action items), while also engaging in covert process (sabotaging a colleague, de-authorising the group leader, working against the group's greater good). In fact, Bion argued that groups always engage in overt and covert processes simultaneously (Bion, 1961). Team leaders, trainers, organisational development consultants, group facilitators and group process consultants all would likely agree that understanding the covert processes in groups and organisations is essential to helping teams and systems engage in the most effective overt processes towards reaching their shared goals. This idea started with Bion's work and has been essential in organisational change efforts since Bion's first formulation.

> Basic assumption life is not oriented outward toward reality, but inward toward fantasy, which is then impulsively and uncritically acted out. There is little pausing to consider or to test consequences, little patience with an inquiring attitude, and great insistence upon feeling. Basic assumption members do not really learn and adapt through experience but actually resist change. So, it seems that the basic assumptions represent an interference with the work task, just as naughty, primitive impulses may interfere with the sensible work of a mature person.
>
> (Rioch, 1975, Pg. 28)

Bion included one positive aspect to basic assumption activity – that he called 'sophisticated' use of basic assumption mentalities (Bion, 1961, Pg. 96). This is when the work task aligns with the basic assumption task. Bion's (1961) theory of group behaviour has become the foundation of the Tavistock model of group behaviour. Bion (1961) viewed the group as a bounded, yet collective entity. For the most part, groups emerge from the acceptance or agreement that a common goal (positive or negative) exists. This manifest aspect of a group is Bion's work (W) group (Bion, 1961, Pg. 129). Bion held that "people come together as a group for the purposes of preserving the group" (op cit, Pg. 63). Rice defined the primary task of a group or sub-group as "the task it must perform if it is to survive" (1965, Pg. 17). Even though groups form, as stated, at an overt level to achieve a common goal, there are also latent or covert aspects within the group that are real (Banet and Hayden, 1977; Bion, 1961; Czander, 1993; Miller, 1993; Rice, 1965). These authors contend that though there is a conscious effort on the part of the group members to pursue the common objective, there are often unconscious hidden agendas that interfere with the completion of work tasks. Furthermore, they suggested that individuals are often unaware of the controls in play, which help to separate their stated intentions from their 'hidden agendas'. The hidden agendas of the individuals within the group collectively make up the latent (covert) aspects of group behaviour, which are referred to by Bion as the Basic Assumptions (ba) group (1961). This covert aspect of the group, though frequently disguised, is a latent motivating force for group members (Banet and Hayden, 1977). This relates also to Bion's (1961, Pg. 65–66) description of group mentality:

> Group mentality is the unanimous expression of the will of the group, contributed to by the individual in ways of which he is unaware, influencing him disagreeably whenever he thinks or behaves in a manner at variance with the basic assumptions. It is thus a machinery of inter-communication that is designed to ensure that group life is in accordance with the basic assumptions. The group's culture is a function of the conflict between the individual's desires and the group's mentality.

Thus, the group's culture emerges and regulates group members' behaviour and provides evidence of the basic assumptions operating within the group. The systems psychodynamics approach thus recognises two groups at play, viz. the W-group and the b/a-group. Both are real, operating and present simultaneously (Bion, 1961; Miller, 1993; Rice, 1965). Banet and Hayden (1977) depicted the W-group as being outwardly focused on the task; while the b/a-group is inwardly focused on itself, and this creates an inevitable tension which is balanced by various behavioural and psychological structures like individual defence systems, ground rules and group norms.

Bion's ideas are used routinely today in organisational development consultancy efforts. He was a change leader whose work is used directly by change leaders today. Bion was one of the first to understand that to drive organisational change, one must address both the overt and covert aspects of organisational life.

The arts at work: The role of the arts in Tavistock organisational practice

Juliet Scott and Heather Stradling

A workshop participant reports her emotions when painting a story of her experience of the Covid-19 pandemic in 2020 onto a two-metre strip of 16 mm film. It references both the enforced measure of social distance and the film as an emblem of the skin and therefore of touch. Later her strip of film is looped together with others, projected and then digitally captured. Through these processes, new meanings and narratives are made as the films are performed with the addition of voiceover narratives. Unconscious stories reveal themselves grappling with expression within these diminutive dimensions, how this relates to scale and time, noticing the attempts to anticipate and control how the story will tell itself when projected. They all have a bearing on practice in organisations.

This is a workshop led by artists Rosalind Fowler and James Holcombe that has evolved over some years where both artists have worked with organisational practitioners in the context of the Tavistock Institute's educational work and through this lens have explored evaluation, storytelling, power and politics, the unconscious and performance. They are now one of a group of eight artists and artist collectives contributing to *Deepening Creative Practice with Organisations* – the Tavistock Institute's programme in five seasons that weaves together the arts and social sciences towards a final 'exhibiting' season that is co-created and curated by the participants, faculty and artist contributors. It combines experiential learning in the Tavistock tradition, with regular embodied practice and interventions, including visual and multi-media arts, dance, theatre and performance art. The working design for the programme envisaged further possibilities such as a sound artist bringing a new sensitivity to awareness of the field, a choreographer drawing attention to questions of inclusion and exclusion. Participants increasingly take active roles in co-design and co-curation as the programme progresses, and in its process, deepen understanding of how psychodynamic concepts and approaches can be intertwined with artistic practice to support the development of organisations.

This could be termed as bringing a new epistemology to working with organisations, but that seems to set the arts somewhat in the shadow of the social sciences as another way of knowing with hierarchical implications around the evidence and quality of that knowledge. The Institute's social science has always worked across disciplines, and supporting the creativity of work groups is at the heart of its purpose. David Armstrong (2017) uses the term 'ethical imagination' to describe an applied social science whose work is less to 'do to' than to 'work with' and support the imaginative coming into being of new ways of organising that is inherent to groups and our survival as a species. It is akin to Norbert Elias's notion of change as an imaginative process that unfolds slowly and iteratively over time (1939). Gordon Lawrence's Social Dreaming methodology where sharing of dreams takes place in a societal context is the coming into being through group sense-making of 'new' thoughts and images (2004).

Since Freud (1910) first considered the life and work of Leonardo da Vinci from a psychoanalytic perspective, the arts have been a source of exploration for the fields of psychology and psychoanalysis. The active contribution of art to the fields of psychoanalysis and psychotherapy have been growing since the development of 'art therapy' as a term in the 1940s – whether art is used as a form of revealing unconscious thoughts, feelings and mechanisms, or understood as a sublimatory tool of expression that in itself supports healing. Donald Winnicott (1990) famously used the squiggle technique with children at his clinic; Laban (1959) wrote about the therapeutic value of dance and there are now numerous trainings for using arts within therapeutic settings. Likewise, psychoanalysis has made a significant contribution to the arts, whether in the expression of psychoanalytic concepts through artistic practice and/or in the critical language used to understand different works of art and their potential conscious and unconscious meanings and communications – psychoanalytic film theory, developed in the 1970s and 1980s, is one example.

Creativity has been a part of the Institute's work for many decades, as articulated by Eric Miller in 'Work and Creativity' (1983). Arts practice has subsequently evolved through a series of different initiatives at the Tavistock Institute where an aesthetic sensibility and curation have been integral – the introduction of a design event at the Leicester Conference (Aram, 2010); the programme of work with the Institute's archive that culminated in a four-day festival celebrating 70 years since its formation in 1947; Juliet Scott's artist in residency and Object Relations exhibition; Social Dreaming illustrations as part of a developmental evaluation; the Arch-A-Live symposium; embodied consultancy (Kelly and Gangjee, 2018); organisational consultancy interventions and finally their formalisation into a programme of work in 2019, Arts and Organisation.

These are the edges where the arts and social science meet and the visual and imaginative storytelling, where the interdisciplinary Tavistock tradition becomes a trans-disciplinary practice in robust exploration of organisation. The directors' opening statement to the Deepening Creative Practice programme promised that their role would be about working with the group to research and practise at the edge of art and organisation, at other edges too and with the interdisciplinary edges between the arts. In the context of Covid-19 and working remotely from each other, it has experimented even more than anticipated in organisational creative co-design and co-curation – exploring the embodied and disembodied, connected and disconnected, competency and incompetency, the seen and unseen – as data that is usually present when working in the same room is missing, such as using all of the senses to be able to read and respond to one another but also playing with new holistic means of expression, understanding and connection in order to contain and work with this century's anxieties, problems and possibilities.

At the time of writing, in the midst of the Covid-19 global pandemic and the #BlackLivesMatters movement, there is potential for lasting, structural changes to society and working life. Recent debates around historic and contemporary barriers, because of unconscious and conscious systemically embedded inequalities, injustices and exploitation, have highlighted how organisations do not operate in a vacuum, separate from the societies and cultures within which they sit, and that therefore, organisations can contribute to a better future. These debates have run alongside questions about the future of office life. Changes in working practices implemented as a response to Covid-19 have combined with the technological improvements that make home working possible for some industries and individuals. And the climate emergency requires radical changes to lifestyles in order to protect the wider world. It is time to build on Miller's 'Work and Creativity', to talk about art and the organisation more specifically.

Miller argued that concepts of creativity and work are polarised in the post-industrial western society, with creativity connected to destructiveness, even though creativity in the workplace is necessary to adapt to societal turbulence. As a result, the work of the artist is institutionalised and valued as the preserve of a few of the 'very best' artists (as defined by those with the power to invest in those artists), and the workplace or business is seen as the place of drudgery, conformity and 'gainful' employment, which looks nothing like play, fun or art. If artistic practice remains removed from organisational life, it perhaps denies the creative, artistic parts of the self and the organisation to be present, thereby limiting the ability to make meaning of, to explore and imagine different and new perspectives and approaches to organisational culture, task and life.

An example of aesthetic practice: sculpting the organisation-in-the-mind (Armstrong, 1997)

An anthropologist, organisational consultant/artist, researcher/therapist/dancer and a consultant/Alexander technique practitioner intwined their many disciplinary backgrounds to design an arts-based intervention to support organisational actors in working through their various notions of organisations-in-the-mind. It iterated into part of a programme of work with a large care organisation which was undergoing a change process towards initiating greater self-leadership in decisions and organisational processes. The aims were to:

- Free up conversations to play with the aesthetics of organisational relationships in the here and now.
- Offer a creative opportunity, with participants making some form of 3-D structure/artefact, expressing current organisational relationships, their inter-connections and contributions to the overarching organisation-in-the-mind.

A workshop was run with the senior leadership team, with an added complexity of giving a small group the task of managing the rest of group, in order to sculpt a representation of the change programme, its relationships to the organisation and environment. Working with found objects, recycled material, chairs, tables, themselves, participants first sculpted the smaller parts, groups that they were members of, and then scaled up into a larger integrated sculpture representing the whole organisation. Organisational dynamics played out quite dramatically, as shown in these extracts from the consultants' working notes (Miller, 1995).

Examples included:

- The focus on carrying out practical tasks. This revealed the organisational culture prioritising efficient and effective task completion i.e. 'leadership is getting the task done' versus a more person-centred approach, which places the end-user first.
- The sculpture task was simplified into a team bonding fun exercise. Laughter and jokes deflected discomfort, photographs and tweeting fetishised the product.
- The rush to intellectualise, rationalise and resist exploring the barriers that are likely to evoke difficult feelings for people as they surfaced their own roles as barriers.
- The tendency to simplify or flatten self-leadership as a concept into 'doing what one wants'. When asked about going to lunch early, one of the responses was, 'well, we did what we are supposed to do, self-leadership!' This didn't acknowledge the complexity of possibilities within that situation such as deepening the exploration of enablers and blockers, challenging the notion of task completion.
- The unconscious will have been strongly expressed through the sculpture, with the experience as a fractal or micro-expression of the organisation overall. What did the sculpture reveal and was the flight to lunch a running away from that?

After lunch we presented our emerging hypothesis to stimulate some deeper thinking about the role of senior leaders in supporting self-leadership in the organisation. There was a mixed response to this ranging from shame/anger to curiosity and agreement. The offered hypothesis was:

> … THAT the managers could not bear the discomfort of the task of exploring barriers and enablers to supporting self-leadership in the organisation, to the extent that managers and managees colluded in rebelling against the 'directors' (those who had given the task) represented by the TIHR consultants.

The sight of this culture and challenging of its associated behaviours by the consultants become available for organisational learning.

It is the quality and rigour of enquiry that is unique to the Institute's vision for the arts. The work could be described as searching for form (Wright, 2009) with the aesthetic criteria of the organisation, noticing its shapes, patterns, inclusions, exclusions, not just beauty but holes, gaps, the pain and sufferings and the other side of that, anaesthesia (Francesetti, 2012). Juliet Scott's work as artist in residence (2016) began as a dialogue with Klein, Winnicott, et al. It is now realising a very different set of relationships where object relations are far more than the psychological searches of expression that first caught her eye in relation to studies of still life but where objects are a vital part of work with complexity and ecology, not least their spiritual dimensions. Antonio Strati's work on organisational aesthetics is rooted in his attendance at the Leicester conference and the opening chapter is centred around the chair (1999), the aesthetic artefact of group relations work. The evidence base for the arts is growing through advances in neuroscience and in relation to wellbeing. Our ambitions reach beyond the therapeutic, however, to collaboration with artists at the edge of chaos, to working as artists in organisations, to bridging the epistemological hierarchies and divides that we know as social defences.

The seriously playful and challenging experience of Deepening Creative Practice so far has highlighted that:

- Everyone has the inherent ability to play and the capacity for creativity – reminding ourselves of this can help the noticing and acknowledgement of the creativity already taking place within organisations that may not otherwise be seen or validated.
- Artistic practice can help bring in a different language to conversations around the organisation and its role and place in society. For instance, concepts of framing, texture and mark-making can lead to conversations more directly related to the 'film' or 'projections' of an organisation or project.
- Alongside systems psychodynamics approaches, the arts can work under the surface of hierarchies and structures, enabling voices from different places to be heard and enabling the 'organisation-in-the-mind' to be expressed. As with arts in psychoanalysis, it can reveal some of the hidden phantasies, unconscious relationships and their connection, or not, to reality.
- Organisational life happens in the imaginal space as much as in the practical achievement of the organisational primary task. Artistic practice can give time, space and a container for the exploration of the non-verbal and symbolic, moving away from stagnant ideas of what communication looks like within organisations, and providing "metaphors that enable insight and allow us to scrutinise the role organisations play in shaping global culture" (Gad, 2015, on Simon Denny's art located in modern processes of organisation).
- Just as the artistry within science is being more recognised (e.g. Kneebone et al., 2018), it is time to recognise the artistry within organisations. Once this happens, then the possibilities for change, for taking risks and moving beyond the narrow perceptions of what work and organisations look like, might help us all be better equipped as citizens of the 21st century.

Taking part in a well-contained artistic activity is enlivening, mind-expanding, invigorating and joyful – why wouldn't we want this to be part of organisational life? As Miller says, perhaps the fear of this being a destructive act is what prevents it from being embraced. However, by not embracing it, then we are perhaps allowing our organisations and societies to self-destruct in other ways. By embracing it, we can perhaps allow our organisations and societies to become truly fit for purpose to meet the needs of the decades ahead.

Case example of working with groups

The following is an example of the use of sub-groups (called Action Learning Sets [ALSs]) comprising people (about 65 senior leaders) from across the organisation to address organisational issues that had eluded the formal hierarchical leadership for many years. The principle behind this method was the loosening up of thoughts, creativity and actionable innovation and capabilities among senior leaders who hitherto operated on a basic assumption of dependency by keeping their heads down, focusing mainly on their bits of the organisation and projecting negative feelings into the rest of the organisation, especially into the executive management, the Chief Executive's Group (CEG).

A unique feature of the ALS method was the way they were integrated into one coherent system of learning and change that dovetailed with the business-as-usual groups in the hierarchy. After each meeting of an ALS, a brief summary of discussion and action points was noted and circulated to the other ALSs as well as to what was called the Internal Referent Group (IRG), comprising the Chief Executive and Deputy Chief Executive and members of the CEG and the two external consultants. The ALSs were encouraged to 'research' their areas of concern and to feel free to approach anyone in the organisation who could assist them in their tasks.

The organisation had 6,500 personnel. A culture change programme is under way involving 5 ALSs, each one focusing on a different theme. One ALS with eight participants from across the organisation is concerned with developing an organisation-wide strategy called the One-Team Strategy, the objective being to create a culture of 'one team' to facilitate changed attitudes, communications and a spirit of collaboration in a system of geographic hubs, siloed teams, isolated specialists and structured divisions between personnel (about 3,500 people) and support staff (about 3,000 people).

The ALS is discussing the relationship between HR Services and Occupational Health, and the absence of 'one team' working around the management of sickness. Occupational Health was considered to be too focused on the individual and not enough on the workforce needs of the organisation. In some areas of the organisation, only 40% of staff were capable of being on duty. The rate of retirement on grounds of ill-health was restricting the work of some sections of the organisation. Attempts at collaboration by HR with Occupational Health, it was said, were thwarted by the interplay of four separate and unintegrated players: the Employer ('needs people to work'), Occupational Health ('too liberal in signing people off sick'), General Practitioners ('because of patient confidentiality, do not speak to/collaborate with the organisation'), manipulative individuals ('have learned how easy it is to play off one part of the system against the other').

The ALS agreed to take action to meet with the Director of HR to discuss the issues identified; the Director of HR would be asked to write to the county's association of GPs about the organisation's aims and intentions around the management of sickness absence and return to work of employees; the Director of HR would be asked to review the role of Occupational Health as advisor on decisions around return to work of employees.

Next up, the ALS discussed problems with Corporate Communications – the difficulties it was having in working together as a team; their poor management practice; it's perception as the 'Cinderella' of the organisation; the expectation of producing documents and statements without first having a full debate on the issues; the lack of clarification of the role of Corporate Communications as a whole; the confusion and failure to realise the potential of its staff. The ALS supported a meeting with the Head of Corporate Communications in order to clarify the nature of and expectations of roles of Corporate Communications staff and the nature of its role in relation to CEG and the organisation. This discussion inevitably raised questions of how the ALS felt about its own internal communications with each other and between the ALS and other units in the organisation. Feelings of not being taken seriously, of not being listened to, were internalised and expressed as lack of confidence in their own ideas, anxiety about approaching senior personnel, frequent statements of 'that won't work' suggesting a lack of a sense of empowerment to bring about change.

In preparation for an up-coming Whole Community Conference on the culture change project, the ALS created a video: "What does the One-Team Strategy mean to me?" by interviewing as many people as possible from around the organisation. The ALS at its meeting reviewed the unedited version of the video prior to presenting it to senior management later in the month. To their shock, the video revealed a range of extremely negative sentiments on the One-Team Strategy, e.g. "I have no pride left in the organisation"; "It's like talking to the wall. We are not listened to, nor consulted"; "There is no 5-year plan. There is no one running the place"; "there is incompetence among the managers, even corruption" (reference to managers employing their friends and relatives); "I don't ever see my manager"; "the one-team strategy is an impossible dream"; "there is no credibility in PDRs (personal development reviews) and not enough investment in people's development"; "people are bored and have nothing to do".

The ALS agreed that more people should be interviewed, and the result should contain positive remarks to balance against the negativity of the first batch of interviews. The ALS would present the video to the Organisational Development Group and fearlessly demonstrate how the One-Team strategy is perceived and experienced by people in the organisation at the present time. The ALS would then coordinate and run feedback groups across the organisation, using the video as a trigger, to address the question: "What do we need to do to help our people develop a One-Team strategy in our workplaces?" Overall, there was a sense of shock at the negative experiences of such a large part of the organisation. By the time of the Whole Community conference, the video was more balanced and showed more sides of people's feelings and hopes for the future. The ALS presented the video as a trigger for inspiration rather than despair and audiences at the Community Conference were visibly moved to do something and to support the ALS and the senior executive team to address this cultural phenomenon in order to fulfil the organisation ambition of becoming one of the Top ten organisations in their sector in the country, which it achieved over the following two years.

Summary

Human beings create social institutions to satisfy their needs as well as accomplish tasks. Bion's theory of groups differentiates between behaviours and activities geared towards rational performance (the Work Group) and those geared to emotional needs and anxieties (the Basic Assumption Group). The Work Group is concerned with the real conscious task of the group, e.g. plan a programme, review activities, study, etc. The Basic Assumption Group is triggered by anxiety and is more likely to manifest when a group is under significant stress. Working concepts applied to group processes include projective identification, psychotic anxiety, symbol formation, schizoid mechanisms and part objects. Organisational and systems theories are integrated with psychoanalytic theories in working with groups to form the basic Tavistock approach termed *systems psychodynamics*. 'Systems' refers to the structural aspects of organisations – design, division of labour, levels of authority, reporting relationships, the nature of work tasks, boundaries, process and activities, its mission, and primary task. 'Psychodynamics' refers to the psychoanalytic perspective on individual, group and social processes from the work of Klein and Bion. 'Systems psychodynamics' in relation to groups brings together the contribution of social psychology (Kurt Lewin, 1947a, b, c, d) and psychoanalysis (Bion, 1961). The aim is to "encourage an analytical and critical approach to the way people perform their roles in the groups to which they belong". Bion was one of the first to suggest that groups and teams can engage in overt processes (working on goals, producing deliverables, fulfilling action items), while also engaging in covert processes (sabotaging a colleague, de-authorising the group leader, working against the group's greater good). A sophisticated use of basic assumptions exists when the work task aligns with the basic assumption task. Individuals are often unaware of the controls in play, which help to separate their stated intentions from their 'hidden agendas'. The arts and social sciences can be woven together combining experiential learning with regular embodied practice, including visual and multi-media arts, dance, theatre and performance art.

Exercise

1 How does your work group manage the tension between (i) its conformist culture and (ii) its creative energies for innovation?
2 In relation to your work group's primary task, what are the advantages and disadvantages of a (i) conformist culture and (ii) creative innovation?
3 Describe how your work group manages its leadership functions and styles around conformity and innovation.

9 The contribution of group relations I

With Leslie Brissett

The flagship group relations conference (Miller, 1989, 1990; Rice, 1965), commonly called the Leicester conference, is an intensive two-week residential event devoted to experiential learning about group and organisational behaviour, with a particular emphasis on the nature of role, authority and leadership. It is a conference designed as a temporary educational institution, comprising both members and staff, which can be studied experientially as it forms, evolves and comes to an end. The conference provides various settings for the here-and-now study of the relatedness of individual, group and organisation. The primary task of the conference focuses on the theme of 'Authority, Leadership, and Organisation' which is generally defined in terms such as "to provide opportunities to study the exercise of authority in the context of interpersonal, intergroup and institutional relations within the Conference Institution".

Group relations theory and practice derives from an academic tradition of over 70 years standing, which grew out of the work of the Tavistock Institute, inspired by the theories of Klein (1959), Winnicott, opens systems theory and especially Bion's (1961) theories on group dynamics. It is a tradition that seeks to reconcile field research with organisational interventions aimed at enhancing organisational and personal effectiveness and well-being. At the heart of group relations theory lies the idea that organisations and groups generate anxiety among their members. This anxiety can become intolerable, triggering a variety of defensive mechanisms some of which are rooted in the individual, others in the group and yet others in the organisation. While defensive mechanisms relieve immediate anxiety, they promote and immerse individuals and groups in a fantasy world, where emotions dominate. This often leads to poor decision-making and miscalculations. Illusions take a grip on individuals' minds in different ways that are almost invariably dysfunctional to the organisation. Within a group relations conference, these processes and dynamics can be revealed and worked with.

The theory and practice of group relations conferences address the following dimensions of organisational experience (see Figure 9.1):

1 The emotional
2 The relational
3 The political

Consultants who have experience of group relations conference gain an added perspective on how they can develop their practice of systems psychodynamics oriented organisational consultancy. The experience of attending

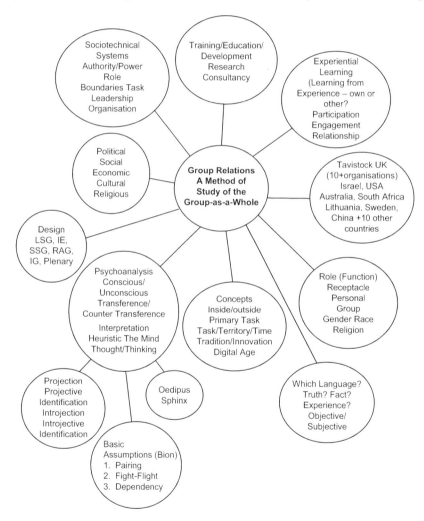

Figure 9.1 Group relations: a method of study of the group-as-a-whole.
Source: © Mannie Sher 2021.

a conference aids the understanding and experience of powerful unconscious forces at play in groups and between groups. This then helps consultants work more effectively in organisations and understand the impact of projections that the role of leader/manager attracts and evokes. Group relations experience provides a means to explore ways in which individual and personal projections link to group and organisational life in the context of their specific environments. Group relations practice provides a means of exploring the resulting enactments or denial of them in an organisational/environmental context. Group relations conferences help consultants understand the defensiveness of individual managers as a reflection and re-creation of the defences of the organisation and how organisational defences are enacted, perpetuated and refined by individual managers. Exploring the links between the emotional dynamics created within and between individuals and groups is fundamental to group relations and the systems psychodynamics models. We include a description of how group relations theory supports and enhances systems psychodynamics and its application to large group interventions, such as search conferences, future search and large group dynamics.

Definitions of Group relations consist of at least a theoretical underpinning, structural and design elements, a primary task, adopting a group-as-a-whole consultative stance and minimum length.

Theoretical underpinning

Group relations has been influenced in a major way by *psychoanalytic theory* — ideas that groups, like individuals, are subject to *conscious and unconscious* drives and motives. Consciousness is the presence of feelings, emotions, desires or lack of them that individuals or groups are aware of consciously; the notion of unconscious process refers to feelings, emotions, etc., that individuals or groups are not aware of, i.e. they do not have access to or the ability to understand them.

> **Transference and countertransference** are two important psychoanalytic concepts used in group relations. Transference is the attribution of feelings, emotions, behaviour and attitudes like fear, love, eroticism, envy, jealousy, competition, etc., onto figures of authority in the present that have their origins in relationships with previous earlier figures of authority, e.g. parents, teachers, bosses. Countertransference describes the feelings, emotions, attitudes, behaviour, etc., aroused in the consultant, coach or teacher, i.e. contemporary figures of authority.
> **Projection**, like transference, describes the attribution of feelings to others, e.g. "I so much want to be more like that person"; or "I am so pleased that I am not like that person".
> **Introjection**, like countertransference, involves the taking in of other's feelings that result in expressions of empathy or compassion.

Projective identification is a psychoanalytic concept that describes the results of someone forcefully trying to change someone else against their will, i.e. making them get caught up uncontrollably in one's own, someone else's or another group's drama.

Introjective identification refers to the subjective experience of being 'projected into' and changing against one's will.

Defences against anxiety refers to the steps taken to preserve the status quo or a state of equilibrium or to prevent being overwhelmed by anxiety, e.g. rigid hierarchies in situations of life and death, e.g. medicine, the military.

Phases of human development. Group relations work requires knowledge of the phases of the human life cycle like birth, dependency, maturation, growth, independence, decline, weakness and death.

The second-most relevant body of theoretical knowledge in group relations is *Open Systems* theory, its four main concepts represented by the word BART:

Boundaries – boundaries are not necessarily a line; they could include a region, like an A&E unit is to a hospital; or an intake committee is to a university.

Authority – the power conferred on one by others to perform a role or function on their behalf.

Role – the rights, obligations and expected behaviour patterns associated with specific positions or social status.

Task – the specific work objective that needs to be accomplished. A primary task refers to the single most required thing that a group/organisation must do to survive.

Other useful concepts from Open Systems theory include:

Leadership – the ability of individuals or groups to lead; to provide guidance or direction.

Inputs, transformations and outputs – these three steps in a process form the basis of sociotechnical systems theory which also forms part of group relations theory. All operations in an organisation produce products and services by changing inputs into outputs using 'input-transformation-output' processes.

Environment – the aggregate of surrounding things, conditions or influences; the social and cultural forces that shape the life of a person or a group or organisation, also referred to as the context.

Representation/delegation – exercising authority on behalf of others which are the processes that lie at the heart of the democratic process.

Discrete bodies of knowledge come together to form new knowledge and, in this regard, we can say a theory of group relations has evolved covering many components of group life in the widest meaning of the word. A group relations theory describes 'relationship', meaning actual relationships and 'relatedness' referring to imagined relationships. Group relations theory incorporates five circles of influence that help to explain phenomena in human relations: the relationship between the inner world of the person's feelings and emotions about the self and others; the relationship between the person and their role; the relationship between the role and group; the relationship between the group and other groups; the relationship between the group and the organisation of which it is a part and relationship between the organisation and its environment. These are five over-arching inter-dependent frameworks, the study of which helps in explaining and understanding human relations.

Another useful theory used widely in group relations is Isabel Menzies Lyth formulation of the functioning of social systems as a defence against anxiety which is described in Vol. 1, Chapter 10.

Structure and design elements

Group relations conferences in the Tavistock tradition are characterised by the presence in the programme of a variety of group experiences for the purposes of the study.

Plenaries

Group relations conferences open and close in plenary sessions. The plenaries further the process of crossing the boundary into and out of the conference. The final plenary additionally allows for studying the process of ending relationships.

Small study groups

Small Study Groups consist of up to 12 participants working with 1 consultant. Their primary task is to learn about the dynamics of small groups and the formation of leadership and followership relationships as they happen in the groups. Small Study Groups are experiential 'here-and-now' events in which the behaviour of the group is placed under a high-resolution microscope and the group has the opportunity to study its own behaviour as it happens with the help of consultancy. The rationale for this is that learning, understanding and knowledge lead to change.

Large study groups

Large Study Groups comprise all the members of the conference working together with consultants. The primary task of Large Study Groups is to provide opportunities for studying the dynamics of large groups and the processes of cohesion and fragmentation, mythmaking and reality-testing as they happen in the groups. Large Study Groups are experiential 'here-and-now' events in which the behaviour of the group is placed under a high-resolution microscope and the group has the opportunity to study its own behaviour as it happens with the help of consultancy. Here too, the rationale for this is that learning, understanding and knowledge lead to change.

Review and application groups

Review and Application Groups provide members with opportunities to reflect on their experiences of the day and how they are taking up their different roles in the conference. Towards the latter half of the conference, these sessions focus on how the members hope to transfer their conference learning into their back-home organisations. This is a bridging exercise between the individual's conference learning and post-conference organisational behavioural practice and has 'here-and-now' and 'now-and-then' aspects to it. The focal question will be: what are we learning in the conference ('here-and-now') that can be applied to our roles in our organisations ('now-and-then')? Green and Molenkamp (2008) suggest the following aims for the Review and Application Groups sessions. The consultancy aims to establish a container and a creative atmosphere for collective learning over ten session series.

Key aims include

1. Creating awareness and understanding of the roles being taken up by participant members and the connections between the groups as the conference proceeds.
2. Facilitating the revelation of conscious and unconscious processes through creative expressive technologies.
3. Developing an awareness of 'system in the mind' in the conference and how it was changing as the conference proceeds.
4. Creating a learning spiral by building on the new insights gleaned in each round, yet being grounded in the participants' conference experiential reality.
5. Developing a collective capability of learners and consultants capable of using creative methods to facilitate transformation.
6. Encouraging exploration of differences as a group, including consultants, and what this may be representing for the system.

Available From: https://www.researchgate.net/publication/277890570_Review_and_Application_Methodologies

Inter-group event

The inter-group event is an opportunity for members to learn about the processes and relationships that form between different groups when they are engaged in a common task. Especially relevant with be learning how to take up representative roles and negotiating and carrying authority on behalf of others. This is an event that combines experiential 'here-and-now' learning with action learning, i.e. the putting into action, within the conference, sets of relationships between groups that derive from the experiential learning of the conference.

Inter-group relations

Organisations have relationships with one another, long before actual meetings between their representatives take place. Members of organisations have shared mental maps of their internal relationships and of their environments. These may consist of phantasies or clear ideas based on intelligence. People tend to idealise the groups which are important to them. This is done by suppressing the less satisfactory aspects or attributing these to other external groups.

Inter-group behaviour

Relations between task and sentient systems

The strength of the sentient system (those relationships based on feelings of loyalty and fidelity) may mean that members seek to preserve it from change. This may cause conflict between the activities of the task system, which demand openness to the environment, and to other groups, and those of the sentient system, directed towards protecting itself from invasion and disruption. Miller and Rice (1967, Pg. 30) distinguish between the task systems and the sentient systems within the organisations. Tasks are conducted by human beings and in organisations individuals are usually organised into groups:

> ... a major constraint on the efficiency of any activity system is that technology has not eliminated, and never will eliminate, the need to mobilize human resources, which bring with them into the enterprise more than the activities they are required to contribute. In the assignment of activities to roles and roles to task groups, human needs may modify task requirements. On the scales of task-system efficiency are superimposed scales of human satisfaction and deprivation.

When people come together in groups some emotional investment in the group can be expected. People derive their identity from their groups, and in this sense, some groups are more important than others. Thus, we may belong to many groups such as sports teams, professional associations, trade unions, political parties, a family, a project team within an organisation or a work group. The task system is made of two interlinked processes, the primary task and the sentient system. The sentient system is the needs of the individuals, feelings, beliefs, stories, practices in which they invest feelings. The sentient system is made up of the social, human processes, symbols, meanings, unconscious group forces, emotionally significant events and experiences. Members of the sentient system have attitudes and beliefs based on their needs and fantasies and the patterns of identification that individuals have built up over time in relation to the role they hold in the organisation. The strength of the sentient system may mean that members seek to preserve it from change. Miller and Rice (1967) used the term sentience to describe the level of emotional commitment and the importance of the group to the individuals within it. The more committed, the stronger the sentience is in the group. The test for the organisational system is that the needs of a task system and the needs of a sentient system need to be balanced, but there is an inescapable tension between the two. According to Miller and Rice (1990, Pg. 264), "sentience is likely to be strongest where task and sentient boundaries coincide ... where members share both a common belief in the objective of the group and complimentary beliefs about their respective contributions to it."

Inter-group behaviour and constructive inter-group exchange

In inter-group relations, it is necessary to decide when to cut off internal discussions about alternative courses of action and take steps to engage with the other group; and when to discontinue inter-group activity and resume normal functioning. Decisions have also to be made about the selection of representatives and definition of their authority. When they return, it is necessary to decide whether to endorse what they have done on behalf of the group, and live with the consequences; or whether to disown what they have done, and hence repudiate the authority vested in them, and endeavour to renegotiate with the other group, with the confusion and loss of credibility this may entail. All these decisions demand that the individual can bear the accompanying feelings of anger, guilt, depression, betrayal or loss, feelings which we have earlier identified as accompanying W-activity.

Recognition of boundaries and authority

Those engaged in inter-group activity only 'know where they are', if they can hold in their minds all the task systems, which are operative. This knowledge will seldom be in the forefront of their minds but will be tacit knowledge determining their behaviour. This entails being able to tolerate the hostility of groups wishing to defend themselves as sentient systems and the seductive pull of others wishing to detach the representative from the group which sent him, and so defend their own boundary by another method. This has been referred to as the capacity to 'stay in role'. While the necessity for representatives to stay in role is most apparent, other members of groups sending and receiving representatives have the same necessity since they also are subject to the pressures and uncertainties of participating in two task systems.

Awareness of time

Transactions between groups take time, and this poses a dilemma for groups, or organisations, whose own ongoing activities depend, at least in part, upon the outcome of a transaction. When two companies are negotiating a possible take-over of one by the other, employees, shareholders and customers can no longer continue as though nothing were happening since their position may be very different if the take-over goes through. Yet they cannot adapt to the new situation since they do not know what it is going to be. The anxiety of waiting for the outcome of inter-group transactions arouses fantasies of interminable negotiations; these are contrasted with equally fantastic instantaneous negotiations, which it is felt could take place if the proceedings were conducted in some other way.

The representative engaged in the inter-group transaction may have the greatest difficulty in maintaining a realistic awareness of the passage of time. He becomes engrossed in his task and imagines his group remaining immobile at the point he left it, like a film, which has been stopped and will be restarted when he returns. He may forget that, if, in fact, his group can do no further work until he returns, then his freedom to develop relationships, explore alternatives and draw up beautifully phrased recommendations is being bought at the expense of making the rest of his group impotent. More usually, however, groups continue to work and change their ideas while their representative is away. He, therefore, represents a group which is increasingly a thing of the past; the policy within which he is working is an anachronism. When he returns to report, he may find that his work is irrelevant to the current preoccupations of the group.

Consulting to the inter-group dynamic

Acceptance of change

From the point of view of groups as sentient systems, the need to have relations with other groups is a demand to tolerate change. Once a group allows its boundary to be breached by incoming or outgoing representatives or by other forms of communication, it is faced with the possibility of having to revise its fantasies about other groups in its environment and about itself, its values and priorities. This arouses fantasies of total disruption and chaos and corresponding defensive activity.

The management of inter-group transactions, therefore, entails the exercise of control through the definition of tasks, roles and authority, setting of time limits, allocation of territory, taking of minutes and other activities.

Such forms of organisation, like any other, constitute defences against anxiety as well as a means of facilitating constructive activity. A measure of the strength of the anxieties, which they are intended to control, is the frequency with which inter-group transactions degenerate into S-activity (survival) and produce bizarre results. Equally frequent are the negotiations, which are so hedged about with procedural regulations, 'talks about talks' and other devices, that the participants have no scope at all for reaching conclusions, which would materially affect the interests of the groups they represent.

Consulting to the inter-group process

The basic stance of the consultant is that consultants use their own feelings to sense what is happening. But consultants do not observe with a detached objectivity that takes away the responsibility of taking account what they are feeling. This may entail feelings of embarrassment, anxiety, anger, hurt, or being pleased. Consultants ask why they are feeling what they are feeling and can attempt to sort out what comes from themselves and what is being projected onto them from organisational members. Consultants can use this as information about the meaning of behaviour, both consciously and unconsciously motivated. If an explanation can be found for the projection, in terms of the specific task of the meeting or process, an interpretation or working hypothesis can be offered about the behaviour of those present, including the consultant. This may be accepted, rejected or ignored. The consultant is primarily concerned only with what is happening 'here and now', and the dynamic relationship between the organisations. The role of consultants is to interpret what is happening in and between organisations in the here-and-now to support learning and development of the parties engaged in the negotiations.

The systems psychodynamics consultant is interested in the authority within the boundary of inter-group relations. Miller and Rice (1967) outline a view of a transactional system that is created when negotiations take place between organisations. It contains four new boundary dimensions:

1 Between Organisation A and Representative A
2 Between Representative A and Organisation B
3 Within Organisation B with the addition of Representative A
4 Within Organisation A with the addition of Representative B

Whole System Event

The Whole System Event, is, as it says, an event that involves all parts of the conference – groups formed by the members and groups formed by the staff – in learning about relationships between parts and wholes; managing differentials of power and influence; how to keep the whole system in mind when one is working in part of it, especially when the system is large and complex and often unknowable. The event involves 'here-and-now' experiential learning.

Over the years, new and innovative group events have been devised and introduced into group relations conference programmes such as the following.

The Management of Resources Event

The Management of Resources Event was designed and introduced by William Halton. The event has a **Management Group and Resource Group.** The aim of the event is to create a plan in which individual named members are authorised to run an event or events which address the assessed learning needs of the members. The Management Group has full authority over all the territories and all the resources of the conference within the boundaries of the event. Each Resource Group must identify its resources, to make them available to the Management Group and to collaborate with all groups in creating and implementing a plan.

Marketplace Event (designed by William Halton)

The aim of the Marketplace event is to explore the dynamics of a marketplace environment without a Management Group. In the marketplace, every organisation is both a supplier and a customer. We supply something to our customers and we, in turn, are customers to other suppliers. In this event, independent groups are formed which have both a supplier and a customer role.

Embodying Role Event

The Embodying Role Event comprises the total conference membership and staff working to explore how paying attention to the whole self – mind, body and spirit – fosters integration and plays a vital part in taking up a role. This is an experiential here-and-now event to practice the (further) awakening of a deeper awareness of internal states as data, thereby increasing access to creative, intellectual and emotional resources.

Presence-in-absence Event

The Presence-in-absence Event opens and closes in Plenary. The task is to study the relationship and relatedness between membership and staff in the here-and-now: how we work together and how we make sense of our roles by exploring the fantasies, assumptions and patterns of relating, bringing sharp focus to issues of authorisation across institutional boundaries.

Notes from the field: the contribution of group relations

By Leslie Brissett

There are some points that WR Bion has stated that we are still yet to fully apprehend, and arguably we need a more mystical framework to do so. When he says, "I cannot here discuss the problems, but need to formulate them for further investigation, thus: Thoughts exist without a thinker. The idea of infinitude is prior to any idea of the infinite. The finite is 'won from the dark and formless infinite'" (Bion, 1967, Pg. 165). I hear this quote as Bion sensing that there is future work to be done by those with an interest in groups and systems that was not possible to be done in his time. These second thoughts are some 10 years after the first Leicester Conference in 1957 and some 53 years before the 2020 Leicester Conference that took place in Bavaria, amid the global coronavirus pandemic.

We have had in place a system of thinking that tells us that biology is the cause of the thinking and meaning-making process: 'Cogito ergo sum', I think therefore I am, has been the basis and structure of how we think about thinking, and therefore how we think about acting and relating. Bion's statement takes us back thousands of years (and simultaneously forwards) into a time where thoughts were believed to pre-exist the thinker. Much of Taoist thought is rooted in the idea that man is an idea in the mind of the void of creation. If we are to engage with the idea that thoughts can exist before we do, then what does that mean for our existence when we are not thinking, "I don't think, therefore I am not", may be one outcome of this logic.

Existential anxiety

Paradox and uncertainty trigger anxiety and psychic defences emerge and continue to exist to assist us to cope with that anxiety. With the passing of the global pandemic and the rise of the deleterious consequences of The Empire, and the rise of the 'like' culture of social media, a new anxiety is emerging, that of Belonging. In 1944, C. S. Lewis delivered a speech in which he says, "Of all the passions, the passion for the Inner Ring is most skillful in making a man who is not yet a very bad man do very bad things …. until you conquer the fear of being an outsider, an outsider you will remain" (Lewis, 1944, Pg. 5). It is this fear of and passion for belonging that may lead to the next round of organisational, environmental or economic disaster, and group relations can illuminate for the individual their propensity to participate and the nature of a system's impact on their behaviour. Perhaps this will enable us to avoid another significant crime against humanity in the form of the transatlantic slave trade or a Nazi Holocaust, to name two in our past.

Seeking to understand authority in human social systems is about to face a resurgence. The levels of corruption, abuse and neglect from all sections of our social systems – police, church, political, economic, education – have left us in need of a remedy. The remedy is one of a super-ordinate goal, a new primary task. By moving authority centre stage, the flagship Leicester Conference is now designated, Task, Authority, Organisation (TAO). When articulated in its acronym as the 'TAO of Tavistock', it allows us the space to consider the transcendence of the systems psychodynamics paradigm into the realm of the existential.

An openness to mysteries

Why is the existential nature of the systems psychodynamics framework in general and group relations in particular so important as we face our next evolutionary step? Arguably, the failure of religion and the consequent loss of a moral compass and an ethical framework to guide humans in a secular world has created a vacuum into which self-serving and corruption have entered. If we consider that the need for a "lived experience of connection" could be a remedy for the internal collapse of the moral structure of modern man, the stage is set for group relations to enter and make a contribution. Group relations cannot be a complete answer to such a wide-ranging programme of destruction, but through its enduring principles of freedom and the centrality of experience, the group relations methodology is a context for discovery.

As we enter the era of full digitalisation across social, economic and political realms, the question of what it is to be human and how humans live and work together will become MORE important, not less. As such, the demand for group relations-oriented persons will increase; our challenge is to prepare the ground for a spreading of the capacity to respond to this demand. What does it mean to be human and how do we live together? These are ancient questions and how we live with and through the questions could be an interesting way into a discussion of our socially constructed world.

Being human in the digital age

Learning the core skill of the anthropologist, "to make the familiar strange and the strange familiar", Horace Miner wrote in "Body Ritual Among the Nacirema", turned a culture upside down so that people could discover a-fresh, what is familiar to them. How we change from a consumer society to a creative society in a sustainable way requires us to revisit some of the early pioneering work of the Tavistock Institute of Human Relations and to take the bold step to live it in daily organisational and social practices. This work begins with the communities of systems psychodynamics practice. Instead of reproducing another century of ego-driven splits and schisms, generating ever more specialisms and disciplines, the challenge is to work collaboratively on the broader, bigger, systemic challenges that require intervention at the level of the 'whole', not the parts.

The nature of the learning in a group relations conference is still unrivalled anywhere in our social milieu. Even in those academic institutions that have shifted their leadership learning to more engaging and experiential methodologies, the pedagogic reliance on teaching and instruction from the teacher to the student demonstrates that even they can still benefit from group relations conference learning.

An early Tavistock Institute collaborator was University of Pennsylvania Wharton School Professor Russell Ackoff. In his work with the Institute's Emery and Trist, the political dimension and the role of democratic processes in the world of work and society were considered in some depth. What they argued in the early 1950s was a prescient, clearly conceived strategy of wholism.

Through their thinking in terms of systems that sought to mobilise the learning capacity of the individual and locate it firmly in the total life world as the context for learning. An illustration of the proliferation of academic disciplines and the impact on our ability to conceive holistically can be illustrated by this quote from Wikipedia describing the influences and the impact of a Spanish essayist, José Ortega y Gasset.

Wikipedia describes him thus: "He worked during the first half of the 20th century, while Spain oscillated between monarchy, republicanism, and dictatorship. His philosophy has been characterized as a "philosophy of life" that "comprised a long-hidden beginning in a pragmatist metaphysics inspired by William James, and with a general method from a realist phenomenology imitating Edmund Husserl, which served both his proto-existentialism (prior to Martin Heidegger's) and his realist historicism".

The requisite discipline to understand the complexity of the social world is enhanced, I advocate, when we can hold in mind the complexity and inherent confusion in trying to make sense of the world. What the Wikipedia entry does is to demonstrate the impact of too much emphasis on dissection and classification. The intellectual pursuit of domains of reductionism and division runs counter to a group relations learning experience.

In group relations, there is the possibility to encounter the full spectrum of the human condition, not avoiding or splitting off the unwanted parts. As such, we can bring all the parts into sharp focus and not lose the broader context to 'see the wood and the trees'.

Group relations as art, science or craft?

Indian Institute of Management, Ahmedabad (IIMA), Professor Ajeet Mathur, in his book Mysteries in Management, says that "All organisations are systems of interpretation and the sense-making function never ceases. Phenomena inside and outside the boundaries of an organisation as unthought knowns and unknown knowables need to be paid attention all the time" (Mathur, 2015, Pg. 156). This quote is reminiscent of the mystery in the writing of Bion quoted earlier, that points us towards a pre-existing infinite that has already a form in a way that we are yet to apperceive. There is an aesthetic sensibility that lives within Mathur's phraseology which invites us to develop and luxuriate in the Keatsian capacity for 'negative capability'. How to listen and not remember and to hear without being wounded is the hallmark or aspiration of the psychoanalytical encounter as described by Bion (1967).

As such, the nature of the learning from a group relations perspective can be articulated as both art and craft. Encounters in group relations utilise the scientific method of observation, testing, hypothesis generation and further testing. Observation in the frame of the quantum physicists is not an objective thing or activity, it is subjective and, at the same time, the observed and the observer become entangled, such that there is no 'other' to be observed. If this quantum entanglement makes its way into our psychic reality and the group relations framework, it could be that we begin to approach what Bion termed 'O'. He said, "I shall use the sign O to denote that which is the ultimate reality, absolute truth, the godhead, the infinite, the thing-in-itself".

Possible future action?

The chapter from Sher and Lawlor states that "While the Double Task approach sits comfortably within the systems psychodynamics canon, it would not feature in Tavistock group relations conferences which instead focus on one task – the primary task – that is more associated with issues of individual and group survival". This view offers one way of making sense of the split between Harold Bridger and A. Ken Rice, who held different views about the capacity and the stress caused when working solely on the group authority relations. This split led to the creation of the Bayswater Institute. What if we, as a group relations community of practice were to be naïve enough to go back to first principles and celebrate the connectivity that has launched new lines of inquiry rather than develop new "isms" seeking their own independence? Could we actually apply our theories to our own actions and thought processes? There is a possibility that Bayswater and Tavistock Institute of Human Relations may be able to work collaboratively and have room for both double task and primary task activity.

In concluding this contribution to the thinking of this book on the future of systems psychodynamics research and consultancy, there is significant scope for us to demonstrate that the impact of group relation conference learning has sway in the real world day to day 'here and now'. We can become our own living laboratory and subject ourselves to rigorous scrutiny and study of the mechanisms of human destructiveness. We could demonstrate that it is possible to work with and through the poison of daily living and that the elements of group relations are designed to work on the primary spirit of the human condition and not the ossification of the primary task of conference methodological narrative.

Summary

A group must have a clear and focused understanding of its task and a structure that protects all participants adequately against the dangers of traumatic re-enactment. Groups share commonality with other people; belong to a society, have a public role and are part of the universal; a feeling of familiarity, of being known, of communion. Membership of a group means taking part in the customary, the commonplace, the ordinary, and the everyday.

(Herman, 1997)

Group relations conferences are devoted to experiential learning about group and organisational behaviour, with an emphasis on the nature of role, authority and leadership. Group relations conferences provide a variety of settings for the 'here-and-now' study of the relatedness of individual, group and organisation. The primary task of group relations conferences provides opportunities to study the exercise of authority in the context of interpersonal, intergroup and institutional relations within the conference institution.

The group relations tradition reconciles field research with organisational interventions aimed at enhancing organisational and personal effectiveness and well-being. At the heart of group relations thinking lies the idea that organisations and groups generate anxiety among their members. Anxiety triggers defensive mechanisms some of which are rooted in the individual, others in the group, and yet others in the organisation. Defensive mechanisms relieve immediate anxiety but they promote and immerse individuals and groups in a fantasy world, where emotions dominate and miscalculations occur. Within group relations conferences, these processes and dynamics can be revealed and worked with. Group relations conferences provide added perspective on the practice of systems psychodynamics-oriented organisational consultancy. Group relations conferences aid the understanding and experience of powerful unconscious forces at play in groups and between groups. Group relations provides a means to explore ways in which individual and personal projections link to group and organisational life in the context of their specific environments. Group relations conferences provide a means of exploring enactments and denial in organisational and environmental contexts. Group relations help understand the defensiveness of individuals as a reflection and re-creation of the defences of the organisation; how organisational defences are enacted, perpetuated and refined by individuals. Exploring the links between the emotional dynamics within and between individuals and groups is fundamental to group relations and the systems psychodynamics paradigm. Group relations consist of a theoretical underpinning, structural and design elements, a primary task, adopting a group-as-a-whole consultative stance and minimum length.

Exercise

1 In your organisation, write a list of all the groups you can think of. What comes to mind about the quality of the relationships between the groups?
2 From your observations, how do the groups feel about each other? What sort of emotions do you see in play?
3 What purpose do they serve?
4 What do the sub-systems put in each other and why do they do that?

10 The contribution of group relations II

With David Armstrong

For a concise and readable account of Group relations theory and practice, The Tavistock Primer II by Charla Hayden and René J. Molenkamp (2004) is very helpful. It is an updated version of the original Primer by Banet and Hayden (1977). In The Tavistock Primer II, the theoretical underpinnings of the educational model have been more thoroughly explored, and the design and structure of conferences have developed in several dimensions as sponsoring organisations and conference directors seek to maintain the relevance of the learning model in the midst of dramatic cultural and institutional changes. The intention of the authors is to continue in the tradition of the first version of the article by making it accessible to people beyond the realm of practicing group relations consultants but to honour the considerable advancements in theory and practice achieved by those within the tradition.

Below, we describe some of the theoretical and practice developments in group relations.

Social dreaming matrix

Controversially, some group relations conferences include a social dreaming matrix; see Lawrence (2003), which is a forum for the exploration of dreams in a matrix in order to derive deeper meaning of the social context in which the matrix exists, i.e. the group relations conference itself. The introduction of social dreaming is controversial for two reasons; firstly, because the search for meaning in the conference goes on in the events themselves and in the Review and Application Groups at the end of each day. Social dreaming matrices as separate events, it is thought, may dilute those experiences; and secondly, dreams usually form part of the different group events anyway where they serve a similar purpose of deepening understanding of unconscious phenomena that may be available for exploration in the conference.

Double task event

Harold Bridger (1990) and Gold and Klein (2004) were part of the remarkable group of social scientists at the Tavistock Institute. Bridger helped to found other institutions including the Bayswater Institute (see: https://www.bayswaterinst.org), which now runs his group relations training model. Bridger's distinctive contribution to systems psychodynamics and group relations lay in several areas. He developed and refined the 'double-task' approach: this involved scrutinising and working with the organisation's primary task, as well as examining and working with the 'process', the secondary task; drawing on his psychoanalytic training, he paid particular attention to the unconscious dimensions of the process. Bridger made a pioneering contribution to understanding and working with the interface between the primary and secondary tasks, dealing with the complex issues that emerge there, and designing methodologies and 'working conferences' that facilitate the mutual development of both tasks. He developed 'working conferences' – 'transitional institutions' (Bridger 1990a), operating on 'double-task' lines – that ran, and continue to run, on a regular basis for the development of managers; these are intended to allow people the space to develop their thinking about organisations in a new way. Bridger, who developed an exceptional skill in the design and running of these, focused squarely on bringing participants' current dilemmas and issues into the working conference.

The Double Task is an approach to group relations favoured by the Bayswater Institute. At one level, the Double Task focuses on people's capabilities to getting the technical or managerial job done; at another, it aims to increase understanding of groups that are engaged in the work. The Double Task provides new ways of seeing teams and increasing effectiveness in team working. While the Double Task approach sits comfortably within the systems psychodynamics canon, it would not feature in Tavistock group relations conferences, which instead focus on one task, the primary task, that is more associated with issues of individual and group survival.

Elements of primary task

Group relations conferences are principally concerned with issues of authority and leadership, two processes that are tightly associated with magic, enchantment and fear, thereby always attracting transference, strong ties and emotions, usually originating in the early development of the individual, that in later life become projected onto the person of the leader. In the conference itself, these early-life projections, identifications, attachments and fears of authority are manifest and experienced in the interpersonal, intra-group, intergroup, institutional and environmental relationships. They are consulted to and interpreted by staff in their consultant and management roles for the purpose of deepening the membership's and the staff's knowledge of the dynamics operating in groups with different tasks and contexts.

The consultative stance

Staff members are appointed to their roles in group relations conferences based on their abilities to work with and in transference and counter-transference phenomena. Their abilities to do so depend on their professional training, past group relations experiences and on having gone through personal psychoanalysis or psychotherapy. These requirements are taken as a minimum standard to enable staff members to have the necessary skills in interpreting group unconscious dynamics; an enhanced ability to work within boundaries; having developed high levels of clarity when working within role and task; capability of working with group-as-a-whole, not individual, phenomena, which distinguishes group relations work from other forms of work with groups. Staff members are also expected to be capable of generating working hypotheses, an interpretation of what is known so far, and an invitation to think about it. Staff members would be expected to be curious and to eschew 'memory and desire', i.e. to desist from influencing people's learning process by imposing their own 'agenda'. Staff members in consultant role would be expected to tolerate 'negative capability', i.e. being able to tolerate not knowing and accepting inaction while learning is going on; giving up the need to have brilliant students, adoring clients, etc.

Length

It is axiomatic that learning about relationships in groups and between groups and how to manage oneself in different roles takes time and will require attendance at group relations conferences of sufficient duration. The original group relations conference, commonly termed the Leicester conference, extends over 14 consecutive days and is residential. Other group relations conferences vary in length between 1 and 12 days and maybe residential or non-residential.

A case example: application of Group Relations to an organisational dilemma

A university requested a social science (group relations) intervention to help resolve tensions and difficulties based on long-standing rivalries between four departments in the Faculty of Science – the departments of chemistry, agriculture, soil sciences and hydrology. These rivalries amplified during the departments' attempts to set up a major joint publicly funded project on global warming and climate change and which required the departments to work closely together, to share budgets and would, if successful, confer huge status on the departments, on the university and benefits to society overall. Failure to work together would face the university with the loss of the project, an important income stream, and pressures to merge or close some departments.

A team of group relations consultants designed and ran a group relations event for 34 senior staff members (the leadership) of the four departments that would, it was hoped, expose the pressure points that exacerbated the competition between them and would provide the necessary framework for developing understanding and insight that would help them take up their respective roles in the project in a more mature collaborative and sustainable manner. The group relations event produced four propositions:

Proposition 1

That the application of group relations (GR) methodology, an abridged version of an Inter-Group event (IG) would clearly demonstrate to the senior staff members of the four departments the complex dynamics of the relationships within and between the different departments as integrated sub-systems in the project.

The 34 participants of the Inter-Group event were invited to self-divide into 2 groups of 8 people each and 2 groups of 9, with the groups asked to ensure a diverse balance of departmental members, grades of seniority, genders and ages. Representatives of the four groups were offered a 'blind' choice to represent one of four sub-systems of the project – chemistry, agriculture, soil sciences and hydrology. The four newly formed groups occupied different spaces in a large room and followed a prepared timetable over two days that consisted of 20 × 30-minute sessions, each with a different group task. The sessions were:

- An introduction to the work.
- Forming into four diversely balanced groups.
- The groups working independently on their identity and structure.
- The groups preparing to deliver the first message to the other three groups.
- Representatives of the groups visiting the other three groups.
- The groups receiving representatives from the other groups to hear their messages.
- The representatives gathering data about how and to what extent their messages were 'heard' and assimilated and bringing data back to their own groups.
- The groups assessing the incoming data about the other three groups' behaviour as well as reflecting on their own behaviour.
- The four groups preparing to communicate the second message to the three other groups and receiving delegates from the other groups.
- The representatives delivering their second messages from their groups to the other groups.
- The delegates assessing again how the groups being visited had changed and adapted since the last message and how they were reacting to the latest message.
- The delegates returning to their groups and the groups assessing incoming data a second time.
- There was a social dreaming matrix on the morning of the second day, and several sessions were devoted to reviewing the work so far and think about how the lessons learned could be applied to their actual departmental internal and external relationships.
- A final plenary session was held for reviewing the totality of the Inter-Group event from the participants' individual perspectives and experiences.

From time to time, the two group relations consultants would visit the groups and assist with any questions. They would also comment on the emerging behavioural dynamics of the groups and the interactions between them. For example, it was noted and commented that the 'chemistry' group seemed to be engaging in a merger with the 'soils sciences' group; their emotional tone appeared to be despondency and a sense of abandonment; the 'agricultural' group lacked leadership and moved about the room as independent operators, tenuously held together by an us-and-them attitude towards the other groups; the 'hydrology' group seemed comfortable in their isolation, saying: "we have the legislative powers and we have the money – they can come to us"; the 'soil sciences' group appeared to be working on-task trying to understand the needs and difficulties of the other groups and struggling to keep communications open between them, but their efforts exhausted them as they were pulled in different directions.

Some participants said dismissively that the exercise felt like a 'role play', but after about 30 minutes, the feeling of being in a role play lifted and the 4 groups experienced for real the deep feelings of competition and emotions of rivalry and envy that corresponded with the original cultures of the four departments. With the help of the consultants, these dynamic relationships and emotions could now be consciously examined and experimented with, with a view to changing them when they eventually returned to their departments after the Inter-Group event.

Proposition 2

That understanding the nature of the dynamics of the four departments in the project as a grouping of sub-systems would lead to improved partnership working of each sub-system individually and of the four sub-systems collectively.

As the groups progressed through the two-day timetable and lived the experiences of being in the 'chemistry', 'agriculture', 'soil sciences' and 'hydrology' groups, whether or not they were actually from those departments, the participants gained greater skills in arguing their cases with the other groups and listening carefully to the arguments of the other groups. People from the 'chemistry' department improved their mobility in and among the three other groups, working to the tasks of each session, they increased their ability to differentiate their roles and make responsible decisions to leave some participants in their group space to receive delegates from the other groups, while other participants fanned out to the three other sub-systems to negotiate for shared resources and other needs. The 'agriculture' group remained stuck in a stubborn independence causing them to be perceived as 'troubled farmers' a role from which it was difficult to emerge. The 'soil sciences' group moved from a state of anxiety about what to do with their rebellious nature to an increased understanding of the need to collaborate with the other groups. Their emotional tone changed showing a greater empathic understanding of the 'hydrology' group despite their haughtiness that came from their greater powers to 'give' or to 'withhold'. They were scornful of the 'agricultural' group and were reluctant to hear what they had to say. The 'hydrology' group was sceptical of the whole process and concentrated solely on the purposes of and the risks to their departmental business with little regard for any wider social concerns. Over the course of the event, they mellowed somewhat and were willing to receive delegations from the other groups.

Proposition 3
That the sub-systems would discover and experience the presence and flow of group unconscious exclusion and inclusion dynamics from the more powerful sub-systems to the less powerful.

Exclusion and inclusion dynamics were evident in the unfolding relationships between the four groups during the event. It was noted that power and status flowed in a singular direction from the 'hydrology' group at the top to the 'soil sciences', to the 'chemists', and finally to the 'agricultural' group at the bottom. It was noted that this kind of power dynamic included some groups and excluded others and was likely to keep all the groups stuck and cut off from the other groups and rendering their collaboration in the project weaker than it should be. The participants were acutely disturbed by this observation as they were introduced to the concept of the 'group and social unconscious', viz. that if unconscious group and Inter-Group dynamics are not exposed, shared, discussed, understood and addressed, the forces that are at play in all human systems could lead to the less powerful and lower status groups to disappear out of mind and therefore not receive the support and attention they need in order to do their work and make the most of their new project opportunity.

Proposition 4
That GR is a powerful instrument for extrapolating from the learning situation (of the event) to managing the external reality of the climate change project.

In the final plenary session, the participants reviewed their experiences from their different roles they had taken up in the IG event. There was general agreement that it had been a powerful learning moment in which the participants discovered how quickly and how permanently one group becomes 'encased' in a role and how the other groups contribute to that identity. Also evident to the dismay of the participants, was how one's group then enacts the unrewarding behaviours that others come to expect of it (or project into it), e.g. entitled, uncooperative and undisciplined ('hydrologists'); arrogant, selfish and indifferent ('agriculturalists'); empathic and understanding ('soil sciences') in conflict with the 'hydrologists', and more seriously, the despair, hopelessness and futility of the 'chemists' who remained permanently burdened with those feelings. Powerful and sometimes disturbing emotions and feelings were evoked by the Inter-Group event experience: someone said: "I will never think of my departmental colleagues in the same way again". Several participants said they saw the value of including and addressing the 'total climate change project system', not just each individual separate department; they saw the powerful application opportunities for improving the project functioning.

Closing statement
The Inter-Group experience aimed to help all participants in the project to notice what they feel or don't feel; what they do or don't do in their intra-group

> and Inter-Group relationships; how they take up their roles and how they work together by being alert to the competition and rivalry and alienation they experience so that change in the culture becomes possible and leads the sub-systems to work together more collaboratively and with improved chances of success and satisfaction.

System psychodynamic approaches to the practice of organisational consultancy

Menzies (1960), in her work with the nursing profession and care-taking institutions, contributed the theory of social defences which she equated with individual defences. Organisational interventions based on this perspective typically involve understanding, interpreting and working through such collective defences, which hopefully result in enlarging the organisations capacity to develop more task appropriate adaptations. A central feature of Menzies's work is the notion that even the most seemingly instrumental, efficient and reasonable patterns of work and division of labour may have social defence properties. In the face of these social defences, she argues for a form of action research and organisational consultation. Menzies describes a collaborative engagement between consultants and their clients to jointly explore the nature of their problems, to generate ideas for change, to test those ideas in practice, and to evaluate the results. Furthermore, because many of the issues involve challenging both individual and social defences, institutional change "inevitably involves a slow, gradual and often painful evolutionary process".

There is a wide spectrum of consultation practice encompassed by the systems psychodynamics perspective. Bain (1998) provides a useful categorisation. He notes that the organisational consultant engages in an analysis of some or all of the following:

1 Roles and role configurations.
2 Structures and organisational design.
3 Work culture and group processes.

The analysis of work culture and group processes is most closely related to the central aim of group relations conferences. It is the most common type of practice taken up by those whose organisational consultation training is almost exclusively based on the group relations conference model. The approach is for a consultant to join regular meetings of a natural work group and to interpret process in a manner like consulting to a small study group. But, in an organisational consultation, there is a marked shift away from interpretations that focus the group's relationship to the consultant to relations between group members themselves, their relatedness to the institution, and their task at hand. A consultant working in this way would be alert to and would selectively interpret the covert and dynamic aspects of the client's organisation and the work groups that comprise it. Often with a focus on how authority is psychologically distributed, exercised and enacted, in contrast to how it is formally invested.

This work would include a consideration of attitudes, beliefs, phantasies, core anxieties, social defences and patterns of relationships and collaboration and how they influence task performance. Consultants would focus on how unwanted feelings and experiences are split off and projected onto individuals and groups that carry them, i.e. their process roles as distinct from their formally sanctioned roles, on behalf of the organisation.

Group relations and the ethical imagination: between past and future

By David Armstrong

In the summer of 1959, as a young would-be social psychologist, hot foot from Cambridge, I joined the staff of the Tavistock Institute of Human Relations in London as a Junior Project Officer. I was to work under the leadership of Eric Trist on an action research programme into the impact of automation on human relations at work. I knew little or nothing about the Tavistock, its history and tradition, the link with psychoanalysis, its reinvention after the Second World War, and its debt to the work of Kurt Lewin and his 'field theory' perspective on social relations in groups and organisations. I knew only that my professor had told me that if I really wanted to be a social psychologist and work in the 'real world' rather than the laboratory, there was only one person and one place it was worth considering, Eric Trist at the 'Tavy'.

Gradually and in the face of early resistances (a mixture of philosophical prejudice and sheer lack of understanding), I became more familiar with what I had known nothing about, familiar from conversation, reading, listening and learning from my 'apprentice masters', on the job, as it were.

At that time, there were two more or less icons, or at least genus loci, whose aura and influence around the place was inescapable: Melanie Klein (in the Clinic) and Wilfred Bion (in the Institute). In particular, it was Wilfred Bion's innovations as a war time psychiatrist and his leadership of what was later to be known as the 'Tavistock group' within military psychiatry that had furnished the groundwork for the later development of 'Group Relations', as a method of exploring, understanding and engaging with the challenges and dilemmas of social and organisational life. Subsequently, Bion had played a central role in the post-war reconstitution of the Tavistock Clinic and the creation of a sister organisation (the Tavistock Institute) based on what had been learned during the war time innovations. Later, working with a variety of different groups (patients, industrialists, staff and students) and drawing on his own emotional experiences in and of them, Bion began to evolve a provisional characterisation of the dynamics of group life and the interplay of conscious and unconscious processes. This he presented in a series of hugely influential papers, eventually published together as *Experiences in Groups* the year after I joined the Institute.

Four years later I was lucky enough to be a member of the last study group taken by Bion in the UK as part of a four month group relations training event at the Tavistock, led by Ken Rice. This experience proved much more disorienting than I had anticipated, in part at least because Bion gave no hint of having written or read *Experiences in Groups*; he seemed to have moved on, though it wasn't immediately clear how or why. I think that it was the puzzle of this that eventually drew me into the field and, give or take an occasional abortive sidetrack, it has remained a constant accompaniment in most of my work, both in training and consultancy ever since.

The puzzles, however, remain, though they are different now. They include questions about the boundary of 'group relations', what's included and what's bracketed out, both in practice and conceptually; the links with other related psychoanalytic or systemic formulations; and perhaps most fundamentally, the issue of applicability, not just what can be learned but what follows from that learning, in the organisational and social worlds we inhabit and inhabit now. What difference, or more exactly what organisational and social difference, does it or might it make. One (or maybe I should just say I) can sometimes sense a missing term, an absence in both the practice and conceptualisation of 'group relations', something like an imaginative deficit, or creative withdrawal.

And this brings me back to the war time origins. For in its origins, group relations was neither a theory nor a method. (You might say it hadn't yet acquired capital letters.) Rather, it was a practical necessity, born of war; how should one select officers, how to meet a shortfall in men putting themselves forward; how to respond to soldiers withdrawn from the front or prisoners of war coming back to civilian life. The group of psychiatrists, psychologists and social scientists gathered around Bion were themselves enlisted and in uniform, working alongside military personnel. In each of their areas of work, they were having to engage with groups, evolving methods and ways of working that had few precedents, at the same time as they were accountable to military command.

Earlier, I referred to 'Group Relations' (with a capital G and R) as a "method of exploring, understanding and engaging with the challenges and dilemmas of social and organisational life". But as regards its origins, this sequence of words is really the wrong way round. 'Group Relations' starts life with engagement; exploration and understanding are a consequence, not a cause.

Looking back, now, at the innovations that Bion and his colleagues were to pioneer: the use of 'leaderless groups' in the selection of military personnel; 'regimental nomination', a remarkable and eventually abortive experiment to involve every soldier in nominating candidates for officer training; the treatment and rehabilitation of soldiers withdrawn from the front; the civil resettlement of returning prisoners of war, one can, I think, retrospectively, trace four associated elements in play which, together, I propose as a working definition of the 'ethical imagination':

- An emergent challenge or dilemma in practical life (for the individual, the group or the social organisation) that carries an implicit developmental undertow.

- An acknowledgement and a belief in human resourcefulness and agency.
- A capacity to reimagine forms of human association.
- The presence or evocation of resistance, internal and/or external.

Consider, for example, Bion and John Rickman's account of their approach to working in a military psychiatric hospital (which appears as a 'Preview' to *Experiences in Groups*). There was no precedence for this, psychiatric, psychoanalytic or otherwise. The originality of their approach, its imaginativeness, turned rather on the suspension of what was already known. It preceded both theory and method, owing little or nothing to either.

Bion and Rickman read the presenting issue, the presence of neurosis, as embedded in the men's real situation, as soldiers withdrawn from the theatre of war. They related to the men as soldiers who happened to be patients, not patients who happened to be soldiers; themselves as soldiers who happened to be psychiatrists. As they were later to put it, the whole therapeutic procedure they evolved turned around a military analogy: to create an organisational framework in which "neurosis can be displayed as a danger to the group (the enemy within), and its display be made the common aim of the group". Though not explicitly stated, this procedure both depended on and owed its apparent effectiveness to an implicit belief in the capacity of the men, simply through being brought into observing and learning from their own experiences in and of the group, to rediscover the capacity for cooperation and courage in addressing the challenges they faced, in short, to come to terms with the forces of resistance, the regressive undertow of response, within themselves. As Bion expressed it in characterising the task of the psychiatrist in such a setting "to become self-respecting men, socially adjusted to the community and therefore willing to accept its responsibilities, whether in peace or war".

In more recent years, in my view, Bion's later explorations in groups, with their emphasis on the regressive pull in group behaviour, have both overshadowed and drawn attention away from the social radicalism of this early venture. That is, the way it was directed to draw out the group's capacity for recovering a sense of internal agency, a capacity that was compromised not only by the group's own internal dynamics but also by what Bion was later to name as "some sort of equilibrium of insincerity … achieved by patients, doctors and the community alike". In the event, after just six weeks, Bion and Rickman's venture was abruptly terminated, and both were summarily dismissed. The exact reasons remain somewhat obscure and contested. It seems likely though that they were, one way or another, a reaction to the way Bion's procedure challenged both the medical and the organisational assumptions on which the whole hospital was run, indeed took those assumptions, with their unquestioned acceptance of conventional hierarchy and professional 'expertise', as part of the problem. On this view, the boundaries of the problem expanded into a wider organisational and social context, as much external as internal, systemic as group.

In a remarkable paper written after the war, now largely ignored, and delivered as his presidential address to the Medical Section of the British Psychological Society, Bion returned to and generalised from this experience.

At one level, his paper can be taken as a plea for colleagues to join him in exploring the ways in which psychoanalysis and related disciplines, including work with groups "had brought a new type of knowledge to humankind, a type of knowledge which, if used, could be the means through which western societies could learn how to surmount their manifold crises and develop to a further stage". At another level, though, perhaps more striking is Bion speculating on the nature of a society's collective discontents. So, at one point, circling around the emotional sources of such discontents, he comments:

> We also have to bear in mind those organisations which in themselves produce problems for the majority of those living in that organisation. It is possible for a society to be organised in such a way that the majority of its members are psychiatrically disinherited.

What he seems to have in mind is the way in which the specialisation of a society and its organisations can restrict the scope for the development of man's political appetite, that is the range of his participation in human affairs and relationships, a kind of 'spiritual drift', he says, "which leads communities into forms of association which are as destructive of the individual as a community without a public health service would be of its physical health". And then:

> Even if we admit that the individual is a more than willing participant in depriving himself of the full range of personal relationships, we still have to bear in mind the educational system of home and school which has allowed him to progress along a path of progressive limitation, without any awareness that he was in fact doing so.

Skip a paragraph and one reads:

> The value of a group decision in an industrial concern may derive from a restoration to the individuals of a group a part of their inheritance. As a prelude to scientific investigation, it is worth speculating on the possibility that the Trade Union movement and now unofficial strikes represent a reaction against psychological disinheritance far more profound than wages or lack of material comforts.

It is as if here Bion is sketching out an agenda for the exercise of an ethical imagination, rooted in a socio-psychological/psychoanalytic understanding but moving towards a more structural opening out that he was himself to pursue. It was this 'opening out' that was to become a hallmark of the Tavistock Institute, separately incorporated within the Tavistock Clinic shortly after Bion's address. For example, in its early explorations of workplace democracy and the autonomous work group, which, originating independently from a spontaneous innovation in the collective practices of a group of South Yorkshire coal miners, were to challenge any assumption of inevitability in the way an organisation was structured, leadership, power and authority distributed.

One might perhaps think of this 'opening out' as both the other side of resistance and simultaneously its source. Something captured, I think, in the model, Bion himself was later to offer (in *Attention and Interpretation*) of the relation between the creative individual, the group and the establishment and the ways in which, within the inner world, the explosive and transformative potential of an emergent thought, which may, unconsciously, be sensed to threaten an existent psychological equilibrium, can evoke a countervailing power that, as it were, claims sovereignty over all development. To take the example, for instance, I have just mentioned, when the Tavistock negotiated to make an in-depth study in the mining industry, drawing from the experience of the Yorkshire miners, "permission was difficult to obtain. Headquarters were nervous about anything like this being studied or published. They sensed it could stir up union relations and would upset traditional managers. They didn't want to touch it so our study was stopped". It's the same pattern, in a different context, as with Bion and Rickman's war time experiment. A pattern to be repeated time and again throughout the Tavistock's history, challenging but also informing both its understanding and its practice.

It is this idea of two sides, the generative and the resistant, and the relation between them, embodied in our past experience, that in more recent years has come to shape how I find myself thinking about our practice and its future. Following, supposedly, in what we take to be Bion's footsteps, I think we have tended to institutionalise a set of practices which, more or less inevitably, focuses more on the resistant than the generative, the regressive pull than the developmental push (Thanatos, I might perhaps say, rather than Eros).

The arena to which many of us owe our first introduction to 'group relations', the Group Relations Conference, specifically sets out, in a way, to elicit regression, the better supposedly to draw attention to unconscious group processes: 'basic assumptions' as against 'work group'. Within the conference, it's as if the latter is taken as simply to do with exploring the former.

There are, though, two reservations that need to be made here. Firstly, at least in my view, it is not the case that unconscious group processes are exclusive to the more regressive forces (Bion's 'basic assumptions'). It is arguable that, concurrently, they may both anticipate and lend meaning to a developmental undertow (Bion's 'work group'). Indeed, were this not the case, it would be difficult to make sense of much of the impact that the work of drawing attention to and interpreting basic assumption functioning can have, even within a conference itself.

Secondly, the self-referential aspect of a conference can somewhat draw attention away from what it is in the work group and or its context that elicits the way basic assumptions emerge and proliferate, what it is that they are defending against. But in the world outside the conference, this is precisely what we need, as it were, to know. To use a phrase brought into this work by one of its early psychoanalytic practitioners, Pierre Turquet, "what's the 'because' clause"? Basic assumptions, like unconscious processes more generally, are but the start of a story. To continue the story, one must interrogate the context and its psychic meaning, both conscious and unconscious. As another of our forebears, Isabel Menzies, half a century ago, was, famously to do, in her study of the nursing service of a training hospital and the ways in which the organisation can unconsciously evolve defensive structures to contain anxiety.

And then? Isabel herself was the first to stress that, in this applied world, interpretation could not be the end of the story; only, as it were, an occupational hazard of the more psychotherapeutically minded practitioner. It is as if it's where interpretation ends that imagination begins, in the entertaining of difference, of the range and possibility of organisational choice. This cannot be foreseen in advance, or to put it another way, the imaginative response cannot just be read off the interpretative work. Nor is it essentially dependent on it. Rather it draws from and depends on other sources, both conscious and unconscious, something illustrated, implicitly, in the coal miner's innovation I referred to earlier.

To give another example, but this time from a community rather than an organisational context, during the later 1970s, after he had left the Tavistock for the United States and then Canada, Eric Trist became involved in a variety of what he described as "four very innovative real world community projects" in the States, in Canada and in Scotland. The last of these comprised a community development organisation that had arisen spontaneously in a low income and deprived area of Edinburgh. Known as the Craigmillar Festival Society, it had begun as a community arts venture inaugurating a 'festival of the poor', with pageants, street theatres, musicals, created by and involving community residents (perhaps symbolically representing a defiant counter to the Edinburgh International Arts Festival). As confidence grew, it expanded and diversified, growing from just being a festival to becoming an all-round community development organisation, drawing up its own Comprehensive Plan for Action as a basis for negotiation with public and policy agencies. This is how Trist described what happened:

> It may seem paradoxical that in a multi-deprived community the tide was turned by activities in the field of the Arts. But paradoxes are apt to contain important meanings. The creation of art in any of its forms is perhaps the most profound and powerful affirmation of life against death that we as humans can make, of harnessing the constructive and positive forces against the destructive and constraining forces. The cultivation of the imagination develops a resourcefulness which enables reality, however grim, to be contended with more innovatively. The Craigmillar folk had nothing else than their imagination to fall back on. They have used it to the full.

At the start of what I have been saying, I talked of sometimes sensing something missing or absent from the practice and conceptualisation of 'Group Relations'. I suggest that this is well captured in Trist's reference to the 'cultivation of the imagination', as a kind of hidden resourcefulness of the Work Group. I don't think we know much about the sources of such a resourcefulness, which perhaps inevitably tends to escape the boundaries of the traditional group relations conference. (As contrasted perhaps with some of the latter-day explorations in social dreaming, with which both this organisation and others in Israel have pioneered.)

But if Group Relations is to re-discover the social and ethical radicalism of its origins, this is the territory, in my view, that it must find ways and allies of engaging in and with. The nature of that engagement, moving out from the boundaries of the conference framework, as also of consultancy driven models, takes one back to how Trist recalled the pattern of the war time projects: of

> "experiencing those with whom he works as travellers on a common journey rather than as clients who have requested particular help"; where the problem or dilemma is "experienced as his also, belonging to both as members of the wider society which it permeates".
>
> The challenges are different now, as much societal as organisational, global as local, less in my view to do with the traditional conference focus on leadership and authority, more with what Bion, in the foreword to *Experiences in Groups*, regretted not having discussed: sovereignty and power. How to engage with those challenges and with what co-travellers; how re-frame what we do and learn again?
>
> I feel as if I were back 53 years in the group with Bion, disoriented by his having seemed to move on and then drawn into the puzzles that remain. Unstable and thereby hopeful.

Cautions – how these derivations and linkages can be misused or misapplied?

According to Gould (2001, Pg. 37) group relations conferences are process orientated and appropriately emphasise non-rational aspects of individual and group behaviour and their impact on task performance. They are designed to show how these processes emerge and function, and thereby provide opportunity for studying them in the here-and-now. But there is limited scope and time for modifying the task or creating new task structures, in contrast to natural work groups and organisations which have more control over time, territory, technology, formal roles, administrative procedures and organisational design. While providing powerful and relevant experiences to any group or organisational situation, they are, at best, partial and cannot substitute for an appreciation of the adaptive value of social defence, an understanding of the impact of organisational structure, and the emotional consequences of how work activities are patterned.

Three related difficulties may become apparent:

1 First conference members may come away from the experience with a 'working theory' of group and organisational life that is, at best, incomplete and, at worst, inadvertently skewed towards the primitive, the non-rational and the maladaptive.
2 If group relations is applied 'wholesale', concretely, and naively in organisational consultation work, it is not likely to be useful in most situations.
3 As Menzies Lyth (1991) points out, the problem most consultation efforts confront is that existing roles, role configurations and the structure of the work at hand may make it impossible to deploy new learning. Therefore, modifications need to be made to the interventions. Interpretative work alone, no matter how accurate, is likely to raise the level of disappointment, cynicism, frustration and disillusionment, making change efforts even more difficult.

Obholzer (2001, Pg. 204) points out that there is little value in merely "commenting on the existence (of unconscious group processes) or drawing attention to them, and possibly speculating about their origin and meaning without addressing issues of what's to be done to address them, by whom, in what role, with what authority and in what time scale".

Hypotheses and insights about organisational dynamics and structure that a consultation team formulates are not fed back via interpretations but via a series of meetings with the client system in the form of seminars/discussion groups in which there is a free exchange of ideas and reactions to the material presented. The 'theory' operates largely in the background and consultants' contributions are in ordinary conversational language in the context of a collaborative relationship with the client. In contrast to Group Relations conferences, organisational interventions do not have the boundary conditions necessary to contain and work with interpretations of unconscious material. The lack of time means that unconscious material cannot be worked through and adaptive defences can be disrupted leaving a disorganised situation for the client and no time to contain over an extended period. Defences can then become more rigid and more resistant to change.

Researching group relations conferences

Tracy Wallach, in her paper, "What do Participants Learn at Group Relations Conferences?" (2014), points out that there is literature describing group relations theory, the conference model and its applications (Banet and Hayden, 1977; Colman and Bexton, 1975; Colman and Geller, 1985; Cytrynbaum and Noumair, 2004; Hayden and Molenkamp, 2004; Miller, 1989; Wells, 1980). But the empirical studies of Group Relations conferences and their outcomes are much fewer in number. In her research of three separate Group Relations conferences, the author reports learning outcomes from these conferences. She poses the following questions:

1 What exactly do participants learn at conferences?
2 How do they learn it?
3 Does learning stick?
4 How does it evolve?
5 Does the learning have impact beyond individuals to the systems in which they work?

She also points out that conference research has been varied in both focus and method. In her survey of the literature, she draws our attention to the studies that have been aimed at understanding group process and functioning from a psychodynamic perspective and at measuring individual member learning, including how individual and conference characteristics impact learning (Lipgar et al., 2004). Research on individual member characteristics has looked at pre-existing levels of subject–object development (Silver, 2001;

Silver and Josselson, 2010), differences in cultural identity (Walker, 1995), or member learning styles as variables (Lipgar et al., 2004). Conference variables studied include conference context (who sponsors the conference and number of conferences sponsored), design (including duration, number of events, and intensity (residential or non-residential), and linkages (i.e. the social and authority ties between staff and members of a conference). Residential conferences of greater intensity and complexity (i.e. longer residential conferences), with strong sponsors (i.e. those who can successfully recruit and finance membership), and authority and social ties between members and staff were found to increase the amount of learning reported by participants (Klein and Astrachan, 1975; Klein et al., 1983, 1989).

Characteristics of conference consulting staff, such as their orientation towards or conceptualisation of their roles, their gender and level of authority (Correa et al., 1988; Cytrynbaum and Belkin, 2004) and the impact of those characteristics on conference dynamics and learning have also been important areas of study (Lipgar et al., 2004; McGarrigle, 1993). Lipgar et al. (2004) used Q methodology to study the relationship between gender and authority in conferences over a period of ten years. Outcomes research for Group Relations conferences focuses on the group process or participant learning measured during (Wheelan et al., 1991) or immediately following a conference (Lipgar and Struhl, 1993; Lipgar et al., 2004; McGarrigle, 1993). Longer-term follow-up studies (at six weeks and three months post-conference) confirmed that conference participants increase their learning about authority, leadership, followership, power dynamics in groups, the group effect on task performance, and interpersonal problems in the exercise of leadership (Klein and Astrachan, 1975; Klein et al., 1989).

Case studies have looked at the long-term impact of group relations conference training on organisational functioning (when a majority of employees have attended conferences) (Menninger, 1975, 1985). Menninger reports mostly positive impact on personal and professional functioning, and on the organisation. This included: changes in attitudes to authority (for individuals in leadership roles, as well as members of teams vis-à-vis management); increased emphasis on treatment community; increased interest in group therapy programme; and establishment of a training programme in family therapy. He also found some negative consequences and inappropriate transporting of group relations to the work setting (Menninger, 1975, 1985). In Northern Ireland, an intervention using both group relations and National Training Laboratory methods was used with communities in conflict. While the results were not entirely clear-cut, many participants reported they had been helped as individuals. For some (not all), their participation enabled them to carry out projects in their communities (Alevy et al., 1974; Doob and Foltz, 1974). Hupkens (2006) conducted a small pilot study consisting of intensive interviews of five people who attended between one and six group relations conferences. For these participants, their perspectives had changed completely, which changed their ways of working with clients and with colleagues. They were able to work more systemically and to work on both content and process levels. For some relatively new people, the impact was not always so positive, as they began to speak up about their experiences in ways that were not always helpful. More follow-up studies, conducted systematically, would greatly enhance our understanding of the processes at work during and after conferences; the variables that contribute to participant learning; and the ways participants make meaning of their experiences.

The data from all of the conferences suggest that for both experienced and inexperienced conference members, the process of learning and making meaning is complex, relational and evolves over time, even beyond conference boundaries. Learning in conferences is cumulative, and returning participants build on their learning from previous conferences. Wallach's research showed that conference learning may be enhanced with more formal follow-up experiences after the conference ends. This is consistent with earlier findings (Klein and Astrachan, 1975; Klein et al., 1989) that conference learning increased when participants and staff had ongoing relationships outside the conference, providing further opportunities to reflect and learn. The ongoing e-mail correspondence and returning several times to the second conference suggests a continuing need to try to work through the whole experience. For study participants in the second and third conferences, the interview process also served as a forum to organise their thoughts and feelings about the conference and contributed to their learning. Opportunities for ongoing reflection may take many forms, from surveys or interviews of conference participants to follow-up meetings. The Boston affiliate of the A. K. Rice Institute routinely offers half-day follow-up application workshops for conference members one to three months post-conference. Such structures offer interested participants an additional outlet for understanding and making meaning of their experiences. Conference sponsors might consider building in some form of follow-up into their conference design as a way to increase learning.

Wallach's findings from three studies to evaluate learning for participants in three separate group relations conferences are consistent with prior research that participants do indeed learn at conferences. The learning may be more personal than systemic, with different obstacles to learning for new participants and veteran participants. It also suggests ways that conference learning may be enhanced through systematic integration of orientation activities before or in the conference and follow-up experiences post-conference to accommodate the evolution of learning over time.

Klein et al. (1988), in their study, highlighted the importance of considering context, design and linkage characteristics of conferences when planning psychological training for professionals. What has been perceived as a constraint in the past (authority and social links) may be a rich opportunity to explore such ties, since work and social relations between members and staff facilitate learning, particularly when both groups share an intense residential experience. Malan et al. (1976) found that patients who benefited the most from the group had prior psychotherapy and were familiar with the treatment format and the therapist's stance. Prior linkages between members and staff may parallel these group therapy findings. In terms of practical implications, they suggest that conference directors keep the following issues in mind when designing training events:

1. Develop a relationship with the sponsoring organisation(s) to facilitate a clear work contract, give legitimacy to the conference and enhance recruitment of committed members with realistic expectations.
2. Hire a diverse staff, some of whom have authority and social links to the membership.
3. Hold the conference in residence, off-site, away from work, to draw a boundary that separates the training from daily activities.
4. If only two days are available for training, use a weekend rather than regular workdays for the event.
5. Have follow-up work to help members integrate the experience and enhance the learning.

These suggestions should facilitate the development of an environment where staff and members can work together to strengthen learning. Because so many of the characteristics studied are confounded, further research is needed (see the Klein et al. (1988) paper for specific details on proposed studies).

Hills (2018) conducted research as a participant observer at a Leicester conference. This two-week residential group relations event has taken place annually since 1959. One small-scale follow-up of participants was taken in 2002, and an elaborate plan for before and after interviews with participants was developed in the early 1980s. However, the researchers 'were never able to secure funding for it. We, therefore, remain reliant on impressionistic and anecdotal evidence, from past members, from people who know them, and from our own observations' (Miller, 1989, Pg. 20). The challenges of researching the conference are considerable. One of these, as Miller notes, is the pedagogic style of the conference and the kind of learning generated:

> "Group relations training" is a misnomer. "Training" implies transmission of skills, acquisition of which should, potentially at least, be measurable. The conference provides a set of experiences, but also explicitly states that authority for making use of the experiences and learning from them rests firmly with the individual member. Outcomes are therefore idiosyncratic and unpredictable.
>
> (Miller, 1989, Pg. 20)

Another challenge is the emotional nature of the work. One description of the Leicester conference describes this as "a contained transitional space which allows members to get in touch with difficult feelings and emotions"

(Brunner et al., 2006, Pg. 45). Participants can find it difficult to put their learning into words, and many reports still integrating the experience, months, or even years, later. The learning may also be deeply personal, as participants adopt a "constructively analytical and critical approach to the way they perform their roles in the groups to which they belong" (Trist and Sofer, 1959, Pg. 6). Although they are learning about the dynamics of groups and organisations, the focus is less on theorising about these and more on having "opportunities to learn about their own involvement in these dynamics" (Miller, 1989, Pg. 9).

At a most basic level, Miller notes, participants learn to identify and label unfamiliar phenomena that are encountered. At another level, they find new ways of classifying the world, particularly noticing "phenomena previously unnoticed or dismissed as irrelevant". However, at a deeper level, which Miller equates to Bateson's (1972) 'level III' learning, there may be "some degree of personality re-structuring—a systemic change" leading some participants, "to make significant changes in their work and personal life: for example, a career move, a job change, a change of partner". Alongside having to find a suitable approach to explore the learning of a complex nature (and finding the resources to do this), researchers have to address the concern, noted by both Trist (quoted by Wallach) and Miller, that the research may disrupt the dynamics of the conference itself. Hills set out to explore a number of questions about learning derived from the conference, and in particular, how different aspects of the conference contributed to learning. In addition, the research explored the challenges inherent in undertaking research into a group relations activity. In relation to the first of these tasks, the results indicated that the learning was highly valued by participants, particularly in terms of increasing their understanding of group dynamics and in feeling more at ease and able to cope in complex, ambiguous and emotionally charged situations, with different aspects of the conference contributing differently to this learning. In terms of the second task, the research demonstrated that useful qualitative and quantitative data could be derived from events of this kind without overly 'interfering' with the event itself and indicated some potential future areas of exploration.

Three research questions were identified:

1 What key learning and insights are generated by the Leicester conference 2012?
2 Which aspects or elements of the conference contribute most to this learning?
3 How do participants make use of this learning on their return to their 'back home' work?

The data required to answer these questions came from three different sources. The researchers attended the conference for two days (just before the mid-conference break and towards the end of the conference), attending two large group events as participant observers and undertaking interviews with participants during breaks in the conference (mainly mealtimes). In addition, online surveys were sent to staff and participants before, immediately after and nine months after the conference. Forty-nine interviews were conducted, representing 76% of all participants and staff (some were interviewed twice). The response rate for the participant questionnaire were 86%, 64% and 18% for the three questionnaires (pre, post and nine months later), respectively.

There were two aims to undertaking this research project: to explore how research, or evaluation, of an event of this kind, could be undertaken, and to gather feedback from participants in the conferences that might be useful for those organising and promoting conferences in the future. In the first aim, the research provided feedback that participants rated their learning experience highly and provided useful feedback about how different aspects of the conference contributed to this learning. The length of the conference and the fact it was residential were particularly important and different events were seen as providing slightly different opportunities to understand group behaviour, to feel comfortable in ambiguous and emotionally challenging situations, or receive personal feedback from consultants and other participants in small group activities. The finding that many felt clearer at the end than they had at the beginning about the relevance of this learning to their work situation is interesting given the fact that most, even those who were in employment, paid for the conference attendance themselves. On the other hand, some used it as an opportunity to review their current career situation and consider possible changes. Participants new to group relations can often take time to get used to the learning style and the challenging and emotional content of some of the sessions, although most people were very appreciative of this by the end of the event. The desire for more 'support', particularly by way of more written or teaching material, goes to the heart of ongoing debates about the group relations approach, which places responsibility for learning firmly in the hands of participants themselves, rather than 'feeding' in pre-digested learning from elsewhere. However, in some group relations traditions, more by way of teaching, lectures or written material is provided than others. The Leicester conference has always been closer to the purely experiential end of the spectrum, although various experiments have been made over the years to provide more formal teaching elements.

Summary

> The downside of attending to the emotional life of groups is that it can swamp the ability to get anything done; a group can become more concerned with satisfying its members than with achieving its goals. Bion identified several ways that groups can slide into pure emotion - they can become "groups for pairing off," in which members are mainly interested in forming romantic couples or discussing those who form them; they

can become dedicated to venerating something, continually praising the object of their affection (fan groups often have this characteristic, be they Harry Potter readers or followers of the Arsenal soccer team), or they can focus too much on real or perceived external threats. Bion trenchantly observed that because external enemies are such spurs to group solidarity, some groups will anoint paranoid leaders because such people are expert at identifying external threats, thus generating pleasurable group solidarity even when the threats aren't real.

(Shirky, 2011)

The design and structure of group relations conferences have developed in several dimensions as sponsoring organisations and conference directors seek to maintain the relevance of the learning model amid cultural and institutional changes. This chapter has built on the advancements in theory and practice achieved by those within the group relations tradition. Group relations conferences are concerned with issues of authority and leadership, two processes that are associated with magic, enchantment and fear, thereby attracting transference, strong ties and emotions, usually originating in the early development of the individual, that in later life become projected onto the person of the leader. Group relations staff members are skilled in working with and in transference and counter-transference phenomena; in interpreting group unconscious dynamics; an enhanced ability to work within boundaries; within role and task; capability of working with group-as-a-whole, not individual phenomena, which distinguishes group relations work from other forms of work with groups. Staff members are skilled in generating working hypotheses, an interpretation of what is known so far, and an invitation to think about it. Learning about relationships in groups and between groups and how to manage oneself in different roles takes time and requires attendance at group relations conferences of sufficient duration. Group relations applied to organisational consultancy includes understanding, interpreting and working through collective defences. The most seemingly instrumental, efficient and reasonable patterns of work and division of labour may have social defence properties. A collaborative engagement between consultants and clients aims to jointly explore the nature of organisational problems, to generate ideas for change, to test those ideas in practice and to evaluate the results. Group relations theory and practice underpin the analysis of organisational cultures. In organisational consultancy, there is a shift away from interpretations that focus the group's relationship to the consultant, to relations between group members themselves, their relatedness to the institution, and their task at hand. A Group relations consultant is alert to and interprets the covert and dynamic aspects of the client's organisation and the work groups that comprise it, often with a focus on how authority is psychologically distributed, exercised and enacted, in contrast to how it is formally invested. Group relations work includes a consideration of attitudes, beliefs, phantasies, core anxieties, social defences and patterns of relationships and collaboration and how they influence task performance; and how individuals take up their work roles. Organisational Role Analysis aims to "disclose meaning to the client - to the organisation-in-the-self and the self-in-the-organisation" (Armstrong). Interpretative work on its own, no matter how accurate, is likely to raise the level of disappointment, cynicism, frustration and disillusionment, making change efforts even more difficult. There is little value in "commenting on the existence (of unconscious group processes) or drawing attention to them, and possibly speculating about their origin and meaning without addressing issues of what's to be done to address them, by whom, in what role, with what authority and in what time scale" (Obholzer A., 1996). Hypotheses and insights about organisational dynamics and structure are not fed back via interpretations but via a series of meetings with the client system in the form of seminars/discussion groups in which there is a free exchange of ideas and reactions to the material presented. The 'theory' operates largely in the background. 'Group Relations Training' is a misnomer. The authority for making use of the experiences and learning from them rests firmly with the individual member. Outcomes are therefore idiosyncratic and unpredictable (Miller, 1989).

Exercise

1 Describe the differences between 'group relations' and working with groups.
2 What are the theoretical roots of the group relations model?
3 Describe the BART concept and apply it to a situation or system you are familiar with.
4 What psychoanalytic concepts are the most relevant in the group relations model, and how can they be helpful in understanding racial-cultural group dynamics?
5 Describe the difference between learning-from-experience and learning from the collected experience of others.
6 Why do you think society places more importance on leadership than on leadership-and-followership?
7 How would you describe the difference between a job and a role?
8 Have you ever been thrust into a role you did not want?
9 What was that like?
10 Have you ever been in an organisation in which its unconscious components were interpreted to you?
11 What was the experience like for you?

11 Systems psychodynamics and organisational consultancy

Social defences are equivalent to individual defences (Menzies, 1960). Interventions based on this perspective typically involve understanding, interpreting and working through such collective defences, which hopefully result in enlarging the organisation's capacity to develop more task appropriate adaptations (see Vol. 1, Chapter 10). A central feature of her work is the notion that even the most seemingly instrumental, efficient and reasonable patterns of work and division of labour may have social defence properties. In the face of these social defences, Menzies Lyth argues for a form of action research and organisational consultation. She describes a collaborative engagement between consultants and their clients as jointly exploring the nature of their problems, generating ideas for change, testing those ideas in practice, and evaluating the results. Furthermore, because many of the issues involve challenging both individual and social defences, institutional change "inevitably involves a slow gradual and often painful evolutionary process". There is a wide spectrum of consultation practice encompassed by the systems psychodynamic perspective. Bain (1998) provides a useful categorisation. He notes that the organisational consultant engages in an analysis of some or all of the following:

1 Roles and role configurations
2 Structures and organisational design
3 Work culture and group processes
4 The analysis of work culture and group processes is most closely related to the central aim of group relations conferences

It is the most common type of practice taken up by those whose organisational consultation training is almost exclusively based on the group relations conference model. The approach is for a consultant to join regular meetings of a natural work group and to interpret process in a manner like how a consultant would function, for example, in taking a small study group.

But, in an organisational consultation situation there is a marked shift away from interpretations that focus the group's relationship to the consultant to relations between group members themselves, their relatedness to the institution and their task at hand. A consultant working in this way would be alert to and would selectively interpret the covert and dynamic aspects of the client's organisation and the work groups that comprise it, often with a focus on how authority is psychologically distributed, exercised and enacted, in contrast to how it is formally invested.

This type of consultation would include a consideration of:

1 Attitudes
2 Beliefs
3 Phantasies
4 Core anxieties
5 Social defences
6 Patterns of relationships and collaboration and how they influence task performance

Through the use of open system theory, focusing on how individuals take up their work roles, the consultant through a series of meetings – often referred to as *organisational role consultations* – consultants might use a variety of assessment and intervention methods, including projective or semi-projective measures such as the production and analysis of mental maps. They might ask for dream material and fantasies stimulated by the social surround of the organisation. They can work from a supportive and interpretative stance. Armstrong (1995) says the aim of an organisational role consultation is to "disclose meaning to the client ... to the organisation-in-themselves and themselves-in-the-organisation". This is a useful intervention in which a manager in a client system has either taken up a new role, needs to assess role performance, considering changing circumstances, or is experiencing chronic difficulties in functioning effectively. These consultations are akin to the Review and Application Groups of group relations conferences, role analysis groups, or application groups. The primary task of these events is to provide opportunities to reflect on their experiences and to examine the connections between such experiences. But a systems psychodynamics consultant needs to exercise caution in how these derivations and linkages can be misused or misapplied. A group relations conference is process orientated and appropriately emphasises non-rational aspects of individual and group behaviour and their impact on task performance. They are designed to show how these processes emerge and function and thereby provide opportunity for studying them in the 'here-and-now'. But there is limited scope for modifying the task or create a task structure of their own; there is limited time, as opposed to natural work groups and organisations who have more control over time, territory, technology, formal roles, administrative procedures and organisational design. While providing powerful and relevant experiences to any group or organisational situation, organisational role consultations are, at best, partial and cannot substitute for an appreciation of the adaptive value of the social defence, an understanding of the impact of organisational structure, and the emotional consequences of how work activities are patterned.

Three related difficulties may become apparent

First, group relations conference members may come away from experience with a 'working theory' of group and organisational life that is, at best, incomplete and, at worst, inadvertently skewed towards the primitive, the non-rational and the maladaptive. If applied 'wholesale', concretely and naively in organisational consultation work, it is not likely to be useful in most situations. The problem most consultation efforts confront is that existing roles, role configurations and the structure of the work at hand may make it impossible to deploy new learning (Menzies Lyth, 1990). Therefore, modifications need to be made in relation to the interventions. Interpretative work alone, no matter how accurate, is likely to raise the level of disappointment, cynicism, frustration and disillusionment, making change efforts even more difficult. Obholzer (2001, Pg. 204) points out that there is little value in merely "commenting on the existence (of unconscious group processes) or drawing attention to them, and possibly speculating about their origin and meaning without addressing issues of what's to be done to address them, by whom, in what role, with what authority and in what time scale". Hypotheses and insights about organisational dynamics and structures that a consultation team formulates are not fed back via interpretations, but via a series of meetings with the client system in the form of seminars/discussion groups in which there is a free exchange of ideas and reactions to the material presented. The 'theory' operates largely in the background and consultants' contributions are in ordinary conversational language in the context of a collaborative relationship with the client. In contrast to group relations conferences, organisational interventions do not have the boundary conditions necessary to contain and work with interpretations of unconscious material. The lack of time means that unconscious material cannot be worked through and adaptive defences can be disrupted, leaving a disorganised situation for the client and no time to contain over an extended period – this represents a lack of containment. Defences can then become more rigid and more resistant to change.

Gould (2000b, Pg. 8) delineates how a consultant would work from within the Tavistock paradigm:

> A consultant working on these aspects of the organisation would be alert to, and selectively interpret, the covert and dynamic aspects of the client organisation and the work groups that comprise it, often with a focus on relatedness and how authority is psychologically distributed, exercised, and enacted, in contrast to how it is formally invested. This work would include a consideration of attitudes, beliefs, phantasies, core anxieties, social defences, patterns of relationships and collaboration, and

how these in turn may influence task performance. Further, in a manner similar to group relations conferences, the consultation work would focus on how a variety of unwanted feelings and experiences are split off and projected onto particular individuals and groups that carry them – i.e. their process roles as distinct from their formally sanctioned role on behalf of the organisation.

Both Czander (1993) and Neumann (1997) consider the entry into the client system as an important process. Czander (1993) considers the crossing of the organisational boundary by the consultant into the client's system as a point for analysis of boundary-related issues in the consultant-consultee relationship. He points out that psychoanalytic consulting maintains that an external boundary forms around all organisations and sub-systems within the organisation. According to Czander (1993), assessment of the boundary issues will give the consultant information on the following aspects of organisational functioning:

a Areas of authority in the organisation.
b How it is delegated?
c Sub-system dependency and autonomy.
d Clarity of task definition.
e How the organisation views multiple tasks?
f How the organisation manages its boundaries?
g Clues concerning the nature of the request for a consultation.
h Issues that precipitated the request for consultation.
i Organisational resistance towards intervention and change.

Czander (1993) highlights the following key activities at the start of a consultancy:

a The nature of the contract between consultant and organisation.
b The consultant's capacity to view and understand his/her entry into the organisation as a microcosm of the organisation's capacity to manage its boundaries.
c The consultant's capacity to conduct an analysis of the dynamics and unconscious forces at play in the consultant-consultee relationship.

Neumann (1997, Pg. 7) underlines entry and contracting as key dynamic processes for the consultant. Difficulties in engaging the client in a diagnostic phase can lead to severe problems for both the client and the consultant.

Working methods and application of theory

Skills, methods, aims and working practices are linked in system psychodynamics organisational consultancy. Systems psychodynamics attempts to develop the capacity for reflection on:

a The emotional experience of task-related work so that these can be better understood and mastered.
b How individuals and teams debate or communicate within the organisation in ways that help or hinder work on the primary task.

A consultant is likely to encourage a realistic rather than a rigidly defensive relationship to the emotional aspects of work. This awareness will help staff gain greater insight into the limits of what is possible in work on the primary task.

Consultants focus on working with the client to:

a Enable them to feel and think through the presenting problem.
b Form their own diagnoses and generate their own solutions.

In systems psychodynamics the task of consultancy is to consider the relations between processes operating across the boundary of different levels of a system. The distinctive emphasis in systems psychodynamics is to bring processes outside of ordinary consciousness into clear focus and understand their meaning. In systems psychodynamics organisational consultancy, the consultant is continually asking, "what is it that is generating the emotional experiences that are being registered by the consultant and by the client?" (Armstrong, 2002, Pg. 89–98). The consultant aims to enable the client to gain awareness of what is happening below the surface within the organisation. The consultant's aim is to help the client rehearse and examine the significance of this awareness and meaning for policy, decision and action. The consultant carries out the consultancy process by the practice of attending to, reflecting on, and making links from the emotional experiences presented through the consultant's engagement with and in the organisation, and in the roles the consultant has taken.

In the systems psychodynamics model, the consultant believes that enlarging understanding, bringing to awareness aspects of the client's experience that are often hidden, un-reflected on, unformulated or simply ignored as not relevant, promotes the client's development. The consultant helps the client reflect on the fit between the motives and intentions driving the action and decision-making in the system. Following on from this, the consultant works to help the client deal with internal resistances, defences and blind spots. Enlarging the client's grasp on the human realities of work and the system is the hallmark of this model, viz. the consultant is always a participant in working with the experience that the client brings. The consultant works to help the client be open to new insights and motivations. The model suggests that a primary preoccupation of systems psychodynamics is in helping the client to extend the repertoire of what can be thought about in charting new courses of action for the system. This is true in relation to organisational structures.

Case example

A consultancy assignment with an oil and gas drilling company in a Central Asian Republic, a former USSR state, set out to evaluate the 'state of the organisation', of The State Oil and Gas Drilling Company (SOaGDC), in relation to its strategic growth objectives of becoming a significant international player in the field of oil and gas drilling. The consultants offered a series of 'working notes' with hypotheses to explain why things were the way they were in SOaGDC and alternatives were proposed. The working notes thus provided an agenda for dialogue with and within SOaGDC as a client system, leading towards shared understandings. By being invited to apply their own expertise, people in the SOaGDC system would tend to feel freer to voice their anxieties and resistances and their ideas for change. The consultants, by not being defensive and not pretending to know the answers, hoped to provide a model for creating a culture of dialogue more widely within SOaGDC as a system.

An initial diagnostic assessment was made to answer the first cut of the questions: (i) *What are the leadership and management development needs of SOaGDC's executive and senior management teams and (ii) what consultancy interventions would address those development needs?*

SOaGDC was established in 2007 as a new company, an offshoot of the parent company, the State Oil Company of the Central Asian Republic, and it was growing rapidly with a current workforce of around 650 people. There was a sense that the senior management groups in the company may not have had the required capabilities and skills to lead the organisation past its current growth phase. The consultants spent four days in the Republic's capital, meeting and interviewing selected senior and middle-ranking managers with a view to acquiring a sense of their leadership capabilities and identifying leadership gaps in the company.

Core business

SOaGDC's core business is drilling, cementing, workover, reinforcement, geophysical assessment and perforation services for oil and gas wells utilising modern techniques and technologies existing in the oil and gas industry. The company provides services through the use of special machinery, equipment, plants and facilities together with their rearrangement, modification and establishment of production infrastructure for air, marine and road transportation for the oil and gas industry. The company also introduces technical know-how in the management of the oil and gas industry, along with provision of technical back-up and other support in repair and operating of relevant plants, equipment and facilities.

The structure of our work – what we did and whom we interviewed

In the formal part of our structure of interviews we spoke to 22 people who had been selected by the General Director on the basis that they displayed reasonably good potential leadership ability. The purpose of the interviews was to deepen our understanding of their perspectives of their roles in the company and to assess the extent of their company-wide vision for the future. A list of questions was compiled that covered the following areas: (i) the person,

(ii) resources, (iii) their understanding of the consultancy initiative, (iv) role and organisation, (v) SOaGDC and its context. The interviews lasted between one and one-and-a-half hours. Fifteen people were interviewed individually, and six people were interviewed in pairs. Meetings were held with the General Director at the end of each day for informal feedback and to gather more information about the background of the project. In this way we could monitor ourselves to ensure that we were working in accordance with the overall objectives of the project and to suggest certain changes to our programme. Two major changes were suggested and implemented: (i) our attendance at a morning conference call meeting of heads of departments at Headquarters with employees on Oil Platforms 11 and 13 and the Stores Depot, and (ii) our visit to the Stores Depot, where we had meetings with the chief of the Depot and the Head of Safety. We visited the three warehouses and the electrical repair shop, where we had the opportunity of speaking to staff and asking questions relating to their work.

We interviewed 1 person at General Director level (Level 1); 3 people at Deputy General Director level (Level 2); 7 Heads of Departments (Level 3); 2 Heads of Services (Level 4); and 9 Specialists (Level 5), i.e. 22 people. We noted that we were not asked to interview representatives of Finance and Economics, and Business Development & New Projects. We also noted there are two vacancies at Deputy General Director level.

Language

As the level of English language capability was variable among the interviewees, we had a good translator for about 75% of the interviews and meetings.

Support

Throughout the project of the visit to SOaGDC in the Republic – travel, accommodation, meals and carrying out the formal part of the interviewing work – we were helped by the staff in the HR Department. They were always available to look after our needs and to arrange the smooth and efficient flow of employees to meetings with us and contributed to the overall keeping of the timetable.

Dinners and formal and informal conversations

We met with the General Director alone on three occasions and socially at dinner on two. These meetings were useful opportunities for us to gather wider impressions and perspectives about SOaGDC specifically and about the oil and gas industry generally. We were inducted into the particularities of drilling and extraction and the huge complexities and inter-relationships between SOaGDC, its parent company, SOCTR, and its contractors and customers. We had the privilege of hearing the General Director's philosophy on the role of energy in today's world and his vision for SOaGDC to become a significant national and international player in oil and gas drilling operations. We were impressed by his ideas on overcoming the limitations in this field by developing new technologies, which he considered to be one of SOaGDC's roles. The General Director shared his doubts and uncertainties about the translation of his vision into practice based on certain gaps in his leadership teams. The struggle, he said, lay in the difference between a leadership that was open to new ideas and willing to take risks and an organisational culture of planned control that had two sources: (i) the residual influences of Soviet education of his people when they were at school and at university; and (ii) the necessity for engineering precision and safety rules that governs the oil and gas industry. Whereas, there could be no room for discretion while on operations on platforms – every action has to be pre-planned, written in manuals and monitored and supervised – strategic leadership of the company required a more fluid, thoughtful, risk-taking stance by senior personnel. These two cultural levels impact differently on operational behaviour and leadership behaviour and the General Director felt that new systems of training and development needed to be introduced into the company so that people could integrate their command-and-control structure with a more transformational and inspirational climate. At the present time, the General Director believes that there is resistance and fear among his senior personnel to taking up leadership roles that are not based simply in trying to satisfy and please the General Director.

The following is a sample of the questions we asked the employees in interviews:

i What is your experience of working in SOaGDC?
ii Describe your daily working schedule?
iii What are your formal processes of appraisal of performance, quality, safety and risk?
iv What is your understanding of what this consultancy is asked to do and why we are speaking to you?
v Describe your relationships with your colleagues within your section/department? And with other sections?
vi What is your experience of the leadership/management of your section/department?
vii What is your experience of the leadership of SOaGDC as a whole?
viii What is your experience of the General Director and of the relationship between the General Director and the rest of the leadership team?
ix Can you describe to us the place/status of SOaGDC in the city, the community and the state?
x How would you describe the organisation in one word – an image or metaphor?
xi What are your career plans?
xii What future do you think SOaGDC needs to work towards?
xiii What, if any, succession issues are there?
xiv What, if any, leadership issues are there?
xv Are there any questions that you were expecting or hoping for that we haven't asked? Is there anything else you want to add that you think we ought to know?

What people told us and why – what were their motives?

Some interviewees welcomed the opportunity of talking and being listened to, and they said they were satisfied with the experience in which they learned more than they thought they would. We encouraged them to tell us about their work in detail which they did; others needed encouragement to focus on their work, especially those who saw the interview as an opportunity to promote themselves. It seemed to us that there was a distinction between HQ people and people from the platforms along these lines. HQ people, being nearer to the General Director (GM) seemed to talk in a manner that positioned them as good followers of the GM, and we heard less from them about future plans, strategic visions and broader conceptualisation of the company within the oil and gas industry. On the other hand, people on the platforms, many of whom had been on the job for many years, expressed great pride in their work, their group and life on the rig generally. They were meticulous in describing safety principles and procedures, and it was a badge of honour for them that life on the platform was safe and that there had been no accidents since the establishment of the company.

Education

Education was underlined as being of primary importance. Education and training were seen as the bases of promotion in the company and were mainly in the realms of scientific and technical training – engineering, safety, ICT, system administration, finance and statistics. Although there were some references to management and leadership, it seemed to us that ideas on these topics are under-developed and rather mechanical – how to make good decisions, how to lead people. Training seems to concentrate on how to solve problems, rather than on training that helps to answer 'why ….' questions. This might be consistent with a highly technical and operational culture, but apart from the General Director, we found little evidence of deep-thought strategic thinking. We wondered if this was the influence of the Soviet system of education that continues to this day; for example, for some, education is seen as an accumulation of credits, certificates and degrees that may be poorly integrated into the philosophy of the company and its leadership. There is a risk that formalised and formulaic education may be applied mechanically without regard to higher levels of thinking and abstraction; in other words, an education that does not take account of over-arching emotional, group and systemic dynamic relationships that impact on individuals, groups, sub-systems, the company as a whole and its contexts – the city, the community, country and the international environment. Putting it another way, it appeared to us that people had been trained ***not*** to think about the politics of the organisation in much the same way that people were discouraged from thinking about or engaging in politics in the previous regime. People were more likely to have a departmental and technical focus and working on problems that can easily be predetermined or pre-planned. Leadership and organisational skills and competencies that rely on, for example, tolerating uncertainty, satisfying competing demands, managing competition and rivalry, or waiting for a way forward to emerge rather than be forced into solutions, seem to be lacking at all levels in the company.

Examples of what people told us

Question: What is it like working here?

> We work 24 hours a day. We gather all the disciplines together to analyse problems and to notify the 8.30 meeting at HQ. It is a good practice.

We must be knowledgeable technically and we need to be patient and not panic. We must be able to listen to people. The emotional temperature on the platforms depends on the tool pushers. We have to have good decisions. If things go wrong, getting angry won't do. We require good explanations. If the worker doesn't change, we inform HQ. We exercise quiet leadership by listening and learning. We investigate quietly and then teach the correct way. Challenges occur when there are deviations from the plans.

(Level 4 Leading Specialist)

There are some difficulties with off-shore staff. There are tendencies for workers to form cliques and rumours increase which we have to put right. We need to communicate with people more frequently to obtain their trust. Working with office managers is easier than working with off-shore people. Sometimes different 'languages' are used by HQ staff and platform employees. People range from university and college graduates to riggers, roustabouts, roughnecks, welders, cleaners, cooks – all are different. Communication with office workers is easier because they are here. In most cases, employees discuss their problems with their managers first; only then are they escalated to HQ. Off-shore people are close to each other. Where there are problems, training does not always help. We need help in using other development approaches.

(Level 4 Leading Specialist)

On Leadership.

We study best practice in leadership, but I don't think we are advanced enough in oil leadership, because everyone here is on a low level. We need good training in leadership if we are to be among the best in the world. Good specialists do not mean people are good leaders. They have to think about the success of the company as a whole and not about their own personal success. They are looking down into their own departments rather than looking and behaving corporately. People think that as long as their department is successful, they need not be interested in the effectiveness of other departments. They avoid risk this way. They hold back in order to keep safe. This attitude is a huge disadvantage for the company. We need long hard training in leadership.

(Level 3 Head of Department)

People at lower levels rely on their supervisors who are sometimes distrusted. Things are not working very well at lower levels. This is probably a left-over from the Soviet period, the old system where you did what you were told. People did not take responsibility but waited for instruction. This is still widespread in operations, creating a fire-fighting culture and attending to the urgency of tasks because of poor planning.

(Level 3 Head of Department)

Question: What is your experience of the GM and of the relationship between the GM and other managers in SOaGDC?

> Managers are in close contact with the GM and are under his influence all the time. The GM is good in selecting people, but people are more devoted to him than to the system, and this affects the practice of our values of quality, safety, novelty, integrity, frugality.
>
> (Level 3 Head of Department)

> The GM wants to retain good relationships with his deputies and he struggles with being a good teacher, a good leader and being strict. He needs leadership training too to help our lower levels of managers, some of whom are good organisers; some are good implementers; and some are not good at delegating and do the work themselves. The GM needs to help them be good leaders and managers.
>
> (Level 3 Head of Department)

Question: Can you describe the place/status of SOaGDC in the city and the country?

> The company has given me a lot. Of all the local oil companies, we are Number 1. Everything is in place and we have certified safe wells. We are well-regarded because we do things properly. We have experienced hard-working, dedicated staff who are learning to improve all the time. We are dependable and locally respected. I trust my company and I am proud of my company. We do a lot for our country. For instance, we dug the first horizontal well to 100% completion. I'm part of this process and that makes me proud.
>
> (Level 2 Deputy General Director)

Question: How would you describe SOaGDC in one word – an image or metaphor?

> An improving and a learning company.
> Promising – we promise the nation.
> Life - struggling to produce more
> Happy faces.
> A star - in the country and in the world.
> A tree - strong roots, always green and growing. Different from other trees. Leaves brightening with the sun.

Question: What future do you think the organisation needs to work towards?

> To be a leading oil company in the Caspian Sea and abroad too. I can see SOaGDC will be a leading company here and an international player.
>
> We need more projects to go international. We have the potential and the right people. We need to restore the role of local oil workers – a new generation, taught in a new way.

Question: What, if any, leadership issues are there?

> Leadership is hollow if it relies on position only. The definition of leadership in our company must be explained. Thought leadership is needed.

For leadership to be developed internally, we need training in coaching, mentoring, succession planning, stress management, negotiating skills, networking skills, acquiring psychological sophistication for recruitment purposes. Many times, our training events do not produce much. People are defended against acquiring new knowledge. Therefore, only interested employees should participate in training … and we need training to fulfil our international ambitions.

Our impressions

Our overall impressions were that people's ability to develop from the 'scientific' and 'technological' to the 'organisational strategic' and 'human potential' was the area where greatest effort and improvement needed to be introduced. Efforts in this area were linked to training people to shift their identification with their departments or divisions towards thinking and behaving more corporately about the company that exists in a changing global economic world that will increase demands for readily available and affordable energy supplies. The difficulties associated with this type of individual and systemic change were structural, cultural and psychological. We viewed these three inter-locking elements as being heavily influenced by the Soviet education system, which dominated the Republic for 71 years and previously in the 19th Century, which we assumed continued into the present, viz, ideas about leadership were considered to reside in one all-knowing and all-powerful individual with the rest of the people in the organisation classified as compliant followers. In this model of leadership it would be rare for 'compliant followers' to demonstrate leadership capability, and the question that the company had to face was what appetite was there in the company and in the company's environment for encouraging new forms of leadership models that would require a fair degree of challenge of the status quo – and all this without compromising safety standards and commitment to the values of the company, including that the company will grow and be profitable.

Learning for leadership

In our conversations with the General Director we heard about his ideas for developing a cadre of new leaders in the company. We observed that his conduct in his role fostered a strong sense of being deferred to by Deputy General Directors and Heads of Departments. This was evident whenever the General Manager travelled abroad for business; he never felt entirely free from the responsibility of answering questions. In our view this spoke to the problems associated with delegation and signalled a model of leadership in his mind and in the minds of his subordinates. This model of leadership was described as passive dependent in which subordinates felt they could not make decisions without authorisation from the General Director, or the basis of their decision-making was to win the General Director's approval, rather than the decision being the right one to make. It is commonly accepted that developing strong leadership qualities in a culture of passive dependency is difficult and much work needed to be done to develop people to fear less, to seek approval less and to take greater risks. This step was measured against two pervasive cultural realities – (i) that work on the platforms requires strict adherence to rules and regulations, and compliance with established guidelines and methods of work; that (ii) the course of the Republic's history and politics had been determined by a small, strong elite who expect and receive loyalty and good behaviour from the citizenry from childhood through to adulthood. Consequently, it was important for the General Director to be clear about what he meant by 'leadership development' for his employees and for the organisational consultants. Leadership development is closely linked to organisational development and the General Director had to consider whether or not he was prepared for such a thorough-going review.

Another source of puzzlement for us was the size of the group at Deputy General Director level. There were 11 positions at Deputy General Director level (two were vacant), and we wondered whether this long line of Deputy General Directors represented another example of command-and-control in the organisation that stifled the proper exercise of leadership. Our initial investigation showed that discussions needed to be held to consider reviewing the internal organisational structure at HQ with a view to streamlining, increasing the span of responsibility of individual Deputy General Directors and strengthening decision-making at lower levels.

The General Director asked the consultants to offer opinions on individuals' capabilities to assume leadership in the company. Focusing on individuals we thought would be a breach of our undertaking to those individuals who spoke to us to whom we promised full confidentiality. In any event, we shared our view that our opinions on individuals would not foster the main task of leadership development as that would require a broader systemic view of structure, role and relationship between all the elements in the organisational chart. We proposed that an organisational review should be conducted in further exploratory discussions with the General Director.

Recommendations

We believed that developing a new cadre of leadership that would be capable of thinking independently, presented certain challenges in this scientific, technical environment and required special educational and development technologies along the lines of learning-from-experience, Action Learning, the study of group relations, systems psychodynamics coaching and mentoring, in which the company's technical tasks in oil and gas drilling could be aligned with strategic leadership and organisational tasks involving as many people as possible.

We proposed the introduction of a significant learning and development programme for SOaGDC leaders and managers to raise the levels of their insight and awareness into, and practice of, the dynamics of leadership in a technology-based organisation.

Establishing and developing a learning environment tested people's thinking abilities, their willingness to take risks, and improved group participation skills and ultimately people's leadership skills. The means for achieving enhanced leadership capability at SOaGDC consisted of formal teaching events leading to certification, on-going interviews, meetings, workshops and other exercises that focused on the meaning and execution of leadership functions in a changing commercial and technological environment.

The place of process

The systems psychodynamics consultant uses process information all the time to gather information or data on the client's situation. The source of this data is varied. It can be feelings generated in the consultancy meeting; it can be through the analysis of documents. The consultant works to help the client to extend the capacity available to manage professional or leadership styles, capabilities, and competencies. Access to the process of organisational life is important for the consultant and client. The consultant then attempts to make sense of this data by attending to it both emotionally and cognitively. If appropriate, the consultant will attempt to feedback on the 'findings' to the client in the form of an interpretation. All the time the consultant is working at the emotional contact with the client system as a method of understanding the system and making a diagnosis that will lead to interventions to solve the presenting problem. In this model, the consultant's mental disposition is such that they can tolerate uncertainty, not knowing, and feelings of confusion ('negative capability') (Sher, 2020).

Also, in this model, the consultant needs to be able to wait on experience before making an interpretation. This means that the consultant reflects on the meaning of an experience before offering it to the client as formulation or interpretation. For this to be possible the consultant needs to have a capacity for empathy. This empathy would show itself by the consultant being able to feel into and for another and the organisation. The consultant needs to have a capacity for some identification with what the organisation is and does.

Working with unconscious processes and the use of interpretation

The systems psychodynamics of organisational consultancy emphasises work with unconscious processes. Many statements relate to skills, methods, aims and working practices linked to their application.

Consultant's methodology

Systems psychodynamics consultants work with unconscious processes that pay attention to:

1 Processes taking place outside of ordinary consciousness.
2 The relations between conscious and unconscious process.
3 Unconscious anti-task tendencies so that these can be better understood and mastered.
4 The 'value' that is attributed to experience, implied motives and intentions.
5 Developing formulations – translating what is happening – as a basis for further exploration.

6 Interpretation as a provisional answer to the question: 'why is this happening?'
7 Risks, hostility, working through resistances, and gearing up clients' readiness for change.
8 Interpretations include speculative links to other elements of the client's organisation.

Miller (1989) describes the methodology of the consultant thus:

> A still more specific derivation from the analyst's role has been the stress laid on examining and using the transference and countertransference within the professional relationship. That is to say, the way the consultant is used and experienced, and also the feelings evoked in him or her, may offer evidence of underlying and unstated issues and feelings in the client system: that which is repressed by the client may be expressed by the consultant.

From the earlier elaboration of the projective identification, introjective identification and reprojection via an interpretation, we see how this illuminates Miller's statement on consultant's methodology. The framework that holds this in place is the proposition that it is necessary to have a 'container – contained' theory as well as its practical application in a structured and organised work group.

Core concepts of the systems psychodynamics model of consultancy

Below is a summary of the core:

1 The application of psychoanalytic concepts to individuals – their 'inner worlds'
2 The application of psychoanalytic concepts to work groups, organisations and environments
3 Theories of organisations and systems
4 Organisational assessment and diagnosis
5 The consultative role and strategies of intervention
6 Authority leadership and leadership transition
7 Management of change and organisational transformation
8 Organisational design and structure
9 Work design
10 Task analysis
11 Role definition
12 Developing human resources
13 Staff development
14 Management theory
15 Strategic planning

16   Boundary maintenance and regulation
17   Sub-system dependency and autonomy
18   Inter-organisational relations (the eco-system)

Systems psychodynamics consultation to team and groups

A systems psychodynamics approach involves an examination of conscious and unconscious conflicts (which might be the result of a team's history and unconscious motives), unhealthy splits between team members or exclusion of team members, problematic relationships with leaders or authority figures, integrating diverse individuals into the team, and difficulty in understanding self and collective anxiety, defences and irrational behavioural processes in the team. The goal of the consultation is to assist the team in exploring its conscious and unconscious processes as team members relating with each other and leadership, and to work on inter-team and organisational relationships with other parts of the system – 'making sense out of nonsense' (Cilliers and Koortzen, 2000, Pg. 13–14) – interpreting behaviour (verbal and non-verbal) in the here-and-now, without presumption of coincidence, without memory or desire. Consulting from this stance implies 'licensed stupidity' (Czander, 1993).

The rationale and hypotheses of the systems psychodynamics approach of teams and organisations

Bennis and Shepard (1956), Wheelan (1994) and Colman and Geller (1985) developed two basic psychoanalytic hypotheses about team behaviour in the work context. These hypotheses look at teams' attempts to study and overcome anxiety, and to study and explore the projections from the rest of the system. Bennis and Shepard (1956) and Wheelan (1994) believe that criteria can be established by which phenomena of development, learning, or movement toward maturity of groups or teams can be identified and studied. From this point of view, maturity for the group means something like maturity for the person. A mature group or team can be identified by its ability to resolve its internal conflicts, mobilise its resources and take intelligent action only if it has a way to consensually validate its experience. Individuals can resolve their internal conflicts, mobilise their resources, and take intelligent action only if anxiety does not interfere with their ability to profit from their experience to analyse, discriminate and foresee.

Anxiety in groups and teams prevents individuals' internal communication systems from functioning appropriately. Under these circumstances, individuals can learn from their experiences only if they are able to overcome their anxiety (Bennis and Shepard, 1956). Similarly, groups or teams need to develop the ability to analyse and study their own anxiety without defensiveness, and to overcome obstacles to valid communication between team members. Using Sullivan's definition of personal maturity (1953), Bennis and Shepard (1956), and Wheelan (1994), contend that a group has reached a state of valid communication or maturity when its members have developed tools for analysing interpersonal experience, the capacity to differentiate between past and present experiences, and the foresight of relatively near future events.

Second, Colman and Geller (1985) point out the importance of projective processes in groups and teams, which affect individuals and others related to them. Mutual projective processes not only impoverish and distort experience of the self and the perceived world but they also affect the behaviour of the world towards the self. Groups, teams, and organisations inevitably create projection systems, in which threatening experiences or feelings are projected on different parts of the system. In a business, for example, incompetence might be projected on the production manager as if the rest of the system has no responsibility for it. This can create personal and interpersonal impoverishment and ineffectiveness. Team development interventions from a psychoanalytic approach offer teams, small groups and internally divided individuals the chance to resolve some of the anxieties and fantasies observable in those settings. Consultants will therefore try to facilitate the development of maturity and the capacity to understand and explore projections from other parts of the system. Several basic assumptions about groups or teams have also been identified in this approach. These assumptions represent specific problematic dynamics, which consultants should work with in team development.

The systems psychodynamics consultancy stance

Cilliers and Koortzen (2002) suggest that when working as a consultant with the basic assumptions of groups and teams in the organisation, the role of the consultant is different from the general role of the consultant (Czander, 1993). Traditionally, the consultant observes, instructs, or helps to solve problems, but these roles are believed to create dependence on the team and its members. The systems psychodynamics model requires consultants to be actively involved with the group, its members, its tasks and its experiences. The presence, person and authority represented by the consultant are part of the team development event, which implies that the team might respond at different levels to the consultant. In our experience, teams sometimes project some of the hostility they feel towards management onto the consultants; this can provide valuable information on the relationship between the two parties in the initial stages of the consultation. A consultant is also required to manage the boundary conditions and to make the team aware of these boundaries (such as task, territory and time). More specifically, a consultant's role can involve exploring why the team needs development. The consultant may want to help the team agree on the outcome of the intervention. This will be part of the entry and contracting process. Here the consultant gains authorisation from the team and the organisation to take up the role. This will involve the consultant devoting time with the team to explain its role, boundaries and impact on the expectations and experiences within the team. Consulting from this position requires two kinds of verbal interventions, namely the consultant asking questions, and formulating and sharing working hypotheses about what is happening. These inputs operate primarily on the cognitive level of team functioning, but the inputs obviously also elicit cognitive, affective and interpersonal behaviour among team members (Czander, 1993). The questions asked by the consultant are sometimes referred to as licensed stupidity, because they have the freedom to ask naive and sometimes childlike questions to encourage the team to make sense out of nonsense i.e. being able to ask the dumb questions that bring out hidden processes. The consultant's working hypotheses are an interpretation of what might be happening in the here-and-now of the group's experience. Both interventions are meant to stimulate awareness. Consultants can explore their working relationship with the team about the role of the consultant. This can help team members explore their experience of the work. The consultant helps the team to work within their boundaries so that the team can act as a container (an emotional container), of the team's anxiety, but at the same time allow team members to work as individuals (Neumann et al., 1997). The consultant is inevitably working with their subjective experiences and using the self as an instrument. This involves a high degree of self-awareness on behalf of the consultant. Being able to distinguish what psychological processes belong to the consultant and what are projections and transference phenomena from the client system and individual is an essential skill for systems psychodynamics consultants. The consultant then may offer working hypotheses and interpretations from their experience in the role.

At the team level, this approach provides an opportunity for team members to study the here-and-now dynamics, processes and relations in the team, which result in an awareness of underlying dynamics and anxieties, and an openness and willingness to explore and study behaviour in the group. If the skills of observation, exploration and studying of team dynamics can be transferred to the team, team members can empower themselves to analyse and explore their own behaviour and team behaviour. If a team can stop the formal agenda of a meeting when it becomes aware of anxiety in the team and spend time on the underlying processes, dynamics and relationships, it can be a valuable process of understanding and resolving the problem. The transferring of observation and exploration competencies can be of great value to team members and make them less dependent on consultations.

Diagnosing teams and evaluating team development interventions

Cilliers and Koortzen (2002) state that traditionally, diagnoses of group behaviour and evaluations of psychoanalytic interventions, whether in the context of individual psychoanalysis or group development, have taken the form of case studies in which a diagnosis was made, the intervention was described, and the impact or effect was analysed qualitatively and thematically. In practice, this means that the consultants use themselves as the instrument of diagnosis, and the evaluation of the intervention is done by describing behavioural changes on the initially diagnosed problematic dimensions (Hunt and McCollom, 1994; McWilliams, 2000). Although this methodology is widely used, it has received severe criticism in the past.

Gutmann et al. (1999) and Levinson (1991) describe diagnostic and intervention procedures that can be summarised as consisting of a diagnostic phase, an intervention phase, and a feedback or evaluation phase. Levinson (1991) describes the importance of data gathering in the first phase of the consultation, starting when the first contact is made. During and after the first meeting, it is important for the consultant to evaluate their own experience (cognitions, emotions and reactions) of the meeting. McCormick and White (2000) believe that when consultants use themselves as instruments of diagnosis, they should pay attention to their emotional responses to a team or organisation and use these to create diagnostic hypotheses.

One's emotional reactions to the team or organisation can be indicative of the emotional state of that team or organisation. Consultants should also pay close attention to their initial perceptions of the organisation, including the negative impressions and feelings about the team or organisation. Consultants should try to understand their common reactions and prejudices so that they can reduce bias in their diagnosis and at the same time postpone judgment to avoid premature conclusions (McCormick and White, 2000). Finally, consultants are encouraged to pay attention to the fantasies and images that occur while gathering information about the system and use these to create diagnostic hypotheses.

The first meeting will enable the consultant to develop an initial diagnosis of the team or organisation but should be followed by a structured process of gathering information (Levinson, 1991). An effective relationship should be developed with the client to gather factual data about the history, policies and procedures and external information relating to the other teams in the system, the competitors and customers. He also mentions the importance of studying the organisational or team structure and responsibilities, the setting or context in which they operate, and the main tasks. Lawrence (1999) points out that the consultant should be aware of what is not being said during information-gathering interviews, as well as the discrepancies between how the team presents itself and the behaviour manifested in the work context.

Once the initial diagnosis has been made, and working hypotheses developed, the consultant will develop a formal plan to study the institution, and an intervention for team development is developed. Gutmann et al. (1999) describe the framework of a workshop in the group relations model as a learning institution. Workshops consisting of different learning events during which opportunities are provided to study the processes and dynamics in the whole team, the relationships between sub-systems in the team and with other teams, and the interpersonal relationships in the team can sometimes be helpful. Consultants present working hypotheses or interpretations of what is happening in the here-and-now and provide opportunities for the team to explore their dynamics. The exploration leads to either supporting or rejecting the hypotheses, and new insights into their own behaviour are facilitated. Alderfer (1980) and Hunt and McCollom (1994) suggest that team members should consider collectively alternative explanations of their experience and what is interpreted by the consultant. This will facilitate a collective acceptance or rejection of possible explanations and solutions. The team also learns this methodology of analysing, exploring hypotheses, and validating to uncover, explore and understand their own dynamics. This is carried over into the work context. Gutmann et al. (1999) point out that important work needs to be done between workshops. During this period, team members might start to experiment with alternative ways of relating to each other; decisions that were made during the first workshop might be implemented, and these changes might create anxiety in the team. Consultants should be available to consult during this process.

According to Long (2000), this is the period in which team members should develop the capacity to be in the presence of others and closely observe their group processes. Examples of this can include denying aspects of team members' identity, including their race, gender and authority. Team members tend to see others the way they want to and not the way they are. The more the team can work with the reality of other team members, the more the team will engage reality and hence be able to work. The author also stresses the importance of developing the ability to internalise other team members. The identification with other team members through the task is an important aspect of this and is especially important after workshops during which interpersonal conflicts can be explored and studied. Finally, Long also mentions the importance of developing the capacity to be able to refer to and negotiate with the internalised team members when forming judgments. Consulting during this phase therefore involves assisting team members in establishing new ways of working together and relating. Further workshops can also be presented if the need exists.

An evaluation of the intervention should consist of a thorough analysis of the diagnosis, the intervention, and the outcomes of the intervention (Levinson, 1991). This is normally presented to the team or organisation in report form and includes recommendations for further development. To do this evaluation, consultants working from this approach have realised that more systematic methods for gathering data, recording intervention processes and analysing the outcomes of the intervention are needed (Baum, 1990; Gummesson, 1991; Shevrin and Dickman, 1980; Guerin 1997; Wheelan et al., 1994; Carew and Parisi-Carew, 1988) (see Vol. 2, Chapters 5 and 6).

Caveats to this approach

Working from a systems psychodynamics approach raises questions of validity and reliability. Care should be taken to provide reasonable checks for the weaknesses of any single method (Baum, 1990; Gummesson, 1991; Shevrin Dickman, 1980). Guerin (1997) developed a methodology plan for the study of the challenges normally faced by researchers. Researchers should use both quantitative and qualitative research methods. Data sources in the form of ethnographic observation, participant interviews and textual coding of recorded meetings would permit the triangulation of data. Empirical-analytical methods should be used for the content analysis of the meeting texts, using the Group Development Observation System protocol (Wheelan et al., 1994).

The key principle to keep in mind is the avoidance of mechanical and formulaic interventions. It is important that the consultant always starts with the idea of tuning into the specific needs of the client system. Listening, self-reflection on the data, working at a mutual diagnosis that the client system is equally involved in and participating as fully as possible is the most important principle to keep in mind. What is to be avoided at all costs is an off-the-shelf solution. The formulaic use of Group Relations methodology is a case in point. All interventions must be based on a sound and provisional diagnosis that can be reviewed and changed in the light of experience and new data.

Skills, methods, aims and working practices in the systems psychodynamics model of organisational consultancy

The *role* of systems psychodynamics consultants is to:

1 Ask questions and seek clarity and understanding of the client's perspective and needs.
2 Pay attention to both the 'hidden' and 'open' messages in clients' communications.
3 Build trust and credibility with the client.
4 Negotiate and agree for sufficient time to be set aside to conduct the consultancy intervention.
5 Develop a collaborative relationship between client and consultant.
6 Test out with the client their understanding of the organisation's work and primary objectives.
7 Agree a contract for the task of the consultation, which would include clarifying expectations of the consulting relationship.
8 Agree on rules around confidentiality.

What *information* would the systems psychodynamics consultant gather?

1 Day-to-day challenges of the client.
2 Objectives of the client system and methods to achieve them.
3 Philosophy of the client.
4 Support measures in existence in the organisation.

What *steps* does the systems psychodynamics consultant take?

1 Participates with the client in diagnosing the problem.
2 Is constructively critical.
3 Shows interest in the client.
4 Make an analysis of the dynamic in the client's system and helps the client understand it.
5 Communicates effectively.
6 Together with the client, always holds the prospect of change in mind.
7 Helps the client stay on task in the consultancy process.
8 Deals with conflict and confrontation.
9 Helps set and manage development objectives.
10 Evaluates achievements and activities.
11 Remains forward-looking and helps the client be pro-active.
12 Retains a creative and innovative outlook.
13 Acts as a catalyst to overcome inertia.
14 Helps clients recognise and define their needs.
15 Helps clients recognise their resources, i.e. personal skills, finance, organisational.
16 Helps the client gather more resources.
17 Finds solutions to problems.
18 Assists clients' attempts to find solutions to identified problems.
19 Helps to evaluate solutions.

What *constructs* may the systems psychodynamics consultant use to help the client understand that?

1 Splitting is an almost inevitable process in organisations, e.g. an organisation's leadership may be 'split' into an idealised good leadership or a vilified bad one.
2 'Unconscious' refers to the hidden aspects of organisational life.
3 Projective process may be used to get rid of unwanted feelings or behaviours in other parts of the organisation.
4 Organisations are complex, where good and bad, right and wrong, us and them, are inextricably linked.
5 Authority is often attacked for no good reason.

6 Through 'spoiling', aspects of the organisation are impaired, weakened, damaged and diminished.
7 Organisations are open systems; required to perform the task of converting inputs into outputs.
8 Work in a system can entail significant anxieties for staff.
9 Defences against anxiety are part of all systems.
10 Systems resist efforts to change them.
11 Change processes expose staff more directly to anxiety.
12 Organisational sub-systems such as teams, or groups of managers, use other sub-systems as repositories for anxiety, criticism, blame, denigration or other unwanted feelings.
13 In a well-functioning organisation, staff and managers will be able to think about the emotional impact and significance of the work.
14 The primary task is the work the organisation must do to survive.
15 Understand the nature of organisation's primary task.
16 Work groups (and organisations) can avoid carrying out the primary task.
17 Anxiety can arise in any part of the system and can have its origins in the personal history of individuals; the demands of the task; the demands in the client/customer group or wider social system.
18 'Containment' describes a basic dimension of human experience, i.e. the relationship between emotion and its 'containment' – the ways in which emotion is experienced or avoided, managed or denied, kept in or passed on so that its effects are either mitigated or amplified.
19 See how these effects happen 'below the surface'.

Summary

Social defences are equivalent to individual psychological defences. Systems psychodynamics interventions involve understanding, interpreting and working through collective (social) defences leading to enlarging the organisation's capacity to develop more task appropriate adaptations. Even the most seemingly instrumental, efficient and reasonable patterns of work and division of labour may have social defence properties. Systems psychodynamics describes a collaborative engagement between consultants and their clients to jointly explore the nature of their problems, to generate ideas for change, to test those ideas in practice, and to evaluate the results. Because organisational 'issues' may challenge both individual and social defences, organisational change inevitably involves a slow gradual and often painful evolutionary process. Organisational consultation interpretations shift the focus from the group's relationship to the consultant to relationships between group members themselves, their relatedness to the organisation and their task at hand. The focus will be on how authority is psychologically distributed, exercised and enacted, in contrast to how it is formally invested. Systems psychodynamics consultants focus on how unwanted feelings and experiences are split off and projected into other individuals and groups that carry them. Systems psychodynamics focuses on how individuals take up their work roles. In *organisational role consultations* consultants might use a variety of assessment and intervention methods, including projective or semi-projective measures such as the production and analysis of mental maps. Systems psychodynamics aims to disclose meaning to the client to the organisation-in-themselves and themselves-in-the-organisation.

Exercises

1 What are the key differences/similarities between group relations consultancy and organisational development consultancy?
2 Discuss the importance of boundary and boundary maintenance in consultancy work
3 In your view, what is the role of emotions in consultancy, and in what ways do emotions manifest in the diagnostic and delivery phases of consultancy?
4 Discuss the role of transference and countertransference in the consultancy relationship. What place does it have in systems psychodynamics consultancy?

12 Defences against anxiety

With Mark Stein

The basics

Institutional anxieties and defences

This chapter will explain the theory of social systems and the defences against anxiety. The chapter will show how the understanding of the nature of anxiety and its influence on human behaviour is an important aspect of the organisational consultant's work. Anxiety is an insidious force, sapping energy and damaging health, undermining job performance and stifling innovation and creativity. Like individuals, organisations can also suffer from symptoms of anxiety. Over the long run, anxiety can reduce an enterprise's strategic adaptability and effectiveness (Gould Wilkinson et al., 1998). The concept of anxiety figures largely in system psychodynamics theory and practice. Accompanying the concept of anxiety is the one of 'containment'. Containment describes a basic dimension of human experience, that is, the relationship between emotion and its containment, the ways in which it is experienced or avoided, managed or denied, kept in or passed on so that its effects are either mitigated or amplified. The capacity to think about anxiety in individuals, groups and organisations is related to the capacity for the containment of anxiety. A basic process for consultants is Bion's 'container–contained' model (Bion, 1967a,b,c).

Linked to anxiety is the notion of defence. Defences are necessary in order to cope with the anxiety that arises as a result of the work, but when these defences are unacknowledged, they can become an organisational way of life and a block to change and learning. Anxiety can arise in any part of the system and can have its origins in the personal history of individuals, the demands of the task, or the demands that exist within the client group or the wider social system. Impulsive action results from the lack of containment of anxiety.

We will describe how these ideas and working practices originated in the seminal work based on Isabel Menzies study of nursing (1960). This classic chapter on the structure of a hospital nursing service has almost iconic status within the field of organisation theory and organisational consultancy. It is required reading for all who were interested in what is now termed the systems psychodynamics approach to organisations (Gould et al., 2001a). In the chapter, Menzies made the original proposition that work in health care and social care organisations entail significant anxieties for staff and that defences against this anxiety can become a dominating aspect of the organisation. Through a detailed explication of the Menzies paper (Menzies, 1960) we will show how contemporary organisational consultants can develop their practice.

We will draw upon Hirschhorn, (1988, Pg. 38), where he outlines the analytic model for boundary management and its implications for anxiety in the social system. The two seminal figures in the development of social defence theory were Elliott Jaques and Isobel Menzies. Below we give a brief description of their history and how they became involved in the Tavistock Institute of Human Relations and the early work at developing systems psychodynamics methodology.

History

Elliott Jaques

Elliott Jaques was the first to put forward a theory of social defence in organisational life. He was a Canadian psychoanalyst, social scientist and management consultant known as the originator of concepts such as 'corporate culture', 'mid-life crisis', 'fair pay', 'maturation curves', 'time span of discretion' and 'requisite organisation', as a total system of managerial organisation (1951, 1953, 1955, 1961, 1964 a,b, 1989, 1995 a,b).

During the Second World War, Jaques served as a Major in the Canadian Army, where in collaboration with Henry Murray of Harvard University, using his education and training, he established the Canadian War Office Selection Boards. He was assigned as liaison to the British Army War Office Psychiatry Division that developed their own War Office Selection Boards. Many of the founders of the Tavistock Clinic and the Tavistock Institute of Human Relations were involved in the work of the War Office Selection Boards. He was a founding member, in 1946, of the Tavistock Institute of Human Relations.

Isabel Menzies Lyth

Isabel Menzies Lyth was born in Fife in 1917, the fourth child of a minister of the Church of Scotland. She took a double first in economics and experimental psychology from St Andrews, where she lectured for some years. Her tutor was Eric Trist, who was to become a leading figure in the field of organisational development. It was through Trist that during the war she was able to spend her vacations from her teaching at St. Andrews, working with the War Office Selection Board and, later, the Civil Resettlement Headquarters of the

British Army. At the end of the war she moved to London and was the only woman in a group of psychiatrists, psychologists, psychoanalysts and social scientists who founded the Tavistock Institute of Human Relations, which offered research and consultation to organisations. Among this group were W.R. Bion, John Bowlby, John Rickman, Jock Sutherland and Elliott Jaques. In this post-war period the influence of Melanie Klein and then Donald Winnicott also imbued the atmosphere of the Tavistock Institute.

As well as her social research, Menzies began psychoanalytic training in London. W. R. Bion was her second analyst. It was an analysis, which she said she undertook for herself rather than the one she had to do for her psychoanalytic training. Therefore, Bion had a great influence on her. In 1957, she qualified as a child analyst and in 1960 became a training analyst of the British Psychoanalytical Society. Throughout her time at the Tavistock Institute of Human Relation she would see her patients in the morning and carry out social research in the afternoon (Dartington, 2008). Menzies had a significant role as a group relations consultant, particularly at the Tavistock Institute's international Leicester conferences on the dynamics of authority and leadership.

The origins of the social defence theory and the centrality of introjection and projection

Hinshelwood (1989) summarises Jaques (1953) development of the social defence theory by asserting that Jaques followed Freud's idea of the aggregating bonds as "one of the primary cohesive elements binding individuals into institutionalised human associations is defence against psychotic anxiety" (Jaques 1953, Pg. 21); and he showed how this results from identification of introjective and projective kinds:

> Individuals may put their internal conflicts into persons in the external world, may unconsciously follow the course of the conflict by means of projective identification, and may re-internalise the course and outcome of the externally perceived conflict by means of introjective identification.

Jaques put forward a hypothesis:

> The specific hypothesis I shall consider is that one of the primary cohesive elements binding individuals into institutionalized association is that of defence against psychotic anxiety. In this sense individuals may be thought of as externalizing those impulses and internal objects that would otherwise give rise to psychotic anxiety and pooling them into the life of the social institutions in which they associate. This is not to say that the institutions so used thereby become 'psychotic'. But it does imply that we would expect to find in group relationships manifestations of unreality, splitting, hostility, suspicion, and other forms of maladaptive behaviour. These would be the social counterpart of, although not

identical with, what would appear as psychotic symptoms in individuals who have not developed the ability to use the mechanism of association in social groups to avoid psychotic anxiety.

(1953, Pg. 497)

Susan Long (2006) summarises Jaques work in the Glacier Metal Company. She describes how he explores this hypothesis through examples in social life and then a specific case study from his work with the company where the dynamics surround the relations between managers and their subordinates within one department. She writes that unable to reach a decision about how to implement a change to payment methods, the management and workers representatives seemed at a deadlock with rising hostility in their talks. Despite these difficulties in the negotiation process, Jaques noticed that work in the department was proceeding with no seeming ill effects or strained relationships. The same people who were in hostile dispute during negotiations were working alongside each other productively. The negotiation task was problematic, the day-to-day work task unproblematic.

According to Long, Jaques explained this through analysis of the unconscious dynamics in the culture. These dynamics are centred on issues of authority and their surrounding unconscious phantasies. The dynamics described include splitting, projective identification and deflection. In particular, the splitting occurs around the different tasks involved in the relations between the workers and their managers. Long reviews Jaques's conclusion that the workers were suspicious of the managers' motives with respect to the payment system and yet comfortable in working with them on a day-to-day basis. This, says Jaques, indicates splitting. He hypothesised that in the minds of the workers the same managers were experienced as 'good' or 'bad' depending upon whether they were relating to them in the work task or in the negotiation task. Projecting their own 'bad impulses' into their representatives who negotiated with the 'bad' negotiating managers allowed for an external 'bad object' to be created as a protection for workers from paranoid anxieties aroused by disturbing internal impulses. Projecting 'good' into the managers in the work situation 'allowed the workers to re-introject the good relations with management, and hence to preserve an undamaged and good object and alleviate depressive anxiety' (Jaques, 1955, Pg. 491). In other words, the workers felt guilt and depressive anxieties due to their projection of 'badness' into the managers and indeed, into their own representatives in the negotiation process. By feeling good about the managers during the work process, this guilt and anxiety was alleviated.

Jaques also describes the managers as holding an idealised view of the workers, which acted, in phantasy, to placate the hostile representatives and to diminish their own depressive anxieties and guilt about unconscious fears of damaging the workers through their daily exercise of managerial authority. These dynamics reinforced one another, and negotiations reached a stalemate. The greater the concessions given by management to the workers, the greater was the guilt and fear of depressive anxiety in the workers, and hence the greater the retreat to paranoid attitudes as a means of avoiding depressive anxiety (Jaques, 1955, Pg. 493).

Following the description of the case study, Jaques moves to the further question of organisational change, stressing the need to understand the dynamics that hold the system in stasis. Long (2006, Pg. 4) writes that in this work Jaques has put forward the following: (i) the central hypothesis of social defence systems, as described above; which includes (ii) the idea that social defences provide a kind of institutional glue or binding function; (iii) the interrelatedness of task and dynamics; (iv) the fact that changes bring about a disruption to the defences established over time and hence change will be resisted for unconscious as well as conscious and more obvious reasons.

Jaques put forward the idea that a social system can act in a unified way 'as if' it was an entity protecting its members from psychotic anxieties. However, beyond the stresses on the individual is the threat to the culture of the workplace, its productivity and capacity to change with a changing context. Obholzer (1999, Pg. 91-92) says:

> The assumption is that there is anxiety specific to and arising from the nature of the work and that the institution defends itself against this anxiety in such a way that the emphasis of the structure is on defence-related rather than work-related functioning .... If this is correct, then it is important for managers to realize that any attempt to alter the specific way in which work is organized in their institution must, by definition mean a disruption of the anxiety-holding system, with a consequent release into the structure of anxiety and resistance to change.

Anxiety, defence and group relations

The idea of the importance of task in shaping workplace anxieties and the social defence systems in institutions has become central to the theory and practice of Group Relations (Rice, 1965; Miller, 1989; French and Vince, 1999; Fraher, 2004a; Nutkevitch and Sher, 2006) and psychodynamic approaches to organisational and institutional life. Obholzer and Roberts (1994) collection of essays and case studies set within the health and social care services illustrate this amply, as do the many cases presented in journals and reported in research theses. Hinshelwood and Skogstad (2000) report on a method of observing organisational dynamics based predominantly on exploring institutions as social defence systems, and their authors provide case studies illustrating the value of such an approach. They use the term 'culture' to define the subjective world that mediates between the task, with its associated anxieties and the defence and thus name their model an 'anxiety-culture-defence model' (2000, Pg. 16). The centrality of the 'social defences against anxiety approach' is again taken up by Hinshelwood and Chiesa (2002).

Anxiety-defence-culture model

The anxiety-culture-defence model described by Hinshelwood and Skogstad (2000) can serve as a general model for social defence theory. It proposes that anxieties originating in people's responses to their work tasks, stimulating primitive anxieties and experienced by many within the organisation (or society) lead to a collective defence. This collective defence becomes part of the culture and structure of the organisation. That is, it becomes part of the way things get done. The anxieties may be part of the primary task, say of nursing, or teaching or accountancy, but they may also be part of associated tasks such as management or taking up 'authority for role' in face of disagreements. Anxieties may arise from normal workplace interactions and communications (Hirschhorn, 1988). Moreover, social defences may operate to protect people from other distressing emotions such as anger, envy or shame.

A real life story

The first part of the executive board meeting of a manufacturing company, flowed smoothly, due probably to the good financial figures just presented. Discussions centred on income, business, technology, customers, etc., and the atmosphere was business-like, collegial and supportive. The more vocal members of the board spoke up, questioning core technological and business aspects of the presentations, nearly always arriving at something more powerful, penetrating and intuitive than the presenter had offered. This raised the level of alertness among the other members of the board.

Timekeeping was good, but at about lunchtime, people started disturbing the meeting by wandering around to get refreshment. By the end of the meeting (six hours), everyone seemed tired and bored.

After lunch, discussions centred on a competitor company that appeared to be catching up with production capability and marketing style. The customer relations person on the board was strongly in touch with customers and bringing data (knowledge) from 'outside' the company to the 'inside'. Members of the board are reassured by his accounts of customer behaviour and expectation, but reactions to his accounts were mixed – the executive board seemed unwilling to take serious note of the reports. 'Out there' seemed far away and somewhat irrelevant. Now in defensive mode, the board unconsciously ignored the possibility of dissatisfied customers changing allegiance and buying from competitors.

Moving on the agenda, the tone of benign indifference persisted when the director of HR spoke about talent management and succession planning. The HR presentation was treated in a similar manner to discussion on customer relations – words are scrutinised, charts and tables are criticised, advice is given to the HR director as if members of executive board think that their expertise in technology, engineering, marketing, budgets, etc., extended to 'people' in a similar way. Again, somewhat defensively, board members seem closed to the idea that 'people issues' have a different, more qualitative, nature than engineering. Without acknowledging it, 'people issues' attracted strong emotional reactions, and the board had to be reminded that the company had agreed structured processes in which people were developed, and hence there was enough remit in letting HR handle that.

In considering social defences against anxiety, one wondered whether there was a mismatch between the high technological sophistication of most of the executive board and the softer 'people' approach of HR. The board seemed to be in difficulty aligning the more descriptive narratives around people and their behaviour with the practical and technological leadership issues in the manufacturing business.

Despite participants of previous leadership programmes having reported that their programme had clear impacts for them – (i) it got them out of their comfort zone; (ii) people learned about other parts of the company; (iii) communications with other parts of the company improved – the board remained anxious about the rate at which the company loses people; why new people leave; and why growing the company's own people with good technical skills, good leadership competencies and good business strategy is so difficult. It seemed that HR was the target of a destructive dynamic for the wider systemic failures to 'hold' people. For example, everyone is required to have a Development Action Plan (DAP) and a People Performance Management Review (PPMR), yet, it turned out that members of the executive board had not done DAPs and PPMRs for their direct reports, signifying that: "I don't need to do them, because I know my people and I can promote them on the basis of my knowledge of them". This caused huge succession issues because senior people did not see their progress in the company based on an identified process but rather on inter-personal relationships. As a result, people development programmes have missed many good 'stars'. Members of the executive board did not take leadership development seriously; they simply did not believe in it. The executive board was deemed to not wish to consider its own failures and this was one possible reason why it had not paid attention to succession issues among senior managers. The gaps in the company's top leadership were in effect the responsibility of the executive board members, but they kept away from the subject and left it to HR to resolve and then challenged HR, in the person of director, for not succeeding, or not succeeding quickly enough.

Executive board members seemed to think that since they have 'made it, they may feel they are above being assessed'. 'Assessment' issues were then left to HR to resolve, and the issues got 'stuck' there – the executive board unconsciously would not allow HR to implement what it could not implement itself.

It was noted that important issues were raised at the end of the meeting when there was no more time to discuss them. For example, the customer relations person wondered how executive board missed an opportunity of appointing a leader from an ethnic minority group to the executive board. The question was put gently and respectfully, but there was an angry reaction when it was discovered that a person from an ethnic minority group had been short-listed but whose name inexplicably fell off the list, and there was no patience or investment of time to find out why. The board had become defensive again in facing difficult and anxiety-making diversity issues.

Conditions for success

Working with social defences is a delicate and subtle business for consultants. The defence is there for a purpose; to protect the individuals and groups from emotional distress and pain. If one confronts the defence head on by making an interpretation or offering a hypothesis that is pitched at too deep a level, i.e. the defence is unconscious and outside of awareness, then this is unlikely to be helpful. The defence will become more strongly entrenched as the anxiety that it is protecting will surface and create disturbance both in the system and the individuals.

Often the defence is in the structure of the system. This shows itself in the organisational structure and most clearly at the boundary of the organisation and its environment. Protecting the individuals and groups from persecutory anxiety usually leads to impermeable boundaries. Consultants if they are self-aware can often spot these defences as they enter the system. How one is introduced to the system, whom you meet and how they convey their organisational story give clues on the culture and the defensive system. As the defensive system is in groups and individuals through projection and introjection the experience that individuals will have is that this is, 'just how things are done here'. Therefore, helping organisations think about the defensive system is usually done through working with groups and teams. The consultant needs to promote a spirit of inquiry. This spirit of inquiry or reflection gives the opportunity to step back and carry out some self-observation. Through this promotion of reflection organisational members can begin to consider how the structures that they have in place either hinder or promote the carrying out of the primary task. These reflective spaces need to connect to the formal system. It is only the formal system through appropriate authorisation that can institute change. Attempts to change or modify the socially defensive system will often provoke strong resistance. The resistance can be through denial and projection. 'It's not our problem', 'it cannot be us; it must be them' (Sher, 2017), 'they don't want to change or collaborate' or 'it's the management's fault', etc. These defensive manoeuvres need careful handling and the underlying anxieties around change and the consequences for staff need acknowledgement.

Theoretical and foundational basis

The centrality of introjection and projection

There is some debate as to how the socially defensive system is constructed and maintained. Elliott Jaques (1953) clearly links the two processes of introjective identification and projective identification and demonstrates how they operate in social relationships. Introjection and introjective identification are complementary to the mechanism of projection and projective identification. Through introjection the individual takes attributes of other people into himself, and they become part of his inner world. In introjective identification the internal world is made up of a whole society of internal objects.

To sum up, according to Jaques (1953),

> Projective identification unconsciously puts internal objects, good or bad, or good or bad impulses, into persons (or things) in the external world. Introjective identification takes persons and things in the outside world into the self, so that what one does comes not from oneself but from the internalised 'other' influencing one's behaviour.

This statement by Jaques (1955) links to the notion that social systems serve as defences against the unconscious anxieties of their members. In other words, the groupings and relationships designed for work not only carry a social component but also are channels for psychic projections and introjections. Actual ways of working may not just be used but distorted by defensive needs, particularly when the task of the enterprise, such as a hospital, itself generates anxieties among those who work in it (Menzies 1960).

Enactment

Gilmore and Krantz (1990) and Mersky (1999) put forward propositions concerning the role of projective identification and enactment. As Gilmore and Krantz note projective identification is little understood or studied by consultants. Gilmore and Krantz suggest that consultant teams (and individuals via supervision) need to create occasions to work on these dynamics. Gilmore and Krantz conclude:

> Learning to understand the impact of projective identification in the consulting relationship can be a vital source of information about the client system's unconscious functioning and about how to work more effectively. If not considered, however, projective identification creates forces that can easily lead consultants to work along pathways that unintentionally collude with their client systems defensive self-understanding or can readily induce consultants into potentially destructive roles.

At the same time as understanding the importance of projective identification in the consulting relationship it is equally necessary to understand introjective identification as a linked process. Individuals use defences but the interactions between individuals create the external reality of the defensive system. Jaques (1955) quotes from Freud's Group Psychology and the Analysis of the Ego (1922) on identification and its primitive nature "identification is known to psychoanalysis as the earliest expression of an emotional tie to another person". He also refers to Paula Heimann's (1973) claim "that introjection and projection may lie at the bottom of even the most complex social processes".

Splitting

Menzies Lyth (1960, Pg. 115) describes the link between projective identification, introjective identification and splitting as it applies to nursing:

> Although, following Jaques, I have used the term 'social defence system' as a construct to describe certain features of the nursing service as a continuing social institution, I wish to make it clear that I do not imply that the nursing service as an institution operates the defences. Defences are, and can be, operated only by individuals. Their behaviour is the link between psychic defences and the institution'. There is a complex and subtle interaction, resulting in a matching between individual and institutional defences. The processes 'depend heavily on repeated projection of the psychic defence system into the social defence system and repeated introjection of the social defence system into the psychic defence system. This allows continuous testing of the match and fit as the individual experiences his own and other people's reactions.' 'The enforced introjection and use of such defences also interferes with the capacity for symbol formation….The defences inhibit the capacity for creative, symbolic thought, abstract thought, and for conceptualisation. They inhibit the full development of the individual's understanding, knowledge and skills that enable reality to be handled effectively and pathological anxiety mastered.

Countertransference

Systems psychodynamically trained consultants attempt to pay attention to their countertransference reactions to gain additional data about the client system. The key concept for this is projective identification. This is the operating mechanism in the countertransferential relationship. If in the consulting relationship there is no attempt to both stay in touch with the client's experience through examination of the countertransference and at the same time an understanding of the impact of introjective identification on the client system then only a limited perspective of the total situation is possible. The consultant's capacity to pay attention to the introjective identification process leads to not fully understanding how the client system may be acting out their internal dynamics in relation to their clients, customers or patients. The clients, customers or patients project into the organisational role-holders, i.e. doctors, nurses, managers, etc., their damaged internal worlds; in turn the role-holders may identify with these damaged projections. The role-holders will have difficulty in understanding the dynamic and in turn project their distress into the wider system such as the management system or the consultant system. In turn, the consultants are in danger of passing on these unconscious processes to their own system management of the work or collusively join in the attack on the management of the department, organisation or client system. Therefore, it would seem important to provide a space for consultants to reflect on the unconscious pressures that they are subject to in order to detoxify the projections and become conscious of the push to enact and thereby to more fully appreciate the state of mind of the organisation.

Sustaining the results

Social defences cannot be got rid of. They serve an important purpose for employees. They protect them from overwhelming anxiety and stress. This is particularly true of organisations that are dealing with life and death issues, i.e. health services, police and armed services. The work of changing the maladaptive social defence system is sustained by working constantly to create a reflective organisation that invests in putting time aside and building into the culture the capacity to question why they do things the way they do. At the same time this needs careful balancing. Too much self-reflection can lead to doubt and confusion and a withdrawal from the environment and the primary task. Working with social defences and the role they have in defending against anxiety requires that the consultant can help the individual and work group work through the issues that are inhibiting progress. The adage of self-reflection leading to paralysis needs to be kept in mind as well as guarding against manic mindless action.

Burning questions

What's the point of trying to work with the social defence system if it is structured into the very being of the organisation? We are not suggesting getting rid of the defence system; that is unrealistic and dangerous. We all need our defences. It is really a question of the degrees and the strengths of the defences that are in place. Consultants need to ask: How well does the defence allow individual to take up their role? How does it hamper them? How well does the defence allow inter-group relationships to flourish? Or does it inhibit creativity and dampen down innovation and excitement? How easy is it to promote reflection? An unwillingness to reflect may show the strength of the defence and indicate the underlying anxiety that it is protecting individuals from.

How to work with a social defensive system

Reflection and learning spaces

Bain (1998) suggests that the most helpful way of working with socially defensive systems is to consciously construct spaces for common reflection on activities, which would allow for a developing awareness of the 'whole', i.e. the organisation and its interconnected parts. As awareness of the social defences against anxiety develops, people would become conscious of them rather than remaining unconscious; other ways of exploring and modifying this anxiety would become possible, so the maladaptive aspects of the social defences can change. Bain describes certain essential features of these 'learning spaces' that are the same in each of the three projects that he described:

1. The agenda for the work of these learning spaces was largely derived from the members of the organisation themselves working on the task of the program.
2. The learning space was not filled up by the CEO or equivalent.
3. The groups came to accept silence at appropriate times rather than filling in the silence with talk.
4. The learning spaces allowed for a stronger connectedness to develop between individuals and organisation.
5. The resistances to change emerged in the relationship of project members to the consultants, which could then be explored in these learning spaces. Working on perceptions of this relationship, the transference helped to deepen insight into work processes, and decreased the power of damaging projective systems, which thereby modified the social defences against anxiety. The process increased the project team's and organisation's capacities for discerning and managing reality.
6. As the social defences against anxiety were modified or changed, the organisation concurrently developed a capacity to learn and develop.

The above spaces for reflection and particularly the resistances to change as they emerge in the transference to the consultants are akin to the process of working through individual psychoanalysis or psychodynamic psychotherapy. Of relevance is the notion of containment. When the social defences are being examined or come to the fore in the consultative process the consultant needs to 'contain' what the client or system cannot bear, in order to comprehend it. The individuals within the system will wish for an experience with the consultant that does cope with the projected parts of the system. The consultant must have the capacity to take in the projections, digest them and re-project them in a tolerable form to the system so that they can be re-introjected in a more benign form. The re-projection is achieved by offering a hypothesis that enables the client system to enlarge its capacity for thinking and reflection. Consultants need to be aware that thinking and reflection is difficult to achieve in a highly defensive system. The defences will show up as splitting, fragmentation and denial. What is under attack is the capacity of the system to think and reflect. This may be felt as a personal attack on the consultant and their methods and ideas. So, it is important to retain a state of mind when this can be understood as the systems defensive reaction to change and its potential threats to the organisational members.

Working through and overcoming resistance

The consultant offers a hypothesis to overcome the resistance to change and the modification of the socially defensive system. Working through is the psychical work that members of the organisation must engage to allow the organisation to accept the below-the-surface phenomena that keep the maladaptive social defence in place. It is a constant process in the relationship with the consultant. The consultants offering hypotheses help the working through. The work consists of showing how the maladaptive social defence interferes with the carrying out of the primary task. This process must be repeated time and time again to enable the organisation to move on from rejection of the hypothesis to a conviction based on the lived experience of organisational members.

How is the social defence system created and maintained?

Menzies Lyth (1988) says that social defences are developed over time because of collective interaction and unconscious agreement among members. Members of the organisation individually protect themselves against anxiety around the task. This defensive behaviour then becomes part of the group culture – i.e. 'this is how we do things here'. This group culture is accomplished through the interplay of conscious and unconscious affect, which is collusion where members unconsciously internalise the potential defence in reducing anxiety, a conscious compromise. Often an individual can feel conflicted over this group culture and compromise. It may conflict with the individual's view of themselves and their values and ideals. Menzies (1988, Pg. 49) comments on this:

> If social defences are forced on the employee, they perpetuate pathological anxiety.... These defences are orientated to the violent, terrifying situations of infancy, and rely heavily on violent splitting which precipitates anxiety. By permitting the individual to avoid the experience of anxiety, they effectively protect the individual from confronting it. Thus, the individual cannot bring the content of the phantasy anxiety situation into contact with reality, therefore, anxiety tends to remain permanently at a level determined more by phantasy than by reality .... They inhibit the full development of the individual's understanding, knowledge, and skills that enable reality to be handled effectively and pathological anxiety to be mastered. Thus, the individual feels helpless in the face of new and strange task or problems.

Menzies never quite describes the psychological mechanism in which these social defence mechanisms manage to 'force internalisation of the social defence'. But Jaques (1961, Pg. 477) suggests:

> Organisations .... provide institutionalised roles whose occupants are sanctioned, or required to take into themselves (force), the projected objects or impulses of other members. The occupant of such roles may absorb the objects and impulses – take them into themselves and become either good or bad objects with corresponding impulses – put them into

an externally perceived ally; or enemy, who is then loved, or attacked. The gain for the individual in projecting objects and impulses and introjecting their careers in the external world, lies in the unconscious cooperation with other members of the institution or group who are using similar projective mechanisms. Introjective identification then allows more than the return of projected objects and impulses. The other members are also taken inside, and legitimised and reinforced attacks upon persecutor, or support manic idealisation of love objects, thereby reinforcing the denial of destructive impulses against them.

Isobel Menzies contribution to understanding organisational life

Menzies describes how a hospital had been finding it increasingly difficult to reconcile staffing needs and training needs. The senior staff felt that there was a danger of complete breakdown in the system of allocating student nurses to practical front-line work with patients while also trying to train them effectively.

Menzies states that she took a position of considering the overt problem as the 'presenting symptom' and to reserve judgement on the real nature of the difficulties until she had completed the 'diagnostic' work. She set up a programme of data-gathering consisting of intensive interviewing, observational studies of operational units, and informal contacts with nurses and other staff. In an interesting footnote she refers to this as a 'therapeutic study' and writes of how the work in later stages shifted from diagnosis to therapy. She states that "presentation and interpretation of data, and work done on resistances to their acceptance, facilitate the growth of insight into the nature of the problem".

Menzies (1960, Pg. 97) notes that as the research proceeded, she "came to attach increasing importance to understanding the nature of the anxiety and the reasons for its intensity". For Menzies, the anxiety is connected to primitive anxieties aroused in the nurse by contact with seriously ill patients. She uses the description of infantile psychic life as elaborated by Freud, and more particularly by Melanie Klein (1959), as a conceptual framework. Above all, Menzies draws on Klein's view that the internal phantasy world of the infant "is characterized by a violence and intensity of feeling quite foreign to the emotional life of the normal adult", seeing infantile-type primitive anxieties aroused for the nurses through intimate contact with patients. Menzies describes how she sees these anxieties mobilised in the nurse around love, hate, aggression and suggests that the main psychological mechanism in use is projection. The nurse projects her own infantile phantasy situation into the workplace, experiencing the work as a deeply painful mixture of objective reality and phantasy.

Alongside anxiety is another crucial theoretical concept, the relationship between emotion and its 'containment', i.e. the ways in which emotion is experienced or avoided, managed or denied, kept in or passed on so that its effects are either mitigated or amplified. The capacity to think, on the part of individuals or groups, is related to the capacity for containment of anxiety (Bion, 1959). Going one step further, Menzies suggests that this to-be-expected anxiety is amplified by the techniques used to contain and modify this anxiety.

Menzies' elaboration of how these defensive techniques are played out in the organisation of the nursing service is discussed in the following sections.

Social systems and defences against anxiety

Organisations thus have both a manifest conscious life and latent unconscious life. The conscious life could be considered to be the way it rationally chooses to manage its primary task, sets goals and objectives, the structures and mechanisms it puts in place to achieve these, and the management of its boundaries to achieve this end and both survive and develop.

Defences against these anxieties will be part of organisational life. These relate to the way in which individuals, groups of individuals and professional groups have used the culture, social structure, working practices and boundaries of any given group or organisation in a defensive way to ward off anxiety or conflict. Menzies identified through action research the socially structured defensive techniques suggested by (1960) as a defence against the anxiety of human encounter in the nursing service of a general hospital.

For ease of exposition Menzies listed them separately, but she suggested that they all operated simultaneously using the early primitive mechanisms of denial, splitting and projection:

1. Splitting up the nurse-patient relationship
2. Denial of the significance of the individual
3. Depersonalisation and categorisation
4. Detachment and denial of feelings
5. The attempt to eliminate decisions by ritual task-performance
6. Reducing the weight of responsibility in decision making by checks and counterchecks
7. The collusive social redistribution of responsibility and irresponsibility
8. Avoidance of change
9. Individual and group defences against anxiety, because of human encounter in the caring professions
10. Over-identification and the denial of difference
11. Use of denial, splitting and or projective identification
12. An anxious urgency to help and care/staff to become victims, niceness – unconditional positive regard
13. Projection of all inadequacies, responsibilities, painful differences and realities elsewhere
14. Rescue fantasies/saviour thinking
15. Turning against the self – I'm not good enough

These defences against anxiety become part of the organisation's system and culture. Organisations will often resist efforts to change them, as change processes expose staff more directly to the persecutory anxiety that they are defending against.

Institutional defences as a source of secondary anxiety

Menzies' conclusions give a powerful picture of dynamic processes at work within an institutionally defensive system. Perhaps the emphases of Menzies' nursing paper militate against its being remembered and taken seriously. The paper illustrates the complex defence system used by the nursing system but does not address adequately what to do about it. This is a point that Isabel Menzies Lyth continued to feel strongly about. She asserted that the paper had been misunderstood and had led people to believe that providing support groups for staff was the answer to anxiety-provoking work. She was firmly opposed to this idea. She thought that the issue of anxiety was over-emphasised, in relation to the other side of the process – containment. She felt that the organisation needed to be designed in a way that offered staff effective containment of their anxieties.

In the shadow of the pandemic

Facing the challenges of Covid-19 and other crises

Mark Stein

In this short note I explore some of the challenges created by the Covid-19 pandemic for us, in our roles as citizens, family members, employees, managers and leaders in organisations. In particular, I draw on my earlier research using systems psychodynamic ideas (Stein, 2004) to help us to understand the crises we may face and how we may address them.

Central to my understanding is that the Covid-19 pandemic signifies a profound failure of the structures and systems that contain us. Indeed, the systems, structures and rituals that we ordinarily use to hold our lives together are suddenly swept away by the pandemic, and we have been left feeling vulnerable, exposed to risks we previously had little or no awareness of, and leading highly constricted lives we had never imagined living.

In my 2004 paper, in a somewhat different context, I introduced the term the 'critical period' to describe such periods of time. I describe the unfolding of such scenarios during which people 'are faced with events that are incongruous, shocking and potentially dangerous' (Stein, 2004, Pg. 1246) and where 'there is invariably the threat of a sudden loss of meaning and the experience that one's view of the world has been violated. People's routines – as well as their customary ways of thinking – are interrupted, leading them to have little idea about how to proceed' (Stein, 2004, Pg. 1246).

Covid-19 is a scenario of this kind, one of a magnitude and duration unprecedented in our lifetime, turning our world upside-down. It has produced feelings of lack of containment and the anxiety that there is no one in authority – government; leaders; authority figures – who are able to look after us, no one able to think of us, deal with our specific problems adequately, and guide us in a way that leaves us feeling comfortable and safe.

What lessons can be learnt from research into earlier crises? In spite of some of the external differences between the various risk scenarios, we can identify three highly problematic activities that, in the face of these anxieties, people engage in. These are: (1) denying, (2) assuming (3) and panicking.

With the first kind of response, denying, because of the magnitude of the challenges and their associated anxieties, there is an inclination to make the assumption that the problem does not exist, or, if it does, that it won't affect us much so that there is no real need to be worried or anxious. The responses of a number of leaders around the world, especially at the early stages of the pandemic, could be seen as examples of denying: in the face of overwhelming evidence that catastrophic events were underway, these leaders concluded either that the problem did not exist, or, if it did, it wouldn't affect them or their constituents much.

Denying occurs when there are known facts that suggest that dangerous or even catastrophic events are imminent, and where these facts make us so anxious that we are inclined to try to obliterate them. For example, for two days during the Three Mile Island nuclear disaster, America's worst, extreme temperature, extreme pressure and extreme radiation readings were explained away as being the result of faulty measuring instruments, rather than being understood as correctly indicating that a potential nuclear catastrophe was unfolding.

'Assuming' is the second type of response which occurs when we have information about an imminent problem or catastrophe, and we make the assumption that someone else of higher or more appropriate authority is addressing the situation in the absence of any evidence that they are doing so. Here too, the anxiety is felt to be so great that we unconsciously 'hand it on' elsewhere, making it the problem of others. During the Cyahogu shipping disaster in the Chesapeake Bay, US, for example, the First Mate saw another ship heading directly towards his ship but did not inform the Captain because he thought the Captain must already be aware of the problem. In fact, the Captain knew nothing about it, and a short while later a collision occurred in which 11 people died.

The third kind of response, panicking, occurs when we are aware of the impending problem, but here the anxiety is felt to be so overwhelming that we cannot think, and, instead, act in haste and without due consideration for the consequences. One example of panic is the police authorities' response during the Hillsborough Football Stadium disaster in Sheffield, UK. With crowds massing outside one of the entrances to the stadium just prior to the football game, the police Match Commander in charge became increasingly anxious, panicky and unable to think. Although he knew that the enclosed spectator 'pens' in the stadium – which led directly from the gates – were getting dangerously full, he panicked and ordered the opening of the gates, leading to severe crushing and the death of 96 people.

> So, what might an appropriate response look like? While there is no easy solution, an appropriate response is one that involves taking the crisis very seriously and trying as best we can to address it. Importantly, although a split-second response is sometimes necessary, more often there is some limited time in which we need to be able to have the capacity to think while – at the same time – keeping in mind the disturbing and conflicting aspects of the situation. Such a response involves using effective and clear leadership to (1) create a safe place for ourselves and others to think about and explore the situation as best we can; (2) explore the challenges, get information and solicit informed opinion about what can be done; (3) facilitate, support and encourage these others to use their perceptual and thinking faculties; (4) bringing the information together and taking decisive action; (5) communicating to others appropriately and (6) monitoring and getting feedback on how it all goes.
>
> This paper received an *Emerald Citation of Excellence*.

Organisations have social defences against anxiety; often these are stimulated by the primary task of the organisation. Social defences may be manifest in the structure, in procedures, communication, roles, culture, and in the espoused theories and actual theories in use. Social defences are 'created' unconsciously by members of the organisation through their interactions in carrying out the primary task. The consultant's task is to aid the organisation's capacity for reflection, thinking and the reduction in maladaptive defence mechanisms that interfere with the carrying out of the primary task.

Summary

Anxiety and its influences on human behaviour are important aspects of organisational consultants' work. 'Containment' is basic to human developmental experience, i.e. the relationship between emotion and its containment, the ways in which it is experienced or avoided, managed or denied, kept in or passed on, mitigated or amplified, affects human performance levels. Anxiety is linked to defence. Defences are necessary to cope with anxiety that arises at work; when these defences are unacknowledged, they become an organisational way of life and block change and learning. Anxiety arises in any part of the system and can have its origins in the personal history of individuals, the demands of the task, or the demands of the client group or the wider social system. Boundary management is important for the containment of anxiety in social systems. Social defence theory is central to the idea of the aggregating bonds binding individuals into institutionalised human associations. Individuals externalise their internal worlds of impulses and internal objects that would otherwise give rise to unbearable anxiety. Workplace anxieties and social defence systems are central to the theory and practice of Group Relations and the understanding of organisational and institutional life. The anxiety-culture-defence model serves as a general model for social defence theory. People's workplace tasks stimulate primitive anxieties and lead to collective group defences. This collective defence becomes part of the culture and structure of the organisation. The defence is there for a purpose – to protect individuals and groups from emotional distress and pain. Social defence systems are constructed and maintained by processes of introjective identification and projective identification. Introjection and introjective identification are complementary to the mechanism of projection and projective identification. Through introjection, individuals take attributes of other people into themselves and the attributes become part of their inner worlds. Conversely, through projection and projective identification, individuals place attributes of themselves into others and the attributes become part of their external and social reality.

Exercise: social systems and defences against anxiety

Briefly ask yourself and list:

1 What are the core anxieties inherent within the nature of my work?
2 What are some of the defences or mechanisms I use in relation to these anxieties and the pressures that accompany them?
3 Would a colleague recognise others that I might not be aware of?
4 What collective defences operate within the organisation in which I work, in relation to these anxieties?

Part IV
Socio-technical systems

In Chapter 13, we will describe the emergence of the concept of the sociotechnical system, which was complementary to the open systems model and served as a reaction to the machine theory of organisation dominant in the earlier decades of the 20th century. In Chapter 13, we show the development of socio-technical systems and design (STSD) and its capacity to connect, work systems which are now complex ecosystems that extend beyond an organization and its employees. Organizations rely increasingly on technologically enabled integration and optimization of a network of multi-faceted connections that are integral to each involved organization's ability to perform effectively and carry out its strategy. The design of any organization extends well beyond the organization's boundaries to include its lateral connections with many elements within the ecosystem. Organization designers must expand the focus from bounded organizations to the design of ecosystems. The design of the technical system that links together the members of the ecosystem will have to occur interactively with the design of the ecosystem's social system.

Sociotechnical systems were devised by Emery and Trist (1960b) to describe systems that involve a complex interaction between humans, machines and the environmental aspects of the work system. With this definition, all aspects, people, machines and context need to be considered when developing such systems using STSD methods. The term sociotechnical system is nowadays widely used to describe many complex systems, but there are five key characteristics of open STS (Badham et al., 2000):

1. Systems should have interdependent parts.
2. Systems should adapt to and pursue goals in external environments.
3. Systems have an internal environment comprising separate but interdependent technical and social sub-systems.
4. Systems have equifinality. In other words, systems goals can be achieved by more than one means. This implies that there are design choices to be made during system development.
5. System performance relies on the joint optimisation of the technical and social sub-systems. Focusing on one of these systems to the exclusion of the other is likely to lead to degraded system performance and utility.

DOI: 10.4324/9781003181507-19

Mumford (2006) outlines STSD. The general aim was to investigate the organisation of work, with early work in STSD focused mostly on manufacturing and production industries such as coal, textiles and petrochemicals. The aim was to see whether work in these industries could be made more humanistic. There has been a revival of interest in sociotechnical approaches as industries have discovered the diminishing returns from investment in new software engineering methods. However, sociotechnical ideas and approaches may not always be explicitly referred to as such (Avgerou et al., 2004). The ideas appear in areas such as participatory design methods and ethnographic approaches to design. Indeed, one of the key tenets of STSD is a focus on participatory methods, where end users are involved during the design process (e.g. Greenbaum and Kyng, 1991).

13 Socio-technical systems

A real life story

The scene is the office of a CEO. I am an organisational development consultant and the CEO is talking to me about the challenge of steering his company's strategy for growth over the next ten years. With a mix of pride and desperation, he describes his feelings about the unique success of the company's product and his apprehension about filling senior leadership posts. His efforts to fill those posts have not been hugely successful. New people are appointed, but there is something about the culture of the company that 'pushes' new people out after about a year in post. The CEO says he fears there is a dynamic operating in the company that makes new staff, although they are well-qualified, feel they do not entirely 'belong to the family' and they leave. He adds that surveying the next level of leadership, i.e. the 70 heads of departments, he cannot see the people with the requisite business skills to develop and run the business at the next level. He is concerned about succession – the present board has people in their late 50s who will be retiring in the next 5-7 years. Who will replace them if new appointees do not stay and the next generation of leaders cannot put people up for board membership?

I think that what the CEO is saying is an example of the psychoanalytic concept of the oedipal conflict which is the conflict with authority figures and the wish to supplant them. In this instance, it is expressed as an inter-group and inter-generational dynamic. In practice, this dynamic gets expressed as subtle, and sometimes not so subtle, expressions by members of the board of insufficient confidence and belief in the leadership capabilities of the next level down – the 70 departmental heads; matched by a collective sense of awe, respect and fear in the group of 70 towards the members of the board, who are regarded as giants and supermen in their fields who are challenged at a price. A stand-off attitude has become entrenched between the two layers of leadership – the board members who are truly strong, expansive and knowledgeable but who also have anxieties about holding onto their sometimes vulnerable positions of power and status; and the group of 70 who are in their 40s and 50s and who are waiting for opportunities for advancement, are rivalrous with their colleagues for promotion;

> who want to be more senior in the company, but don't feel authorised by the board.
>
> The key organisational dynamic can be summarised as idealising from below; and infantalizing from above. What is hidden is the rivalry between old and young; there is an impasse between two projective processes. The CEO's feelings of pride and desperation are two aspects of the fragmentation processes in the company that have been projected into him. In conceptual terms, it is about killing the father and the presence of murderous feelings on both sides.
>
> Psychoanalytically, the aim of this consultancy intervention was 'working through', i.e. reflecting, thinking and taking appropriate action. Before genuine and useful 'working through' could take place, resistance in the participants required considering the impossibility of reflection because of the fear of unconscious murderous rage towards the 'father' and 'castration' of the people below him.
>
> Technically, as consultant, I am required to speak truth to power, telling the CEO something difficult and reminding him of realities of the company and the limitations of my consultancy. Inevitably, I am faced with 'negative therapeutic reactions' i.e. taking one step forwards followed by two steps backwards, as the board struggles with its group unconscious phantasy of the CEO who is experienced as a brilliant scientist but a brutal manager and their sometimes futile attempts to introject him as a benign good object. In the midst of the CEO's 'working through' in relation to his position in the board's mind as the 'father' CEO, the feelings that come to the surface in the board are a mixture of hatred of the interpretations and a resistance to owning these dynamics.

The basics

The sociotechnical model provides the structural contribution to organisations through the approach to job and organisational design. Every organisation is made up of people (the social system) using tools, techniques and knowledge (the technical system) to produce goods or services valued by customers (who are part of the organisation's external environment).

In this chapter, we will describe the emergence of the concept of the sociotechnical system, which was complementary to the open systems model and served as a reaction to the machine theory of organisation dominant in the earlier decades of the 20th century. The 1930s and 1940s had seen the emergence in the United States of the 'human relations' or motivational school of management (e.g. Mayo 1933; Roethlisberger and Dickson 1939). This drew attention to the informal organisation, which sometimes supported but often subverted, the performance of the enterprise. Organisational effectiveness depended on meeting the needs – both overt and unrecognised – of the employees. The influence of this school was literally incorporated into the name of The Tavistock Institute of Human Relations and the Institute's first major project with the Glacier Metal Company (Jaques, 1951a, b) concentrated on the motives and drives of workers and managers with little attention to the technology and production processes themselves. Studies of work organisation in coal mining (Trist and Bamforth, 1951; Trist et al., 1963) brought the mechanistic and human relations perspectives together, asserting the proposition that an effective form of work organisation was an organisation of two systems – the psycho-social and the technico-economic (cf. Emery and Trist, 1960). This proposition was tested experimentally from 1953 onwards, initially in Indian textile mills with positive results (Rice, 1958, 1963; Miller, 1975). The application of the STS concept to the design of semi-autonomous group working has become widely disseminated. It has also been applied to organisational change of larger systems (Rice, 1963; Miller and Rice, 1967).

History

According to Susman (1976), the use of autonomous work groups largely came from the application of STS (Cummings, 1978; Emery and Trist, 1960b; Susman, 1976). The "use of autonomous groups involves a shift in focus from individual methods of performing work to group methods", and the rationale for making the shift in focus results from "the proposition that a group can more effectively allocate its resources when and where required to deal with its total variance in work conditions, than can an aggregate of individuals each of who is assigned part of the variance" (Susman, 1976, Pg. 183).

Self-regulating work groups within sociotechnical systems (STS)

An important outcome of Emery and Trist's early work on semi-autonomous work groups in organizations *is greater productivity and worker satisfaction* (Cummings, 1994, Pg. 268). They revealed that improvements in the technical system do not always result in higher productivity or effectiveness if the social system is not supportive and able to cope with any stresses it places on its members (Cummings, 1994, Pg. 287).

The use of work groups as the basic building block for work design can give the organization the ability to meet the demands stemming from either the environment or the interdependent social and technical components. Probably the most popular application of STS theory has been the development of self-regulating work groups (Cummings, 1981, Pg. 250–271). Alternatively referred to as self-leading or self-managing teams, self-regulating work groups include members performing interrelated tasks (Manz, 1990, Pg. 273–299). Such groups control members' task behaviours. Self-regulating work groups have responsibility for a whole product or service and make decisions about task assignments and work methods.

In self-regulating work groups, the group sets its own production goals within broader organizational limits and may be responsible for support services, such as maintenance, purchasing and quality control. Team members are generally expected to learn all the jobs within the span of control of the group and usually are paid based on knowledge and skills rather than seniority. When pay is based on performance, the group rather than individual performance measures are used.

> Autonomous groups manage coordination on a real time basis through informal adjustments among group members rather than relying on supervisors to perform coordination functions. Contrasted with traditional teamwork, in which individuals perform mainly specialized tasks, autonomous group members are more flexible, making cooperation easier. About one half of all socio-technical system experiments involve the establishment of autonomous groups to increase cooperative effort, improve training, heighten motivation, enhance problem solving and improve organizational flexibility.
> (Pasmore and Woodman, 1989. Pg. 98)

The mining industry

The second project undertaken by the Tavistock Institute following the work with the Glacier Metal Company was in the mining industry (Trist and Murray, 1993). The concept of open systems theory was first applied to an actual organisation by Trist and Bamforth (Trist and Bamforth, 1951). Following the nationalisation of the British coal mining industry in 1948, mechanical methods were increasingly introduced into mines and these had a considerable effect on the behaviour of the miners and the productivity of the mines. Trist and Bamforth spent over two years in close discussion with face workers to discover the effect of the introduction of the new technology of mechanical coal cutters resulting in the 'longwall' method of mining. Before the introduction of mechanical methods, the basic working unit was a pair of miners with one or two assistants, who were all self-chosen and who made their own contract with management regarding the amount of coal to be hewn and the wages to be paid. The pair were virtually self-managing for all aspects of the task. With the introduction of mechanisation these working practices could not be sustained. These technological changes inevitably caused changes in the way individual miners were organised and affected their working and personal relationships. In their attempt to adapt to the new mechanisation, certain behaviours occurred among the workers, which Trist and Bamforth said were defences against anxiety and hindered the overall effectiveness of the primary task – to extract coal. According to Rice (1958):

> Trist and Bamforth showed that the introduction of the three-shift longwall cycle into British mining resulted in the breakdown of an established social system at the coal face. A new social system came into being, characterised by maladaptive mechanisms, as a defence against the social

and psychological consequences of the new technology. The concept of a sociotechnical system arose from the consideration that any production system requires both a technological organisation, equipment and process layout – and a work organisation relating to each other those who carry out the necessary tasks. The technological demands place limits upon the type of work organisation possible, but a work organisation has social and psychological properties of its own that are independent of technology.

The conclusions of this study were simple and precise. "A qualitative change will have to be effected in the general characteristics of the method – the longwall – so that a social as well as technological whole can come into existence" (Trist and Bamforth 1951).

The relationship between technology and social structures

The special contribution of the early Tavistock pioneers lay in their analysis of the interrelation between the technological and the social structures in an organisation and how each influences the other. We will describe how the STS concept was developed to refer to the major components within organisational systems: (i) the technological aspects of machinery, (ii) the particular method of working and (iii) the social aspects that involve the interpersonal relations between employees. We show how these components are interlinked with each other and changes in one automatically cause changes in the other, creating a perspective of the whole system acting as a sociotechnical system whose total effectiveness depends on the balance achieved between the social and the technological components. Work in the mining industry 'gave a first glimpse of the emergence of a new paradigm of work' in which the best match would be sought between requirements of the social and technical systems (Trist and Murray, 1993, Pg. 38).

Research and consultancy

The formalisation of the ideas of the sociotechnical system was contributed to by many people, but notably, Rice and Miller (Miller and Rice 1967; Miller 1976) who began to combine the approach with systems theory as it emerged in the 1960s and 1970s. According to Hinshelwood and Chiesa (2002, Pg. 151), the 'discovery' of systems theory by the Tavistock tradition rejuvenated consultancy work. Emphasis on the system, and how systems behave, was particularly suitable to research that relied upon commissions from industry and business. But managers required a means of handling the system, not necessarily understanding where the problems came from. Increasingly, stress was laid on system maintenance (Miller, 1993) and the problems of role, boundary, task and aspects of leadership and authority (Rice, 1965). Though 'effecting change' had often been the original reason for the commission, increasingly there was an interest in an 'understanding mode' that was more in keeping with a psychoanalytic approach.

The Tavistock Institute's central sociotechnical/open systems model was developed during the 1950s and 1960s:

> A work organisation can be conceived of in terms of the separate dynamics and requirements of its 'technical sub-system' and its 'social sub-systems'. Both have a role in achieving performance of an overall organisational task, and the requirements of one constrain the other without fully determining possibilities. In principle, it is possible to come to an accommodation or 'joint optimisation' of the two, such that both overall task performance requirements (the technical) and the socio-psychological needs of workers (the social) are catered for. These social-psychological requirements include the need for some form of autonomy at the level of individual jobs, and where appropriate, workgroups.
> (Holti, 1997, Pg. 214)

Holti (1997, Pg. 218) describes an 'enabling concept' – several important insights and assumptions which are in line with classic sociotechnical work and makes sociotechnical work more able to deal with the range and complexity of issues that have to be faced in designing or redesigning contemporary work organisations. We argue that a range of concepts needs to be drawn upon and combined with socio-technical work towards the development of a meta-framework of sociotechnical analysis.

A reformulation of the STS approach was necessary to consider the diversity and interworking of theory and practice within the development of social science. Holti (1997) puts forward the following addition to classic STS theory that "in analysing the functioning and contradictions of work organisations, greater insight can usually be achieved by taking more aspects than is customary of the 'psycho-social whole' into consideration, by conducting and inter-relating analyses at different levels". He argues that STS theory needs to incorporate the dimension of conflict that is not just caused by the mismatch of the social and technical systems, but that conflict is also inherent due to social and economic interests in the social system of the enterprise. This perhaps also connects to the early difficulties that were faced by the Tavistock pioneers when they did not include the unions in work redesign or that the unions were unwilling to engage with the redesign efforts. These conflicts are over matters such as pay, grading opportunities for advancement and job security.

Holti describes what he calls 'a number of important insights and assumptions' which are in line with classic **sociotechnical** work but also mark a new development. Holti claims that these ideas form the 'enabling' concept to make **sociotechnical** work more able to deal with the range and complexity of issues that must be faced currently in designing or redesigning work organisations. He questions the reliance on general systems theory which originally derived from the biological sciences and its adequacy for conceptualising the varied forms of conflict that are part of the fabric of work organisations. He argues that a range of concepts needs to be drawn upon and combined with *socio-technical* work. He offers a meta-framework of *sociotechnical* analysis that incorporates four different conceptual levels that are needed for successful system change and redesign:

1 **The political and economic.** Here we are concerned with the conscious struggles for resources, influence and control that occur as members of an organisation set about furthering what they see as legitimate personal, group and organisational objectives.
2 **The logistical and cognitive.** This level of analysis concerns the constraints placed on an organisation by the finite capacity of individuals and groups to process information, and the configurations of systems of planning, execution and control which may be effective in addressing the information-processing demands of an organisational task. Here we are concerned with the organisations and the individuals within it to process information and develop capacities for better decision-making.
3 **The cultural.** This level concerns the interpretative framework, the sets of assumptions, values and strategies for going about their working lives that people learn when they join an organisation and become involved in its life. Change can challenge and disrupt these assumptions and potentially lead to resistance.
4 **The psychodynamic.** Here we are concerned with the unconscious processes that shape the way individual and groups experience each other in the organisation. Dynamics uses concepts of 'projective process' and 'splitting' to illuminate the way that different groups or individuals may 'carry' or represent conflicting aspects of the pressures impinging on an organisation, so that they are each protected from facing dilemmas and contradictions, blaming others for the hostile ideas they represent. Holti emphasises the need to provide secure conditions within which individuals and groups can develop understanding of these processes. Like Mumford (1996, 2003), we think Holti is referring to the need for consultants to provide containment when they are working with these issues.

Circumstances that promote achievement

The sociotechnical approach to organisational design

The Tavistock Institute group developed a set of guidelines and principles to assist themselves and other consultants and managers concerned with improving the design of work situations. According to Mumford (2003), the role of the consultant is to help the users of the system analyse their own needs and problems, evaluate alternative solutions and arrive at design decisions. The design principles of the sociotechnical approach were enhanced as research and action advanced. A key contributor to this development was Fred and Merrelyn Emery (1978a, b).

Mumford (2003) helpfully summarised Albert Cherns's elucidation of the principles from his paper in *Human Relations* (Cherns, 1976). William Pasmore (1985) described the key insights of the sociotechnical approach as listed by Trist and Murray (1993, Pg. 324) in *The Social Engagement of Social Science: The Socio-Technical Perspective:*

1 The work system should be conceived as a set of activities making up a functioning whole rather than a collection of individual jobs.
2 The work *group* should be considered more central than individual jobholders.
3 Internal regulation of the work system should be regulated by its members, not by external supervisors.
4 The underlying design philosophy should be based on redundancy of parts (multi-skilling vs. single skilling). Its members should have more skills than the system normally requires.
5 The discretionary component of work is as important to the success of the system as the prescribed component.
6 The individual should be viewed as complementary to the machine rather than an extension of it.
7 The design of work should be variety-increasing rather than variety-decreasing for the individual and the group so that learning can take place for organisational adaptation.

Much earlier, Emery (1978a, b) added to these insights by stating that each member of the work group should have:

1 An optimal level of variety
2 Learning opportunities
3 Scope for making decisions
4 Organisational support – training, good supervision, etc.
5 A job recognised as important by the outside world
6 The potential for making progress in the future

Conceptual basis

Implications for organisational consultants and change agents working with a STS approach and design

According to Mumford (2003), the consultant's role is to help the design group to choose and implement an appropriate problem-solving methodology, to keep the members interested and motivated towards the design task, to help them resolve any conflicts, and to make sure that important

Socio-technical systems

design factors are not forgotten or overlooked. The consultant must in no circumstances take decisions for the design group or persuade them that certain things should not be done. The consultant's role is to help the design group systematically to analyse their own problems and needs and arrive at an organisational solution that solves the problems and meets the needs. She states the consultant should help the design group with:

1. Clarification of the task and overcoming doubts as to their capacity to tackle the problems
2. Offering information on how other organisations have tackled similar problems
3. Organising visits to other companies
4. Inviting experts to talk to the group on possible options
5. Helping keep up the morale of the group as it works through the distinct phases of anxiety and uncertainty at the start; maintaining the group's capacity to work as it begins to feel overwhelmed by data and the reaction of other groups around it.

Mumford suggests that several skills are required by the consultant such as flexibility and tact. The skills in helping the group members communicate easily and accurately with each other are important skills. The consultant must be able to get on with people, have easy and pleasant social manners and be able to run a meeting democratically and ensure that relationships within the group stay friendly and constructive. This requires patience, control, enthusiasm and the ability to create and maintain positive attitudes. The managing of conflict and different ideas and perceptions is crucial. Conflicts of ideas and interests need to be recognised, brought out into the open and discussed, and solution must be arrived at which meet the approval of all members. We think Mumford here is talking about the psychoanalytic concept of 'containment' that is central to managing the inevitable anxieties connected to redesign.

The following are Eric Trist's (1981, Pg. 33) guidelines for improving the design of work systems:

1. An initial scanning is made of all the main aspects – technical and social – of the *selected target system* – that is, the department or plant to be studied.
2. The *unit operations* – that is, the transformations (change of states) of the material or product that takes place in the target system – are then identified, whether carried out by people or machines.
3. An attempt is made to discover the *key variances*. A variance is defined as a weak link in the system where it is difficult to achieve required or desired norms or standards. A variance is key if it significantly affects (1) either the quantity or quality of production and (2) either the operating or social costs of production.

4 Variances should be documented showing:
  i where the variance occurs and why
  ii where it is first observed
  iii where and how it is corrected
  iv who does this
  v what they must do to correct it
  vi what information they need to correct it
  vii what other resources are required
5 A separate inquiry is made into the social system's members' perceptions of their roles and role possibilities as well as constraining factors, including:
  i A brief description of the organisational structure: who works with whom
  ii A description of the relationships required between workers for the optimal production of the product
  iii A note on the extent of work flexibility: the knowledge each worker has of the jobs of others
  iv A description of pay relationships – the nature of the pay system, differentials, bonuses, etc.
  v A description of the workers' psychological needs
  vi The extent to which the present work structure and roles meet these needs.
6 Attention then shifts to *neighbouring systems*, beginning with the support or maintenance system. An assessment should be made of how the system of support and maintenance in operation impacts on and affects, the targeted system. The same should be done for the system that supplies materials and services to the change area.
7 Attention then shifts to the *boundary-crossing systems* on the input and output side – i.e. supplier and user systems.
8 The target system and its environment are then considered in the context of the *general management system* of the organisation regarding the effects of policies or development plans of either a technical or social nature.
9 Proposals for change – the consultant gathers all the information and after discussions with the different groups works at arriving an agreed action plan.

Self-regulating work groups within STS

Appelbaum (1997, Pg. 452–463) points out that an important outcome of Emery and Trist's early work is that developing semi-autonomous work groups in organizations can lead to greater productivity and to worker satisfaction. Emery and Trist (1965, Pg. 21–32) revealed that improvements in the technical system do not always result in higher productivity or effectiveness if the social system is not supportive and able to cope with any stresses it places on its members. The use of work groups as the basic building block for work design can give the organization the ability to meet the demands stemming from either the environment or the interdependent social and technical components. Such groups can control members' task behaviours. STS theory as an intervention strategy has many strong points but must be utilized within a strategic change plan for organizational development rather than an isolated strategy for development. Appelbaum suggests that self-managed teams are not easy to implement. They require organizational changes and investments of time and resources to make them work. The changes and contextual supports require organizational commitment and investment. Without the willingness to make this investment, an organization is unlikely to sustain the performance and quality benefits that can arise from the implementation of work teams.

Supporting the outcomes

Structured work design and STS analysis – textile mills and car manufacture

One of the earliest accounts of a comprehensive organisational re-design according to sociotechnical principles was undertaken by Rice (1958) in textile mills in Ahmedabad, India. Here, as elsewhere, the sociotechnical redesign led to a radically different organisation that, it was argued, was now jointly optimised. Indeed, the "reorganization was reflected in a significant and sustained improvement in mean percentage efficiency and a decrease in mean percentage damage [to goods] ... the improvements were consistently maintained through-out a long period of follow up" (Trist, 1981, Pg. 1-67). No doubt encouraged by a growing body of similar findings, STS theory, for a time at least, experienced the same kind of commercial buy-in currently enjoyed by business process re-engineering, lean production and six sigma.

The most famous example of sociotechnical design is undoubtedly that undertaken at Volvo's Kalmar and Uddevalla car plants (Hammerstrom and Lansbury, 1991; Knights and McCabe, 2000; Sandberg, 1995; Auer and Riegler, 1990, Lindholm and Norstedt, 1975, Lindholm,1990). While many commercial instantiations of STS theory are criticised for their limited degree of 'technological' change, choosing to focus instead on the altogether less expensive aspects of 'socio' and 'organisational' change (Pasmore et al., 1982), the Volvo case study embraced the principles based on a clean slate approach and on a scale heretofore not yet experienced.

The defining feature of the Kalmar plant's design was a shift from a rationalistic style of hierarchical organisation to one based on smaller groups. In Volvo's case, the change was radical. The production line, the mainstay of automobile manufacture since the days of Henry Ford, literally disappeared. It was replaced by autonomous group work undertaken by well-qualified personnel, "advanced automation in the handling of production material; co-determination in the planning and a minimum of levels in the organisation" (Sandberg, 1995, Pg. 147). In Volvo's case, the parts for the cars were organised as if they were kits, with each member of the team completing a proportion of the kit and the team effectively building a whole car independently of other teams. In terms of agility it was quickly observed that "model changes [...] needed less time and less costs in tools and training" compared to a similar plant that was organised around the traditional factory principle (Sandberg, 1995, Pg. 149).

Obviously, such teams still needed to be related to the wider system, which required someone to work at the system boundaries to "perceive what is needed of him and to take appropriate measures" (Teram, 1991, Pg. 343–356). In command-and-control terms, this new organisation shifts the primary task of commanders (or managers) away from processes of internal regulation to instead being more outwardly focused (Trist, 1978). At Volvo, not only had the assembly line disappeared but so too had the role of supervisor. In its place was a roving post called a "lagombud" (or 'group ombudsman') "who relates to other groups and to the product shop manager" (Sandberg, 1995, Pg. 148). This is an important conceptual difference. Managers and commanders now take up a form of executive, coordinating function, 'designing behaviours' rather than arduously 'scripting tasks' (e.g. Reynolds, 1987).

Variations in STS analysis

According to Neumann et al. (1995, Pg. 110), there are several variants of STS analysis in use: the 12-step method for Shell UK by Michael Foster (1967,1972) and colleagues at the Tavistock Institute; the work restructuring method developed by Schumacher in the UK; and one developed by Lou Davis (1975, 1979, Pg. 3–15) in the United States. All these 'STS' methods have been adopted with some success by leading international corporations and local companies. Neumann states that the principal features are, however, similar. At the heart of STS is the concern to get a better match between the needs of the task and human needs for greater involvement, autonomy and responsibility in the workplace (Neumann, 1989, Pg. 181–182).

Worker involvement

The Tavistock approach to STS developed over time (Mumford, 1996). In the early years, the coal mining work had a therapeutic and expert orientation due to the clinical backgrounds of many researchers. But by the time they were working with the Norwegian industrial democracy experiments, they had evolved into a group that believed in the participation and involvement of workers in the design of their own work situation. Mumford reminds us that designing and implementing STS is always going to be difficult; for success, it requires the following:

1 Enthusiasm and involvement of management
2 Involvement of lower-level employees and unions
3 training, information and good administration
4 Skill
5 Leadership
6 Conviction

Summary

Organisations and ecosystems are the total collective efforts of groups of people producing goods, services or functions. Organisations are made up of people with requisite technical and specialist skills who contribute to the production of goods, services or functions.

Organisations are groups of people who temperamentally fit well into teams, who are willing to work cooperatively and who are willing to face the constraints and challenges of economic and social trends, and who seek to enjoy the practical and emotional rewards of successful teamwork. Organisations are social constructs that provide for sentient feelings – a sense of emotional connectedness that comes from group membership, a sense of loyalty and cohesion – as well as providing frustrations that sometimes require a re-ordering of one's thinking and ways of behaving – a re-learning of modes of being in the world. Organisations are complex entities, combining innovation and the use of new technologies with people of different skills to produce goods, services or functions. Organisations are places where technology is changed and developed, are places where work systems are organised that affects the ways people experience themselves, their social identities, their work and the society of which they are members. Organisations are containers of people's desires, ambitions, pride, passions and love, as well as the sources of anxiety about the possible failure to achieve these life's satisfactions. Organisations are the necessary and desired agglomerations that fulfil certain human needs, as well as serve as a source of frustration and fear that people's individuality might be used for the organisation's collective purposes. Organisations are objects of mixed feelings that are mediated by leadership that takes account of competing interests and decides what constitutes the greatest good for the greatest number. A truly comprehensive understanding of organisations comes about through the help of concepts derived from systems psychodynamics and psychoanalysis.

Exercise

1. Reflect and describe whether your work group has any of the features of a semi-autonomous work group.
2. What barriers are there in your work group for it becoming more fully a semi-autonomous work group?
3. How might these barriers be overcome?

14 Summary

Multiple theories

Systems psychodynamics consultancy work and organisational theory is made up of a many-stranded, highly theoretically driven model. Practitioners place different emphases on certain theoretical constructions. The group of practitioners represented in the Obholzer's and Robert's *The Unconscious at Work* (1994) place more emphasis on psychoanalytic theory and its application as a means of understanding organisational process. But unlike the psychoanalytic literature on the treatment of individuals, not much has been written about the application of the specific theories of projective identification and introjective identification as key processes for organisational consultants to work with. The exceptions are Jaques (1955), Menzies (1960) and Krantz (1989), who draw heavily from the interplay of projection and introjection within the transference and countertransference relationship of psychoanalyst and analysand.

Social systems as a defence against anxiety

In the systems psychodynamics literature, the theory of social systems as a defence against anxiety is the way in which the projective and introjective processes that occur in intra-psychic life are applied to encompass organisational systems and the individuals within them. But the application of these ideas as a consulting methodology is poorly theorised. Specifically, the relationship of introjection and projection in the consulting relationship is not made explicit in the numerous case studies. In particular, the location of the good and bad object in the systems psychodynamics consulting relationship is an interesting question which we examine more closely in the interplay of a consulting relationship by consultants in the field.

A distinct paradigm

The systems psychodynamics literature clearly suggests that the differing theoretical strands could be described as a container or distinct paradigm. The different locus of analysis from a sociotechnical framework, as opposed to a purely psychoanalytic or group relations one, is difficult to sustain in the field of real-world consultancy. But we argue that the human relations aspect of the organisation as well as its structural properties must be viewed as interlinking systems that impact and influence each other. When confronted with real world problems as a working consultant, one is pushed back to familiar and safe ground to work from. The anxiety from the client system and the competitive nature of the consultancy world impact on the consultant to stay with the familiar. Our view is that the model of systems psychodynamics consultancy is limited if it does not contain an integrated psychoanalytic and group relations perspective. Consultancy work that does not have an in-depth understanding and application of unconscious processes of individuals and groups can have only limited success in solving complex and enduring 'people problems'.

The sociotechnical

Both open systems theory and sociotechnical theory need to be applied in consultancy practice. The rather limited contribution of developments within the sociotechnical literature in the United Kingdom may have led to an emphasis on the clinical aspects of the theory; in North America and the Netherlands and Scandinavia, sociotechnical systems have seen developments and application. The dynamic processes that are illuminated by psychoanalytic theory have a limited application if they are not connected to the structural properties of the organisational system. The sociotechnical model best provides this structural contribution because the sociotechnical systems approach to the job and organisational design considers every organisation to be made up of people (the social system) using tools, techniques and knowledge (the technical system) to produce goods or services valued by customers, who together with suppliers and other stakeholders are part of the organisation's external environment. Sociotechnical systems show how organisations are designed and how the design impacts both their performance and the satisfaction of their members and stakeholders. Within the model, *changing* the design of the technical system affects the social system and vice versa. It argues that the most effective arrangements will be those that integrate the demands of both. Ours is a dual concern with the social and technical systems. This is known as *joint optimisation;* peak performance can only be achieved when the needs of both systems are met. In organisational design, *work design* is the application of sociotechnical systems principles and techniques to the humanisation of work.

The aims of work design are:

a Improved job satisfaction
b Improved through-put
c Improved quality
d Reduced employee problems, e.g. grievances, absenteeism

Characteristics of joint optimisation are:

a Self-managing work teams – groups take collective responsibility for performing a set of tasks as well as some self-management – more delegation of decision-making.
b Whole tasks – work is not broken up into many operations. The task is organised into a meaningful whole.
c Tasks are made whole by incorporating functions that previously were performed by other services or units.
d Flexibility in work assignments – to create individual skills development. Mutual learning helps reinforce coordination and team-wide planning activities.
e The team determines how its members rotate through or learn a larger set of tasks.

According to Stokes (1994), the conceptual model as outlined above is of little use unless the practitioner consultant holds the model in mind as a set of theoretical lenses. These lenses ideally should be used in conjunction with the emotional experience of contact with the client system. Time spent reflecting on one's own emotional experiences and thoughts is also prerequisite for this method of consultancy.

Summary of basic theories: the application of systems psychodynamics in consultancy and training

> The Tavistock approach to thinking about and understanding organizational behaviour strengthens the consultant who works with systems and their sub-systems. Systems psychodynamics-oriented consultants can train human resources personnel and organizational leaders and managers in this way of thinking and understanding.
> (Koortzen and Cilliers, 2002, Pg. 272)

In the systems psychodynamic paradigm, the consultant works at understanding the conscious and unconscious processes in the individuals and the system. Interpretations are offered as working hypotheses. A consultant could choose to interpret individual and group behaviour in the here-and-now. A judgement has to be made how ready the client is for certain aspects of their dynamic process to be brought to their attention. Czander suggests that consulting from this stance implies 'licensed stupidity' giving the consultant freedom to ask very naive and sometimes childlike questions. (Czander, 1993). Another way to put it is having permission to ask the 'dumb questions' and describing the elephant in the room.

The consultant may decide to look at the way a variety of defence mechanisms are used by individuals and groups to manage their anxiety in the organisation. The way authority is exercised in different systems needs to be attended to. Once the consultant has started working, they will be able to see the nature of interpersonal relationships within the organisation. They can see the relationships and relatedness with authority, peers and subordinates and the leadership practices and management of boundaries; and how the sub-systems relate to each other. Often inter-group relationships between sub-systems or departments are points of conflict or disturbance. 'Making sense out of nonsense', results from exploring the possible unconscious meanings of organisational events that can be inferred from verbal and nonverbal behaviour, occurrences and nonsense happenings, and in non-coincidences in the here-and-now of the client-consultant relationship.

In summary, a systems psychodynamics consultant will work with:

1. Individuals and groups as they manage their anxiety in the organisation through the use of various defence mechanisms.
2. The modes of exercising authority in the different systems of the organisation.
3. The nature of the interpersonal relationships within the organisation.
4. The relationships and relatedness with authority, peers and subordinates.
5. Leadership practices and the management of boundaries.
6. Intergroup relationships between sub-systems (departments, divisions, etc.).
7. The sociotechnical systems inherent in identity, roles, tasks, space, time and structural boundaries.
8. Management of individual and organisational anxiety.
9. The environmental context of which the organisation is a part.

Here is a summary of the key concepts that inform consultancy practice related to the systems psychodynamics model of consultation.

Psychoanalytic theory

Splitting in organisations can take a collective form. Groups of individuals or even the majority of organisational members may collectively split the organisation or its leadership into idealised good parts and vilified bad parts. Invariably, good parts are invested with love and introjected (taken in and identified with), while bad parts become legitimate targets of hate and are scapegoated. The concept of splitting is an important concept to have in mind when taking up the role of consultant. It may be necessary to draw the client's attention to evidence of the phenomena of splitting.

The unconscious refers to the hidden aspects of organisational life

Institutions have unconscious tasks alongside conscious tasks. The unconscious is central to the systems psychodynamics model of consultation. It may be important to interpret unconscious processes to the client, but this is a matter of judgement and needs discretion in terms of how ready the client is able to process such a working hypothesis or formulation. There is an interaction between conscious and unconscious dynamics in an organisation. The idea of projection can also be helpful. Projection can be thought of as perceiving someone else as having one's own characteristics. With projective identification, this involves a more active getting rid of something belonging to the self into someone else.

The understanding of projective processes is key. Projection is a ubiquitous process and while it may have some short-term benefits for defences against anxiety, in the long run, it leads to a depletion of the client's capacity for thinking, decision-making and action. Projection is an important process for understand meaning and function in organisations.

The depressive position (DP) is associated with the view that the world is a complex place where good and bad, right and wrong are inextricably linked both in the minds of individuals and groups and in the outer world of reality and time. The paranoid schizoid (PS), position is associated with a view that divides up the world into extreme good and extreme bad and is characterised by persecutory anxiety. DP and PS as processes should be borne in mind and potentially drawn to the client's attention. One can often offer a working hypothesis on DP and PS forces in consultation work.

Envy and spoiling

Envy needs to be thought about in consultancy work. Envious attacks in organisational life need to be understood and, therefore, envious attacks should be recognised and worked with. Linked to envy is spoiling. Spoiling attacks in organisational life can have a very destructive effect on individuals and the systems functioning.

Organisational life and organisational functioning

Work in organisations can entail significant anxieties for staff. Defences against anxiety will be part of organisational life. Defences as a process are essential to understand. Bringing the client's attention to the defensive process can help improve performance. We must bear in mind that organisations resist efforts to change them. Change processes expose staff more directly to anxiety; therefore, defences against anxiety become part of the organisation's system, which then become part of the organisation's culture. Organisational sub-systems such as teams or groups of managers may tend to use other sub-systems as repositories for anxiety, criticism, blame, denigration, competition or other unwanted feelings. It is likely that an improvement in the functioning of an individual team or organisational sub-system will entail an increase in conscious anxiety and emotional pain in other parts of the system. Processes outside of ordinary consciousness may operate at the level of an individual, group or of the organisation as a whole. Understanding and working with systems psychodynamics concepts above, involves the disciplined use of regular reflective meetings at all levels in the organisation and the development of trust between consultant and client.

The nature of the working relationships between roles, the extent and clarity of roles with authority and decision-making powers for furthering the primary task is central to understanding how well or badly an organisation is functioning. In a well-functioning organisation there will be a capacity among staff and managers to think about the emotional impact and significance of the work undertaken with respect to the primary task. Emotional experience is understood as an expression of the relatedness between individual, group and organisation. All these processes create the organisational culture which becomes part of the 'accepted' way that work is done.

Bion

Bion's work on group dynamics is fundamental within the systems psychodynamics model. For organisations to survive, they must perform a primary task. Work groups may avoid carrying out the primary task, for example, Obholzer's assertion that the NHS's conscious primary task is complicated by its simultaneous unconscious task of saving us from death, which can distort the NHS's ability to take up the primary task which is to treat ill people within the resources that are available. The functioning of a group is best understood by reference to Bion's Basic Assumptions, i.e. the emotional states of groups and organisations that keep them locked in their unconscious primary tasks. An organisational or group that is in a basic assumption mode of thinking and behaving is likely to perform poorly.

Group relations and the systems psychodynamics model

Group relations addresses:

a The emotional dimensions of organisational experience.
b Relational dimensions of organisational experience.
c Political dimensions of organisational experience.

Group relations helps organisations understand the impact of projections that the role of manager attracts and evokes. Group relations provides a means to explore ways in which individual and personal projections link to organisational life. Group relations provides a means to explore the resulting enactment or denial of them in an organisational context. The defensiveness of individual managers is a reflection and re-creation of the defences of the organisation. The defences that are characteristic of an organisation are enacted, perpetuated and refined by individual managers. Exploring the links between the emotional dynamics created within and between individuals and groups is the work of group relations. This link is fundamental both as a method of learning from experience and as a focus of organisational enquiry into processes of change. Group relations make the underlying emotional and unconscious processes within and between systems visible and available as an aspect of organisational learning and change. Group relations aims for institutional transformation.

This includes:

a   Transformation of systems and roles.
b   The need for an awareness of emotional and relational dynamics.
c   The transformation of the resistances and defences that are evoked.
d   The recognition of the institutional aspects of collective experience and action as the place where links between the individual and the organisation can be revealed.

The focus of group relations is the system rather than the group. A systems view emphasises that the whole and their parts are dynamically interrelated in complex and important ways. Group relations practitioners address interactions between the individual, group and the broader systems in which these sub-systems are embedded (e.g. organisations, communities and societies, local, national and international). Group relations offers a framework for understanding and for intervening in systems whether from: 'inside' or from 'outside'. Systems psychodynamics consultants utilise concepts from group relations in their practice as consultants. Sometimes they design consultancy interventions derived from a group relations model.

Work, anxiety and containment and the application of a systems psychodynamics model of organisational consultancy

Work

Freud (1927, S. E., 21:5–56) noted that:

> … although men are not spontaneously fond of work, every civilisation rests on a compulsion to work. Work gives the individual a secure place in a portion of reality, in the human community. It offers the possibility of displacing libido, - narcissistic, aggressive, or erotic - on to work, and on to the human relations connected with it. Work has a value and is indispensable to the preservation and justification of existence in society. Work activity is a source of special satisfaction, if it is freely chosen, as a means of sublimation; it makes possible to use inclinations or instinctual impulses in socially constructive ways. And yet, as a path to happiness, work is not highly prized as other possibilities of satisfaction. Most people work under the stress of necessity, and this natural human aversion to work raises difficult social problems.

Henrick (1943, 12:311–329) concluded that work is not primarily motivated by sexual need or associated aggressions, but by the need for the efficient use of the muscular and intellectual tools, regardless of what secondary needs, i.e. self-preservative, aggressive or sexual, work performance may also satisfy. Work provides primary pleasure through efficient use of the central nervous system for the performance of well-integrated ego functions, which enable individuals to control or alter their environment. Work capacity is important for normal ego organisation, biological survival, and a sense of individual usefulness to society. Work is an essential function, but alongside the study of defence mechanisms, anxiety and the super-ego, systems psychodynamics includes studies of work as integrated functions by which we perceive, appraise and manipulate the environment.

In our society, work as an activity takes on increasingly greater significance as a source of pleasure, or a means of obtaining the resources for later pleasures. It is a source of self-esteem, a social gratification, the fulfilment of an ego-ideal, the attainment of the role of a mature adult, the useful and pleasurable utilisation of time, and the achievement of psycho-social success. Work becomes one of the top contenders for resource expenditure. Social change and economic change affect social values in which getting a job, holding a job, advancing in a job, retiring from a job, or losing a job become significant human concerns.

Lawrence (1982) in considering the psychic and political consequences of work, explores the problem of hostility and aggression in the work enterprise:

> The fact that these emotions exist in industrial and other enterprises and that the ego finds ways of defending against bad experiences is not an issue; what is more difficult to establish is the complex way in which these feelings are dealt with.

Menninger (1942) regarded work as a method whereby aggressive and destructive energies are sublimated:

> It is easy to see that all work represents a fight against something, an attack upon the environment. The farmer ploughs the earth, he harrows it, tears it, pulverises it; he pulls out weeds, he cuts them or burns them; he poisons insects and fights against drought and floods. To be sure, all this is done to create something, for which reason we can call it work and not rage. The destructiveness is, so to speak specialised or selectively directed and a net "product" is obtained.

Freud viewed work as an inescapable and tragic necessity, a task of socialising and civilising people and thus preserving the species. He took work for granted, fulfilling a religious duty, or it may be pleasurable, creative or have an inter-personal texture. Freud distinguished work from love, pleasure, consumption and freedom. He regarded work as a curse for most people mitigated by the fear of boredom, which can be even greater than its irksomeness. Work is directed towards the avoidance of hunger. Freud placed love and work as the two main keystones of life. Developing this theme, Klein (1937) saw these two factors 'forever linked' in the unconscious, because of the infant's experience in food and love coming from the same source.

> Security was first afforded to us by our mother, who not only stilled the pangs of hunger, but also satisfied our emotional needs and relieved anxiety. Security attained by satisfaction of our essential requirements is, therefore linked with emotional security.

By the same token, threats from the individual (inadequate education, skills and capacities) or social dislocation (markets, wars, pandemics) to obtaining a livelihood and self-preservation can be felt as a loss of love and produce apathy or an urge for vengeance.

Anxiety and containment

Containment describes a basic dimension of human experience that is the relationship between emotion and its 'containment' – the ways in which it is experienced or avoided managed or denied kept in or passed on so that its effects are either mitigated or amplified. The capacity to think on the parts of individuals or groups is related to the capacity for containment of anxiety. Anxiety is a working concept and informs consultants in their practice. Anxiety as a process is important to understand and work with. Consultants can bring the client's attention to anxiety as a process. While defences are necessary to cope but when ignored or denied they can become an organisational way of life and a block to change and learning. Anxiety can arise in any part of the system and can have origins in:

a   The personal history of individuals.
b   The demands of the task.
c   The demands that exist within the client group or wider social system.

A necessary process for consultants is the 'container – contained' model from Bion (1967a,b,c). Impulsive action can often result from the lack of containment of anxiety.

The capacity to think about work involves reflecting on the relationship between all five of the following elements:

a   The nature of the task.
b   Difficulties in undertaking the work.
c   The symbolic significance of communication associated with the work process.

d The relationship between the individual and the aims of the wider organisation.
e The relationship between the small work group and the aims of the wider organisation.

Management in a well-functioning organisation ensures the provision of constant opportunities for staff to think about the task of the organisation. A consultant works to promote the capacity for learning from the experiences of the members of the organisation and system.

Systems psychodynamics model of organisational consultancy

Systems psychodynamics consultancy attempts the following:

To develop the capacity for reflection on the emotional experiences of technical task-related work so that these can be better understood and mastered. Consultants should consider boundary maintenance and regulation to be a key source for organisational diagnosis. Consultants can examine how individuals or teams debate or communicate within the organisation in ways that help or hinder work on the primary task. A consultant is likely to encourage a realistic rather than a rigidly defensive relationship to the emotional aspects of work. This awareness will help staff gain a greater insight into the limits of what is possible in achieving the primary task.

A consultant will often focus on working with the client to:

a Enable them to feel and think through the presenting problem.
b To form their own diagnoses and generate their own solutions.

In the systems psychodynamics model, the task of consultancy is to consider the relations between processes operating across the boundary of different levels of a system. The distinctive emphasis in the systems psychodynamics model is to bring processes outside of ordinary consciousness into clear focus and understand their meaning. In organisational consultancy, one is continually asking oneself what is generating the emotional experiences of the group that are being registered? Consultants aim to enable the client to gain awareness of what is happening below the surface within the organisation; to help the client rehearse the significance of this awareness and meaning for policy decision and action. The consultant attends to and reflects on and makes links from their emotional experiences presented through the consultant's engagement with and in the organisation. In this model, the consultant believes that enlarging understanding by bringing to awareness aspects of the client's experience that are often hidden or simply ignored as not relevant promotes the client's development. In this model, the consultant helps the client reflect on the fit between the motives and intentions driving the action. The consultant helps the client deal with internal resistances, defences and blind spots. Enlarging the client's grasp on the human realities is a particular hallmark of this model. The consultant is always a participant in working with the experience. The consultant helps the client be open to new insights and motivations; extend the repertoire of what can be brought to bear in charting new courses of action; extend the repertoire of what can be brought to bear in thinking about organisational structures.

Consultants may carry out the following activities with clients:

a   Ask questions and probe for clarity/understanding of the client's issues.
b   Pay attention to both the 'hidden' and 'open' messages that the client is giving.
c   Attempt to understand the client's perspective and needs.
d   Build trust and credibility between the client and the consultant.
e   Suggest ideas on any initial problems that the client presents.
f   Test out with the client their understanding of the work group and its primary preoccupation.
g   Negotiate and agree a contract with the client on the task of the consultation and the fee to be paid for it.
h   Explore and clarify expectations of consultant and client in the consulting relationship.
i   Negotiate and agree that time needs to be set aside to process, examine and review the work of the consultant and the client. For example, questions such as "How have things gone thus far? Are we both satisfied with progress? How could we have done things better? What should we do next?"
j   Negotiate and agree that consultation is a collaborative relationship between the client and the consultant.
k   Negotiate and agree rules around confidentiality?
l   Agree on evaluation of the consultancy.

As a systems psychodynamics consultant, you will be interested and active in:

a   Day-to-day problems of your client.
b   The objectives of the client and methods to achieve them.
c   The philosophy of the client.
d   Supporting of the client's work.
e   Constructively critical of the client's work.
f   Interested in the client's work.
g   Diagnose problems.
h   Analyse the dynamics in the client's system and helping the client understand it.
i   Communicating effectively with the client.
j   Thinking about change.
k   Staying on task in the consultancy session.
l   Dealing with conflict and confrontation in the session.

272 Socio-technical systems

m Developing objectives and managing them.
n Evaluating their achievements and activities.
o Helping the client be pro-active in the consultancy session.
p Being creative and innovative in working with the client.
q Acting as a catalyst and overcoming inertia to work on serious problems.
r Offering solutions to organisational problems.
s Recognising and defining their needs.
t Recognising the resources – personal skills, finance, organisational.
u Planning how to gain more resources.
v Selecting or creating solutions to problems.
w Adapting and carrying out solutions to identified problems.
x Evaluating solutions.

The consultant works to help the client to extend the repertoire of what can be brought to bear in managing professional or leadership style capabilities and competencies. In accessing the process of organisational life, the aim is for consultant and client to attend to and interpret emotional experiences. In this model, the consultants' mental disposition is such that they can tolerate uncertainty, not knowing and feelings of confusion (negative capability). In this model, the consultant needs to be able to wait on experience before making an interpretation. The consultant needs to have a capacity for empathy (to feel into and for another and into the organisation). The consultant needs to have a capacity for some identification with what the organisation is and does.

Transference and countertransference dynamics

The systems psychodynamics model of organisational consultancy works with transference and countertransference dynamics. In the consultancy relationship, transference and countertransference to the consultant is an important source of information about the unconscious life of the organisation. Consultants can have in mind the idea of transference and countertransference. They may choose to speak about transference and countertransference to the client. But drawing attention to transference and countertransference may not be helpful, so one may avoid drawing attention to transference and countertransference. This is the difference between working in the transference and working with the transference as a working practice. In the process of understanding consultancy activity, the consultant learns about the team's/organisations/systems pattern of conscious and unconscious functioning through attention to their own experiences of being with the working groups as they work with the consultants. In the consultancy relationship, the consultant's countertransference is an important source of information about the unconscious life of the organisation. The consultant's capacity to interpret transference and countertransference phenomena is part of helping consultees develop their own capacity for thinking about work-related emotional experience. In the transference, consultants have access to the organisation by asking questions about the client's picture of 'the organisation-in-the-mind'. The evolution of the picture of 'the organisation-in-the-mind' is the work that the consultant and client will engage in day by day.

The systems psychodynamics model of organisational consultancy and unconscious processes

Systems psychodynamics consultants work with unconscious processes with the following ideas in mind. In the systems psychodynamics model, consultants pay particular attention to processes taking place outside of ordinary consciousness; the relations between conscious and unconscious process; raising awareness of anti-task tendencies in the individual or work group so that these can be better understood and mastered.

The systems psychodynamics model of organisational consultancy and aims

Systems psychodynamics consultants have the following aims: to listen and tune in to everything their senses are picking up from meetings with clients; to pay attention to the shifting feelings they become aware of in themselves, in particular, the unexpected or surprising. The practice of letting oneself be open to the associations that come into one's mind as one listens to or observes the client is a distinctive feature of the systems psychodynamics model (images, memories, recollections of earlier material, questions, etc.)

In this model, the consultant needs to have knowledge of and training in:

a   Psychoanalytic thinking
b   Group relations
c   Systemic thinking

Consultants help clients look at the 'value' that is attributed to an experience where value may have to do with implied motive or intentions. Consultants may develop formulations, a formulation being the consultant's translation of what is happening. Consultants give a formulation to the client as a basis for further exploration. The offering of a formulation entails risks, facing hostility, working through resistances, depending on the client's readiness. Interpretation is a provisional answer to the question 'why is this happening?' Interpretations involve making speculative links to other elements of the client's and the organisation's situation.

Systems psychodynamics model – understanding and testing from the inside

The systems psychodynamics model is about a way of working with experience: prerequisites for working as a consultant in this model are practice in 'reflective awareness' – this may include the experience of individual therapy and group relations. Another prerequisite is experience in organisational roles as manager, leader, professional union official, and employer, for example. The systems psychodynamics model encompasses three domains – the social, the psychoanalytical and the ecological. The 'social' refers to the human systems dimension of the organisation and how these interact with its structural aspects. These include:

a Design
b Division of labour
c Levels of authority
d Reporting relationships
e Nature of its work tasks
f Processes and activities
g Mission and primary task

The 'psychoanalytic' refers to concepts that provide an understanding of individuals, groups and social processes, especially those that function at the irrational and unconscious level. Psychoanalytic concepts include splitting, projection, defences against anxiety, envy, spoiling, contempt, etc.

The 'socioecological' refers to turbulent environments, complexity, open systems theory, systems thinking.

The 'social', 'psychoanalytical', 'sociotechnical' and 'socioecological' bodies of knowledge are combined to form the systems psychodynamics model and consultancy is the application of these ideas in practice.

References

Abraham, K., (1924). A short study of the development of the libido, viewed in the light of mental disorders. In: Frankiel, R. V. (Ed.) (1994), *Essential papers on object loss*. Pgs. 72–93. New York: New York University Press.
Abraham, F., (2013). The Tavistock Group. In: M. Witzel and M. Warner (Eds.), *The Oxford handbook of management theorists*. Oxford: Oxford University Press. http://www.tavinstitute.org/projects/the-tavistock-group/
Ackoff, Russell L., (1974). *Redesigning the future*. New York: John Wiley & Sons.
Ackoff, Russell L., (1978). *The art of problem solving*. New York: John Wiley & Sons.
Ackoff, Russell L., (1981). *Creating the corporate future*. New York: John Wiley & Sons.
Ackoff, R. L. and Emery, F. E., (1972). *On purposeful systems: An interdisciplinary analysis of individual and social behavior as a system of purposeful events*. New Brunswick, NJ: Aldine Transaction.
Ackoff, Russell L. and Greenberg, D., (2008). *Turning learning right side up: Putting education back on track*. Philadelphia: Wharton School Publishing.
Alban, B. T. and Bunker, B., (1997). *Large group interventions: Engaging the whole system for rapid change*. San Francisco: Jossey-Bass.
Alderfer, C. P., (1980). Consulting to under-bounded systems. In: C. P. Alderfer and C. L. Cooper (Eds.), *Advances in experiential social processes*, Vol. 2. Pgs. 267–295. New York: Wiley.
Aldrich, H., (1971). Organizational boundaries and inter-organizational conflict. *Human Relations*, 24(4): 279–293.
Alevy, D. I., Bunker, B. B., Doob, L. W., Foltz, W. J., French, N., Klein, E. B., and Miller, J. C., (1974). Rationale, research, and role relations in the Stirling workshop. *The Journal of Conflict Resolution*, 18(2): 276–284.
Allcorn, S. and Diamond, M., (2003). The cornerstone of psychoanalytic organizational analysis: Psychological reality, transference and countertransference in the workplace. *Human Relations*, 56(4): 491–504.
Allen, P. M., (1998). Evolutionary complex systems: Models of technological change, complexity in social science. In: G. Altman and W. Koch (Eds.), *New paradigms for the human sciences*. Berlin and London: Walter de Gruyter.
Amar, D., (2004). Motivating knowledge workers to innovate: A model integrating motivation dynamics and antecedents. *European Journal of Innovation Management*, 7: 89–101.
Ambrose, A., (1989). Key concepts of the transitional approach to managing change. In: L. Klein (Ed.), *Working with organisations, papers to celebrate the 80th birthday of Harold Bridger*. Loxwood: Kestrel Print.

Appelbaum, S., (1997). Socio-technical systems theory: An intervention strategy for organizational development. *Management Decision*, 35(6): 452–463.

Aram, E., (2010). *The aesthetics of group relations, a talk given at the AK Rice Institute's 40th anniversary symposium.* Chicago, IL: A.K. Rice Institute.

Argyris, C. (1964) *Integrating the individual and the organization.* New York: Wiley.

Armstrong D., (1995). The Psychoanalytic Approach to Institutional Life: Why So Little Impact? *Group Analysis*, 28(1): 33–45.

Armstrong, D., (1997). The organization-in-the-mind: Reflections on the relation of psychoanalysis to work with institutions. *Free Associations*, 7(41): 1–14.

Armstrong, D., (2002). Making present: Reflections on a neglected function of leadership and its contemporary relevance. *Organisational and social dynamics*, 2(1): 89–98. London: Karnac Books. *Also in*: R. French, (2005). *Organisation in the Mind.* London: Karnac.

Armstrong, D., (2004). The analytic object in organizational work. *Free Associations*, 11(1): 79–88.

Armstrong D. G., (2005a). The analytic object in organisational work. *The organisation in the mind*, Pgs. 44–54. London: Karnac. Paper also presented at the annual meeting of the International Society for the Psychoanalytic Study of Organisations. London, 1995.

Armstrong, D., (2005b). *Organization in the mind: Psychoanalysis, group relations and organizational consultancy.* London: Karnac.

Armstrong, D., (2005c). The work group revisited: Reflections on the practice of group relations. In: D. Armstrong and R. French (Eds.), *Organization in the mind: Psychoanalysis, group relations, and organizational consultancy – occasional papers 1989-2003*, Pgs. 139–150. London: Karnac.

Armstrong, D., (2014). The 'Tavistock Group' within War Psychiatry in Britain. Paper presented at a *Conference on Psychoanalysis and Totalitarianism*. London: Unpublished, 2012.

Armstrong, D., (2017). Psychoanalytic study and the ethical imagination: The making, finding, and losing of a tradition. *Organisational and Social Dynamics*, 17(2): 222–234.

Armstrong, D. G., Bazalgette, J. and Hutton, J., (1994). What does management really mean? In: R. Casemore et al. (Eds.), *What makes consultancy work?* London: South Bank University Press.

Arnaud, G., (2012). The contribution of psychoanalysis to organization studies and management: An overview. *Organization Studies*, 33(9):1121–1135.

Association for Coaching, (2020). *Global statement from the professional bodies for coaching, mentoring and supervision.* Available from: https://cdn.ymaws.com/www.associationfor coaching.com/resource/resmgr/email_images/global_new/AGREED_JOINT_STATEMENT_on_CC.pdf

Auer, P. and Riegler, C., (1990). *Post-Taylorism: The enterprise as a place of learning organizational change. A comprehensive study on work organization changes and its context at Volvo.* Stockholm/Berlin: The Swedish Work Environment Fund/Wissenschaftszentrum fur Sozialforschung. Available from: https://www.researchgate.net/publication/277890570_Review_and_Application_Methodologies

Avgerou C., Ciborra C., and Land F., (2004). *The social study of information and communication technology.* Oxford: Oxford University Press.

Badham, R., Clegg, C., and Wall, T., (2000). Socio-technical theory. In: W. Karwowski (Ed.), *Handbook of ergonomics.* New York, NY: John Wiley.

Bain, A., (1982). *The Baric experiment.* Occasional Paper No. 4. London: Tavistock Institute.

Bain, A., (1998). Social defences against organizational learning. *Human Relations*, 51(3): 422–425.

Bain, A., (2000). The role of organizational consultant as socio-analyst. *AISA Working Paper* (4), 1–8.

Bain, A. and Barnett, L., (1982). *The design of a day care system in a nursery setting for children under five.* Occasional Paper No.8. London: Tavistock Institute.

Bales, R. F., (1950). *Interaction process analysis; a method for the study of small groups.* Boston, MA: Addison-Wesley.

Balint, M., (1968). *The basic fault: Therapeutic aspects of regression.* London: Tavistock.

Bánáthy B. H., (1996). *Designing social systems in a changing world.* New York: Plenum Press.

Banet, A. G., Jr. and Hayden, C., (1977). A Tavistock primer. In: J. E. Jones and J. W. Pfeiffer (Eds.), *The 1977 annual handbook for group facilitators.* San Diego, CA: University Associates.

Bastedo, M. N., (2006). Open systems theory. In: Fenwick W. English (Ed.), *The Sage Encyclopedia of educational leadership and administration.* Thousand Oaks: Sage.

Bateson, G., (1972). *Steps to an ecology of mind: Collected essays in anthropology, psychiatry, evolution, and epistemology.* Chicago and London: University of Chicago Press.

Baum, H. S., (1990). *Organizational membership: Personal development in the workplace.* Albany, NY: State University of New York Press.

Bazalgette, J. and Quine, C., (2014). *Finding freedom to make a difference.* Pg. 194. London: Grubb Institute. Available from: https://www.grubbinstitute.org.uk/wp-content/uploads/2014/12/034_Finding-Freedom-to-Make-a-Difference.pdf

Beer, S. A., (1959). *Cybernetics and management.* London: English Universities Press.

Beer, S. and Leonard, A., (1994). *The systems perspective: Methods and models for the future.* AC/UNU Millennium Project Futures Research Methodology. Chichester: John Wiley & Sons, Available from: http://citeseerx.ist.psu.edu/viewdoc/download?doi=10.1.1.20.9436&rep=rep1&type=pdf

Beinum, H. van., (1990). *Observations on the development of a new organisational paradigm.* Stockholm: The Swedish Centre for Working Life.

Benjamin, J., (1998). *Shadow of the other: Intersubjectivity and gender in psychoanalysis.* London: Taylor & Frances/Routledge.

Benjamin, J. (2004). Beyond doer and done to: An intersubjective view of thirdness. *Psychoanalytic Quarterly,* 73: 5–45.

Bennis, W. G., and Shepard, H. A., (1956). A theory of group development. *Human Relations*, 9: 415–437.

Bertalanffy, L. von, (1950a). The theory of open systems in physics and biology. *Science*, 3: 23–29.

Bertalanffy, L. von, (1950b). An outline of general system theory. *British Journal of the Philosophy of Science*, 1: 134–165.

Bertalanffy, L. von., (1950). The theory of open systems in physics and biology. *Science*, 3: 23–29. [Also in F. E. Emery (Ed.), (1969). *Systems thinking: Selected readings.* Pgs. 70–85. Harmondsworth, UK: Penguin Books.]

Bertalanffy, L. V., (1968). *General system theory: Foundations, development, applications.* New York: George Braziller.

Bion, W. R., (1948). Psychiatry at a time of crisis. *British Journal of Medical Psychology XXI*, Vol. 21 Part 2, 181–189.

Bion, W. R., (1948–51). Experiences in groups: I-VII. *Human Relations*, 1948-51: 1–4.

Bion, W. R., (1959). Attacks on linking. *International Journal of Psychoanalysis*, 40: 308–315. *Also in: Second thoughts* (1967). Pg. 103–109. London: Heinemann.

Bion, W. R., (1961). *Experiences in groups and other papers.* London: Tavistock Publications. [Reprinted London: Routledge, 1989; London: Brunner-Routledge, 2001.]
Bion, W. R., (1962). *Learning from experience.* London: William Heinemann. [Reprinted London: Karnac Books.]
Bion, W. R., (1967a). *Second thoughts.* Pgs. 36–64, 120–166. London: Heinemann.
Bion, W., (1967b). *Second thoughts.* Pgs. 143–145. London: Heineman. [Reprinted 1984 London: Karnac.]
Bion, W., (1967c). Notes on memory and desire. *The Psychoanalytic Forum,* 2: 272–280.
Bion, W. R., (1970). *Attention and interpretation.* London: Tavistock Publications.
Bjerknes, G., and Bratteteig, T., (1995). User participation and democracy. A discussion of Scandinavian Research on system development. *Scandinavian Journal of Information Systems,* 7(1): 73–98.
Bjerknes, G., Ehn, P., and Kyng, M., (1987). (Eds.), *Computers and democracy.* 434 pages. Aldershot, Brookfield USA, Hong Kong, Singapore, Sydney: Avebury. (1988). *Organization Studies,* 9(1), 131–133.
Blackman, J. S., (2004). *101 defences. How the mind shields itself.* New York: Brunner-Routledge.
Bohm, D., (1951). (revised 2012). *Quantum theory.* North Chelmsford, MA: Courier Corporation.
Bohm, D., (1980). *Wholeness and the implicate order.* London: Routledge.
Brazaitis S. J., (2017). Wilfred Bion's organization change legacy: Without memory or desire. In: D. B. Szabla, W. A. Pasmore, M. A. Barnes, and A. N. Gipson (Eds.), *The Palgrave handbook of organizational change thinkers.* London: Palgrave Macmillan.
Bridger, H., (1985). Northfield revisited. In: *Pines M (1985) Bion and group psychotherapy.* Pgs. 87–107. London: Routledge and Kegan Paul.
Bridger, H., (1990a). Courses and working conferences as transitional learning institutions. In: E. Trist and H. Murray (Eds.), *The social engagement of social science: A Tavistock anthology,* Vol. I. Pgs. 221–245. Philadelphia: University of Pennsylvania Press. Available from: http://www.moderntimesworkplace.com/archives/archives.html
Bridger, H., (1990b). The discovery of the therapeutic community: The Northfield experiments. In: E. Trist and H. Murray (Eds.), *The social engagement of social science.* Pgs. 68–87. London: Free Association Books. Available from: www.moderntimesworkplace.com
Brissett, L., Sher, M., and Smith T. (2020). *Dynamics at boardroom level: A Tavistock primer for leaders, coaches and consultants.* London: Routledge.
Brunner, L. D., Nutkevitch, A., and Sher, M., (2006). *Group relations conferences.* London: Karnac.
Brunning, H., (2001). Six domains of executive coaching. *Journal of Organisational and Social Dynamics,* 1(2): 254–263.
Brunning, H., (Ed.), (2006). *Executive coaching: Systems-psychodynamic perspective.* London: Karnac.
Brunning, H., (2014). *Psychoanalytic essays on power and vulnerability.* London: Karnac.
Brunning, H. and Khaleelee, O., (2021). *Danse macabre and other stories - a psychoanalytic perspective on global dynamics.* London: Phoenix Publishing House.
Burton, M., (2003). Review of systemic intervention: Philosophy, methodology, and practice by Midgley G. (2000). *Journal of Community and Applied Psychology,* 13(4): 330–333.
Butler, J., (1993). *Bodies that matter: On the discursive limits of 'sex'.* London: Verso.
Butler, J., (1997). *The psychic life of power: Theories in subjection.* London: Routledge.
Butler, J. (2004). *Precarious life: The power of mourning and violence.* London: Verso.

Cabrera, D. (2014). In search of universality in systems thinking. Plenary for 58th Meeting of the International Society for the Systems Sciences, Washington, D.C. https://www.crlab.us/#dr-derek-cabrera-s-plenary-for-58-th-meeting-of-the-international-society-for-the-systems-sciences-at-the-school-of-business-at-george-washington-university-washington-dc, (17) (PDF) A Unifying Theory of Systems Thinking with Psychosocial Applications. Available from: https://www.researchgate.net/publication/281672363_A_Unifying_Theory_of_Systems_Thinking_with_Psychosocial_Applications [accessed Sep 24 2021].

Cabrera, D., and Cabrera, L. (2015). *Systems thinking made simple: New hope for solving wicked problems in a complex world.* Ithaca, NY: Odyssean Press.

Campbell, D. and Gronbaek, M., (2006). *Taking positions in the organisation.* London: Karnac.

Campbell, D. (2007). *The socially constructed organisation.* London: Karnac.

Campbell, D., and Huffington, C. (2008). *Organizations Connected A Handbook of Systemic Consultation.* London: Routledge.

Capra, F., (2002). *The hidden connections.* London: Harper Collins.

Carew, D. K., and Parisi-Carew, E., (1988). *Group development stage analysis: Matching leader behaviours with team development.* (Available from Blanchard Training and Development, Inc.,) 125 State Place, Escondido, CA 92025).

Chapman, J., (1999). Hatred and corruption of task. *Socio-Analysis: the Journal of the Australian Institute of Socio-Analysis*, 1(2): 127–150.

Checkland, P., (1999). *Systems thinking, systems practice.* Chichester, UK: Wiley.

Chen, D. and Stroup, W., (1993). General system theory: Toward a conceptual framework for science and technology education for all. *Journal of Science Education and Technology*, 2(7): 447–459.

Cherns, A., (1976). The principles of sociotechnical design. *Human Relations*, 9(8): 783–792.

Child, C., Junge, K., Iacopini, G., and Stock, L., (2012). *Unpublished Report: Evaluation of Tower Hamlets Prevent Projects.* London: Tavistock Institute of Human Relations. https://www.tavinstitute.org/wp-content/uploads/2012/12/Tavistock_Projects_Tower-Hamlets-PVE_evaluation_final_report.pdf https://www.tavinstitute.org/projects/evaluation-of-tower-hamlets-prevent-projects/. Accessed May 2019.

Chin, R., (1961). The planning of change. In: W. Bennis, K. Benne, and R. Chin (Eds.). *Readings in applied behavioural sciences.* Pgs. 110–131. New York: Holt, Rinehart and Winston.

Cilliers, F., and Koortzen, P., (2000). The psychodynamic view of organizational behaviour. *The Industrial-Organizational Psychologist*, 38(2): 59–67.

Cilliers, F., and Koortzen, P., (2002). The psychoanalytic approach to team development. In: Rodney L. Lowman (Ed.), *The California school of organizational studies handbook of organizational consulting psychology: A comprehensive guide to theory, skills, and techniques.* California School of Organizational Studies at Alliant International University. San Francisco: Jossey-Bass.

Cilliers, F. and Koortzen, P., (2005). Working with conflict in teams: The CIBART model. *HR Future*, October: 51–52.

Clement, S., Jaques, E., and Lessem, R., (1994). *Executive leadership: A practical guide to managing complexity.* Oxford: Blackwell Publishing.

Cohen, S. G. and Ledford, G. E., (1994). The effectiveness of self-managing teams: A quasi-experiment. *Human Relations*, 47(1): 13–43.

Colman, A. D. and Bexton W. H. (Eds.), (1975). *Group relations reader 1*. Pgs. 3–10. Washington: A. K. Rice Institute.

Colman, A. D. and Geller, M. H., (1985). *Group relations reader 2*. Jupiter, FL: A. K. Rice Institute.

Cooke, B. and Burnes, B., (2013). The Tavistock's 1945 invention of organization development: Early British business and management applications of social psychiatry. *Business History*, 55(5): 768–789.

Coombe, P., (2020). The Northfield experiments — a reappraisal 70 years on. *Group Analysis*, 53(2): 162–176.

Cordery, J. L., Mueller, W. S., and Smith, L. M., (1991). Attitudinal and behaviour effects of autonomous group working. *Academy of Management Journal*, 34(2): 464–476.

Correa, M. E., Klein, E. B., Stone, W. N., Astrachan, J. H., Kossek, E. E., and Komarraju, M., (1988). Reactions to women in authority: The impact of gender in learning in group relations conferences. *Journal of Applied Behavioral Science*, 24: 219–233.

Coveney, P. and Highfield, R., (1995). *Frontiers of complexity: The search for order in a chaotic world*. New York: Fawcett Columbine.

Cummings, T., (1978). Self-regulating work groups: A socio-technical synthesis. *The Academy of Management Review*, 3(3): 625–634. Retrieved May 1, 2020, from www.jstor.org/stable/257551

Cummings, T., (1981). Designing effective work groups. In: P. Nystrom, and W. Starbuck, (Eds.), *Handbook of organizational design: Remodelling organizations and their environments*, Vol. 2. Oxford: Oxford University Press.

Cummings, T., (1994). Self-regulating work groups: A socio-technical synthesis. In: French, W., Bell, C. and Zawacki, R. (Eds.) *Organizational development and transformation*, 4th ed., Pgs. 268–277. Burr Ridge, IL: Irwin Publishing.

Curle, A., (1947). Transitional communities and social re-connection. *Human Relations*, 11(2): 240–288.

Cytrynbaum, S. and Belkin, M., (2004). Gender and authority in group relations conferences: implications for theory and research. In: S. Cytrynbaum and D. Noumair (Eds.), *Group dynamics, organizational irrationality, and social complexity: group relations reader 3*, Pgs. 443–455. Jupiter, FL: A. K. Rice Institute.

Cytrynbaum, S. and Noumair, A., (2004). *Group relations reader 3*. Jupiter, FL: A. K. Rice Institute.

Czander, W., (1985). *The application of social systems thinking to organizational consulting*. Washington, DC: University Press.

Czander, W. (1993). *The psychodynamics of work and organisations*. New York: Guilford Press.

Czander, W. M and Eisold, K., (2003). Psychoanalytic perspectives on organizational consulting: Transference and countertransference, *Human Relations*, 56(4): 475–490. London: Tavistock Institute.

Dartington, T., (2008). Guardian Obituary, Isabel Menzies-Lyth. https://www.theguardian.com/science/2008/feb/20/1

Davar, E., (2020). On teaching Winnicott: The charms and challenges of Winnicott's concepts, *Organisational & Social Dynamics*, 20(1): 48–59.

Davis. L., (1979). Optimizing organization-plant design: A complementary structure for technical and social systems. *Organizational Dynamics*, Autumn: 3–15.

Davis. L. and Cherns, A. (Eds.), (1975). The quality of working life. *Cases and Commentary*, Vol. 2. New York: The Free Press.

De Board, R., (1978). *The psychoanalysis of organizations: A psychoanalytic is approach to behaviour in groups and organizations*. London: Routledge.

de Maré, P., (1972). *Perspectives in group psychotherapy: A theoretical background*. London: George Allen and Unwin.
De Vries, M. F. R. K., (1992). The motivating role of envy: A forgotten factor in management theory. *Administration & Society*, 24(1): 41–60.
De Vries, M. F. R. K., (1994). The leadership mystique. *Academy of Management Perspectives*, 8(3): 73–89.
De Vries, M. F. R. K., (2007). *Coach and couch*. London: Palgrave.
De Vries, M. F. R. K., (2020) *Journey to the Coronavirus Land eBook*. Available from: https://www.kdvi.com/research_items/859
Denworth, L., (2020). The biggest psychological experiment in history is running now. *Scientific American*. Available from: https://www.scientificamerican.com/interactive/the-biggest-psychological-experiment-in-history-is-running-now
Devane, T. and Holman, P. (Eds.), (2007). *The change handbook – group methods for shaping the future*. San Francisco: Berrett-Koehler.
Dicks, H. V., (1970.) *Fifty years of the Tavistock clinic*. London: Routledge and Kegan Paul.
Doob, L. W., and Foltz, W. J., (1974). The impact of a workshop upon grass-roots leaders in Belfast. *The Journal of Conflict Resolution*, 18(2): 237–256.
Duberley, J. and Johnson, P., (2000). *Understanding management research*. London: Sage.
Ehn, P. and Kyng, M. (Eds.), (19870). *Computers and democracy*. 434 pages. Aldershot, Brookfield USA, Hong Kong, Singapore, Sydney: Avebury. (1988). *Organization Studies*, 9(1), 131–133.
Eijnatten, van, F. M., (1992). *The socio-technical systems design (STSD) paradigm: A full bibliography of English-language literature*. (Release FBEL 03T ed.) (TU Eindhoven. Fac. TBDK, Vakgroep TandA: monografie; Vol. 009). Eindhoven: Technische Universiteit Eindhoven.
Eijnatten, F. M. Van., (1998). Developments in socio-technical systems design (STSD). In: P. Drenth, T. Henk and C. De Wolff (Eds.), *Handbook of work and organizational psychology*, Vol. 4, Pg. 61. Organizational Psychology, Psychology Press, London: Taylor and Francis.
Eijnatten, F. M. Van and Van Der Zwaan, A. H., (1998). The Dutch IOR approach to organizational design: An alternative to business process re-engineering? *Human Relations*, 51: 289–318.
Eisold, K., (2005). Using Bion. *Psychoanalytic psychology*, 22: 357–369.
Elias, N., (1939). *The civilizing process*. Oxford, UK: Blackwell Publishers.
Emery, F. E. (Ed.), (1969). Introduction. In: *Systems thinking*. Harmondsworth UK: Penguin Books.
Emery, M., (1993a). Introduction to the 1993 edition. In Emery, M. (Ed.), *Participative design for participative democracy*, Pgs. 1–6. Canberra: Centre for Continuing Education, Australian National University.
Emery, M., (1993b). *Participative design for participative democracy*. Canberra: Australia National University, Centre for Continuing Education.
Emery, M., (1996). The search conference: Design and management of learning. In: F. E. Emery, E. Trist and H. Murray (Eds.), *The social engagement of social science: A Tavistock anthology: The socio-technical perspective*, Vol. III, Pgs. 599–613. Philadelphia: University of Pennsylvania Press. Available from: http://www.moderntimesworkplace.com/archives/archives.html

Emery, M., (1998). *Searching: The theory and practice of making cultural change*. Amsterdam: John Benjamins Publisher.

Emery, M., (2000). The current version of Emery's open systems theory. *Systemic Practice and Action Research*, 13: 623–643.

Emery, F. E. and Emery, M., (1974) *Responsibility and social change*. Canberra: Australia National University, Centre for Continuing Education.

Emery, M. and Emery, F., (1978a). Searching: For new direction, in new ways for new times. In: J. W. Sutherland (Ed.), *Management handbook for public administrators*, Pgs. 257–301. New York: Van Nostrand Reinhold Co.

Emery, F. and Emery. M., (1978b). Searching: For new directions. In:J. W. Sutherland (Ed.), *New ways … for new times. In management handbook for public administration*. New York: Van Nostrand.

Emery, F. and Emery. M., (1993). The participative design workshop. In: E. Trist, F. Emery and H. Murray (Eds.), *The social engagement of social science: A Tavistock anthology: The socio-technical perspective*, Vol. II, Pgs. 599–613. Philadelphia: University of Pennsylvania Press. Available from: http://www.moderntimesworkplace.com/archives/archives.html

Emery, M. and Purser, R., (1996). *The search conference: A powerful method for planning organizational change and community action*. San Francisco: Jossey Bass.

Emery, F. E., and Thorsrud, E., (1964). *Form and content of industrial democracy. Some experiments from Norway and other European countries*. Oslo: Oslo University Press. (Also published in London: Tavistock (1969), and in Assen: Van Gorcum (1969).)

Emery, F., and Trist, E., (1960a). *Report on the Barford Conference for Bristol/Siddley, Aero-Engine Corporation*. Document no. 598. London: Tavistock.

Emery, F. E., and Trist, E. L., (1960b). Sociotechnical systems. In: C. W. Churchman and M. Verhulst (Eds.), *Management science: Models and techniques*, Vol. 2. Oxford: Pergamon.

Emery, F. and Trist, E., (1965). The causal texture of organizational environments. *Human Relations*, 18: 21–32. *Also in:* Emery & Trist: The Causal Texture of Organizational Environments, Vol. III: The Socio- Ecological Perspective, Tavistock Anthology. University of Pennsylvania Press. Available from: www.moderntimesworkplace.com

Emery F. E., Trist E. L., Churchman C. W., and Verhulst M., (1960). Socio-technical systems. *Management science models and techniques*, Vol. 2, Pgs. 83–97. Oxford: Pergamon Press.

Ettinger B., (2006). *The matrixial borderspace (essays from 1994–1999)*. Minneapolis, MN: University of Minnesota Press.

Fairbairn, W. R., (1952). *Psychoanalytic studies of the personality*. London: Routledge and Kegan Paul.

Fayol, H., (1949). *General and industrial management*. Translated by C. Storrs. London: Sir Isaac Pitman & Sons.

Federici, S., (2012). *Revolution at point zero: Housework, reproduction, and feminist struggle*. Common Notions. Oakland, CA: PM Press.

Fenichel, O., (1945). *The psychoanalytic theory of neurosis*. New York: W. W. Norton & Co.

Fisher, J. V., (2006). The emotional experience of K. *International Journal of Psychoanalysis*, 87: 1221–1237.

Flood, Robert L., (2010). The relationship of systems thinking to action research. *Systemic Practice and Action Research*, 23: 269–284.

Ford, A., (2010). *Information feedback and causal loops. Modeling the environment*. Washington: Island Press.

Foster, A., (2001). The duty to care and the need to split. *Journal of Social Work Practice*, 15: 1.

Foster, M., (1967). *Developing an analytical model for socio-technical analysis.* London: Tavistock, Document HRC 7 I HRC 15.

Foster, M., (1972). An introduction to the theory and practice of action research in work organizations. *Human Relations*, 25(6): 529–556.

Fotaki, M., (2010). Why do public policies fail so often? Exploring health policy making as an imaginary/symbolic construction. *Organization*, 17: 703–720.

Fotaki, M., (2017). Relational ties of love: A psychosocial proposal for ethics of compassionate care in health and public services. *Psychodynamic Practice*, 23: 181–189.

Fotaki, M., (2019). Feminist ethics: Embodied relationality as a normative guide for management and organizations. In: C. Neesham and R. Macklin (Eds.), *Handbook of philosophy of management*. New York: Springer.

Fotaki, M. and Harding, N., (2013). Lacan and sexual difference in organization and management theory: Towards a hysterical academy? *Organization*, 20: 153–172.

Fotaki, M. and Harding, N. (2017). *Gender and the organization: Women at work in the 21st century.* London: Routledge.

Fotaki, M., Islam, G., and Antoni, A. (Eds.), (2020). *Business ethics and care in organizations*, Chapter 1, Pg. 1–3. London: Routledge.

Fotaki, M., Long, S., and Schwartz, H., (2009). Special issue on psychoanalytic perspectives on organizations: What can psychoanalysis offer organization studies today?. *Organization Studies*, 30: 451–452.

Fotaki, M., Long, S., and Schwartz, H. S., (2012) What can psychoanalysis offer organization studies today? Taking stock of current developments and thinking about future directions. *Organization Studies*, 33(9): 1105–1120. Available from: https://www.research.manchester.ac.uk/portal/en/publications/what-can-psychoanalysis-offer-organization-studies-today-taking-stock-of-current-developments-and-thinking-about-future-directions(651e88e9-c573-42c2-b392-876b192cd281)/export.html#export

Foucault, M., (1970). *The order of things: An archaeology of the human sciences.* London: Tavistock Publications.

Foulkes, S. H., (1948). *Introduction to group-analytic psychotherapy: Studies in the social integration of individuals and groups.* London: Maresfield Reprints, 1984.

Foulkes, S. H. and Anthony, E. J., (1957). *Group psychotherapy: The psychoanalytic approach.* London: Maresfield Reprints, 1984.

Fraher, A. L., (2004a). *A history of group study and psychodynamic organizations.* London: Free Association Books.

Fraher, A. L., (2004b). Systems psychodynamics: The formative years of an interdisciplinary field at the Tavistock Institute. *History of Psychology*, 7(1): 65–84.

Francesetti, G., (2012). Pain and beauty: From the psychopathology to the aesthetics of contact. *British Gestalt Journal*, 21(2): 4–18.

François, C., (2004). *International Encyclopaedia of systems and cybernetics.* 2nd ed. Munchen: K. G. Saur North America Research.

Fraser, N., (2016). Contradictions of capital and care. *New Left Review*, July/August: 99–117.

French, R., (2000). *'Negative Capability', 'Dispersal' and the Containment of Emotion.* Paper presented at the ISPSO Symposium, London.

French, R. and Simpson, P., (2010) The 'work group': Redressing the balance in Bion's experiences in groups. *Human Relations*, 63(12): 1859–1878.

French, R. and Vince, R. (Eds.), (1999). *Group relations, management and organization.* Oxford: Oxford University Press.

Freud, S., (1910). Leonardo da Vinci and a memory of his childhood. In: *The standard edition of the complete psychological works of Sigmund Freud*, Vol. 11, Pgs. 59–137. Translated by James Strachey. London: Hogarth Press.

Freud, S., (1911). Formulations on the two principles of mental functioning. *The standard edition of the complete psychological works of Sigmund Freud*, Vol. XII, Pgs. 213–226. London: Hogarth Press.

Freud, S., (1917). Mourning and Melancholia. *The standard edition of the complete psychological works of Sigmund Freud*, Vol. XIV (1914–1916): On the History of the Psycho-Analytic Movement, Papers on Metapsychology and Other Works, Pgs. 237–258. London: Hogarth Press.

Freud, S., (1922). *Group psychology and the analysis of the ego*, Pgs. viii + 134. Translated by J. Strachey. London and Vienna: International Psycho-Analytical Press.

Freud, S., (1927). The future of an illusion. *Standard Edition*, 21: 5–56.

Friedman, R. (2014). Group analysis today—Developments in intersubjectivity. *Group Analysis*, 47(3): 194–200.

Friend, J., (1992). Connective planning: From practice to theory and back. In: E. Trist, F. Emery, and H. Murray (Eds.), *The social engagement of social science, a Tavistock anthology: The socio-ecological perspective*, Vol. 3, Pgs. 439–469. Philadelphia: University of Pennsylvania Press. Available from: www.moderntimesworkplace.com

Friend, J. and Hickling, A., (1997). *Planning under pressure: The strategic choice approach*, 2nd ed. Oxford: Heinemann.

Gabriel, Y., (1999). *Organizations in depth*. Thousand Oaks, CA: Sage.

Gabriel, Y., (2016). Psychoanalysis and the study of organization. In: R. Mir, H. Willmott, and M. Greenwood (Eds.), *The Routledge companion to philosophy in organization studies*, Pgs. 212–224. Abingdon, UK: Routledge.

Gabriel, Y. and Carr, A., (2002). Organizations, management and psychoanalysis: An overview. *Journal of Managerial Psychology*, 17(5): 348–365.

Gad, A., (2015). Culture hacking: Inside (and outside) Simon Denny's work. In: S. Denny (Ed.), *Products for organising*. London: Serpentine Gallery. Available from: https://www.serpentinegalleries.org/whats-on/simon-denny-products-organising/

Gazzaley, A. and Rosen, L. D., (2016). *Ancient brains in a high tech world*. Cambridge, MA: MIT Press.

Gell-Mann, M., (1994). *The quark and the jaguar*. New York: W. H. Freeman.

Gharajedaghi, J., (1985). *Toward a systems theory of organization*. Inter-systems Publications. Available from: https://openlibrary.org/publishers/Intersystems_Publications.

Gilmore, T. N. and Krantz, J., (1985). Projective identification in the consulting relationship: Exploring the unconscious dimensions of a client system. *Human Relations*, 38(12): 1159–1177.

Gilmore, T. and Krantz, J., (1990). The splitting of leadership and management as a social defence. *Human Relations*, 43(2): 183–204.

Ginzberg, C., (1983). Clues: Morelli, Freud, and Sherlock Holmes. In: U. Eco and T. A. Sebeok (Eds.), *The sign of three: Dupin, Holmes, Peirce*, Pgs. 81–118. Bloomington: Indiana University Press.

Ginzberg, C. and Davin, A., (1980). Morelli, Freud, and Sherlock Holmes: Clues and scientific method. In: Carlo Ginzburg and Anna Davin (Eds.), *History workshop*, Vol. 9, Pgs. 5–36. Oxford: Oxford University Press.

Gleick, J., (1987). *Chaos: Making a new science*. New York: Viking Press.

Gold, M., (1992). Metatheory and field theory in social psychology: Relevance or elegance? *Journal of Social Issues*, 48(2): 67–78.

Gold, S. and Klein, L., (2004). Harold Bridger - conversations and recollections. *Organizational and Social Dynamics*, 4(1): 1–21.

Goodwin, B., (1995). *How the leopard changed its spots: The evolution of complexity*. New York: Scribner.

Gosling, R., (1994). The everyday work group. In: B. Sievers and D. Armstrong (Eds.), *Discovering social meaning: A Festschrift for W. Gordon Lawrence on the occasion of his 60th birthday*. Waltham, MA: Unpublished.

Gould, L., Stapley, L., and Stein, M. (Eds.), (2001a). *The systems psychodynamics of organizations*, Pgs. 1–15. London: Karnac Books.

Gould, L. J., Stapley, L. F., and Stein, M., (2001b). *The systems psychodynamics of organisations*, Pg. 8. London: Karnac.

Gould, J., Wilkinson, J., Voyer, J., and Ford, D., (1998). *Overcoming organisational anxiety*, Pgs. 1–16. Waltham, MA: Pegasus Communications. ISBN-10: 1883823196; ISBN-13: 978-1883823191

Gould, L., Wilkinson, J., Voyer, and Ford D., (2021).Overcoming organizational anxiety. Available from: https://thesystemsthinker.com/overcoming-organizational-anxiety/ http://www.sba.oakland.edu/ispo/html/1999Symposium/mersky1999.htm https://www.researchgate.net/publication/232607906_Developments_and_Thinking_about_Future_Directions_What_Can_Psychoanalysis_Offer_Organization_Studies_Today_Taking_Stock_of_Current

Green, Z. and Molenkamp, R., (2008). Review and application group consulting methodologies. A.K Rice Institute. Available from: https://www.akriceinstitute.org/

Greenbaum, J. and Kyng M., (1991). *Design at work: Cooperative design of computer systems*. Hillsdale: NJLEA.

Gregory, E. and Murray, H., (1975). Unpublished report to evaluate the effectiveness of policy on race relations within the Civil Service. Available from: http://tihr-archive.tavinstitute.org/home-page/

Griffin, D. and Shaw, P., (2000). *Complexity and management: Fad or radical challenge to systems thinking*. London: Routledge.

Guerin, M. L., (1997). Teamwork at Barton Company: A psychodynamic perspective. Available from: http://www.sba.oakland.edu/ispo/htmll/1997Guer.htm

Gummesson, E., (1991). *Qualitative methods and management research*. Thousand Oaks, CA: Sage.

Gustavsen, B., (1985). *Workplace reform and democratic dialogue: economic and industrial democracy*, Vol. 6. London: Sage.

Gutmann, D., Ternier-David, J., and Verrier, C., (1999). From envy to desire: Witnessing the transformation. In: R. French and R. Vince (Eds.), *Group relations, management, and organization*, Pgs. 155–172. New York: Oxford University Press.

Hall, K. and Savery, L. K., (1987). Stress management. *Management Decision*, 25(6): 29–35.

Halton, W., (1994). Some unconscious aspects of organisational life: Contributions from psychoanalysis. In: A. Obholzer and V. Roberts (Eds.), *The unconscious at work*. London: Routledge.

Hammerstrom, O. and Lansbury, R. D., (1991). The art of building a car: The Swedish experience re-examined. *New Technology, Work and Employment*, 6(2): 85–90.

Hammond, D., (2003). *The science of synthesis: Exploring the social implications of general systems theory*. Colorado: University Press of Colorado.

Hayden, C. and Molenkamp, R., (2004). The Tavistock primer II. In: S. Cytrynbaum and D. Noumair (Eds.), *Group dynamics, organizational irrationality, and social complexity: Group relations reader 3*, Pgs. 135–158. Jupiter, FL: A. K. Rice Institute.

Heimann, P., (1973). Certain functions of introjection and projection in early infancy. In: M. Klein, P. Heimann, S. Isaacs and J. Reviere, *Developments in psychoanalysis*, Pgs. 122–168. London: The Hogarth Press and the Institute of Psychoanalysis.

Henrick, I., (1943). Work and the pleasure principle. *Psychoanalytic Quarterly*, 12: 311–329.

Herman, J. L., (1997).*Trauma and recovery: The aftermath of violence: From domestic abuse to political terror.* New York: Basic Books.

Hills, D., (2018). Research into Learning at the Leicester Conference. *Organisational & Social Dynamics*, 18(2): 167–190.

Hinshelwood, R. D., (1989). *Dictionary of Kleinian thought*. London: Free Association Books.

Hinshelwood, R. D., (1994). *Clinical Klein*. London: Free Association Books.

Hinshelwood, R. D. and Chiesa, M., (Eds.), (2002). *Organisations, Anxieties and defences: Toward a psychoanalytic social psychology*. London: Whurr Publishers.

Hinshelwood, R. D. and Skogstad, W. (Eds.), (2000). *Observing organisations: Anxiety, defence and culture in health care*. London: Routledge.

Hinshelwood, RD (2003) Group mentality and 'having a mind'. In: Pines, M, Lipgar, B (eds) Building on Bion: Volume 1, Roots. London: Jessica Kingsley, pp. 181–182.

Hirschhorn, L., (1988). *The workplace within: Psychodynamics of organisational life*, Pgs. 10–11. MA: MIT Press.

Hirschhorn, L., & Barnett, C. K. (Eds.). (1993). The psychodynamics of organizations. Philadelphia: Temple University Press.

Hirschhorn, L., (1997). *Reworking authority: Leading and following in the post-modern organization*. Cambridge, MA: The MIT Press.

Hobbs, D., (2020). Moving to new styles of leadership. *Critical Eye*. Available from: https://www.criticaleye.com/inspiring/community-update.cfm?m=392CF07EEF2DDF78&id=1079

Hoggett, P., (1996). Review of the: *The Unconscious at Work: Individual and Organisational Stress in the Human Services*. London: Routledge, 1994. http://human-nature.com/free-associations/hogg.html

Holti, R., (1997). Consulting to organisational implications of technical change. In: J. E. Neumann, K. Kellner and A. Dawson-Shepherd (Eds.), *Developing organisational consultancy*. London: Routledge.

Hornstrup, C., et al., (2005). *Systemisk Ledelse*. DPF. Dansk psykologisk Forlag.

Huffington, C., Armstrong, D., Halton, W., Hoyle, L., and Pooley, J. (2004). *Working below the surface*. London: Karnac Books Ltd.

Hunt, J. and McCollom, M., (1994). Using psychoanalytic approaches in organizational consulting. *Consulting Psychology Journal*, 46(2): 1–11.

Hupkens, L., (2006). Applying group relations learning to the daily work of consultants and managers. In: L. D. Brunner, A. Nutkevitch, and M. Sher (Eds.), *Group relations conferences: Reviewing and exploring theory, design, role-taking and application*, Pgs. 138–150. London: Karnac.

Hutchins, E., (1991). The social organization of distributed cognition. In: L. B. Resnick, J. M. Levine, and S. D. Teasley (Eds.), *Perspectives on socially shared cognition*, Pgs. 283–307. Washington, DC: American Psychological Association.

Hutton, J., Bazalgette, J., and Reed, B. (1997). Organisation-in-the-mind. In: J. Neumann, et al. (Eds.), *Developing organisational consultancy*. London: Routledge.

Hutton, J., Bazalgette, J., & Armstrong, D., (1994). What Does Management Really Mean? In: R. Casemore, et al (eds.) *What Makes Consultancy Work - Understanding the Dynamics*. London: South Bank University Press, pg. 185–203.

Isaacs, S., (1952). The nature and function of phantasy. In: J. Riviere (Ed.), *Developments in psychoanalysis*, Pgs. 76–121. London: Hogarth Press.

Izod, K., (2017). *A Relational Systems Psychodynamic Approach to the Understanding of Group and Organisational Processes: The Construction of 'The Relational Terrain'*. Available from: http://repository.tavistockandportman.ac.uk/2036/1/Izod%20thesis.pdf

Izod, K. and Whittle, S. R. (Eds.), (2009). *Mind-ful consulting*. London: Karnac.

Izod, K. and Whittle, S. R. (Eds.), (2014). *Resource-ful consulting: Working with your presence and identity in consulting to change*. London: Karnac.

Jackson, M. C., (2000). *Systems approaches to management*. New York, NY: Kluwer/Plenum.

Jackson, M. C., (2019). *Critical systems thinking and the management of complexity*. Chichester: Wiley.

Jacobs, R., (1998). *Real time strategic change*. San Francisco: Berrett-Koehler.

Jameson, C., (2010). The short step from love to hypnosis: A reconsideration of the Stockholm syndrome. *Journal for Cultural Research*, 14(4): 337–355.

Jaques, E., (1948). Interpretive group discussion as a method of facilitating social change: A progress report on the use of group methods in the investigation and resolution of social problems. *Human Relations*, 1(4): 533–549.

Jaques, E., (1951a). *The changing culture of a factory: A study of authority and participation in an industrial setting*. London: Tavistock; reissued New York: Garland, 1987.

Jaques, E., (1951b). Working through industrial conflict: The service department at the Glacier Metal Company. In: E. Trist and H. Murray (Eds.), *The social engagement of social science. Volume 1: The social psychological perspective*, Pgs. 379–404. London: Free Association Books (1990). Available from: www.moderntimesworkplace.com

Jaques, E., (1953). On the dynamics of social structure: A contribution to the psychoanalytic study of social phenomena deriving from the views of Melanie Klein. In: *The social engagement of social science. Volume 1: The social psychological perspective*, Pgs. 420–438. London: Free Association Books (1990). Available from: www.moderntimesworkplace.com

Jaques, E. (1955). Social systems as a defence against persecutory and depressive anxiety. In: M. Klein, R. Heimann, and R. E. Money-Kyrle (Eds.), *New directions in psychoanalysis*, Pgs. 478–498. New York: Basic Books.

Jaques, E., (1961). *Equitable payment: A general theory of work, differential payment, and individual progress*. London: Heinemann.

Jaques, E., (1964a). Social-analysis and the Glacier Project. *Human Relations*, 17: 361–375.

Jaques, E., (1964b). *Time-span handbook: The use of time-span of discretion to measure the level of work in employment roles and to arrange an equitable payment structure*. London: Heinemann.

Jaques, E., (1989). *Requisite organization: The CEO's guide to creative structure and leadership*. Aldershot: Gower.

Jaques, E., (1990), *Creativity and work*. Madison: International Universities.

Jaques, E., (1995a). *Requisite organization: total system for effective managerial organization and managerial leadership for the 21st century*. London: Gower.

Jaques, E., (1995b). Why the psychoanalytical approach to understanding organizations is dysfunctional. *Human Relations*, 48(4): 343–349.

Kapoor, A., (2016). Finding, making, and taking role, a case study from the complexity of inter-agency dynamics. In: *Transforming experience in organisations a framework for organisational research and consultancy*. London: Routledge.

Kauffman, S., (1995). *At home in the universe*. Oxford: Oxford University Press.

Kay, J. and King, M., (2020). *Radical uncertainty*. London: Bridge Street Press.

Kegan, R., (1994). *In over our heads. The mental demands of modern life*. Cambridge: Harvard University.

Kelly, R. and Gangjee, Z. H., (2018). The yoga event in the Leicester Conference model. In: E. Aram, C. Archer, R. Kelly, G. Strauss, and J. Triest (Eds.),*Doing the business of group relations conferences: Exploring the discourse*, Belgirate Vol. V. London: Routledge.

Kenny, K., and Fotaki, M. (2015). From gendered organizations to compassionate borderspaces: Reading corporeal ethics with Bracha Ettinger. *Organization*, 22: 183–199.

Klein, J. A., (1991). A re-examination of autonomy in the light of new manufacturing practices. *Human Relations*, 44: 21–38.

Klein, L., (2005). Working across the gap. The practice of social science in organisations. Karnac, London.

Klein, M., (1928). Early stages of the oedipus conflict. *The International Journal of Psychoanalysis*, 9: 167.

Klein, M., (1935). A contribution to the psychogenesis of manic depressive states. *The International Journal of Psychoanalysis*, 16: 145–174.

Klein. M., (1937). Love, guilt and reparation. In: *Love, guilt and reparation and other works*. London: Hogarth Press.

Klein, M., (1940). Mourning and its relation to manic depressive states. *The International Journal of Psychoanalysis*, 21: 125–153.

Klein, M., (1945). The Oedipus complex in the light of early anxieties. *The International Journal of Psychoanalysis*, 26: 11–33.

Klein, M., (1946). Notes on some schizoid mechanisms. *The International Journal of Psychoanalysis*, 27: 99–110.

Klein, M., (1948). *Contributions to psychoanalysis 1921–1945*. London: The Hogarth Press.

Klein, M., (1952). Some theoretical conclusions regarding the emotional life of the infant. In: M. Klein, P. Heimann, S Isaacs, and J. Riviere (Eds.), *Developments in psychoanalysis*. London: Hogarth Press.

Klein, M., (1957). *Envy and gratitude*. New York: Basic Books. [Reprinted London: Karnac 1977.]

Klein, M., (1959), Our adult world and its roots in infancy; republished (1963) in *Our adult world and other essays*. London: Heinemann. Also in: A. Colman and M. Geller (Eds.), (1985). *Group relations reader 2*, Pgs. 5–20. Washington: A. K. Rice Institute.

Klein, M., (1961). *Narrative of a child analysis*. London: Hogarth.

Klein, E. B. and Astrachan, J. H., (1975). Mental health students' reactions to a group training conference: Understanding from a systems perspective. *Social Psychiatry*, 10: 79–85.

Klein, E. B., Correa, M. E., Howe, S. R., and Stone, W. N., (1983). The effect of social systems on group relations training. *Social Psychiatry. Sozialpsychiatrie. Psychiatrie Sociale*, 18(1): 7–12.

Klein, M., Heimann, P., and Money-Kyrle, R. E., (1955), *New directions in psychoanalysis*. London: Tavistock. [Reprinted London: Karnac, 1977.]

Klein, E. B., Stone, W. N., Correa, M. E., et al. (1989). Dimensions of experiential learning at group relations conferences. *Social Psychiatry Psychiatric Epidemiology*, 24: 241–248. Available from: https://www.researchgate.net/publication/227154498_Dimensions_of_experiential_learning_at_group_relations_conferences

Kling, R. and Gerson, E., (1978). Patterns of segmentation and intersection in the computing world. *Symbolic Interaction*, 1(2): 24–43.

Kling, R. and Scacchi, W., (1980). Computing as social action: The social dynamics of computing in complex organizations. *Advance in Computers*, 19: 249–327.

Kling, R., (1977). The organizational context of user-centered software design. *MIS Quarterly*, 1(Winter): 41–52.

Kling, R., (2000). Learning about information technologies and social change: The contribution of social informatics. *The Information Society*, 16(3): 217–232.

Kneebone, R., Schlegel, C., Spivey, A. (2018, December). Science in hand: How art and craft can boost reproducibility. *Nature*, 564: 188–189.

Knights, D., and McCabe, D., (2000). Bewitched, bothered and bewildered: The meaning and experience of team working for employees in an automobile company. *Human Relations*, 53(11): 1481–1517.

Kohon G., (1986). *The British School of psychoanalysis*. London: Free Association Books.

Kolb, D. and Frohman, A., (1970). An organization development approach to consulting. *Sloan Management Review*, 12(1): 51–65.

Koortzen, P. and Cilliers, F., (2002). The psychoanalytical approach to team development. In: R. L. Lowman (Ed.), *Handbook of organisational consulting psychology*. San Francisco: Jossey-Bass.

Krantz, J., (1989). The managerial couple: Superior-subordinate relationships as a unit of analysis. *Human Resource Management*, 28: 161–175.

Krantz, J., (1990). Lessons from the field: An essay on the crisis of leadership in contemporary organizations. *The Journal of Applied Behavioral Science*, 26(1): 49–64.

Krantz, J., (2006). Leadership, betrayal and adaptation. *Human Relations*, 59: 221–240.

Krantz, J., (2014). Personal communication.

Kuhn, Thomas S., (1970). *The structure of scientific revolutions*. Enlarged, 2nd ed. Chicago: University of Chicago Press.

Laban, R., (1959). The educational and therapeutic value of dance. *Laban Art of Movement Guild Magazine*, 22(May, Special Commemorative Number): 18–21.

Lacan J., (2006). *Ecrits*. Trans. B. Fink. W.W. New York: Norton & Company.

Lawlor, D., (2009). Test of time: A case study in the functioning of social systems as a defence against anxiety: Rereading 50 years on. *Clinical Child Psychology and Psychiatry*, 14(4): 523–530.

Lawlor, D. and Webb, L., (2009). An interview with Isabel Menzies Lyth, with a conceptual commentary. *Organizational & Social Dynamics*, 9(1): 93–137.

Lawrence, G., (1977). Management development … some ideals, images and realities. *Journal of European Industrial Training*, 1(2): 21–25.

Lawrence, G., (1982). *Some psychic and political dimensions of work experiences*. Occasional Paper No. 2. London: Tavistock Institute of Human Relations.

Lawrence, G., (1983). Unemployment and Strain as Sources of Renewal. *Personnel Management Review*, November.

Lawrence, W.G., (1994). The Politics of Salvation and Revelation in the Practice of Consultancy. In: R. Casemore, et. al. *What Makes Consultancy Work - Understanding the Dynamics*. London: South Bank University Press, pg. 87.

Lawrence, W. G., (1997). Centering the sphinx for the psychoanalytic study of organisations. Paper presented at the ISPSO Symposium, Philadelphia.

Lawrence, W G., (1999). *Exploring individual and organizational boundaries: A Tavistock open systems approach*. London: Karnac.

Lawrence G. W., (2000). *Tongued with fire: Groups in experience*. London: Karnac.

Lawrence, G., (2003). Social dreaming as sustained thinking. *Human Relations*, 56(5): 609–624.

Lawrence, W. G., (2004). *Introduction to social dreaming: Transforming thinking*. London: Karnac Books.

Lawrence G. W., (2006). Executive coaching, unconscious thinking, and infinity. In: H. Brunning (Ed.), *Executive coaching - systems psychodynamic perspective*. London: Karnac.

Lawrence, G. W., Bain, A., and Gould, L., (1996a). The fifth basic assumption. *Free Associations*, 6(1: 37): 2855.

Lawrence, W. G., Bain, A., and Gould, L., (1996b). The fifth basic assumption. In: W. G. Lawrence (Ed.), *Tongued with fire: Groups in experience*. London: Karnac.

Lawrence G. W. and Miller, E., (1982). Psychic and political constraints on the growth of industrial democracies. In: M. Pines and L. Rafaelsen, (Eds.), *The individual and the group*, Pgs. 399–403. New York: Plenum Press.

Le Bon, G., (1896). *The crowd. A study of the popular mind*. Paris: Adansonia.

Lear, J., (2008). *Radical hope: Ethics in the face of cultural devastation*. Harvard: Harvard University Press.

Leighton, E., (2020). The science of a successful return to work. *HR Review*. Available from: https://www.hrreview.co.uk/inside-hr-webinars/science-of-successful-return-to-work

Leiper, R., (1994). Evaluation: Organisations learning from experience. In: A. Obholzer and V. Z. Roberts (Eds.), *The unconscious at work*. Oxford: Routledge.

Leith, M., (1996). Organizational change and large group interventions. *Career Development International*, 1(4): 19–23.

Leith, M., (2019). *Creating Collaborative Gatherings using Large Group Interventions*. Available from: http://jackmartinleith.com/documents/creating-collaborative-gatherings-using-large-group-interventions.pdf

Leleur, S., (2014). The meaning of system: Towards a complexity orientation in systems thinking. *International Journal of Systems and Society*, 1(1): 22.

Levinson, H., (1991). *Organisational diagnosis*. Cambridge, MA: Harvard University Press.

Lewin, K., (1935). *A dynamic theory of personality – selected papers*. New York: McGraw Hill.

Lewin, K., (1936a). Causal connections in psychology. The historical and the systemic concept of causality. *Principles of topological psychology*, Pgs. 30–40. New York: McGraw Hill.

Lewin, K., (1936b). *Principles of topological psychology*. New York: McGraw Hill.

Lewin, K., (1944). A research approach to leadership problems. *The Journal of Educational Sociology*, 17(7): 392–398.

Lewin, K., (1947a). Frontiers in Group Dynamics, part 1: Concept, method and reality in social science: Social equilibria and social change. *Human Relations*, 1: 5–41.

Lewin, K., (1947b). Frontiers in Group Dynamics, part 2: Channels of group life: Social planning and action research. *Human Relations*, 1: 143–153.

Lewin, K., (1947c). Frontiers in Group Dynamics: Concept, method and reality in social science; social equilibria and social change. *Human Relations*, 1(1): 5–41.

Lewin, K., (1947d). Frontiers in Group Dynamics: II. Channels of group life; social planning and action research. *Human Relations*, 1(2): 143–153.

Lewin, K., (1948). Field theory and learning. In: D. Cartwright (Ed.), *Field theory in social science & selected theoretical papers*, Pgs. 212–230. Washington, DC: American Psychological Association.

Lewin, K. and Cartwright, D. (Eds.), (1951). *Field theory in social science*. New York: Harper.

Lindholm, C., (1990). *Inquiry and change*. New Haven, CT: Yale University Press.

Lindholm, R. and Norstedt, J.P., (1975). *The Volvo Report*. Stockholm: Swedisch Employers' Confederation SAF.

Lipgar, R. M. and Struhl, S., (1993). *Group relations research progress report: Contextual and methodological issues in the study of gender and authority in Tavistock group relations conferences, or 'it depends'*. Paper presented at the Community or Chaos, Marina Del Rey California, 6–9 May 1993.

Lipgar, R. M., Bair, J. P., and Fichtner, C., (2004). Integrating research with group relations conferences: Challenges, insights and implications. In: S. Cytrynbaum and D. A. Noumair (Eds.), *Group dynamics, organizational irrationality, and social complexity: Group relations reader 3*, Pgs. 417–442. Jupiter, FL: A. K. Rice Institute.

Lippit, A. M., (2005). *Atomic light*. Minnesota: University of Minnesota Press.

Lippit, R. and White, R. K., (1939). The 'social' climate of children's groups. In: R. Barker, J. Kounin, and H. Wright (Eds.) (1943), *Child behaviours and development*. London: McGraw-Hill.

Loewenthal, K. M., (1996). Book review: The unconscious at work: Individual and organizational stress in the human services. *Human Relations*, 49(9): 1241–1252.

Long, S., et al., (1997). *Collaborative Action Research in an Organisation: Can Psychoanalytically Informed Thinking Deepen the Collaboration?* Paper presented at the ISPSO Symposium, Philadelphia.

Long, S., (2000). *The internal team: A discussion of the socio-emotional dynamics of team (work)*. Available from: http://www.sba.oakland.edu/ispso/html/2000Synposium/

Long, S. and. Harney, M., (2013). The associative unconscious. *In: Socioanalytic methods: Discovering the hidden in organisations and social systems*. London: Karnac.

Long, S., (2006). Organisational defenses against anxiety: What has happened since the 1955 Jaques paper? *International Journal of Applied Psychoanalytic Studies*, 3(4): 279–295.

Long, S. D., (2008). *The perverse organisation and its deadly sins*. London: Karnac.

Long, S., (2010). Images of leadership. In: H. Brunning and M. Perini (Eds.), *Psychoanalytic perspectives on a turbulent world*. London: Karnac.

Long, S. (Ed.), (2013). *Socioanalytic methods: Discovering the hidden in organisations and social systems*. London: Karnac.

Long, S., (2016). *Transforming experience in organisations a framework for organisational research and consultancy*. London: Routledge.

Long, S., Dalton, D., Faris, M., and Newton, J., (2010a). Me and my job: Transforming performance appraisals through role conversations. *Socio-Analysis*, 12: 39–55.

Long, S. and Manley, J. (Eds.), (2018). *Social dreaming: Philosophy, research, theory and practice*. London: Karnac.

Long, S. D., Penny, D., Gold, S., and Harding, W. (2010b). A shared vision: Using action research/learning for work culture change in a cardiology department. In: J. Braithwaite, P. Hyde, and C. Pope (Eds.), *Culture and climate in health care organizations*. London: Palgrave McMillan.

Mackay, J., (2019). *Course material for the coaching for leadership programme*. London: Tavistock Institute of Human Relations.

Maier, M. and Rechtin E., (2000). *The art of systems architecting*, 2nd ed. New York: CRC Press.

Main, T. F., (1946). The hospital as a therapeutic institution. *Bulletin of the Menninger Clinic*, 10(3): 66–70.

Main, T. F., (1989) The ailment. In: T. F. Main and J. Johns (Eds.) (1989), *The ailment and other psychoanalytical essays*, Pgs. 12–35. London: Free Association Books.

Malan, D. H, Balfour, F. H. G, Hood, V. G., and Shooter A., (1976). Group psychotherapy: A long-term follow-up study. *Arch Gen Psychiatry*, 33: 1303–1315.

Manz, C. C., (1990). Beyond self-managing work teams: Toward self-leading teams in the workplace. In R. Woodman and W. Pasmore (Eds.), *Research in organizational change and development*, Pgs. 273–299. Greenwich, CT: JAI Press.

Mathur, N., (2015). Paper tiger: Law, bureaucracy, and the developmental state in Himalayan India. Cambridge: Cambridge University Press.
Mayo, E., (1933). *The human problems of an industrial civilization*. Cambridge, MA: Harvard.
McCann, J. and Selsky, J. W., (1984). Hyperturbulence and the emergence of type V. *Academy of Management Review*, 9 (3).
McCollom Hampton, M., (1999). Work groups. In: Y. Gabriel (Ed.), *Organizations in depth*. London: Sage.
McCormick, D. W. and White, J., (2000). Using one's self as an instrument for organizational diagnosis. *Organizational Development Journal*, 18(3): 49–62.
McDermott, R., (1999). Why information technology inspired but cannot deliver knowledge management. *California Management Review*, 41(4): pp. 103–117.
McDermott, R., Snyder, W. M., and Wenger, E., (2002). *Cultivating communities of practice: A guide to managing knowledge*. Boston: Harvard Business School Press.
McGarrigle, E., (1993). *Ego ideals and the role behavior of the small group consultant*. Paper presented at the Chaos or Community, Marino Del Rey, CA, 6–9 May 1993.
McKenna, D. D. and Davis, S. L., (2009). Hidden in plain sight: The active ingredient of executive coaching. *Industrial and Organisational Psychology*, 2(3): 244–260.
McLemore, J. R. and Neumann, J. E., (1987). The inherently political nature of program evaluators and evaluation research. *Evaluation and Program Planning*, 10(1): 83–93.
McQuaid, D., (2020a). Employees willing to take a pay cut for remote working. *HR Review*. Available from: https://www.hrreview.co.uk/hr-news/strategy-news/employees-willing-to-take-a-pay-cut-for-remote-working
McQuaid, D., (2020b). *Lockdown has left employees feeling anxious, depressed and sleepless*. Available from: https://www.hrreview.co.uk/hr-news/wellbeing-news/lockdown-has-left-employees-feeling-anxious-sleeplessness-and-depressed/
McWilliams, N., (2000). On teaching psychoanalysis in anti-analytical times: A polemic. *American Journal of Psychoanalysis*, 60(4): 371–339.
Medeiros-Ward, N., Watson, J. M., and Strayer, D. L., (2015). On supertaskers and the neural basis of efficient multitasking. *Psychonomic Bulletin & Review*, 22: 876–883.
Menninger, K. A., (1942). Work as sublimation. *Bulletin of the Menninger Clinic*, 6: 170–182.
Menninger, R. W., (1975). The impact of group relations conferences on organizational growth. In: A. D. Colman and W. H. Bexton (Eds.), *Group relations reader 1*, Pgs. 265–280. Jupiter, FL: A. K. Rice Institute.
Menninger, R. W., (1985). A retrospective view of a hospital-wide group relations training program: Costs, consequences and conclusions. In: A. D. Colman and M. H. Geller (Eds.), *Group relations reader 2*, Pgs. 285–298. Jupiter, FL: A. K. Rice Institute.
Menzies, I., (1960). A case-study in the functioning of social systems as a defence against anxiety: A report on a study of the nursing service of a general hospital Isabel. *Human relations*, 13: 95. Also In: Menzies-Lyth, I., (1988). *Containing anxiety in institutions*: Free Association Books, Pgs. 43–85.
Menzies, I. E. P., (1970). *The functioning of social systems as a defence against anxiety. A report on a study of the nursing service of a general hospital*. London: The Tavistock Institute of Human Relations. Also In: Menzies Lyth, I., (1988). *Containing anxiety in institutions: Selected essays*, Vol. 1. Free Association Books.
Menzies Lyth, I., (1988). *Containing anxiety in institutions*, Vol. 1. London: Free Association Books.
Menzies Lyth, I., (1989a). A psychoanalytic perspective on social institutions. In: *The dynamics of the social. Selected essays*, Vol. 2, Pgs. 26–44. London: Free Association Books.

Menzies Lyth, I., (1989b). *The dynamics of the social: Selected essays*, Vol. 2. London: Free Association Books.

Menzies Lyth, I., (1990). A psychoanalytic perspective on social institutions, In: E. Trist and H. Murray (Eds.), *The social engagement of social science: A Tavistock anthology. Vol. 1, The socio-psychological perspective*. London: Free Association Books. Available from: www.moderntimesworkplace.com

Menzies Lyth, I., (1991). Changing organisations and individuals: Psychoanalytic insights for improving organisational health. In: M. Kets de Vries (Ed.) (1991), *Organisations on the couch: Clinical perspectives on organisational behavior and change*. San Francisco: Jossey-Bass.

Mersky, R. R., (1999). Falling from Grace – When Consultants Go Out of Role: Enactment in the Service of Organisational Consultancy. Paper delivered at the *International Society for the Psychoanalytic Study of Organisations*, 1999 Symposium. Toronto Canada

Midgley, G., (2000). *Systemic intervention: Philosophy, methodology, and practice*. New York, NY: Kluwer Academic.

Midgley, G., (2003). *Systems thinking*. Thousand Oaks, CA: Sage.

Miller, E. J. (1959). Technology, territory, and time: The internal differentiation of complex production systems, *Human Relations*, 12(3): 243–272.

Miller, E. J., (1975). Socio-technical systems in weaving, 1953-70: A follow-up study, *Human Relations*, 28: 349–386.

Miller, E. J. (1976). Role perspectives and the understanding of organisational behaviour. In: E. J. Miller (Ed.), *Task and organisation*, Pgs. 1–18. Chichester: Wiley.

Miller, E. J., (1977). Organizational development and industrial democracy: A current case-study. In: C. Cooper (Ed.), *Organizational development in the UK and USA: A joint evaluation*, Pgs. 31–63. London: Palgrave McMillan.

Miller, E., (1983). Work and creativity. *Occasional Paper no 6*. London: The Tavistock Institute.

Miller, E. J., (1989). The "Leicester" model: Experiential study of group and organisational processes. *Tavistock Institute Occasional Paper No. 10*. London: Tavistock.

Miller, E. J., (1990). Experiential Learning in Groups I: The development of the Leicester model. In: E. Trist and H. Murray (Eds.), *The social engagement of social science, Vol.1. The socio-psychological perspective*, Pgs. 165–185. London: Free Association Books. Available from: www.moderntimesworkplace.com

Miller, E. J. (1992/1993). *Tavistock Institute Review*. London: Author.

Miller, E. J. (1993). *From dependency to autonomy: Studies in organisation and change*. London: Free Association Books.

Miller, E., (1995). Dialogue with the client system, use of the 'working note' in organizational consultancy. *Journal of Managerial Psychology*, 10(6): 27–30.

Miller, E. J., (1997). Effecting organisational change in large complex systems: A collaborative consultancy approach. In: J. Neumann, K. Kellner, and A. Dawson-Shepherd (Eds.), *Developing Organisational Consultancy*, Pgs. 187–212. London: Routledge.

Miller, E., (1998). A note on the protomental system and "groupishness": Bion's basic assumptions revisited. *Human Relations*, 51: 1495–1508.

Miller, J. H. and Page, S. E., (2007). *Complex adaptive systems: An introduction to computational models of social life*. Princeton: Princeton University Press.

Miller, E. and Rice, A. K., (1967). *Systems of organization: Tasks and sentient groups and their boundary control*. London: Tavistock.

Mohanty, C. T. (2003). *Feminism without borders: Decolonizing theory, practicing solidarity*. Durham, NC: Duke University Press.

Montuori, A. (Ed.), (2015). *Journeys in complexity: Autobiographical accounts by leading systems and complexity thinkers*. New York: Routledge.

Morgan, G., (1993). Organisational choice and the new technology. In: E. L. Trist and H. Murray (Eds.), *The social engagement of the social sciences: A Tavistock anthology Vol. 2: The socio-technical perspective*. London and Philadelphia: University of Pennsylvania Press.

Mostafa, M., (2005). Factors affecting organizational creativity and innovativeness in Egyptian business organizations: An empirical investigation. *Journal of Management Development*, 24: 7–33.

Mumford, E., (1996). *Systems design: Ethical tools for ethical change*. London: Macmillan.

Mumford, E., (2003). *Redesigning human systems*. London: Idea Publishing Group.

Mumford, E., (2006). The story of socio-technical design: Reflections in its successes, failures and potential. *Information Systems Journal*, 16: 317–342.

Muthusamy, S. K., Senthil, K., and White Margaret, A., (2005). Learning and knowledge transfer in strategic alliances: A social exchange view. *Organization Studies*, 26(3): pp. 415-441.

Muthusamy, S. K., Wheeler, J. V., and Simmons, B. L., (2005). Self-managing work teams: Enhancing organizational innovativeness. *Organization Development Journal*, 23(3): 53–66. Available from: SSRN: https://ssrn.com/abstract=687892

Nagel, C., (2020). *Covid19 presents us with the 4th narcissistic blow to humankind: Not only leaders need to recollect their human qualities*. Offenbach am Main: Nagel & Company Consulting. Available from: http://www.nagelcompany.com/files/blog/essays/COVID19_as_the_4th_narcissistic_blow_to_humankind-Claudia_Nagel_April_2020.pdf

Netland, T. H., et al., (2008). *The new importance of socio-technical systems research on high-tech production systems*. SINTEF Technology and Society N-7465 Trondheim, Norway. Available from: https://www.researchgate.net/publication/254912675_The_new_importance_of_socio-technical_systems_research_on_high-tech_production_systems

Neumann, J. E., (1989). Why people don't participate in organisational change. *Research in Organizational Change and Development*, 3: 181–212.

Neumann, J. E., (1997). Negotiating entry and contracting. In: J. E. Neumann, K. Keller, and A. Dawson-Shepherd (Eds.) (1997), *Developing organisational consultancy*. London: Routledge.

Neumann, J. E., (1999). Systems psychodynamics in the service of political organizational change. In: R. French and R. Vince (Eds.), *Group relations, management, and organization*, Pgs. 54–69. Oxford, England: Oxford University Press.

Neumann, J. E., (2002). Preparing for succession and structural renewal in a religious community. Unpublished consultation report. Dr. Jean Neumann, Tavistock Institute London.

Neumann, J. E. and Bryant, D., (1989). *Organisational factors in shipping casualties*. Unpublished research report. London: The Tavistock Institute of Human Relations.

Neumann, J. E. and Hirschhorn, L., (1999). The challenge of integrating psychodynamic and organizational theory. *Human Relations*, 52(6): 683–695.

Neumann, J. E., Holti, R., and Standing, H., (1995). *Change everything at once! The Tavistock Institute's guide to developing teamwork in manufacturing*. Didcot Oxfordshire: Management Books 2000.

Neumann, J. E., Keller, K., and Dawson-Shepherd, A., (1997). *Developing organisational consultancy*. London: Routledge.

Neumann, J. E. and Sama, A., (2010). *Infrastructure for integrating health and social care*. Unpublished consultation report. Kent, UK: Canterbury Christ Church University.

News of companies that have gone bust in the UK (2020). Company Rescue. Available from: https://www.companyrescue.co.uk/guides-knowledge/news/

Newton, J., Long, S. and Sievers, B., (2006). *Coaching in depth. The organisational role analysis approach*. London: Karnac.

Nossal, B., (2007). *Psychodynamics and Consulting to Organisations in Australia*: Doctoral Thesis Available from: https://researchbank.rmit.edu.au/eserv/rmit:9775/Nossal.pdf

Nutkevitch, A. and Sher, M., (2006). Group relations conferences: Reviewing and exploring theory, design, role-taking and application. In: L. Brunner, A. Nutkevitch, and M. Sher (Eds.), *Group relations conferences: reviewing and exploring theory, design, role-taking and application*, Pgs. 3–13. London: Karnac.

Nystrom, P. C., Keshavamurthy, R., and Wilson, A. L., (2002). Organizational context, climate and innovativeness: Adoption of imaging technology. *Journal of Engineering and Technology Management*, 19: 221–247.

Obholzer, A., (1994). Authority, power and leadership. In: A. Obholzer and V. Z. Roberts, *The unconscious at work*, Pgs. 43–45. London and New York: Routledge.

Obholzer, A., (1994). Managing social anxieties in public sector organisations. In: *The unconscious at work: Individual and organisational stress in the human services*. London: Routledge.

Obholzer, A., (1999). Managing the unconscious at work. In: R. French and R. Vince (Eds.), *Group relations, management and organization*, Oxford: Oxford University Press.

Obholzer, A., (2001). The leader, the unconscious, and the management of the organisation (Pg. 196–215) In: J. Gould, L. Stapley, and M. Stein (Eds.), *The systems psychodynamics of organisations*, Pgs. 197–296. London: Karnac.

Obholzer, A. and Roberts, V. (Eds.), (1994). *The unconscious at work: Individual and organisational stress in the human services*. London: Routledge.

Obholzer, A. (1996), "Psychoanalytic contributions to authority and leadership issues", Leadership & Organization Development Journal, Vol. 17 No. 6, pp. 53–56.

Painter, B., (2009). STS Theory – From the Industrial to the Knowledge Age. In: http://moderntimesworkplace.com/good_reading/GRWorkRed/STS_Theory_-_From_Industrial_To_Knowledge_Age.pdf. Accessed 5 February 2019.

Palmer, B., (2002). The Tavistock paradigm: Inside, outside and beyond. In: R. D. Hinshelwood and M. Chiesa (Eds.), *Organisations, anxieties and defences*. London: Whurr.

Palmer, S., and Whybrow, A. (Eds.), (2007). Psychodynamic and systems-psychodynamic coaching. In: V. Z. Roberts & H. Brunning (Eds.), *Handbook of coaching psychology - a guide to practitioners*, Pgs. 253–277. London: Routledge.

Parsadh, A., (2020). *Why psychodynamically informed leadership is critical now and beyond COVID-19?* Available from: LinkedIn https://www.linkedin.com/pulse/why-psychodynamically-informed-leadership-critical-now-adrian-parsadh/

Parsons, T., (1951). *The social system*. New York: The Free Press.

Pasmore, W. A., Francis, C., Haldeman, J., and Shani, A., (1982). Sociotechnical systems: A North American reflection on empirical studies of the seventies. *Human Relations*, 35(12): 1179–1204.

Pasmore, W. A., (1985). Social science transformer: The socio-technical perspective. *Human Relations*, 48: 1–22.

Pasmore, W. A., (1988). *Designing effective organizations: The sociotechnical systems perspective*. New York: John Wiley.

Pasmore, W. A. and Woodman R. W. (Eds), (1989). *Research in organizational change and development*, Vol. 2, Pgs. 1–57. Greenwich, CT: JAI Press.

Pattison, N., (2020). Why mental health and wellbeing must be on the agenda. *HR Review*. Available from: https://www.hrreview.co.uk/analysis/neil-pattison-why-mental-health-and-wellbeing-must-be-on-the-agenda

Pava, C., (1983a). *Managing new office technology: An organizational strategy*. New York: Free Press.

Pava, C., (1983b). Designing managerial and professional work for high performance: A sociotechnical approach. *National Productivity Review*, 2: 126–135.

Pava, C., (1986a). *Managing new office technology: An organizational strategy*. New York: Free Press.

Pava, C., (1986b). Designing managerial and professional work for high performance: A sociotechnical approach. *National Productivity Review*, 2: 126–135.

Peirce, C. S., (1931). *The collected papers of Charles Sanders Peirce, Vol. I: The principles of philosophy*. Cambridge, MA: Harvard University Press.

Peters G. and Beishon, J. (Eds.), (1972). *Systems behaviour*. London: Harper and Row.

Petriglieri, G., (2017). Psychoanalyzing the World's Problems Won't Solve Them. Available from: https://hbr.org/2017/01/psychoanalyzing-the-worlds-problems-wont-help-us-solve-them. Accessed 24 January 2017.

Petriglieri, G. and Petriglieri, J. L., (2020). The return of the oppressed: A systems psychodynamic approach to organization studies. *The Academy of Management Annals*, 14(1), 411–449. Available from: https://sites.insead.edu/facultyresearch/research/doc.cfm?did=66021

Petriglieri, G., and Petriglieri, J. L., (2010). Identity workspaces: The case of business schools. *Academy of Management Learning & Education*, 9(1): 44–60.

Porra, J. and Hirscheim, R., (2007). A lifetime of theory and action on the ethical use of computers. A dialogue with Enid Mumford. *Journal of the Association for Information Systems*, 8(9): 467–478.

Prigogine I. and Stengers, I., (1984). *Order out of chaos*. London: Bantam.

Quine C. and Hutton, J. M., (1992). *Finding, Making and Taking the Role of Head Teacher*. Available from: https://www.grubbinstitute.org.uk/wp-content/uploads/2014/12/031_Integration-in-Behaviour.pdf

Reed, B. D. and Armstrong, D. G., (1988a). *Notes on professional management*. London: Grubb Institute.

Reed, B. and Armstrong, D., (1988b). *Professional management*. London: The Grubb Institute.

Revans, R., (2011). *ABC of action learning*. London: Routledge.

Reynolds, C. W., (1987). Flocks, herds, and schools: A distributed behavioural model. *Computer Graphics*, 21(4): 25–34.

Rice, A. K., (1953a). Book review: Human problems in technological change. *Human Relations*, 6(4): 411–412. https://doi.org/10.1177/001872675300600407

Rice, A. K., (1953b). Productivity and social organization in an Indian weaving shed: An examination of some aspects of the socio-technical system of an experimental automatic loom shed. *Human Relations*, 6(4): 297–329.

Rice, A. K., (1958). *Productivity and social organisation: The Ahmedabad experiment: Technical innovation, work organisation and management*. London: Tavistock Publications. [Reprinted 2001. Abingdon: Routledge. ISBN 0-415-26469-3.]

Rice, A. K., (1963). *The enterprise and its environment*. London: Tavistock. Publications.

Rice, A. K., (1965). *Learning for leadership: Interpersonal and intergroup relations*. London: Tavistock Publications. [Reprinted 1999, Karnac Books.]

Rickman, J., (1957). *Selected contributions to psychoanalysis*. London: Hogarth Press. [Reprinted 2003 with a new preface. London: Karnac Books.]

Riesenberg-Malcolm, R., (2001). Bion's Theory of containment. In: C. Bronstein (Ed.), *Kleinian Theory: A contemporary perspective*, Pgs. 165–180. London: Whurr.

Rioch, M. J., (1975). Group relations: Rationale and technique. In: A. D. Colman and W. H. Bexton (Eds.), *Group relations reader 1*, Pgs. 3–10. Washington: A. K. Rice Institute.

Roberts, V. Z. and Jarrett, M., (2006). What is the difference and what makes a difference, a comparative study of psychodynamic and non-psychodynamic approaches to executive coaching. In: Brunning H. (Ed.), *Executive coaching -systems psychodynamic perspective*. London: Karnac.

Roberts V.Z. & Brunning H., (2007). Psychodynamic and systems-psychodynamic coaching. In: Palmer S & Whybrow A., (Eds)., Handbook of coaching psychology-a guide to practitioners. Routledge p 253–277

Roethlisberger, F. J. and Dickson, W. J., (1939). *Management and the worker: An account of a research program conducted by the western electric company, Hawthorne works*. Chicago: Harvard University Press.

Rosenfeld, H., (1947). Analysis of a schizophrenic state with depersonalization. *The International Journal of Psycho-Analysis*, 28: 130–139. [Reprinted (1965) in Rosenfeld, *Psychotic States*. Hogarth, Pg. 13–33.]

Rosenfeld, H., (1952). Notes on the analysis of the super-ego conflict in an acute schizophrenic patient. *The International Journal of Psycho-Analysis*, 33: 111–131. [Reprinted (1965) in Rosenfeld, *Psychotic States*. Hogarth, Pg. 180–219.]

Russell, J., (2021). Self-managed work teams. Available from: https://russellconsultinginc.com/resources/whitepapers/the-disciplines-of-self-managed-work-teams-mastery-leads-to-self-management-success/

Sagoe, Isaac K. II. (1994). Why are self-managed Teams So Popular? *Journal for Quality and Participation*, 17(5): 64–67.

Samuels, A., (2020). Psychotherapy and politics: Learning from the political trickster. Paper presented at Psychoanalysis and the Public Sphere: Social Fault Lines.

Sandberg, P. R., (1995). Socio-technical design, trade union strategy and action research. *In:* E. Mumford, R Hirschheim, G. Fitzgerald, and A. T. WoodHarper (Eds.), *Research methods in information systems*. Amsterdam: North Holland.

Schafer, R., (2003). *Insight and interpretation. The essential tools of psychoanalysis*. London: Karnac.

Schein, E. (1988). *Process consultation, its role in organizational development*. Reading MA: Addison-Westley Publishing.

Schein, E., (2016). *Humble consulting: How to provide real help faster*. Oakland: Berrett-Koehler.

Schuler, D. and Namioka, A. E., (1993). *Participatory design: Principles and practices*. Mahwah, NJ: Lawrence Erlbaum Associates.

Schwarz, E., (1996). *Streams of systemic thought*. Neuchâtel, Switzerland. Available from: https://stream.syscoi.com/2019/06/10/some-streams-of-systemic-thought-schwarz-extended-durant-iigss-hadorn/

Scott, J., (2016 and 2017). *Exhibition: Object relations at reimagining human relations in our time*. Swiss Church London and Helmsley Arts Centre.

Segal, H., (1950). Some aspects of the analysis of a schizophrenic. *The International Journal of Psycho-Analysis*, 31: 268–278.

Segal, H., (1964). *Introduction to the work of Melanie Klein*. Heinemann: London [Revised edition Hogarth, (1973)].

Sentil, K., (2021) Why self-managing teams smarter than smartest leaders. Available from: https://www.linkedin.com/pulse/why-self-managing-teams-smarter-than-smartest-leaders-senthil-kumar

Shani, A.B. & Sena, J.A., (2000). "Knowledge Management and new product development: learning from a software development firm", Proceedings of the Third International. Conf. on Practical Aspects of Knowledge Management (PAKM2000), Basel, Switzerland.

Shapiro, E. R. and Carr, A. W., (1991). *Lost in familiar places: Creating new connections between the individual and society*. London: Yale University.

Sher, M., (2013). *The dynamics of change: Tavistock approaches to improving social systems*. London: Routledge.

Sher, M., (2017). *"It cannot be us; it must be them": Understanding and working with projective dynamics in the value chain helps to reduce blame, time, waste (inventory) and cost*. https://www.tavinstitute.org/projects/projective-dynamics-value-chain/

Sher, M., (2020). Organisational diagnosis. https://www.youtube.com/watch?v=y-vn9CE2sow. Accessed 10 September 2020.

Shevrin, H. and Dickman, S., (1980). The psychological unconscious: A necessary assumption for all psychological theory? *American Psychologist*, 35, 421–434.

Shirky, C., (2011). *Cognitive surplus: Creativity and generosity in a connected age*. London: Penguin.

Silver, J., (2001). *A constructive developmental approach to Tavistock group relations conference learning: A narrative study*. Unpublished Dissertation. Fielding Graduate Institute.

Silver, J. and Josselson, R., (2010). Epistemological lenses and group relations learning. *Organizational and Social Dynamics*, 10(2): 155–179.

Sitter, L., de, Hertog, J. den, and Eijnatten, F. van., (1990). *Simple organisations, complex jobs: The Dutch socio-technical approach*, Paper presented at the Annual Conference of the American Academy of Management, San Francisco.

Smith, M. Marco. B., Ball, P., and van der Meer R.,. (2008). Factors influencing an organisations ability to manage innovation: A structured literature review and conceptual model. *International Journal of Innovation Management*, 12: 655–676.

Sofer, C., (1961). *The organisation from Within: A comparative study of social institutions based on a sociotherapeutic approach*. London: Tavistock.

Sofer, C., (1972). *Organisations in theory and practice*. London: Heinemann

Sprigg, C. A., Jackson, P. R., and Parker, S. K., (2000). Production team working: The importance of interdependence and autonomy for employee strain and satisfaction. *Human Relations*, 53(11): 1519–1543.

Stacey, R. D., (1991). *The chaos frontier: Creative strategic control for business*. Oxford: Butterworth Heinemann.

Stacey, R. D., (1992). *Managing the unknowable: The strategic boundaries between order and chaos*. San Francisco: Jossey Bass.

Stacey, R. D., (1993). *Strategic management and organizational dynamics*. London: Pitman.

Stacey, R. D., (2000). *Strategic management and organisational dynamics: The challenge of complexity*. 3rd ed. London: Pearson Education.

Stacey, R. D., (2001). *Complex responsive processes in organizations: Learning and knowledge creation*. London: Routledge.

Stacey, R. D., (2003a). *Complexity and group processes: A radically social understanding of individuals*. New York: Brunner-Routledge.

Stacey, R. D., (2003b). Learning as an activity of interdependent people. *Learning Organization*, 10: 325–331.

Stacey, R. D., Griffin, D., and Shaw, P., (2000). *Complexity and management: Fad or a radical challenge to systems thinking?* London: Routledge.

Stapley, L. F., (1996). *The personality of the organisation. A psycho-dynamic explanation of culture and change.* London: Free Association.

Stapley, L.F., (2006). Individuals, groups and organisations beneath the surface. London: Karnac.

Stein, M., (1997). Envy and leadership. *European Journal of Work and Organisation Psychology*, 6(4): 453–465.

Stein, M., (2000a). The risk taker as shadow: A psychoanalytic view of the collapse of Barings bank. *Journal of Management Studies*, 37(8), 1215–1229.

Stein, M., (2000b). After Eden: Envy and the defences against anxiety paradigm. *Human Relations*, 53(2): 193–211.

Stein, M., (2003). Unbounded irrationality: Risk and organizational narcissism at long term capital management. *Human Relations*, 56(5): 523–540.

Stein, M., (2004). The critical period of disasters: Insights from sense-making and psychoanalytic theory. *Human Relations*, 57(10): 1243–1261.

Stein, M., (2005). The Othello Conundrum: The inner contagion of leadership. *Organization Studies*, 26(9): 1405–1419.

Stein, M., (2007). Oedipus Rex at Enron: Leadership, Oedipal struggles, and organizational collapse. *Human Relations*, 60(9): 1387–1410.

Stiehm, J. H. and Townsend, N., (2002). *The U.S. Army War college: Military education in a democracy*, Pg. 6. Philadelphia: Temple University Press.

Stokes, J., (1994). The unconscious at work in groups and teams: Contributions from the work of Wilfred Bion. In: A. Obholzer and V. Zagier Roberts (Eds.), *The unconscious at work: individual and organizational stress in the human services*, Pgs. 19–27. London: Routledge.

Stokes, J., (1994). What is unconscious in organisation? In: R. Casemore et al. (Eds.), *What makes consultancy work*. London: South Bank University Press.

Stokoe, P., (2011). The healthy and the unhealthy organisation: How can we help teams to remain effective? In: A. Rubitel and D. Reiss (Eds.), *Containment in the community: Frameworks for thinking about antisocial behaviour and mental health*. London: Karnac Books.

Stokoe, P., (2020). *The curiosity drive: How inquisitive thinking develops the mind and protects society.* Bicester: Phoenix Publishing House.

Strati, A., (1999). *Organization and aesthetics.* Thousand Oaks, CA: Sage.

Sullivan,. H. S., (1953). *Interpersonal theory of psychiatry.* New York: W.W. Norton.

Sullivan, C. C., (2002). Finding the Thou in the I: Countertransference and parallel process analysis in organizational research and consultation. *The Journal of Applied Behavioural Science*, 38(3): 375–393.

Susman, G. I. (1976). *Autonomy at work: A sociotechnical analysis of participative management.* New York: Praeger Publishers.

Tang, H. K., (1999). An inventory of organizational innovativeness. *Technovation*, 19: 41–52.

Tavistock Clinic., (1945). Memorandum for Dr. Alan Gregg on Proposed Developments in Social Psychiatry at the Tavistock Clinic, London; An appreciation of the present situation and a request for financial assistance for specific purposes. In: *Rockefeller Foundation Archives. Sleepy Hollow.* New York: Rockefeller Archive Center, 1945 Box 196, series 200R, Record Group (RG) 1.1.

Teram, E. (1991). Interdisciplinary teams and the control of clients: A sociotechnical perspective. *Human Relations*, 44: 343–356.

Thamhain, Hans J., (1990). Managing technologically innovative team efforts toward new product success. *The Journal of Product Innovation Management*, 7: 5–19.

Trist, E., Higgin, G., Murray, H., and Pollock, A., (1963). *Organisational choice: Capabilities of groups at the coal face under changing technologies: the loss, rediscovery and transformation of a work tradition*. London: Tavistock Publications.

Trist, E., (1981). *The evolution of socio-technical systems*. Occasional Paper, 2. Ontario Quality of Working Life Center. Available from: https://www.google.com/search?q=trist+1981&rlz=1C1GCEU_enGB827GB837&oq=&aqs=chrome.0.69i59i45 0l8.7779433847j0j7&sourceid=chrome&ie=UTF-8

Trist, E., (1983). Referent organizations and the development of inter-organizational domains. *Human Relations*, 36: 269–284. (See Trist, E. L., 'Reference Organizations and the Development of Inter-Organizational Domains', Vol. III: *The Socio-Ecological Perspective*, Tavistock Anthology. University of Pennsylvania Press.) Also available from http://www.moderntimesworkplace.com/archives/archives.html

Trist, E., (1985). Working with Bion in the 1940s: The group decade. In: M. Pines (Ed.), *Bion and group psychotherapy*, Pgs. 1–46. London: Routledge and Kegan Paul.

Trist, E. L., and Bamforth, K. W., (1951). Some social and psychological consequences of the Longwall method of coal-getting. *Human Relations*, 4(1): 3–38.

Trist E., Emery F., and Murray. H., (eds) (1997) *The social engagement of social science*, Vol. 3. The socio-ecological perspective. Philadelphia: University of Pennsylvania Press.

Trist, E., and Murray, H., (1990a). Historical overview: The foundation and development of the Tavistock Institute to 1989. In: E. Trist and H. Murray (Eds.), *The social engagement of social science: A Tavistock anthology*, Vol. 1. Philadelphia: University of Pennsylvania Press. Available from: http://www.moderntimesworkplace.com/archives/archives.html

Trist, E. and Murray, H. (Eds.), (1990b). *The social engagement of social science, Volume 1: The socio-psychological perspective. A Tavistock anthology*. London: Free Association Books. Available from: www.moderntimesworkplace.com

Trist, E. and Murray, H. (Eds.), (1993). *The social engagement of social science: Volume II: The socio-technical perspective*. Philadelphia: University of Pennsylvania Press. Available from: http://www.moderntimesworkplace.com/archives/archives.html

Trist, B. and Murray, H., (1997) *The social engagement of the social sciences: A Tavistock anthology London Vol. 3: The socio-ecological perspective*. Philadelphia: University of Pennsylvania Press.

Trist, E. L. and Sofer, C., (1959). *Exploration in group relations*. London: Tavistock Institute of Human Relations and Leicester University Press.

Tronto, J., (1995). Caring as the basis for radical political judgments. *Hypatia*, 10: 141–149.

Truex, D., Baskerville, R., and Klein, H., (1999). Growing systems in an emergent organization *Communications ACM*, 42(8): 117–123.

Turquet, P., (1974). Leadership: The individual and the group. In: G. S. Gibbard (Ed.), *Analysis of groups*. San Francisco: Jossey-Bass.

Turquet, P. M., (1975). Threats to identity in the large group. In: L. Kreeger, (Ed.), *The large group: Dynamics and therapy*. London: Constable.

van Alstyne, Marshall, (1997). The State of Network Organization: A Survey in Three Frameworks. *Journal of Organizational Computing and Electronic Commerce*, 7(2–3): 83–151.

Vince, R. and French, R. (Eds.), (1999) *Group relations, management, and organization*. Oxford: Oxford University Press.

Waldrop, M., (1992). *Complexity: The emerging science at the edge of chaos*. London: Penguin.
Walker, E. M., (1995). *Cultural identity and intergroup relations: A look at the truth and consequences of 'diversity'*. Paper presented at the Twelfth Scientific Meeting of the A. K. Rice Institute, Washington DC, May 10–13, 1995.
Wallach, T., (2014). What do participants learn at group relations conferences? *Organizational and Social Dynamics*, 14(1): 13–38.
Weatherill, R., (1994). *Cultural Collapse*. London: Free Association Books.
Weber, L., (2017). The end of employees. *The Wall Street Journal*. Available from: https://www.wsj.com/articles/the-end-of-employees-1486050443
Wegner D. M., et al., (1987). Paradoxical effects of thought suppression. *Journal of Personality and Social Psychology*, 53: 5–13.
Weick, K. and Ashford, S., (2001). Learning in organizations. In: F. Jablin and L. Putnam (Eds.), *The new handbook of organizational communication: Advance in theory, research, and methods*, Pgs. 704–731. Thousand Oaks, CA: Sage.
Weisbord, M. R., (1987). *Productive workplaces*. San Francisco: Jossey-Bass.
Weisbord, M. and Janoff, S., (1995). *Future search: An action guide to finding common ground in organizations and community*. San Francisco: Berrett-Koehler.
Wells, L., (1980). The group-as-a-whole: A systemic socio-analytical perspective on interpersonal and group relations. In: C.P. Alderfer and C.L. Cooper (eds). Advances in experiential social processes, 2: 165–198.
Wells, L. (1980). The group as a whole: A systemic psychoanalytic perspective on interpersonal and group relations. In: C. P. Alderfer & C. Cooper (Eds.), *Advances in experiential social processes*, Vol. 2, Pgs. 50–85. New York: John Wiley.
Western, S., (2019). *Leadership: A critical text*. London: Sage.
Western, S., (2020). Covid-19: An intrusion of the real: The unconscious unleashes its truth. Available from: Academia.edu www.academia.edu/42201252/Covid-19_An_intrusion_of_the_Real_The_unconscious_unleashes_its_Truth
Wheelan, S. A., (1994). *Group processes: A developmental perspective*. Boston: Allyn & Bacon.
Wheelan, S., Michael, T., Abraham, M., Krasick, C., Verdi, A., McKeage, R., Johnston, F., and Whiteling, V., (1991). *The group relations conference as a laboratory for the study of organizational and societal processes: Methods, findings and a call for collaboration*. Paper presented at the Transformations in Global and Organizational Systems: Changing Boundaries in the 90's. The tenth scientific meeting of the A. K. Rice Institute, St. Louis, Missouri.
Wheelan, S. A., Verdi, A., and McKeage, R., (1994). *The group development observation systems: Origins and applications*. Philadelphia: PEP Press.
White, A., (2014). *Psychoanalysis goes to war (eventually) a prehistory of the Tavistock Institute*, A talk by Alice White. Available from: https://www.tavinstitute.org/projects/psychoanalysis-goes-war-eventually/
Whittle, S. R. and Stevens, R. C. (Eds.), (2013). *Changing organizations from within: Roles, risks, and consultancy relationships*. Farnham: Gower.
Whitworth, B., (2009), A brief introduction to socio-technical systems. In: Claude Ghaoui (Ed.), *Encyclopedia of information science and technology*, 2nd ed., Pg. 394–400. Hershey: Idea Group Publishing.
Wilson, B., (2001). *Soft systems methodology – conceptual model building and its contribution*. Hoboken, New Jersey: J.H. Wiley.
Winby, S., and Mohrman, S. A., (2018). Digital sociotechnical system design. *The Journal of Applied Behavioral Science*, 54(4): 399–423.
Winnicott, D., (1965). *Maturational Processes and the Facilitating Environment: Studies in the Theory of Emotional Development*. London: Hogarth Press.

Winnicott, D. W., (1971). *Therapeutic consultations in child psychiatry.* London: Hogarth Press and the Institute of Psycho-Analysis.

Winnicott, D., (1990) *Maturational processes and the facilitating environment: Studies in the theory of emotional development.* London: Karnac Books.

Wright, K., (2009). *Mirroring and attunement: Self realisation in psychoanalysis and art.* Hove: Routledge.

Zaleznik, A., (1989). *The managerial mystique: Restoring leadership in business.* New York, NY: Harper Collins.

Zwetsloot, Gerard, (2001). The management of innovation by frontrunner companies in environmental management and health and safety. *Environmental Management and Health,* 12: 207–214.

Index

Note: *Italicized* page numbers refer to figures, **bold** page numbers refer to tables

A. K. Rice Institute 196
abductive logic 102–103
Abraham, K. 16
Ackoff, R. 35, 176
action learning sets (ALSs) 123–127, 161–162
Advanced Organisational Consultation (AOC) Programme 17
aesthetic practice 158–160
Ahmedabad Manufacturing and Calico Printing Co. 15
Alderfer, C.P. 221
Allcorn, S. 16
alpha function 74, 82, 84
Ambrose, A. 16
anal stage 66
anxiety: and change 57; container for 7; and containment 226, 269–270; definition of 94; existential 175–176; and group relations 230; institutional 226–227; institutional defences as source of 241; secondary 241; in teams and groups 217
anxiety-culture-defence model 231
Appelbaum 256–257
Aram, E. 1
Archer, C. 1
Armstrong, D. 1, 16, 88, 115–116, 116–117, 119–135, 130, 131–133, 136–151, 145–150, 156, 187–193
Arnaud, G. 65
Arts 156–160
associative unconscious 101–102
authority: definition of 94, 167; and open systems theory 167; recognition of 171–172
automobile manufacture 257–258
awareness of time 172

Bain, A. 16, 128, 186, 202, 236–237
Balint, M. 66
Bamforth, K. 19, 27, 44, 250–251
Bánáthy, B.H 34
Banet, A.G., Jr. 180
basic assumption activity 154
basic assumption dependency (b/aD) 20, 128
basic assumption fight/flight (b/aF/F) 20, 128
basic assumption pairing (b/aP) 20, 128
basic assumptions group mentality 129–131
basic assumptions mentality 127–129
basic assumptions theory 82, 92
Bastedo, M.N. 40
Bateson, G. 35, 198
Bayer 15
Bayswater Institute 178, 181
Bazalgette, J. 98
Beckhard, R. 141
Benjamin, J. 76, 91
Bennis, W.G. 217, 218
Benson, A. 1
Bion, W. 7, 15, 20, 24, 27, 49, 69, 74, 81, 87, 115, 117, 187, 226, 266; basic assumption groups 154; *Experiences in Groups and other papers* 119, 131–132, 187–190, 193; group mentality 154; Northfield experiments 119–123; theory of group behavior 122; theory of groups 119–135, 152; theory of thinking 82–83; work group mentality 129–131; work groups 153–154
BlackLivesMatters movement 157

Index

blindness of faith 148
Bohm, D. 35, 101
boundaries: definition of 94; external 39; internal 39; in open systems model 40, 167; recognition of 171–172
boundary-crossing systems 256
Bowlby, J. 15
Brazaitis, S.J. 152–153
Bridger, H. 15, 121, 178, 181
Brissett, L. 1, 116, 164–179
British Operational Research Society 15
Browne, L. 15
Brunning, H. 1, 93–113
Burnes, B. 15
Butler, J. 76
buzz sessions 140

Calico Mills 19
Capra, F. 34, 35
Care 75, 77
Carr, W. 16, 18
Centre for Applied Social Research (CASR) 15
Centre for Organisational and Operational Research (COOR) 15
change: acceptance of 172–173; and anxiety 57; processes 57
Chapman, J. 16
Checkland, P. 35, 42
Chen, D. 36
Chern, A. 254
Chid, C. 1
chief executive's group (CEG) 161
Chiesa, M. 230, 251
China 31–33
Churchill, W. 115
Cilliers, F. 21, 22, 129, 218
circular model of organisational development intervention. 59
Civil Resettlement Units (CRUs) 14
climate change project 182–186
coaching: in the Covid world *111*; executive 107–112; for leadership 93–97; models *108*
coal mining 19
Colman, A.D. 217, 218
complexity theory 30
Confucianism 31–32
conjectural knowledge 103
consciousness 58, 93, 113, 166
consultancy relationship 87
consultant-client relationship 117

consultations, inter-group 172–174
consultative stance 182
container for anxieties 7
container-contained model 82, 117, 226, 269
containing leadership 89
containment: and anxiety 226, 269–270; in consultancy 83; definition of 82; and emotion 239–240
contingency theorists 40
Cooke, B. 15
corporate communications 162
countertransference 8, 51, 81–82, 92, 116, 166, 235–236, 272–273; *see also* transference
Covid-19 pandemic 110–111, 157–158, 241–243
Craigmillar Festival Society 192
critical systems thinking 36
The Crowd (Le Bon) 121
curiosity 83
Cyahogu shipping disaster 242
Czander, W. 21–22, 26–27, 47–48, 49–51, 68, 74, 205

Da Vinci, L. 157
Dartington, T. 18
Davar, E. 150
Davin, A. 103
Davis, L. 258
De Maré, P. 121
De Vries, M. F. R. K. 23
Deepening Creative Practice programme 156, 157, 160
defences against anxiety 226–244; case example 231–232; creation and maintenance of social defence system 238–239; definition of 167; and emotion 239–240; and enactment 234; and institutional anxieties 226–227; and introjection 233–236; learning spaces 236–237; and organisational life 239–240; overcoming resistance 237–238; overview 226–227; and reflection 236–237; and social systems 240–241; social systems as 261; and splitting 235–236; success factors in 233; *see also* anxiety
defensive mechanisms 164
delegation 167
dependency 152
depressive position (DP) 265
Diamond, M. 16

Dicks, H, 14, 15
double task events 181
Doyle, C. 103
dreams 102
drive theory 76
Duberley, J. 5

eco-systems 44–45
Edinburgh International Arts Festival 192
ego 234
Eisold, K. 49–51
Elias, N. 156
embodying role event 174
Emery, F. 15, 19, 35, 140–141, 254, 256
Emery, M. 44–45
emotional experience 88
emotional links 82
emotional pain 71, 79
enactment 234
environment 9, 167
envy 74–75, 265
epistemophilic instinct 132
equifinality 21, 34
ethical imagination 156, 188–189
Ettinger, B. 77
Evaluation Development Review Unit (EDRU) 15
exclusion dynamics 185
executive coaching 107–112; coaching 107–108; and Covid-19 110–111; post-Covid-19 111–112; six domains of *109*; steady state 108–109; systems psychodynamics coaching 107–108
existential anxiety 175–176
existential primary task 94
Experiences in Groups and other papers (Bion) 119, 120, 131–132, 187–188, 193
external boundaries 39
extreme ultraviolet light (EUV) 145

Fairbairn, R. 66, 67–68, 78
faith 148
Fayol, H. 40
Feedback 36, 38
feminist psychoanalysis 75–77
Fenichell, O. 152
fight-flight 152
Fisher 83
Flood, R.L. 35
Ford, H. 258
formal task 94
Forster, M. 258
Fotaki, M. 1, 65, 75–77

Foucault, M. 76, 78
Foulkes, S.H. 121
Fowler, R. 156
Fraher, A.L. 17, 19
free association 86
French, R. 16, 129
Freud, S. 21, 24, 66–69, 76, 157, 234, 267, 268–269
Frohman, A. 58–59
Future Research 141
Future Search 142

Gabriel, Y. 16, 23
Geller, M.H. 217, 218
general management system 256
general practitioners 161
genital stage 66
Gharajedaghi, J. 21
Gilmore, T. 16, 234
Ginzberg, C. 103
Glacier Metal Company 6, 15, 18, 229, 237, 248, 250
glacier project 18–19
Gold, M. 181
Gosling, J. 1
Gould, L. 2, 6, 18–19, 47, 68–69, 128, 193
Green, Z. 169
group behaviour theory 122–123
group dynamics 115–118, 134–135
group mentality 122, 154
group psychology 234
group relations: applications of 152–153; as art and craft 177; consultative stance 182; contributions of 164–179, 179–201; and defences against anxiety 230; definition of 188; dimensions of *166*; double task events 181; existential anxiety and 175–176; length 182; organisational applications of 152–153; and organisational dilemma 182–186; primary tasks 181; social applications of 152–153; social dreaming matrix 180; and systems psychodynamics 266–267; thinking 152; training 197
group relations conferences 164–166, 191, 203; aims of 169; characteristics of consulting staff 195; design and practice 27, 134; difficulties in 193–194; emotional nature of 197–198; issues in designing training events 197; large study groups 168–169; learning in 196; long-term impact of 195–196;

organisational experience and 165–166; pedagogic style of 197; plenaries 168; primary task of 152–153; research 194–199; review and application groups 169; small study groups 168; *see also* Leicester Conference
Group Relations Programme 17
group relations theory 19–21, 90, 116–117, 133, 139
Group Relations Training Programme (GRTP) 21
groups 7, 20, 21; anxiety in 218; basic assumptions mentality 127–129; and organisational life 136; working with 136–151, 152–163
Grubb Institute 93, 101
Guttmann, D. 220, 221

H drive 83–84
Halton, W. 69, 70, 72, 174
Hammond. D. 34
Hampton, M.C. 128
hard systems 35–36
Harding, N. 77
Hargreaves, R. 14, 15
Harris, R.T. 141
hate 82
Hayden, C. 180
Healthy Organisation model 85
Heiddeger, M. 177
Heimann, P. 234
Henrick, I. 268
Hills, D. 1, 197
Hillsborough Football Stadium disaster 242
Hinshelwood, R.D. 66, 228, 231, 251
Hirschborn, L. 16, 26, 97, 227
Hoggett, P. 10
Holcombe, J. 156
Hollymoor Hospital 120
Holti, R. 252–253
Huffington, C. 16
human behavior approach 43
human development, phases of 167
Human Relations (Chern) 16, 254
Human Resources Centre (HRC) 15
human resources (HR) 161
Hunt, J. 221
Husserl, E. 177

identification 89
identity 94
inclusion dynamics 185

individuals, working with 93–113
Industrial Productivity Committee 16–18
Industrial Welfare Society 140
inputs 167
'inside-out' perspective 22–23
Institute of Operational Research (IOR) 15
institutional anxieties 226–227
institutional theorists 40
integrated perspectives: environmental approach 43–44; process approach 43–44; and systems theory 43; theories 43–44
inter-group behaviour 170–171; constructive inter-group exchange and 171–172
inter-group dynamics 172–173
inter-group event 169–170, 183–184
inter-group process 173–174; embodying role event 174; management of resources event 174; marketplace event 174; presence-in-absence event 174; whole system events 173–174
inter-group relations 170
internal boundaries 39
internal objects 74, 78
internal referent group (IRG) 161
An Introduction to Systems Psychodynamics: Consultancy Research & Training (Lawlor and Sher) 1, 27
Introjection 82–83, 89, 117, 142–145, 166, 233–234
introjective identification 73–74, 142–145, 167
Izod, K. 90–91

Jackson, M.C. 35
James, W. 177
Jaques, E. 6, 15, 27, 71, 74, 117, 227, 228–230, 233–234, 238–239
Jarrett, M. 107
Johnson, P. 5
joint optimisation 262–263
Judge, M.-Y. C. 1

Kahn, R. 40, 44
Katz, D. 40, 44
K-drive 83–84
Keats, J. 102
key variances 255–256
Khaleelee, O. 1, 18
Klein, M. 66, 74, 76, 78, 122, 152, 181, 187, 196, 269; depressive position

69–71; epistemophilic instinct 132; object relations theory 21, 68; organisational life 239–240; paranoid schizoid position 69–71
knowing 82
Kolb, D. 58–59
Koortzen, P. 21, 22, 129, 218
Krantz, J. 16, 27, 234
Kuhn, T.S. 5

L drive 83–84
Laban, R. 157
Lacan, J. 76
large group intervention 140–141
large study groups 168–169
Lawlor, D. 2, 178
Lawrence, G. 40, 102, 111–112, 128, 130, 133, 156, 220, 268
Lawrence, P. 16, 44
Le Bon, G. 121
leadership 167, 211–214; coaching for 93–97; containing 89
Lear, J. 133
learning from experience 84
learning spaces 236–237
Lectio Divina 147–149
Leicester Conference 21, 134, 157, 175; emotional nature of 197–198; pedagogic style of 197; primary task of 164; see also group relations conferences
Leicester Conferences – A Working Conference for the study of organisational life (Bion) 7
Leiper, R. 11
Leith, M. 141
Leonard, A. 35
level III training 198
Levinson, D.J. 220
Lewin, K. 15, 16, 20, 35, 142
Lewis, C.S. 175
linking 82
Lippitt, F. 142
Loewenthal, K. 11
Long, S. 1, 16, 93–113, 221, 229–230
Lorsch, J. 44
love 82
Luff, M. 15
Lyth, I,M. 18

Main, T.F. 121
Malan, D.H. 197
management group 174
management of resources event 174

Massachusetts Institute of Technology (MIT) 16
Mathur, A. 177
matrixial borderspace 77
Maturana, H. 35
Mayo, E. 40
McCollom, M. 221
McCormick, D.W. 220
Me-ness (b/aM) 128, 129
Menninger, K.A. 268
mental images 88
Menzies Lyth, I. 15, 27, 52, 57, 116, 117, 168, 186, 191, 193, 202, 226–228; defences against anxiety 240; institutional defences as a source of secondary anxiety 241; on organisational life 239–240; social defences 238; on splitting 235
Mersky, R.R. 234
metaphors 10
Midgley, G. 35–36
Miller, E. 3, 6, 19, 21, 26, 40, 58, 91–92, 116, 157–158, 160, 170–171, 173, 197, 198, 216, 251
Miner, H. 176
mining industry 250–251
Molenkamp, R.J. 169, 180
Montouri, A. 34
Moore, G.E. 54
Moore's law 54
Morelli 103
Morgan, G. 44
mother-infant relationship 67–68, 78, 86
Mumford, E. 253–255, 258–259
Murray, H. 9, 10–11, 13, 16, 254

Nagel, C. 110
National Health Service 14
National Training Laboratories 16, 20
neighbouring systems 256
Neumann, J.E. 17, 18, 59, 205, 258
neurosis 189
normative task 94
Northfield Military Hospital 115, 119–123
nursing training programme 18–19

Obholzer, A. 1, 74, 116, 194, 230, 266
object relations 122; basic concepts in 66–67; definition of 66; development of 67–69; history of 67–69; and splitting 66, 67
object relations theory 21, 26
objects 78

occupational health 161
official task 94
One-ness (b/aO) 128–129
one-team strategy 161, 162
open exploration 146
open systems 21, 26, 37–39, 65, 139; boundaries in 40; development of 252; diagram 42
opens systems theory (OST) 19, 29, 37, 40, 167
oral stage 66
Ordowich, C. 1
organisation experience 165–166
organisational consultancy 116, 208–209; activities 205; case example 207–214; core concepts of 216–217; difficulties 204–205; dinners 208; and education 210; goals of 206; impressions 213; language in 208; and leadership 211–212, 213–214; methodology 215–216; motives of participants 209–211; orgnisational role consultations 203; place of process 215; recommendations 214; scope of 202–203; structure of 207–208; supports in 208; system psychodynamic approaches to 186–187; systems psychodynamics model of 202–225, 270–273; unconscious processes in 215–216; working methods 205–206
organisational design 253–254
organisational development consultancy cycle 58–59
organisational development (OD) 140
organisational dilemma 182–186
organisational functioning 265–266
organisational life 136, 265–266
organisational role analysis (ORA) 97–99, 101–107; and abductive logic 102–104; aims of 101; and associative unconscious 101–102; case examples 103, 104; conducting 105–106; defined 101; and socioanalysis 104; and transforming experience model 105; use in organisations 106
organisational role consultation (ORC) 93, 113, 203; and group relations conferences 203
organisation-in-the-mind 88, 93, 97, 98–100, 113
organisations 21, 26; open systems 29, 37–40, 139; primary tasks 38, 39–40; as a social system 139

organization functioning 205
Ortega y Gasset, J. 177
outputs 167
'outside-in' perspective 22–23

Painter, B. 1
pairing 152
Palmer, B. 7, 49
paranoid schizoid position, depressive position 69–71
paranoid schizoid (PS) 265
Parsons, T. 34
Participative Design Workshop process 141
Passmore, W. 254
Peirce, C. 102
personal maturity 218
person/role/organisation (P/R/O) model 109
Petriglieri, G. 22–23
phases of human development, phases of 167
phenomenological primary task 94
pictures-in-the-mind 88, 89
plenaries 168
post-Covid-19 111–112
post-traumatic stress disorders (PTSD) 119
presence-in-absence event 174
Prigogine, I. 6, 35
primary tasks 10–11, 38, 39–40, 92, 94, 181
projection 72, 82, 117, 166, 233–234
projective identification 70–71, 72–73, 167
psychoanalysis 3, 65–79; applications of 81–92; emotional pain 71; envy 74–75; feminist 75–77; introjective identification 73–74; object relations 66–69; overview 65–66; paranoid schizoid position 69–71; projective identification 72–73; splitting 71–72; and systems psychodynamics 83–87; unconscious 69
psychoanalytic theory 21, 26, 166; envy 265; organisational functioning 265–266; organisational life 265–266; spoiling 265; unconscious 264–265

Quine, C. 98

Rawlings, J. 15
reflection 236–237
relational 90–91; terrain 90; turn 91

representation 167
resource dependency theorists 40
resource group 174
Revans, R. 35
revelation, politics of *112*
reverie 74
review and application groups 169, 180, 203
Rice, A.K. 6, 14, 19, 24–25, 27, 39–40, 122, 140, 170–171, 173, 178, 188, 250–251, 257
Rickman, J. 119–121, 189
Roberts, V.Z. 107, 230
Rockefeller Foundation 15
role 94, 167
role consultation 99–100, 113
Royal Army Medical Corps 121
Russell, J. 136

Sagoe, I.K. 137
salvation, politics of *112*
Schindler-Rainman, E. 142
scientific management 43
Scott, J. 1, 115, 116, 152–163, 157
Search Conferences 142–145
secondary anxiety 241
Self-Help Alliance project 15
self-managed teams 136
self-regulating work groups 249–250
self-regulation 38
Senge, P. 34, 44
sentient systems 170–171
shell shock 119
Shell UK 15, 258
Shepard, H.A. 217, 218
Sher, M. 2, 25, 178
Short Course Intervention 84
Simon, H. 44
Simpson, P. 129
Skogstad, W. 231
small study groups 168
social defence theory 18–19; and anxiety 230; case example 231–232; creation and maintenance of social defence system 238–239; and enactment 234; and group relations 230; history 227–228; Jacques's role in development of 227; learning spaces 236–237; Menzies Lyth's role in development of 227–228; and organisational life 239–240; origins of 227–230; overcoming resistance 237–238; and projection 233–236; and reflection 236–237; and splitting 235–236; success factors in 233; working with social defences 236–237
social defences 202
social dreaming 102, 133, 156; matrix 180
The Social Engagement of Social Science: The Socio-Technical Perspective (Murray) 254
social life theory 76
social structures 251
social systems 117, 240–241, 261
socio-ecological domain 9–10
socio-psychological domain 9–10
socio-technical systems (STS) 9–11, 19, 44–45, 65, 91, 247–260; basics of 248–249; cultural level 253; development of 252; and group relations 139; history 249; joint optimisation 262–263; logistical and cognitive level 253; in mining industry 250–251; organisational consultancy 254–256; organisational design 253–254; political and economic level 253; psychodynamics level 253; real life story 247–248; research and consultancy in 251–253; self-regulating work groups in 249–250, 256–257; and social structures 251; and structured work design 257–258; thinking 30; variations in analysis 258; work design 262–263
sociotherapy 92
Sofer, C. 6, 13, 23–24
soft systems 36
sophisticated group 20
spiritual drift 190
splitting 56–57, 67, 70, 71–72, 78, 234, 264
spoiling 265
Stacey, R.D. 6
Stafford Beer, A. 35
steady state 108–109
Stein, M. 1, 241–243
Stokoe, P. 1, 81–92
Stradling, H. 1, 115, 116, 152–163
strangeness 148
Stroup, W. 36
sub-systems 37, 184–185
Sullivan, A. 218
Sullivan, C.C. 16
Susman, G.I. 249
Sutherland, J.D. 15
Swanson, R.A. 34
system-environment interactions 36
systems 29–30, 34–35; concept 43; properties 42–43

Systems of Organisation (Miller and Rice) 19
systems psychodynamics 5, 30, 47–60; application of 263–264; and capacity for reflection 205–206; case study 54–56; coaching 107–108; consultancy 48–53; core concepts of 7; as distinct paradigm 261–262; geneaology of 4; group relations 266–267; multi-disciplinary and multi-theoretical nature of 5; and organisational consultancy 202–225; organisational development consultancy cycle 58–59; overview 1–3; paradigm 3–7; as protection from risk 261; splitting phenomena 56–57; working methods 49–53
systems psychodynamics coaching, post-Covid-19 111–112
systems psychodynamics consultancy 186–187, 263–264, 270–273; activities 205; aims of 273; and capacity for reflection 205–206; case example 207–214; constructs used in 223–224; core concepts of 202–225; counter-transference in 272–273; dinners 208; ecological domain 274; and education 210; formal and informal consultations 208–209; goals of 206; impressions 213; information gathered in 223; language in 208; and leadership 211–212, 213–214; methodology 215–216; motives of participants 209–211; orgnisational role consultations 203; place of process 215; psychoanalytical domain 274; rationale and hypotheses 217–218; recommendations 214; roles and responsibilities of 271–272; roles of consultants 222; scope of 202–203; social domain 274; stance 218–220; steps in 223; structure of 207–208; supports in 208; team development interventions in 220–222; team diagnosis in 220–222; for teams and groups 217; transference in 272–273; unconscious processes in 215–216, 273–274; understanding and testing from inside 273–274
Systems Psychodynamics: Innovative Approaches to Change, Whole Systems & Complexity 1
systems psychodynamics perspective 21–22
Systems Psychodynamics: Theorist and Practitioner Voices from the Field 2

systems science 34
systems theory 3, 34–35; definition of 36–37; goals of 34; and integrated perspectives 43
systems thinking 29, 32, 34–35; as a conceptual framework 36; socio-technical 30; waves of 35–36

TAO (task, authority, organisation) 175
Taoism 32, 175
tasks 40, 94, 167; double task events 181; existential primary 94; formal 94; normative 94; official 94; phenomenological primary 94; primary 10–11, 38, 39–40, 92, 94, 181; sentient systems and 170–171
Tavistock and Portman NHS Trust 1
Tavistock Clinic 1, 13, 14, 15, 187
Tavistock Group 16
Tavistock group 187
Tavistock group consultants 23–25
Tavistock Institute 14–15, 140, 141; in China 31–33; coal mining 19; early work 16–18; glacier project 18–19; group relations theory 19–21; history of 13–25; income 15; key figures 15–16; major projects 18; nursing training programme 18–19; opens systems theory 19; research units 15; social defence theory 18–19; sociotechnical systems 19
Tavistock Institute of Medical Psychology 1
Tavistock Primer II 180
team(s): anxiety in 218; development interventions 220–221; diagnosis 220–221
teamwork 40
temporary safe environment 7
territory 40
textile mills 257–258
thirdness 76
thoughts 87–88
time 40
time awareness 172
transactions 40
transference 8, 51, 81–82, 92, 116, 166, 272–273; *see also* countertransference
transformations 167
Transforming Experience in Organisations (Long) 105
transforming experience model 105
trans-subjectivity 77

Trist, E. 9, 10–11, 13, 15, 16, 19, 20, 27, 35, 44, 116, 137, 137–141, 149, 187, 192, 198, 250–251, 254, 255, 256
Turquet, P. 128, 191

Unconscious 69, 115, 166, 264–265
Unconscious at Work 10–11
unconscious phantasies 84, 88, 117
unconscious processes 58, 215–216, 273
Unilever 15
unit operations 255

Varela, F. 35
variances 255–256
Volvo 257–258
Von Bertalanffy, L. 20, 21, 26, 34, 35, 37, 40

Wallach, T. 194, 196, 198
War Office Selection Board (WOSB) 14
Weisbord, M. 141

We-ness 128
Western, S. 201
Western Electric Company 136
Wharncliffe Memorandum 120
Wheatlety, M. 44
Wheelan, S. 217, 218
White, A. 220
whole system events 173–174
Wilson, A.T.M. 14
Wilson, B. 35
Wilson, T. 15
Winnicott, D. 66, 67, 78, 150, 157
Woodward, J. 44
Work 267–269
work design 262–263
work groups 20, 116, 152–155; evolution of 145–150; mentality 129–131; self-managed 137–140; self-regulating 249–250, 256–257

Zaleznik, A. 23

Printed in the United States
by Baker & Taylor Publisher Services